global risk/global opportunity

global risk/global opportunity

Ten Essential Tools for Tracking Minds, Markets & Money

Shlomo Maital
D.V.R. Seshadri

Response
Business books from SAGE
Los Angeles ▪ London ▪ New Delhi ▪ Singapore ▪ Washington DC
www.sagepublications.com

First published in 2010 by

Response Books
Business books from SAGE
B1/I-1 Mohan Cooperative Industrial Area
Mathura Road, New Delhi 110 044, India

SAGE Publications Inc
2455 Teller Road
Thousand Oaks, California 91320, USA

SAGE Publications Ltd
1 Oliver's Yard, 55 City Road
London EC1Y 1SP, United Kingdom

SAGE Publications Asia-Pacific Pte Ltd
33 Pekin Street
#02-01 Far East Square
Singapore 048763

Published by Vivek Mehra for Response Books, typeset in 10/13 pt Georgia by Star Compugraphics Private Limited, Delhi and printed at Chaman Enterprises, New Delhi.

Library of Congress Cataloging-in-Publication Data

Maital, Shlomo.
    Global risk/global opportunity: ten essential tools for tracking minds, markets & money/ Shlomo Maital, D.V.R. Seshadri.
        p. cm.
        Includes index.
    1. Financial risk management.   2. Investments, Foreign.   3. Investments.   4. Economic forecasting.   5. Business forecasting.   I. Seshadri, D.V.R., 1957– II. Title.

HD61.M25   658.15'5—dc22   2010   2010017044

ISBN: 978-81-321-0443-8 (PB)

The SAGE Team: Qudsiya Ahmed, Swati Sengupta, Sanjeev Kumar Sharma, and
                        Trinankur Banerjee

To the young generation of managers everywhere—may you tirelessly and
  fearlessly seek opportunities to create value for others, and in doing so, make the
  world far better for all.
And for our grandchildren
  Tal, Aharon, Maya, Romema, Tuvya, Shoshana, Agam, Tzfanya, Neta, and Ayala.

Shlomo Maital

To Generation Next of the world, who have onerous challenges in the road ahead
  and consequently will encounter risks along the way, and also huge opportunities.
  Here is wishing them that they may achieve their dreams.
To our just-born granddaughter Yamini Srikari, the archetype of GenNext.

D.V.R. Seshadri

Contents

List of Tables

List of Figures

List of Boxes

List of Action Learning Exercises

List of Case Studies

Foreword

It is said, "judgment comes from experience," but "good judgment comes from bad experience!" The latest book by the authors on *Global Risk/Global Opportunity* could not have chosen a more apt time than 2010. Business managers everywhere will regard the 10 essential tools as a wonderful addition to their quiver.

Business managers today are split in two groups; those who "faced" the year 2008 and those who were not at the forefront facing the challenge. The situation today is akin to the world born after the years of Great Depression and the one before 1929. The business perspective, assessment and outlook on risk and opportunity has undergone a remarkable change depending upon which side of the time-line one stands. As one reads through the insightful chapters in this book, it becomes evident that risk is an integral part of our lives, something which cannot be wished away. It needs to be handled and the same is illustrated in a lucid manner with practical case studies.

In my business experience, organizations (read, managers) have often failed to articulate the "risks" that their business faces. Often, in organizations, "scenarios" are developed with statistical mumbo-jumbo. Truly big surprises—or as I term them— nightmarish scenarios are seldom thought of, let alone properly stated. Consequently, we hear post event exclamations and, of course, unpleasant consequences. One plausible explanation for this lack of imagination is the inability of contrarian views to exist in the organizations. The speed of work, inordinate focus on action and the seemingly all pervasive "we know it all" attitude due to easy access to information is making companies (and slowly people) bereft of interactions that encourage painting of "uncertainty".

Another pitfall exhibited by businesses is the overpowering influence of an uncertain "event" and a concomitant failure in assessing the underlying "risk". For example, higher cost of raw materials (or an inordinate hike in commodity prices) is an "event", whereas the inability to pass it on to a firms' buyers is the "risk". The corrective actions taken by the firm to mitigate the ill effect of an "event" will be completely different from addressing the "risk" and the doors of opportunity that the accompanying risk opens.

In today's complex organizations, irrespective of being an MNC or otherwise, one would often come to a situation where the same event is seen as an "opportunity" by one part of the company and as a "risk" by the other part. Strengthening exchange rate, for instance, is one such event and is posed as a risk or an opportunity to different parts of the organization at the same time.

Reading through the tools described in this rather unique book on macro-economics, it is apparent that risk management has to be an ongoing exercise as opposed to being a periodic brainstorming exercise that a Chief Executive calls for when hit by an event. Risk assessment and analysis need to become pre-emptive as opposed to being like a post-mortem analysis. It needs to be far more inclusive in terms of areas that business managers think about in order to allow them to open the window to the world; to be able to build sustainable and agile organizations in a risky, yet opportune world; and to create a future that is stronger and more promising than the present.

Peeyush Gupta*
Kolkata, India
March 2010

---

* Peeyush Gupta is Chief of Marketing and Sales, Flat Products, Tata Steel; the archetypical global senior manager, who deals with global risk and global opportunity scenarios on a daily basis.

To the Reader

SETTING EXPECTATIONS

Before launching any project or venture—and well before building a project timetable and plan—successful managers always ask one key question: When the project is completed, how will I know if it was successful?

Unless you measure success, you cannot truly learn from your experience, because you cannot tell whether the results of your action were what you planned. Until you decide how to measure success, you have not determined what your concrete goals are. And without defining concrete goals, how can you know how to proceed or where to lead?

So let us begin our journey together through this book with these vital questions:

- *What are your goals?*
- *What are your expectations in working through this book?*
- *And when you've finished reading it, how will you know if your time has been well invested?*

Experienced management educators call this process *setting expectations*. We almost always begin our workshop sessions by allocating at least an hour or two to this process.

May we offer as an initial suggestion the following six goals for our book? Readers are of course invited to adapt and alter them according to their needs and preferences:

Objectives of *global risk/global opportunity*

- To understand what it means to think and act like a global manager with a true global perspective.
- To learn how to analyze global risk and always relate to global risk as a form of concrete business opportunity—going far beyond the well-known risk-as-opportunity cliché.

- To build a set of useful clearly understandable tools that will enable managers to assess and track global risk and see risk where others see only return.
- To enhance skills in analyzing a new market or country or geography, as an initial key step in doing business in that country—a kind of *due diligence*, not the variety used before acquiring a company, but what one does before venturing into a new and unfamiliar country, market and geography.[†]
- To constantly sharpen those risk-analysis skills by engaging in action learning exercises that apply the 10 essential tools to analysis of risk in a new and perhaps unfamiliar country—or in a familiar country where new insights are sought.
- To understand how global risk can be analyzed, assessed, and causally understood, in ways that offer insights into likely future scenarios.

Memo

One day, a memo similar to the following one may land on your, our reader's, desk. The 10 essential tools in this book are designed to help you respond to it effectively, and professionally.

From: CEO
To: Global Risk/Global Opportunity Reader
Date: 8.00 a.m., Monday
Re: New market

We are thinking of investing in India [or Chile, Costa Rica, Ghana, Belgium, Kazakhstan, or New Zealand]. Perhaps we can sell our middle-to-low price products there. Or even our high-end products. Maybe, do some component outsourcing there. Maybe even build an assembly operation. Maybe site some of our Research and Development there, especially for local-market product adaptation. Maybe beyond that, develop a new product line there. Maybe all of those. Maybe none of them.

Because we are a bit late in this game—some of our competitors are already there—we need to move fast. So by 8 a.m., Friday, I want you to submit a concise laser-sharp report that answers the question, *Should we invest in this country? Why or why not?*

I want a *big-picture* report. Your job is to peel away the outer layers of the *onion*. Tell us about the economy. Is it true that it now has high inflation? Why? Will it continue? What are its growth drivers? Trade patterns? Strong and weak points? Competitiveness? Debt? Interest rates? Credit market? Work force?

[†] *Due diligence* is defined as the process of investigation into the details of a potential investment, such as an examination of operations and management of a company or business division, and the verification of material facts; usually performed prior to acquisition of the company in question. Here we use it as a generic term, related to examining the business environment (*material facts*) for an entire country.

We see major opportunities there, but want to evaluate the risks that always are attendant on such opportunities. If you do your job well, with the outer layer, we can proceed from there to the inner layers, analyzing our industry and our specific products and services and their potential there.

Good luck. If you do this well, you may end up leading our whole operation there. That is why it is crucial for you to do this macroeconomic *due diligence* well. A year from now, you do not want to be blindsided by something you failed to see today.

I'm sticking this memo onto a book you may want to use, *Global Risk/Global Opportunity*. Since you have so little time to carry out this mission, you may find it helpful as a kind of analytical template. *Do this right! A lot is at stake here.*

Oh, and while you're at it, take a quick big-picture look at global markets in general. How fast, or slow, will we emerge from the current global downturn? We have to get our timing right.

After reading our book, you, our reader should be able to conduct a serious *due diligence* analysis of India's economy and society, or any economy and society, and write a terse 10-page report for your CEO that contains all the vital information needed to set the stage for deeper industry and product analyses. You should also be capable of analyzing big-picture trends in global markets, while integrating minds (psychology and emotion), markets (aspects of demand and supply in key markets), and money (the availability, and cost of credit and liquidity). You should know how to build vivid tangible scenarios as the foundation for effective global strategies (our first of the 10 tools, described in the first chapter).

MACROECONOMICS?

Readers will note, with perhaps a small degree of perplexity, that while this book is largely about global macroeconomics, and the 10 tools are drawn from this discipline, we do not use the term in the title. This is purposeful. Physicist Stephen Hawkins, author of the best-selling *A Brief History of Time*, notes that every equation in a book cuts its sales by half (his book has only one: $E = mc^2$). We believe that the term *economics* in a book title has the same effect. There is good reason for this.

Macroeconomists have in large part created a closed world whose jargon-ridden language is obscure and murky for the uninitiated. Moreover, textbooks in macroeconomics are written largely for students of economics. But the needs of global managers are utterly different. They do not need to understand the language of macroeconomics, and its body of knowledge as an end in itself. Rather they need the *insights* and *wisdom* of macroeconomic tools, so that they can better navigate the treacherous waters of global risk, and better understand what risks the future holds, and how they can be transformed into business ventures. Global managers need a toolbox, not a mathematical theory. We offer 10 tools, mostly originating in the realm of macroeconomics.

The authors have many years of combined experience in teaching and working with global managers. In this book, we apply the acid test of relevance to our writing. We ask, for each of the 10 tools: Is this tool useful? Is it relevant? Is it proven? Does it bring powerful insights to managers seeking to explore new countries, markets and geographies, and trying to avoid unseen risks? Can the global managers with whom we work use these tools, after some practice, to truncate risks, and seize opportunities?

For two decades, the first author (Maital) taught a course whose content resembled the contents of this book at MIT Sloan School of Management. Maital recalls an epiphany, a life-changing event. A young woman, a talented senior manager from IBM, became exasperated with the mathematics and jargon the instructor was bombarding the classroom and its innocent victims. She stood up and asked: Why do we need to know this? That question had, in the instructor's experience, never before been asked. It was always assumed by economics students that if the professor was teaching something, then it was *by definition* a vital part of the arsenal of everyone aiming to become a professional economist, and thus had to be learned. Economists, after all, study economics, and economics is what the economics professor teaches.

But *managers reject this premise.* They want to know whether a body of knowledge is useful, and if so, can it be used to help them achieve their global management goals? They accept unconditionally the statement by social psychologist Kurt Lewin that the only true test of a theory is whether it can be used successfully to achieve defined results.

That epiphany, and the resulting shift in perspective, facilitated by the question of the IBM manager, forever altered Maital's approach and perspective. The results-oriented toolbox perspective is, of course, part of the DNA of the second author, who has recorded many years of hands-on senior management experience. And it is the perspective taken in this book.

THE STRUCTURE OF THIS BOOK

There are 10 chapters. Each chapter features an analytical tool that can help you carry out your due diligence exercise. The tools are logically linked, and presented in a sensible order. Each tool is accompanied by detailed action learning exercises, and each chapter has mini case studies illustrating the key principles with real-world examples.

Chapter one: Global crisis 2007–2009: Risks and opportunities

This chapter explains the nature and origins of the global capital market crisis that began in the United States in 2007 (as the so-called *sub-prime mortgage* crisis) and spread elsewhere. It shows the dynamics of this crisis, and analyzes how independent-thinking managers could have recognized early warning signals long before the bubble burst. It discusses the growing amplitude of global business fluctuations, and stresses the importance of scenario analysis and planning—transforming uncertainty into risk by exploring various scenarios, and attaching probabilities to each.

The key tool in this chapter is **Tool #1: Scenario Planning—How to dispel denial by making worst-case scenarios concrete and believable.**

Chapter two: What is your story? How to build powerful global narratives

This chapter helps you understand why it is vital for managers to acquire their own macroeconomic analytic tools, and develop their own perspective on key trends in global markets. You should know what *teleology* (the study of cause-and-effect) means, and why becoming good at understanding teleology in global markets is important. You should also understand how a systems thinker uses dynamic feedback loops to understand fundamental causality as it unfolds in world markets. You should be able to use the GELT model (geopolitics, economics, lifestyle, technology) to identify key global trends, and build a narrative from them that translates insights into global trends, to create business opportunities.

The featured tool in this chapter is: **Tool #2: GELT—Geopolitics, Economics, Lifestyle, Technology**. A related tool is the concept of teleology—understanding the world as interrelated causal feedback loops. With practice you should become expert at analyzing unfolding global trends as a cause-and-effect system shown as a feedback loop, and at identifying those feedback loops that reflect *bubble* psychology.

Chapter three: Risk management with telescopes and microscopes

This chapter helps managers understand why they need a unique kind of vision, able, with one eye, to zoom out on the global marketplace (*telescope*) and, with one eye, to zoom in on the business DNA of the organization he or she leads or manages (*microscope*). The chapter examines the failure of conventional risk-assessment models, such as *value-at-risk*, and focuses on how to analyze systemic (big-picture) risk.

The featured tool in this chapter is: **Tool #3: Zoom Out, Zoom In with Telescope and Microscope.** A related tool is that of feedback loops, used in the chapter to show how feedback can generate leveraging-driven bubbles, in which assets are bought with growing amounts of debt, raising asset prices, and encouraging further leverage; this process reverses, when asset prices decline, leading to further asset sales to reduce debt, causing further asset price declines, and so on.

Chapter four: A country is a business

This chapter helps managers perceive countries as businesses, and develop the ability to *read* a country's basic GDP data as if it were a business profit-and-loss statement, drawing strategic conclusions about the country's market size, saving and investment, growth orientation, and future prospects, useful for guiding business decisions. Countries *are* in many ways like businesses. Each country, like a business, has a set of *Profit and Loss* statements, or ones similar to them, that when used judiciously can reveal a lot about the company's, or the country's, basic soundness, its dynamism, prospects, and its expected future performance. Macro accounting can show managers where a country's resources come from, who uses them, whether a country is future-oriented, where it is building its assets, whether it is selling what it makes, and why it is (or is not) growing.

The tool developed in this chapter is: **Tool #4: Gross Domestic Product—The Financial Statement of a Country.** Managers will be able to go well beyond press reports of GDP to analyze, on their own, the meaning of the underlying GDP components, and how they change.

Chapter five: Analyzing engines of growth

Growth is crucial for businesses, and no less crucial for countries. After reading this chapter, you should know how to measure for any country, and any period, the underlying reasons the country did (or did not) enjoy economic growth, measure the adequacy of a country's net saving, and compute what parts of it are used for investment at home and abroad, and gauge how fast the country's capacity to produce GDP is growing. You should then be able to gauge, from the country's growth drivers, whether the country aligns with your company's growth strategy. This chapter will enable managers to understand whether a country's growth can be sustained in the long-term.

The analytical tool featured in this chapter is: **Tool #5: Engines of GDP Growth—Which GDP Components Drive Growth (or Decline)?** Using this tool, managers can build striking graphs and charts showing how growth drivers evolve and change.

Chapter six: Money talks—Interest rates listen

This chapter deals with money, and the price of money, the rate of interest. Credit is the oxygen of businesses. Understanding money and credit is vital for a global manager. This chapter helps the reader understand what money is, why it is hard to define and even harder for the Central Bank of a country to control, how to track money supply, how money is related to inflation, how money is related to economic momentum, and why the rate at which money turns over, or changes hands (velocity) is a crucial, and often-overlooked variable. It explains why desperate efforts of Central Banks worldwide to inject liquidity into national economies do not always succeed. After reading this chapter, managers should understand how to measure whether interest—the cost of money—is expensive or cheap, whether to borrow, or reduce debt and lend, who controls interest rates and how they do it, and why interest rates have become so volatile and hard to predict. Managers should also understand how, in a world where capital flows quickly, and easily from one country to another in search of higher return, such capital flows have radically changed the policy options of nations.

The analytical tool is: **Tool #6: Economic Momentum.** This is a very old and simple theory that links the quantity of money, and the rate at which it changes hands with GDP, or economic momentum. This tool shows why *minds* (psychology) drive the rate at which money changes hands, an oft-ignored variable that is at least as important as the quantity of money and credit available. A related tool is that of *real* (inflation-adjusted) interest rates, which help managers to gauge accurately when credit is expensive, and when it is relatively cheap.

Chapter seven: Tracking booms and busts

Why has America experienced a dozen recessions since World War II? What causes booms and busts? After reading this chapter, you should understand the basic forces driving recessions, and economic slowdowns, the link between consumer spending, and recession (including consumer debt and inventories), and the key role played by the trade deficit and government budget deficit, and how they interact. You should understand the business-cycle theory of J.M. Keynes. Very often, though not always, global economic crisis, and downturns follow close on the heels of global financial collapse. After reading this chapter, managers should know why business trends driven by demand-side forces differ strategically from those driven by supply-side forces, know how to track both demand and supply, why the stock market reacts differently to demand supply forces, and know how to evaluate current stock prices, and judge their long-term behavior based on underlying supply and demand forces. Managers should understand how inflation and deflation impact stock prices, and should know the key difference between demand-pull and cost-push inflation.

The analytical tool is: **Tool #7: Twin Deficits—Budget and Trade Deficit.** This simple tool shows how to track two key deficits, and to use them in order to help predict whether the economy will contract or expand in the near term. A related tool is **The Real Dow-Jones Average:** stock averages adjusted for inflation. This tool helps managers gain a true historical perspective on equity prices, with a view to knowing when they are based on *irrational exuberance*, that is, *bubbles*, and when they are justified by future profit and growth prospects.

Chapter eight: Tracking trade and forex

The crucial engine of growth in world markets since 1990 has been trade, which historically has grown twice as fast as global GDP. *Managers need to* understand how to analyze the crucial foreign-exchange cash flow performance of countries, using the Balance of Payments statement—for the purpose of analyzing countries' performance, stability, credit worthiness, and future prospects. The objective: to help managers better understand the ability of countries to sell successfully in foreign markets and to attract foreign capital. In addition, understanding a nation's external debt position is vital in assessing country-specific risk. After reading this chapter, managers will understand how interest rates drive exchange rates, why official exchange rates may not reflect true currency value, how to gauge future changes in exchange rates and why exchange rates have become exceedingly volatile. They will know how to measure whether a currency is priced too high or too low, in terms of dollars.

The main analytical tool is: **Tool #8: Balance of Payments—Orderly Account of Transactions Between People and Businesses of One Country with Other Countries.** Managers will learn how to *read* Balance of Payments statements to reveal potential sources of global risk and will understand why Balance of Payments trends signal looming crisis long before such crisis actually unfolds. A related supplementary tool is **Purchasing power parity exchange rates (PPP),** which helps managers to evaluate whether national exchange rates are consistent with long-run underlying values.

Chapter nine: Non-economic risks

In addition to the various risks related to the economic situation of the country discussed in chapters 1 to 8, managers should also be aware of several other country risks. These include political risks, environmental risks, risks of terrorism, risks stemming from societal factors, risks of war, and so on. Companies could be impacted by these factors, now more so than ever before. This chapter provides a framework to analyze these risks, through various case studies.

The main analytical tool is: **Tool #9: Assessing and Tracking Non-economic Risk.** Managers will learn how to map the various other types of risks, beyond those related to conventional market forces, that impact a company, how to quantify them, and through this deeper understanding of these risks, ensure that their companies are not adversely impacted by the manifestation of these risks.

Chapter ten: Country "due diligence"—Integrating the ten tools

Managers will read this concluding chapter with the objective of acquiring a systematic checklist of questions that can help analyze the business prospects and potential of any country using the 10 essential macroeconomic tools, and adding to them, non-economic factors related to culture, politics and ethics. The checklist will include questions related to application of the ten tools, and in addition, will explore such key issues as: ease of doing business; perceived lack of corruption; and the four dimensions of global competitiveness. This checklist will help global managers systematically conduct *due diligence* examinations of new geographies, before expanding their organizations' businesses into them. It shows how managers with global mindsets can become experts linking global *macro* trends with local *micro* conditions—a capability that is essential, if managers are to anticipate future global crises and transform them into, first, survival, and second, into growth opportunities, for their organizations.

The main tool is: **Tool #10: Checklist for Country "Due Diligence" Analysis.**

We have chosen to begin our journey in Chapter One with an in-depth analysis of the global crisis of 2007–2009—its underlying causes and dynamics. We try to answer Queen Elizabeth's question: why did no one foresee the crisis? And US ex-President Bush's question: how did we get here?

Acknowledgements

My friend and mentor Professor Lester Thurow, MIT Sloan School of Management, and Chair of TIM—Technion Institute of Management, taught me most of what I know about globalization, and above all showed me that being an economic educator is a worthy profession. I served for more than a decade as TIM academic director, and in interacting with some 200 Israeli companies and 1,500 managers, found that often teachers learn more from their students than students learn from their teachers. I am deeply grateful to my close friend, and co-author Professor D.V.R. Seshadri. Some friendships survive only one book collaboration; ours has become even stronger in this, our second book, and I look forward to working with him on a third. I am thankful to MIT Sloan School of Management Professor Edward Roberts, who offered me a life-changing opportunity to teach economics to his Management of Technology M.Sc. students 25 years ago. My wife Sharona has endured me for nearly 43 years; she is my friend, companion, partner, wife, and sometimes, co-author, and I cannot imagine life without her. Finally, I owe a huge debt to my country, Israel, which daily gives meaning to my life and my work.

—Shlomo Maital

I would like to express my sincere thanks to the Almighty for having connected me to Professor Shlomo Maital several years ago. He has been my friend, philosopher and guide, and our partnership has grown stronger with the passing years. Our relationship has grown from strength to strength over the years. I am eternally grateful to my Gurus who have guided me over the years, whose ever-present and infinite grace has been instrumental in making me what I am. I would like to sincerely record my heartfelt appreciation to Prema, my dear and loving wife for 27 years, who has over the years stood by me like the Rock of Gibraltar, as we jointly went through life in its vicissitudes. She, along with our lovely daughters, Divya and Nitya, as well as our gentle and genial son-in-law, Lakshminarayana, have provided me a strong and robust emotional tapestry to embark on this project. Our first grandchild Yamini, born during this book project, has enhanced the richness of this emotional support and strength. To the many managers of companies in India, with whom I have interacted over the years, in my various teaching assignments, I am profoundly grateful, for sharing their perspectives that have shaped in many ways parts of this book. Ms Shobitha Hegde and Mr T.A. Krishnamurthy provided much needed research and administrative support respectively, leaving me free to work with Professor Shlomo Maital on this book project. I have had the good fortune of being associated in a teaching capacity with two top management educational institutions in India, IIM Bangalore and IIM Ahmedabad. I express my sincere gratitude to both these institutes for their ongoing support.

—**D.V.R. Seshadri**

(The reader is asked to turn the book upside-down to see the reverse image)

Introduction: Two Tales

THE ECONOMISTS' NEW CLOTHES

Once there was a Queen. Her name was Elizabeth II (Elizabeth Alexandra Mary) and she ruled, and still rules, the United Kingdom. She became Queen in 1952 at the tender age of 26, when her father George VI died of a coronary thrombosis.

She was an exemplary queen whose English was perfect. She always spoke politely and diplomatically.

But one day, on November 5, 2008, she and her husband, the Duke of Edinburgh, went to the Mecca of Economics, LSE—London School of Economics—to dedicate a new eight-floor academic building. The building cost USD 113 million.

Dressed impeccably in a white suit and matching hat, the Queen was uncharacteristically rude. She asked bluntly about the global financial and economic crisis that began in 2007.

"Why did no one see it coming?" she asked.

Some of those present quietly chuckled, and recalled the beloved Hans Christian Anderson story.‡

"The Queen is very well dressed," they thought. "It is we who are nude."

THE PRESIDENT'S OLD CLOTHES

Once there was a President. His name was Bush, and he did not speak perfect English. He was known as Bush II, because his father Bush I had also been President. He ruled over a land known as the United States of America. His reign ended on January 20, 2009.

Bush II wore fine clothes from a wardrobe he called *unregulated free-market capitalism*. He had been known to make many others wear the same clothes in the past.

---

‡ In the story, a vain emperor employs two swindlers to weave him fine new clothes. They weave cloth they say can be seen only by those who are not stupid. The Emperor then parades through the capital showing off his finery. The people applaud his finery. Then, a small child cries out, "But he has nothing on!"

One day, some two months before the Queen's blunt question, on September 18, 2008, Bush II put on his finest capitalist suit. He went to the Roosevelt Room in his home, the White House. His experts told him that a leading investment bank had gone bankrupt, and a leading global insurance company had to be bailed out, at a cost to the federal budget of USD 85 billion. Credit markets had frozen, and banks were refusing to lend money.

"How did we get here?" he asked, bewildered.[§]

His advisors looked at Bush II. They did not hear his question. Because suddenly, Bush II was wearing only his underwear.

Of course, Bush II immediately bundled his entire wardrobe into trucks, and tried to give it away.

But strangely, no one wanted his old clothes.

We, the authors, have come together to answer the questions of Elizabeth II and Bush II, by supplying managers and leaders of businesses with tools that illuminate the past, but more important, help to strategize the future.

We will show how independent-thinking managers, using basic economic tools, can track the three elements that together drive the world's complex, and somewhat unstable economic system: minds, markets and money, and transform global risk into business opportunities.

[§] Jo Becker, Sheryl Gay Stolberg, and Stephen Labaton, "The Reckoning: White House Philosophy Stoked Mortgage Bonfire", *New York Times*, December 20, 2008 (nyt.com).

Chapter 1

Global crisis 2007–2009: Risks and opportunities

LEARNING OBJECTIVES

- After reading this chapter, you should understand the basics of scenario planning, why it is important and how great organizations use it to meet large unexpected challenges.
- You should understand what contrarian thinking is, and how it can protect managers from resorting to herd mentality, or groupthink.
- You should know the difference between an *analyst* and a *strategist*, understand which thinking predominates in your own mind, and know why both types of mindset are crucial for meeting global challenges.
- You should grasp how America's response to the 2000–01 dot.com bubble[1] directly led to the 2001–07 housing bubble, and why this bubble ultimately collapsed.
- You should know what organizational resilience is, and why it is of growing importance; you should be able to gauge your own resilience, and that of your organization.
- You should understand what a *tipping point* (critical mass) is, and how it causes markets to shift quickly from bullish to bearish sentiment and vice versa.
- You should understand how, and why markets are driven by the interaction of minds (market psychology), and money (cost, and availability of credit and liquidity), and how to track the dynamics of changing market sentiment.

---

[1] The dot.com bubble that unfolded in 2000–2001 in USA and many other countries was the inevitable fall-out consequent to the realization that many overly hyped companies that were born as a consequence of the pervasive availability of the Internet, but with very tenuous business models and that obtained significant easy funding during the boom cycle, were found to be essentially hollow in terms of ability to generate wealth for their shareholders on a sustained basis. This realization resulted in widespread panic, with investors rapidly seeking to pull out their investments, resulting in large investments in these companies virtually going up in smoke almost overnight.

TOOL #1

Scenario Planning

How to dispel denial by making worst-case scenarios concrete and believable.

MINDS, MARKETS, AND MONEY

This chapter focuses on the crisis in global capital, goods, and labor markets in 2007–2009, its causes and the opportunities it creates. Our objective is to drill home to our readers, two key points, or truths, and offer some practical tools to help reinforce those points and enable their implementation on a daily basis.

- The vital importance for global managers to build and sustain an *independent mindset*. Think for yourself! Economists' macroeconomic forecasts are notoriously inaccurate, especially in predicting downturns and bubble collapses.[2]
- Be sure to track *moods, emotions, and psychology* in markets, not just the so-called *fundamentals*. In the end, markets are driven by buying and selling behavior, and buying and selling is powerfully influenced by the emotions and feelings of those engaged in the market. It has been said that financial bubbles burst when the prevailing emotion in markets shifts from *greed* (generating bullish behavior) to *fear* (generating bearish behavior). This transition happens very quickly, sometimes within a matter of days! Sensing this transition is a vital part of best-practice global risk management! Later in this chapter, we will explain (by using *tipping point* analysis) why these transitions happen quickly, and how independent–thinking managers can keep their hands on the pulse of market moods and mindsets.

---

[2] Ormerod, Paul, "The Impossibility of Accurate Macro-Economic Forecasting", *Economic Affairs 1997* 17, no. 1 (1997): 44–49. Ormerod claims that the macro-economic short-term forecasting record in the West over the past thirty years is very poor, and that such inaccuracy is a deep and inherent property of the data itself. The economic forecasting record simply cannot be improved. Much economic policy still focuses on short-term intervention based on short-term forecasts. But such efforts are futile because forecasts of sufficient accuracy over time cannot be made.

The perils of groupthink and herd mentality

Global capital markets in particular are driven by herd mentality. Herd mentality is characterized by groupthink—the tendency of groups of people to think alike, often in denial of existing realities—and is especially common in capital markets, during *bubbles* (unrealistic appreciation in asset prices). Groupthink is a term first coined by author William Whyte, in a 1952 article in Fortune magazine. In the latter stages of financial bubbles—the most dangerous periods of all—it is vitally important to avoid groupthink, to think independently, to question existing *herd* assumptions, and to develop tools that foster and buttress this independent mindset.

Definition: *Groupthink* is a type of thought exhibited by group members who try to minimize conflict and reach consensus without critically testing, analyzing, and evaluating ideas. Individual creativity, uniqueness, and independent thinking are lost in the pursuit of group cohesiveness, as are the advantages of reasonable balance in choice and thought that might normally be obtained by making decisions as a group. During groupthink, members of the group avoid promoting viewpoints outside the comfort zone of consensus thinking. A popular column in the US business daily *Wall Street Journal* is called "Heard on the Street". It could just as well be "Herd on the Street".[3]

One way to think independently is to practice *contrarian* thinking.

ACTION LEARNING

Contrarian Thinking

Ask yourself, at the present time:

- What are the prevailing common assumptions about local and world markets?
- What are the implications, if some or all of these assumptions are completely wrong or in other words, if the precise opposite is true?

Example: American and world capital markets assumed US housing prices would continue to rise, even though no asset price can rise forever.

(Action Learning continued)

---

[3] Source: http://en.wikipedia.org/wiki/Groupthink (accessed January 28, 2010).

(Action Learning continued)

> Some risk-management models did not even allow for simulating a decline in housing prices![4] Negative numbers could not be entered.
>
> Those who explored the implications of *declining* housing prices found ways to avoid enormous risk.
>
> A second example: Many economists predict that the US economy will lead a world recovery, beginning in the third quarter of 2009. What if the recovery is delayed by a year or more? What if the groupthink assumption is utterly wrong?

Author Irving Janis wrote a pathbreaking book on groupthink.[5] There he defined it as "a mode of thinking that people engage in when they are deeply involved in a cohesive in-group, when the members' strivings for unanimity override their motivation to realistically appraise alternative courses of action." In capital markets, groupthink occurs when large profits are accruing from activities that stem from high but concealed risk. Few of those enjoying such profits are willing to put an end to the *party*.

One way to avoid groupthink is by tracking a small number of key variables that can alert us about the looming danger.

Groupthink can lead to rapid, often unexpected shifts in market sentiment, from raging optimism to despondent pessimism and then back again. This is known as a *tipping point* phenomenon.

ACTION LEARNING

One Picture is Worth a Thousand Words

Graphs of key variables can alert us about looming crises.

What three graphs do you have in front of your desk, in your workspace, that you view daily, that serve to alert you to potential risks and market declines? Do you update them regularly?

(Action Learning continued)

---

[4] "An investment analyst named Steve Eisman called Standard & Poor's (a bond rating agency) [in early 2007] and asked what would happen to default rates if real estate prices fell. The man at S&P could not say (what would happen to default rates if real estate prices fell); *its model for home prices had no ability to accept a negative number* for the rate of growth of real estate prices. 'They were just assuming home prices would keep going up,' Eisman says." Source: Michael Lewis, "The End", www.portfolio.com. http://notes.kateva.org.2008/12/michael-lewis-on-end-of-wall-street-my-my.html. (accessed January 18, 2010).

[5] Janis, Irving L. *Victims of Groupthink* (Boston: Houghton Mifflin Company, 1972).

(*Action Learning continued*)

> Figure 1.4 shows an example (Median House Prices/Median Family Income). Tracking this graph regularly would have shown how out-of-line (with incomes) house prices had become in the United States and how difficult it would be in future for ordinary households to maintain mortgage payments. Another example has been shown in Figure 2.12 (Chapter Two) which shows America's trade deficit and budget deficit; had managers and investors been tracking these continually, alarm bells should have sounded in 1999 or 2000, years before the global collapse.

TRACKING MINDS—TIPPING POINT ANALYSIS

Malcolm Gladwell's 2002 book *The Tipping Point* shows how a critical mass of persons can develop and suddenly change a market or an election.[6] His book summarizes in popular fashion a wide variety of results developed by experts in game theory over five decades.

Figure 1.1 shows a *tipping point* or critical-mass model of markets, based on the proportion of participants and investors who are *bears* or *bulls*. In Wall Street parlance, a *bear* is someone who thinks asset prices will fall. Being bearish is to be pessimistic. A *bull* is someone who thinks asset prices will rise. Being bullish is to be optimistic. The proportion of bulls and bears in a market is crucial because it determines whether there is net supply or net demand for assets (The origin of the term *bears* and *bulls* is not precisely known, though there are many theories).

On the x-axis, we show the proportion of participants in capital markets who are *bears*. On the y-axis, we show the *perceived average profit*. The *bulls* line shows the perceived average profit from being a *bull*. It declines as the proportion of bears rises, because the more bears there are, the more likely it is that asset prices will fall. The bears' line shows the perceived average profit from being a bear, which too declines. Those who are bears can profit, in a down market, from short-selling. Bears profit in a down market since they sell stocks short. The price of stocks drops, then they buy them back and replace them, and pocket the difference between the price at which they sold and the price at which they bought the stocks. However, if too many bears practice the same strategy, profits diminish. The bear line is shallower than the bull line, because bear profits based on short-selling are less sensitive to the number of bears than are bull profits. Bulls lose money when bears predominate, because the assets they hold lose value. Bears may lose opportunities, when bears predominate, because their profit-making strategies are diluted, but their actual losses may be small.

---

[6] Malcolm Gladwell, *The Tipping Point* (Boston: Little Brown, 2002).

FIGURE 1.1   Tipping Point Model of Financial Crises

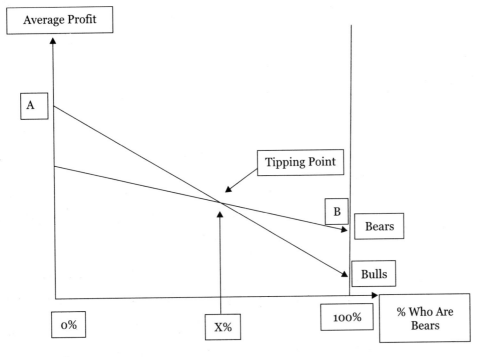

Source: Authors.

Note: The figure shows *average profit* from financial transactions, on the y-axis, as a function of the percentage of investors who are *bears* (expect falling asset prices), on
the x-axis. The *tipping point* is X percent. That is, if the percentage of bears exceeds
X percent, then it becomes more profitable to be a bear than a bull (or optimist, who
expects rising asset prices), and everyone becomes a bear—the equilibrium point is
B, with 100 percent bears and prolonged market downturn. As long as less than X
percent of investors are bears, then the equilibrium point is *A*, where everyone is a *bull*.

In this analysis, there are three key points: The tipping point X (the point where
the two lines intersect), as well as two other points shown in the figure: point A and
point B.

- If the proportion of bears is less than X percent (the tipping point), it pays
  more to be a bull than a bear. The market dynamics, then, are such that the
  proportion of bears declines, ultimately going to zero (Point A).
- If the proportion of bears is X percent or greater, it becomes more profitable
  to be a bear than a bull. The proportion of bears then grows until it embraces
  all the participants (point B).

A rumor, random market decline or major bankruptcy can rapidly create the X percent coalition of bears needed to *tip* the market.

Moreover, changes in markets, for example, the sudden change in perceived risk, and hence in risk premiums, may cause *bearish* views to be perceived as more profitable (note: the reality here is immaterial, what matters is what market participants *think*), and bullish views to be perceived as less profitable. Thus, in Figure 1.2, the bull profit line shifts downward and the bear profit line shifts upward. This shifts the tipping point from X percent (which may be large) to Y percent (which may be quite small). If the actual proportion of bears exceeds Y percent, but is less than X percent, a market that previously tended toward bullish views can suddenly become totally bearish.

Of course, the opposite is also true. The *minds* of markets can shift equally quickly from bearish to bullish, creating a tipping point majority toward optimism. This, in our view, is how huge global capital markets can shift and decline, or explode upward, almost overnight.[7]

It is important to understand, as a former Soros trader notes,[8] that it does not matter if your perceptions are right. What matters is whether your perceptions are shared by others. According to Thomas Law, in psychology, perception is reality. This is why we include *minds* in our subtitle, along with *markets* and *money*. Skilled investors judge the prevailing mindset, buy on bullish sentiment, and sell just before that sentiment changes. But such exquisite timing is very rare and exceedingly difficult.

SYSTEMS THINKING

One of the most difficult and challenging aspects in tracking global risk is what is called *big-picture thinking*—analyzing market ecosystems, rather than individual pieces of the system. One of the most common risk management models is the so-called value-at-risk model.[9] It has a major weakness, one that proved fatal for many

---

[7] The markets have become incredibly volatile, especially since Lehman Brothers sank into bankruptcy in September, 2008. Since then, the S&P [500 stock index] has moved more than 5 percent in either direction on 18 days. *There were only 17 such days in the previous 53 years,* according to calculations by Howard Silverblatt, an index analyst at S&P Vikas Bajaj, "Markets Limp Into 2009 After a Bruising Year", www.nyt.com, January 1, 2009. http://www.nytimes.com/2009/01/01/business/economy/01markets.html. (accessed January 18, 2010).

[8] Shown in the video "The Great Crash" (*Frontline*, Public Broadcasting System, 2001).

[9] Value-at-Risk is best defined with an example: If a portfolio of stocks has a one-day 5 percent Value-at-Risk of USD 1 million, there is a 5 percent probability that the portfolio will fall in value by more than USD 1 million over a one day period.

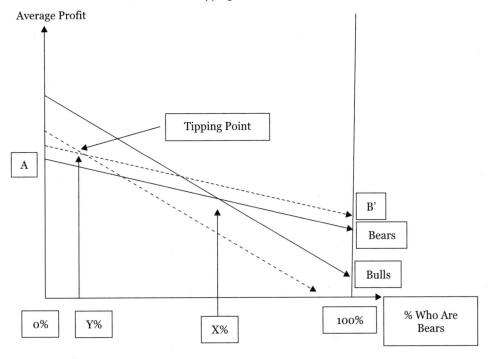

FIGURE 1.2 Shifts in Tipping Point Based on Market Sentiments

Source: Author.

Note: In financial markets, in times of uncertainty, the perceived profit from *bearish* behavior rises (the dotted line), and the perceived profit from bullish behavior declines (dotted line), as investors become aware of risks they ignored previously. This reduces the tipping point from X percent to Y percent. If the existing proportion of bearish investors is greater than Y percent, then very quickly the market equilibrium and *mood* can shift from *fully bullish* (point A) to *fully bearish* (point B'). This shift can happen very quickly, as it did during the 2007–08 financial collapse. The figure shows how a relatively small upward shift in the *perceived-profit bears* line (and a relatively small downward shift in the *perceived-profit bulls* line) can lead to rapid massive shifts in the market.

highly sophisticated organizations (see the case study in the Appendix to Chapter 3). It is this—it focuses on specific portfolios, rather than on systemic global risk.

Culture expert Richard Nisbet, in his fascinating book on East-West differences in thinking, offers the following puzzle:[10]

---

[10] Richard E. Nisbet, *The Geography of Thought: How Asians and Westerners Think Differently—And Why* (London: Nicholas Brealey, 2003).

ACTION LEARNING

Chicken, Cow, Grass

 Which of the three does not belong?

A majority of Western respondents answer, grass. Chicken and cow are both forms of meat that we eat, while grass is not.

A majority of Asian respondents answer, chicken. Cow and grass form an ecosystem, as cows eat grass.

This puzzle reveals differences in patterns of thinking. Western thinking is logical, teleological, and seeks causal links and categories, while Eastern thinking is holistic, systemic, and seeks relationships.

Global managers need both. *They need both Western and Eastern thinking.*

Global managers need the logical skills that can link unrelated events in cause-and-effect chains—a vital tool discussed at length in Chapter One. But perhaps even more important, they need the holistic skills that help them understand complex systems and how the various parts link together—because global goods, labor, capital, and information markets form an intricate ecosystem whose interactions are complex and not easy to grasp. Only systemic holistic thinkers can even hope to grasp it. Skill at big-picture systemic thinking is a key part of the armory of top global managers. This is a focus of this first chapter.

CASE STUDY

Paper-Rock-Scissors

 There is a children's game known as paper-rock-scissors. Two children simultaneously, with their fingers and hand, gesture one of the three. Scissors cut paper, rock defeats scissors, and paper defeats rock as paper can wrap around the rock. Here is a global version. In America, the recession has reduced consumer spending on toys. Many of the world's toys are made in China. So Chinese factories have greatly slashed their production. Cardboard is a major component of toys. So China's imports of recycled paper have declined.

Britain is a major world supplier of recycled paper. The reason is that Britain is the world's fifth largest consumer of paper products, importing

(*Case Study continued*)

(Case Study continued)

7.6 million tons out of its 12.5 million tons of paper consumption in 2005.[11] Britain, therefore, has a lot of paper to recycle, and has a well-organized recycling system. The price of recycled British paper, once as high as USD 144/ton, dropped drastically in 2008, falling to USD 22/ton. At that price, it does not even pay to collect the waste paper. A profitable business model was shredded by global scissors. Hence, in the global teleology, the *minds* of the American consumers have impacted the money and markets for British recycled paper, via Chinese factories.

The global collapse of 2007–09 was systemic in nature. It can only be understood by first, understanding the crisis that preceded and led to it (2000–01, the so-called *dot.com* crisis), and then, by examining the causalities that together created the *perfect storm* of 2007.

Part of big-picture thinking is the ability to have double vision—to zoom in on the organization's short-term business and markets, while at the same time zooming out on long-term strategic aspects of global eco-systems. In other words, analyst-thinking together with strategic-thinking. (see Box 1.1)

BOX 1.1   Analyst or Strategist?

Reader: ask yourself, are you primarily an analyst or a strategist?

Definition:

- Analyst: An employee of a brokerage or fund management firm who studies companies and makes buying and selling recommendations on stocks of these companies.
- Strategist: Those who weigh broad market sentiment and macroeconomic factors in order to assess the overall business environment as an aid to those making buying and selling recommendations.

Chances are, if you are a manager, you are closer in your skills to an analyst. Almost by definition, managers zoom in on the DNA of their organization and their business units—the competitive strengths and weaknesses, competitive climate, products and services, and the forces of competition. This zoom-in capability is essential. Unless you understand deeply the inner nature of your business culture, strategy, resources, and ecology, you cannot manage effectively.

Our book *Innovation Management: Strategies, Concepts and Tools for Growth and Profit* (Response 2007) sought to provide skills at such business analysis, in the realm of entrepreneurial innovation.

(Box 1.1 continued)

---

[11] Source: www.digital-publishing.co.uk/statistics/paper-consumption.html (accessed January 28, 2010).

(*Box 1.1 continued*)

Yet at the same time, if *all* you understand is the zoom-in DNA, chances are you will miss major global opportunities and be afflicted by unanticipated disastrous risks. True global managers are always analysts, with one eye, and strategists, with the second eye. The strategic second eye requires world class *zoom-out* ability—skill in grasping global trends as they unfold, or perhaps even before they fully unfold, and *linking and integrating them with the DNA analysis of the organization*. Indeed, global managers must call upon the vital *third eye*, which in Indian tradition is the intuition or sixth sense that gives us wisdom beyond what ordinary vision provides. This third eye combines the skills of analysis and strategy. It provides the ability to zoom out, on the global stage, and zoom in, on the business DNA, *at one and the same time*—a feat ordinary eyes are not capable of fulfilling.

In brief, *Global Risk/Global Opportunity* aims at making the reader a skilled and effective global strategist. The combination of powerful analyst and insightful strategist is a winning combination all global managers share.

In times of global boom and growth, the vital core competency is that of the analyst. But inevitably, when global managers only have analyst skills, they are blindsided by the inevitable downturns, slowdowns, and crises that occur after periods of boom. This can result in disaster for themselves and for their organizations. Thus, especially in times of rising asset prices and global growth, global managers keep a sharp strategic eye on global trends and assess global risk. Wise global managers who combine both, personalities of analyst and strategist, avoid huge pitfalls and losses that clever managers utterly miss and then labor to extricate themselves from. Risk is consistently and persistently underestimated in times of boom—then equally consistently overestimated in times of bust and crisis. Managers who combine analytical and strategic skills avoid both pitfalls.

Investment banks employ both analysts and strategists. Here is how one observer describes their relative importance.

ACTION LEARNING

Are You an Analyst? Or a Strategist? Or Both?

Rank your abilities as analyst or strategist, in the following areas:

- Are you primarily a short-term thinker, or do you invest, plan, and act long-term?

Short-term (analyst)   Long-term (strategist)

⊥__⊥__⊥__⊥__⊥__⊥__⊥__⊥__⊥__⊥__⊥__⊥__⊥__⊥__⊥

- Do you primarily track developments in your own industry and markets, or within a broad range of markets and industries?

(*Action Learning continued*)

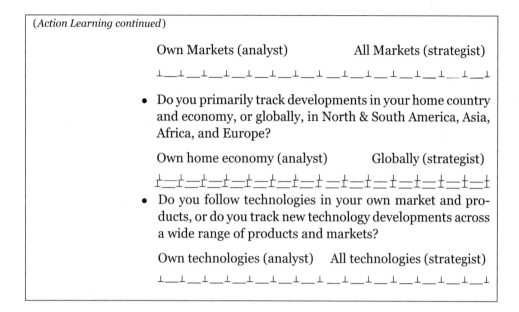

(Action Learning continued)

Own Markets (analyst)   All Markets (strategist)

- Do you primarily track developments in your home country and economy, or globally, in North & South America, Asia, Africa, and Europe?

Own home economy (analyst)   Globally (strategist)

- Do you follow technologies in your own market and products, or do you track new technology developments across a wide range of products and markets?

Own technologies (analyst)   All technologies (strategist)

THE ROLE OF HISTORY

How did the current global system evolve? Who designed it? What are its flaws? How will it change and evolve in the future? These are all questions related to history and to prediction. Prediction cannot be solid if it is not based on understanding the past. That is why our book has many mini case studies of historical episodes. History never repeats itself. But only by understanding history can global managers understand why and how the future will be different from the past.

Many young managers today are largely unaware that globalization is old hat. Indeed, Globalization 1.0—the first version, that unfolded in the 19th century—was in many ways far more *global* and far less flawed than Globalization 2.0, the system designed at Bretton Woods, NH, USA, during a three-week period from 1 to 20 July, 1944. Globalization 1.0 had a global currency—pound sterling. It had a global integrated trading system, based on flow of goods and services between Great Britain and its colonies in Asia, Africa, and North America. It even had an Internet—the telegraph, known as The Victorian Internet.[12] The ability of the telegraph to transmit information instantly to every part of the world was an enormous technological revolution, at least as sweeping as that created by the Internet.

---

[12] See, Tom Standage, *The Victorian Internet: The Remarkable Story of the Telegraph and the Nineteenth Century's On-line Pioneers* (New York: Berkley Trade, 1999).

Globalization 1.0 crashed and burned, in the wake of World War I and the Great Depression that followed, as countries engaged in competitive currency devaluations to try to *export* the unemployment they suffered to other countries. World trade soon evaporated. Some experts believe that the global financial crisis of 2007–08 may have a similar disastrous impact on global trade and capital flows. New York Times columnist Paul Krugman observes that "today's high degree of global economic interdependence, which can be sustained only if all major governments act sensibly, is more fragile than we imagine".[13] And who among us are willing to bet on major governments acting sensibly?

If nationalism killed globalization in the 1920s and 1930s, can it occur again? This may or not occur. But clearly, a broad knowledge of 19th century economic history will equip global managers with vital tools needed to understand 21st century trends.

After reading this book, we hope our readers will have a clear historical perspective, and will see unfolding events now and in the future as part of an entire historical development and evolution, unfolding over two centuries, rather than as a series of isolated perplexing individual events that are seemingly unrelated.

RELEVANCE, TIMELINESS, AND TOPICALITY

The British poet John Keats died young; he was only 25. On his tombstone he ordered that the following words be written: "Here lies one whose name was writ in water."

Keats' name, of course, became immortal, far from being "written on water". But at times, those who write about global risk wish they had written on water. World markets change so frequently, so rapidly and so extensively, that a book on global risk that aspires to be relevant and topical is necessarily obsolete the moment the ink dries. A very early version of this text was completed in September, 1997. Because it failed to address the unfolding Asian crisis that began with the collapse of the Thai baht in July, 1997, it had to be scrapped. The same thing happened repeatedly, as crisis overtook crisis.

This version, the last, will seek to relate to timely and topical events, such as the global liquidity crisis that began in July 2007. But it will do this in full awareness that such analysis will seem dated, perhaps even erroneous, within a year. Deep understanding of events in global markets requires some distance in time to fully grasp their nature. Hence, many of our country case studies will be taken from the past. We have chosen the 10 tools in our toolbox specifically to enable managers to

---

[13] Paul Krugman, "The Great Illusion", New York Times, Op-Ed, August 15, 2008.

address the challenges of the future, but largely choose to explain and implement those tools using historical examples. One reason is that like assembling a 1,000-piece jigsaw puzzle, making sense of global events demands a systemic holistic grasp—and putting together the pieces in the puzzle requires careful reflection. Often the key pieces are precisely those not seen or reported by the media.

TRACKING MONEY AND MARKETS: HOW SOLVING ONE CRISIS CREATED ANOTHER

Chapter Two will focus on some of the long-run structural aspects of the 2007–09 global crisis. In this chapter, we look at the short-run aspects—how the well-meaning efforts to deal with one crisis (the dot.com bubble collapse in 2000–01) created the conditions that caused another, far worse crisis in 2007.

On March 9, 2000, the electronic NASDAQ (National Association of Securities Dealers Automated Quotations) market featuring mainly technology stocks collapsed, falling quickly from a level of over 5,000 to around 1,250, losing some three-fourths of its value. The dot.com bubble had been created when investment banks floated initial public issues of companies which had little or no revenues and no profits, but whose dot.com name created public perceptions of huge future profits—perceptions fed by the analysts of the same investment banks whose television appearances and published opinions pushed those same stocks.[14] At the time, the Dow Jones 30 Industrial Stock Index, based on blue-chip stocks, also slumped, though far less—about 20 percent, from around 11,000 to about 9,000.

It is important to note that many of the key underlying events that led to creating an unsustainable bubble *were not directly observed or observable by most of the market participants. Their actions were based on the implicit trust and faith placed in market experts, especially the investment banks.* That trust collapsed almost in the twinkling of an eye, on September 15, 2008. On that day Lehman Brothers, a leading American investment bank founded in 1850, declared bankruptcy, in the face of huge losses due to positions in sub-prime mortgages and securities backed by them. Shock waves echoed throughout capital markets, where investors had assumed the collapse of a 158-year-old investment bank would never be allowed by the Federal Reserve. Once lost, investor trust is extraordinarily difficult to restore. And the collapse was two-sided. Investors lost faith in those who mediated their actions. And banks lost faith in those to whom they were lending. As a result, liquidity (*money*) declined rapidly and drastically, despite desperate efforts by the American Central Bank, the

---

[14] See dot.com, *Frontline* (Public Broadcasting System), 2002.

Fed, to pump liquidity into the system. These efforts were equivalent to *pushing on a string*, because the Fed can push liquidity into the banking system, but if banks are reluctant to lend those reserves (instead holding them to bolster their crumbling balance-sheet position), and if borrowers are reluctant to borrow, avoiding debt during times of deflation and downturn, then credit markets will remain frozen. And this is precisely what happened, not only in America but in Britain and other countries, too (See Chapter Six for a fuller discussion of money and credit).

GLOBAL CRISIS 2007: CAUSE-AND-EFFECT

Often, organizations solve one crisis by creating another. For example, fierce cost-cutting can temporarily combat shrinking profit margins, but may lead to bankruptcy if the cuts include investments in innovation and Research and Development (R&D). Countries, too, do the same. Here is how America created a large crisis by myopically dealing with a much smaller one.

On March 9, 2000, equity prices on the NASDAQ electronic stock exchange collapsed. The NASDAQ exchange lists mainly technology stocks. From 1996, when Netscape (the company that pioneered Internet browsers) floated its initial public offering (IPO) of shares and astonished the world with its rapid ten-fold rise in share prices, Wall Street understood it had stumbled on a powerful money machine. A great many other technology companies had IPO's, even though most had little or no revenue and very flimsy underlying business models. The resulting bubble collapsed on March 9, 2000. The collapse spread to other parts of the capital market and equity prices in general went into decline, with the Dow Jones 30 Industrial Stock Index falling by some 20 percent.[15]

To prevent the capital market decline from creating a deep and prolonged recession, US Federal Reserve Chair, Alan Greenspan, initiated a rapid and unprecedented sharp cut in interest rates (Figure 1.3) in January 2001. Within 12 months, by January 2002, Federal Funds interest rates (the very-short-term interest rate set by America's Central Bank—see Chapter Six) had fallen from 6.5 percent down to 1.75 percent. They were to fall even further, to 1 percent. This sharp fall in interest

---

[15] The Dow Jones 30 Stock Industrial Average is the simple sum of the price of 30 leading American stocks, and was first published in 1896. (It is adjusted for stock splits.) The 30 companies are mainly traditional industrial ones: 3M, Alcoa, American Express, AT&T, Bank of America, Boeing, Caterpillar, Chevron, Citigroup, Coca-Cola, DuPont, ExxonMobil, GE, General Motors, HP, Home Depot, IBM, Intel, Johnson and Johnson, J.P. Morgan Chase, Kraft, McDonald's, Merck, Microsoft, Pfizer, Procter and Gamble, United Technologies, Verizon, Wal-Mart and Walt Disney.

FIGURE 1.3   United States, Federal Funds Interest Rate; House Price Index, 2000–2008

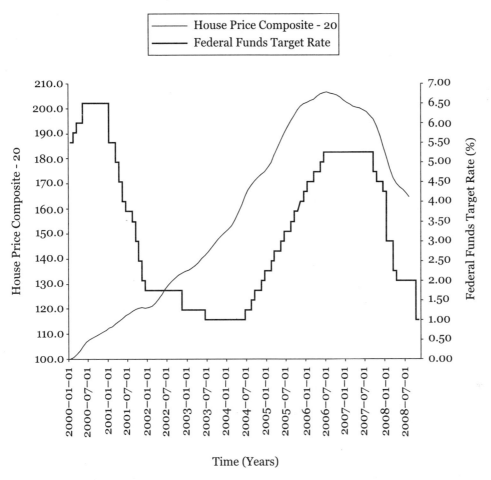

Time (Years)

Source: A. Tishler, Tel Aviv University, Tel Aviv, Israel.

rates was accompanied by a massive expansion in credit and in the money supply (Discussed in detail in Chapter Six).

Why did Greenspan slash interest rates so drastically? Greenspan sought to stimulate the housing market, a major source of economic activity, demand, and employment. Lower interest rates stimulate mortgage lending, create housing demand, boost housing prices, and lead to even further demand for housing. And indeed, this is what happened. As Figure 1.3 shows, housing prices quickly doubled. A housing bubble resulted.

How do we know it was a bubble, and that housing prices rose to unrealistic levels? Figure 1.4 shows the ratio of average house prices to median annual family income, from 1978 through 2008. The bubble is clearly visible. When house prices rose to four times median family income, from the long-term norm of about 2.75, in July 2006, it became clear that the price of houses had soared beyond the levels of income available to support mortgage payments. House prices began to decline. That decline set in motion a string of events that ultimately toppled major banks, crashed equity prices, and spread throughout the world.

FIGURE 1.4   United States, House Prices/Median Family Income, 1978–2008

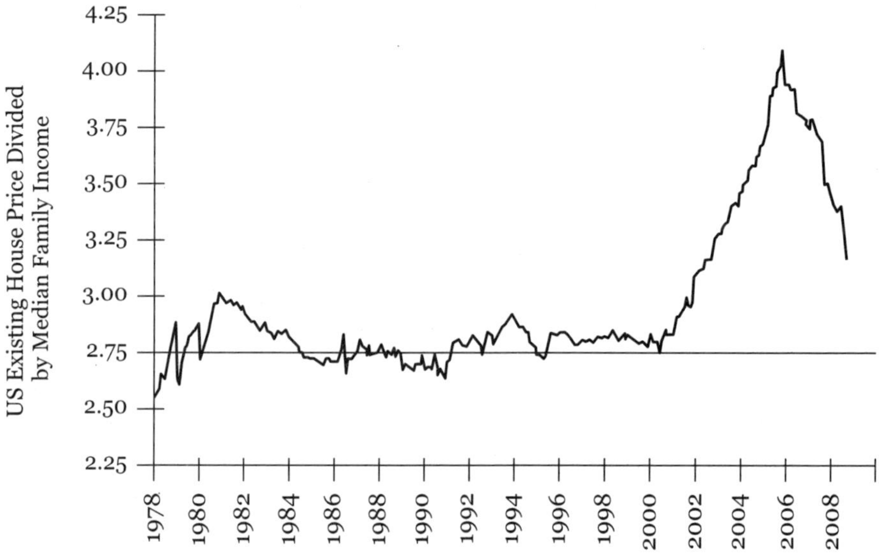

Source: A. Tishler, Tel Aviv University, Tel Aviv, Israel.

A major contributing factor to the housing bubble collapse was the recognition of Alan Greenspan and America's Fed (its Central Bank) that it had created an unsustainable bubble, that inflation was accelerating, and that interest rates were at unsustainable low levels (Indeed, real interest rates—the difference between nominal rates and the rate of inflation—had become negative, a sure sign that money had become excessively cheap). In the summer of 2004, Greenspan and the Fed began to raise interest rates almost as rapidly as they had slashed them (see Figure 1.3). By the summer of 2006 interest rates were back to 5 percent. In June 2007, it occurred to participants in capital markets that risk premiums no longer reflected reality. The reasons are given in later chapters. There ensued a chain of events, described below, that led to a scenario very few had anticipated: Global capital market collapse.

An important question arises: Historically central banks are cautious in changing interest rates, because capital markets do not favor rapid changes either upward or downward. Why then did America's Fed slash interest rates so rapidly and drastically, only to raise them almost equally drastically? Was this a key source of instability that ultimately toppled America's capital markets and the world's? And, had managers worldwide been equipped with basic macroeconomic tools, would they have perceived the enormous dangers inherent in this irresponsible policy of the US Fed?

How many managers had Figures 1.3 and 1.4, or their equivalents, tacked on the wall in their offices? If they had, would they have been better equipped to anticipate the collapse of the bubble and prepare for it?

UNDERSTANDING THE 2007 CAPITAL MARKET COLLAPSE

The great uncertainty of all data in war is a peculiar difficulty, because all action must, to a certain extent, be planned in a mere twilight, which in addition not infrequently—like the effect of a fog or moonshine—gives to things exaggerated dimensions and unnatural appearance.

Gen. Carl Von Clausewitz[16]

The German general von Clausewitz famously spoke of *the fog of war*. Today the world is wrapped in a *fog of peace*. Thick fog enshrouds global capital markets. Few understand clearly what exactly happened that led to the rapid collapse of asset prices, culminating in the 7 percent decline in the Dow Jones Average on Thursday, October 9, 2008, exactly one year after the Index reached its all-time high. During the week that ended on October 10, 2008, the decline in the Dow Jones Index amounted to 20 percent, the steepest one-week fall since the Dow Jones was created in 1896.

Here is our attempt at explaining for our readers, what exactly caused this huge train wreck, based on six key principles.

1. In capital markets, it is not stocks, bonds, and other paper assets that are bought and sold. It is RISK!

   Sophisticated bankers and financial experts bought contracts they did not fully understand. American International Group (AIG), a huge global insurance

---

[16] Clausewitz Carl Von 1873, trans., Colonel J.J.Graham, *On War*. Chapter 2, paragraph 24 (London: N. Trubner), Also available at http://www.clausewitz.com/readings/On war1873/TOC.htm

and financial company, bought assets known as Credit Default Swaps (CDS), insuring companies like Lehman Brothers against credit default. They treated these contracts like regular insurance. They were not. They failed to estimate the enormous downside risk these contracts entailed. The result destroyed the company, even though this part of AIG's business was very small compared to its conventional global insurance business.

CASE STUDY

June 13, 2007: The Day the World Changed Forever[17]

 On Wednesday, June 13, 2007, the world changed forever. Sophisticated investors rediscovered the above principle: that it is *risk* that is priced in capital markets, not assets. The day before, on June 12, the interest-rate spread between 10-year US Treasury bonds (riskless) and junk bonds (high risk) shrank to only 2.4 percentage points. The return on junk bonds was 7.7 percent, and on Treasuries, 5.3 percent, despite the hugely massive difference in risk levels. On June 13, investors finally woke up. They sensed the detachment from reality, and began pricing risk properly. Yields on Treasuries fell, and on junk bonds, rose. By April, 2008 the price of junk bond risk was 7 percent. That is, junk bonds carried yields 7 percent higher than riskless Treasuries or AAA-rated bonds (see Figure 1.5). An immediate consequence was that risky bonds, including securities backed by sub-prime mortgages fell drastically in price.[18] (This is because there is an inverse relation between bond prices and their yield, or interest rate.) This, in turn, set in motion a chain of events that ultimately bankrupted major banks and investment houses and initiated the global crisis.

2. In global capital markets, one form of risk is consistently underestimated. It is called *perfect storm risk*.

Once every decade or so, factors combine that singly are fairly uncommon, and taken together, are even more uncommon, but when combined, they destroy the world. This is called *perfect storm risk*. In July, 2007, sub-prime mortgage default, global inflation, rising oil prices, and the falling dollar,

---

[17] Based on Geoff Colvin, "Why the Party's Over", *Fortune* May 5 (2008): 126.

[18] Sub-prime mortgage holders are those with low incomes, who probably should not have qualified for a mortgage in the first place.

FIGURE 1.5 Risk Premium: Junk Bonds vs. AAA and BAA Bonds, 2006–2008, and Chain of Major Collapses of Investment Banks

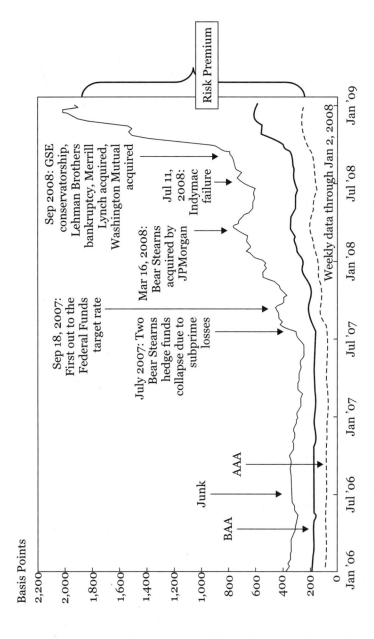

Source: Council of Economic Advisors, Economic Report of the President, 2009 (p. 52).

Note: Junk Bonds are high risk; AAA bonds are very low risk and BAA Bonds are moderately low-risk.

combined together to create a perfect storm. This has happened before. We had a perfect storm like this during the *Asian contagion* of 1998. The result was to cause the hedge fund known as Long Term Capital Management (LTCM) to incur liabilities of some USD 1 trillion.[19] Had not Alan Greenspan and the American Fed come to the rescue (even though they were not authorized to do so, because LTCM was registered in the Cayman Islands), there would have been a financial collapse similar to the one the world is witnessing today. Greenspan's bailout gave LTCM enough time to *unwind* its huge liabilities without destroying world markets or knocking over the banks from which it had borrowed billions. We should have realized then that the world might not be so lucky the next time. This is that next time.

3. Be sure to understand the dynamics of the industry in which you do business.

The global insurance company American International Group (AIG) came within days of bankruptcy and was bailed out by the US Treasury to the tune of USD 85 billion. Why?

AIG failed to understand that a financial innovation known as *default risk insurance* is not like life insurance. (see Case Study: Credit Default Swaps). AIG's big mistake was to treat the risk of default on mortgage-backed bonds, which it insured, like regular insurance, charging premiums of about 2 percent (for example, on a USD 10 million liability, it charged USD 200,000 a year in insurance premiums). In normal times, this is adequate. But in a *perfect storm* financial crisis, it is not. AIG is an insurance company. It understands insurance. It apparently did not understand complex derivative markets. The result was fatal.

Rule: Do business in areas you understand.

When you insure people's lives, it is impossible for all the insured people to die on the same day. If they did, AIG would be broke. But when you insure companies' bonds, it is entirely likely that all these bonds *die* on the same day, because in a global crisis this is what happens. Markets become *sellers only*, and then nobody's bonds are worth anything. AIG failed to take this into account.

---

[19] A hedge fund is an investment fund allowed by regulators to invest in a broader range of assets than other investment funds, including shares, debt, commodities, and so forth. It is called a hedge fund, because it hedges risk by investing in a wide range of assets, spreading risk and thus reducing it.

4. Capital markets will regularly have major crises, every five years or so. It is *baked into the cake*.

Former assistant secretary of Commerce Norman Rothkopf once said, "One thing we all agree—there will be another crisis, it is 'baked into the cake'."[20] He said this in 2000, after the Asian crisis saw Asian currencies collapse and then saw Russia default on its debt in August, 1998. He was right. There are fundamental flaws in global capital markets that lead to repeated crises. One of those flaws is the *talent asymmetry* of regulation (see below).

5. In the contest between Wall Street and the bodies that regulate their activities, Wall Street will always win, finding a way to outflank the regulators even when the latter are trying their best. This is what we refer to as *asymmetry of regulation*.

The Bush Administration had consistently appointed regulators who fought to minimize government regulation of capital markets and allow investment banks to do whatever they pleased. But even when regulators are tough—as they are likely to be under the new Democratic Administration—the contest is unfair. Regulators are government employees, paid government salaries. Wall Street *innovators* are paid Wall Street bonuses, which can add up to millions of dollars yearly, many times what a regulator earns. What are the chances that an MIT (Massachusetts Institute of Technology) whiz kid financial engineer can outflank a government bureaucrat? Probably 100 percent. This is what happened with so-called *credit default swaps* (CDS)—the derivative market that soared to some USD 65 trillion, greater than world GDP.

Credit default swaps (CDS) are insurance contracts sold by the insurer, the *seller*, to the insured, the *buyer*. These insurance policies pay damages if an asset (like a mortgage-backed bond) is in default. A typical premium might be 2 percent of the default value J.P. Morgan, the bank that invented them, called them *swaps* rather than *insurance*, because calling them *insurance* would have subjected them to regulation by the bodies that regulated insurance. Swaps are, under the Commodity Futures Modernization Act of 2000, specifically unregulated. Huge losses from CDS's ruined Lehman Brothers, Bear Stearns, AIG, and other financial services institutions. Warren Buffet, head of Berkshire Hathaway, widely regarded as the world's leading investment guru, once

---

[20] Source: CD: The Great Crash, Frontline, PBS, 2001.

called CDS's "financial weapons of mass destruction". His intuition was right. (see Case Study).

CASE STUDY

Credit Default Swaps

 Once, there was a great bank named J.P. Morgan, named after its founder, financier John Pierpont Morgan. In 1994, J.P. Morgan gave a small group of young M.I.T. graduates in financial engineering, an assignment. We lend money, the bank said. The law makes us keep cash reserves to back those loans. But we want to use those reserves to lend more money. Find a way. They did. Why not insure the loans, said the young geniuses, so there is no risk? Then, J.P. Morgan need not hold reserves. We will call these insurance contracts *credit default insurance*. For instance, the global insurance company American International Group (AIG) will insure default on mortgage-backed bonds, at a premium of 2 percent a year. To illustrate, J.P. Morgan will insure USD 10 million in bonds by paying AIG USD 200,000 as insurance premium every year. If the bonds become worthless when people default on their mortgages, AIG pays J.P. Morgan USD 10 million. *Wait!* said the experts. Let's call them credit default swaps (CDS), because, if we call them *insurance*, they will be subjected to government regulation. According to the Commodity Futures Modernization Act (2000), *swaps* are specifically exempt from any government regulation. Wow, what a loophole! So yearly, the market for these CDS's doubled. It soon equaled some USD 65 trillion, larger than world Gross Domestic Product. The CDS market became a great Las Vegas in the sky.

Then, the perfect storm happened. One company after another went into default. AIG could not pay. It was as if everyone who held a life insurance policy died on the same day. Warren Buffett expresses his concerns with derivatives, referring to the Wild West unregulated CDS market as "weapons of mass destruction".[21] One company after the other failed and like dominos, began to knock over other companies. The US government had to bail them out. The credit default swap turned into a financial swamp.

---

[21] Helen Simon, "Are Derivatives Financial Weapons of Mass Destruction", www.investopedia.com (accessed January 25, 2010).

6. In a perfect storm, one *domino* topples another, amplifying the impact by a thousand times.

In meteorology, a perfect storm is a rare joining of atmospheric conditions, all occurring at the same time that creates especially ferocious weather disturbances. A perfect storm occurred in global capital markets in 2007–08. When AIG found it could not pay its debts, in the CDS realm, its losses (like a hot potato) threatened to topple other institutions (Lehman Brothers, major banks). They would have lost billions, and that in turn would have made them unable to pay their debts, in turn toppling even more banks. To some degree this has happened rapidly, even before America and Europe could develop strong bailout strategies. Governments need to act extremely rapidly, to stop the dominos from toppling one another. But because of the thick *fog* enveloping markets, such rapid action is rarely possible or likely.

There is perhaps one additional principle. After the crisis, you can always look back and see clearly what touched it off, but can never see this while it is happening. According to Stephen Labaton, writing in the *International Herald Tribune*, a meeting of the American Securities Exchange Commission on April 28, 2004, that lasted less than one hour, led to a decision that directly caused the current crisis. On that day, five American investment banks, led by Goldman Sachs, pressed the SEC to exempt their brokerage units from a rule limiting the amount of debt they could incur. This would free funds so they could invest in CDSs. The SEC quickly agreed. The individual who *led the charge* was named Henry (Hank) Paulsen, the same Hank Paulsen who was appointed US Secretary of the Treasury on May 30, 2006, and as such had to craft the bailout plan to save banks from the very disaster his 2004 *charge* caused.

The "fog" described by von Clausewitz still exists. No one knows for sure what the magnitude of potential losses are, from Credit Default Swaps, because, being unregulated, they are traded *over the counter*, hence no one knows for sure what they are worth.

The enormous sum America's Congress has allocated for its bailout, USD 700 billion, sounds adequate, but it is miniscule compared to the potential CDS losses, in a USD 65 trillion market. We are still in the eye of the *perfect storm*, and no one knows how much more damage it will cause.

As the following case study shows, not all Central Bankers succumbed to excessive credit creation or bubble creation. Some were anti-Greenspan.

CASE STUDY

INDIA[22]

 It is interesting that India avoided much of the *bubble* damage because of a courageous leader.

India had a bank regulator who was anti-Greenspan. His name was Dr Y.V. Reddy, and he was the governor of the Reserve Bank of India. Seventy percent of the banking system in India is nationalized, so a strong regulator is critical, since any banking scandal amounts to a national political scandal as well. And in the irascible Reddy, who took office in 2003 and stepped down in September 2008, it had exactly the right man in the right job at the right time.

"He basically believed that if bankers were given the opportunity to sin, they would sin," said one banker who asked not to be named because, well, there's not much percentage in getting on the wrong side of the Reserve Bank of India. For all the bankers' talk about their higher lending standards, the truth is that Reddy made them even more stringent during the bubble. Unlike Alan Greenspan, who did not believe it was his job to even point out bubbles, much less try to deflate them, Reddy saw his job as making sure Indian banks did not get too caught up in the bubble mentality. About two years ago, he started sensing that real estate, in particular, had entered bubble territory. One of the first moves he made was to ban the use of bank loans for the purchase of raw land, which was skyrocketing. Only when the developer was about to commence building could the bank get involved—and then only to make construction loans (Guess who wound up financing the land purchases? US private equity and hedge funds, of course!). Then, as securitizations and derivatives gained increasing prominence in the world's financial system, the Reserve Bank of India sharply curtailed their use in the country. When Reddy saw US banks setting up off-balance-sheet vehicles to hide debt, he essentially banned them in India. As a result, banks in India wound up holding onto the loans they made to customers. On the one hand, this meant they made fewer loans than their US counterparts because they could not sell off the loans to Wall Street in securitizations. On the other hand, it meant they still had the incentive—as US banks did not—to see those loans paid back.

Seeing inflation on the horizon, Reddy pushed interest rates up to more than 20 percent, which of course dampened the housing frenzy. He increased risk weightings on commercial buildings and shopping mall construction; doubling the amount of capital banks were required to hold in reserve in case things went awry. He made banks put aside extra capital for every loan they made. In effect, Reddy was creating liquidity even before there was a global liquidity crisis.

(Case Study continued)

[22] Joe Nocera, "How India avoided a crisis", *International Herald Tribune*, December 19, http://www.nytimes.com/2008/12/20/business/20nocera.html?_r=1&scp=2&sq=nocera&st=nyt. (accessed January 18, 2010).

(*Case Study continued*)

Did India's bankers stand up to applaud Reddy as he was making these moves? Of course not. They were naturally furious, just as American bankers would have been if Greenspan had been more active. Their regulator was holding them back, constraining their growth! Deepak Parekh of HDFC felt that while he had been saying for some time that Indian real estate was in bubble territory, he was still unhappy with the rules imposed by Reddy. "We were critical of the central bank," he said. "We thought these were harsh measures."

"For a while we were wondering if we were missing out on something," said Ms Kochhar of ICICI. Banks in the United States seemed to have come up with some magical new formula for making money: make loans that required no down payment and little in the way of verification—and post instant, short-term, profits.

As Luis Miranda, who runs a private equity firm devoted to developing India's infrastructure, put it: "We kept wondering if they had figured out something that we were too dense to figure out. It looked like they were smart and we were stupid." Instead, India was the smart one, and they were the stupid ones.

Ms Kochhar said that the underlying risks of having "a majority of loans not owned by the people who originated them" was not apparent during the bubble. Now that those risks have been made painfully clear, every banker in India realizes that Reddy did the right thing by limiting securitizations." At times like this, you tend to appreciate what he did more than we did at the time," said Mr Kapoor.

ON THE VITAL NEED FOR MANAGERIAL RESILIENCE

The plain truth is, no matter how well managers practice scenario planning, and no matter how many graphs they tack up on their wall to track global minds, markets and money, the world will remain a highly unstable place in the foreseeable future and that uncertainty will doubtless increase. Again, America serves as an example.

Figure 1.6 shows net income after tax for American corporations as a percent of GDP. Figure 1.7 shows the year-to-year change in net income, for the period 1962–2008.

Engineers who understand signal processing, or electrical signals, will quickly perceive that the amplitude of fluctuations in net income has been growing for some 40 years. It may also be true that the frequency of such fluctuations is growing. The financial sector has apparently been a major contributing factor. Figure 1.6 shows that when financial profits are included, corporate profits peaked at 6 percent of GDP in 2006. In that year, financial services accounted for fully 40 percent of all corporate profits in America. This is another indicator that, had we tracked it carefully, it would have given strong signals that a major bubble was about to collapse.

An important implication of these two figures is that managers and leaders worldwide will, in future, need to have in their core competency toolbox, the ability to react quickly and vigorously to unexpected events—a quality known as resiliency. As strategy guru Gary Hamel notes, the world is becoming turbulent faster than organizations are becoming resilient. He notes that over the past four decades, the

FIGURE 1.6   United States: Net Income, Incorporated Businesses, as Percentage of GDP, 1962–2008

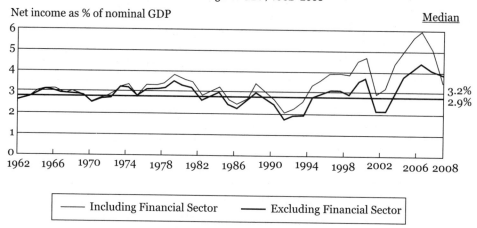

Source: Financial Crises—Past and Present, by David Cogman and Richard Dobbs, McKinsey Global Research Institute, McKinsey Quarterly, December, 2008, p. 3.

FIGURE 1.7   United States: Year-to-Year Percentage Change in Net Income, 1962–2008

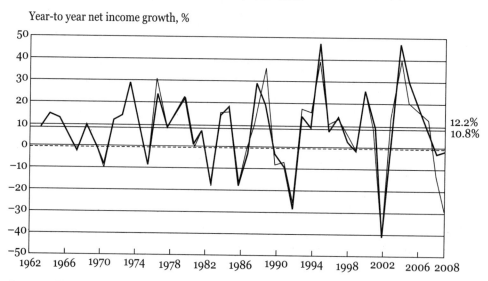

Source: Financial Crises—Past and Present, by David Cogman and Richard Dobbs, McKinsey Global Research Institute, McKinsey Quarterly, December, 2008, p. 3.

volatility of the earnings of the 500 Standard and Poor companies has increased by nearly 50 percent.[23]

Hamel notes that resilient organizations overcome four challenges:

- Cognitive: resisting denial, facing brutal facts, and recognizing threats and challenges.
- Strategic: ability to adapt strategies quickly to changing business environments.
- Political: organizational politics tend to resist major shifts in capital allocation and closing of unprofitable businesses; resilience demands these measures.
- Ideological: Peter Drucker defines a manager as someone who does things right; and a leader as someone who does the right things. Resilient organizations constantly examine if they are doing the right things, in the face of market turbulence, and react quickly if the answer is negative. This requires ideological flexibility. Google, for example, has strategically repositioned itself from being a pure Internet search engine company, to becoming the world's largest media company that gains billions of dollars in revenues from selling advertising. This requires enormous resilience. Not all organizations are capable of it.

Is your organization resilient? This action learning exercise will test it.

ACTION LEARNING

Organizational Resilience

Note: This exercise can be applied to you the reader, personally, or to an organization for which you work or have worked in the past.

- In your organization's culture, are there stories about how managers and leaders stepped forward in times of challenge and crisis, to react quickly and lead the organization out of trouble?
- Does your organization regularly examine potential life-threatening threats and discuss how to face them?
- Are you, and your organization's leaders, able to describe convincingly, in past tense, a scenario in which your organization's technology, products and business design quickly become obsolete and irrelevant, and the organization disappears?
- Do managers in your organization regularly take responsibility far beyond their authority and job definitions, in order to meet challenges that arise unexpectedly?

---

[23] Gary Hamel and Liisa Valikangas, "The Quest for Resilience," *Harvard Business Review* 81, no.9 (2003): 52–63.

Resilient organizations have the key ability to do what management guru Jim Collins calls "face the brutal facts".[24] When they do so, they are far better equipped to undertake transformative change, a key element of resilience. One approach to encouraging the ability to face the brutal facts is to engage in scenario planning—the main tool presented in this chapter.

Tool #1

Scenario Planning[25]

Scenarios differ in important ways from forecasts.

- A forecast defines the present situation, describes the future situation and indicates a single path followed from the present to the future. Many forecasts do not in fact define the path or causality but only the end result. Forecasters often prefer to keep their forecasting models as *black boxes*, to preserve their intellectual property. Some forecasting models are so complex that even their constructors do not fully understand them.
- A scenario is simply a story, describing *vividly* what may happen and how it will come about. Because it is vivid, it is believable, even though improbable. Scenario analysis:

  (*a*) describes perceived current realities as a *mental map* (and which may differ widely among members of the group constructing them);

  (*b*) defines several alternative *images of the future*, in tangible, concrete form; and

  (*c*) describes paths that could be followed that generate these scenarios.

Scenario planning is a vital, perhaps indispensable, tool for turning risk into opportunity, by carrying out the necessary task of defining and recognizing potential risks, including some that are *unthinkable*. Scenarios become an opportunity for a strategic conversation, in which participants outline their personal *teleologies*

---

[24] Jim Collins, *Good to Great: Why Some Companies Make the Leap—And Others Don't*, (New York: Harper Business, 2001), 85.

[25] This section is based in part on: Peter Cornelius, Alexander van de Putte, Mattia Romani, "Three Decades of Scenario Planning in Shell", *California Management Review*, Fall 48, no. 1 (2005): 92–109.

(cause-and-effect theories—see Chapter Two). It is the process of scenario planning that is valuable, not just the product, because it *mines* the strategic insights of several minds and produces the opposite of what Irving Janis has called "groupthink" or herd mentality. The process can inoculate organizations against mental *blind spots*—inability to see risks, that are somewhat hidden and potentially life-threatening. The objective of scenario planning, and the measure of its success, is the degree to which it prepares the organization for a wider range of possibilities, opportunities and eventualities, and helps the organization make rapid decisions in crisis while other organizations are frozen by the depth and enormity of the strategic surprise.

Here is a case study showing successful implementation of scenario planning. The global petroleum company Royal Dutch Shell used scenario planning to gain key competitive advantage in the turbulent conditions of 1972–73.

CASE STUDY

Scenario Planning at Royal Dutch Shell, 1972

 The British–Dutch global oil company Royal Dutch Shell weathered the 1973–74 oil embargo and oil price spike better than its competitors. The main reason was that it was prepared for it. But how? Pierre Wack, who together with Arie de Geus led Shell's scenario planning, claims that forecasts tend to be wrong because they are implicitly or explicitly based on the assumption that the future will be much like the present. But it is precisely when this assumption is wrong, and when *discontinuities* develop that utterly change the global rules of the business game, that forecasts become most misleading and dangerous. This is what happened in 2007–09. Scenario planning helps organizations explore the implications of a rapid and radical change in business conditions and environment. The process is vital in dissipating a common and widespread characteristic of human psychology—'minds'—known as denial, the rejection of scenarios that embody decline, loss, crisis, and collapse. In the 2007–09 global economic crisis, denial persisted at the highest levels, even when it was transparently clear that a huge global downturn was underway.

At Shell, a study known as the "Survey of World Political and Economic Conditions for the Years 1985–2000" was conducted in 1972, and portrayed six vivid tangible scenarios for economic growth, oil supply and oil prices. The scenarios foresaw a disruption in oil supply and production. Shell undertook contingency planning, to define what the company would do if this scenario occurred. As a result, when the Yom Kippur War broke out

(Case Study continued)

(Case Study continued)

on October 6, 1973, oil prices quadrupled and drivers queued for gasoline in America and in Europe, Shell was better prepared than its competitors. It knew what it had to do and did it. It did not need to waste valuable time to strategize the radically new and dangerous situation. Nor were its managers and leaders in a state of denial.

Later, in 1982, scenarios were developed that showed steep and rapid declines in the price of oil. Again Shell found itself prepared for an event that many other organizations were surprised by.

The Method

There are many varieties of scenario planning. Shell's variant uses a *zoom in* approach.

- It begins by a PEST (Political Economic Social Technological) analysis, examining global trends and developing global scenarios. [See Chapter Two for a variant on this, which we call, GELT (Geopolitics, Economic, Lifestyle, Technology) analysis.]
- Shell then zooms in on implications of the global scenario for country or business level.
- The scenario then zooms in further, to the project level (for example, oil and gas exploration projects).

A major objective of this book is to provide managers and leaders with appropriate macroeconomic tools to facilitate strong scenario analysis at the global and country levels. The 10 tools contained in this book, which describe such concepts as GDP, interest rates, money and credit, trade, foreign exchange, capital flows, equity prices, inflation and deflation, and budget and trade deficits, are indispensable in conducting such global and country scenario planning.

GLOBAL OPPORTUNITIES

What, then, are the opportunities arising from what appears like undiluted folly and disaster?

Readers are invited to consider their own insights. Here is only one view.

The flimsy structure of global financial services changed almost overnight. The Wild West unregulated behavior of American investment banks ended with the bankruptcy of Lehman Brothers, and the redefinition of leading investment banks as banking holding companies, subject to the regulatory supervision of commercial banks. Thousands of persons employed on Wall Street, in financial services, have been shown on television leaving their offices forever, carrying boxes of personal effects.

In our interactions with young students, we encounter many who have deep passion and interest in financial engineering and financial services, but who assume that because of the collapse, there is no future in this realm.

We counsel the opposite. In any industry, when the rules of the game are being radically rewritten, there are huge opportunities for persons with energy, wisdom and creativity. The financial services industry is a vital and integral part of the global economy. Global business and trade is dependent on a smoothly-operating global capital market. Hence, the financial services industry will be reinvented and reborn. Those who lead this process—leaders with courage and vision—will do both good for society and do well for themselves. We urge all those who seek careers in financial services not to abandon them, while cautioning that the road ahead may well be rocky for several years.

For those in other industries, we note that the global shortage of liquidity and credit creates new opportunities for business models that economize on this now-scarce resource. Those who see ways to save money, and to do business without it (a process known as boot-strapping), can do well. Those with courage enough to launch new businesses, in a time when it is widely assumed (*groupthink*) that global recession makes entrepreneurship impossible, will enjoy a rare situation with a low level of competition and with a loaded generous global market for talent.

But how can leaders and managers build powerful businesses on insights into global trends and risk? Our next chapter offers a systematic, disciplined approach known as GELT.

Chapter 2

What is your story? How to build powerful global narratives

LEARNING OBJECTIVES

- After reading this chapter, you should understand why it is vital for managers to acquire their own macroeconomic analytic tools, and develop their own perspective on key trends in global markets.
- You should understand precisely what a global manager is, and how a global manager thinks and acts on that thinking.
- You should know what *teleology* (the study of cause-and-effect) means, and why becoming good at understanding teleology in global markets is important.
- You will learn how a systems thinker uses dynamic feedback loops to understand fundamental causality as it unfolds in world markets. You should be able to construct feedback loops that identify the key dynamic processes occurring in global markets.
- You should be able to use the GELT model (geopolitics, economics, lifestyle, technology) to identify key global trends and build a narrative from them that leads to global strategies.
- You should be familiar with the recent history of global markets, and have in your mind a teleological account of events as they unfolded from November 9, 1989 to the present.

TOOL # 2

GELT—Geopolitics, Economics, Lifestyle, Technology

With this tool you will be able to construct persuasive narratives (teleologies) about key global macro-trends, and use them to identify global business opportunities, often arising from contexts that appear to primarily, contain risk.

Additional tools related to GELT are: Feedback Loops: causal connections among variables, with *input* leading to *output*, feeding back to *input*, and so on. Many key global processes, especially those that drive asset prices, and financial crises, are feedback loops. With practice you should become an expert at analyzing unfolding global trends as a cause-and-effect system. You must practice understanding the teleology that unfolded in the past, in order to grasp the teleology unfolding in the present and future.

INTRODUCTION: JORMA OLLILA, GLOBAL MANAGER

In this chapter, we will define in concrete terms what it means to be a global manager, and will begin providing the reader, tools to achieve this goal, and thus raise your global perspective to a new and higher level.

In management, by far the best way to understand concepts is through stories—which are sometimes given the boring name, *case studies*. Our book contains many such stories.

So we chose to begin our book with a great story—how a truly global manager built a remarkable global company known as Nokia, through a deep insight obtained from watching an event—the fall of the Berlin Wall—that hundreds of millions *watched*, all over the world, but few truly *saw*. The manager in question is Jorma Ollila.

FALL OF THE WALL AND THE RISE OF NOKIA

The background to our case study is the startling events of November 9, 1989, the day the Berlin Wall fell. Ollila was then a mid-level manager at the Finnish conglomerate Nokia. Nokia at the time was in considerable difficulty. With the disintegration of the U.S.S.R., a key customer of Finland and Nokia, Nokia was about to lose its main market. While on vacation with his family in southern France, Ollila watched the fall of the Wall on television. He saw a huge business opportunity that others did not.

CASE STUDY

Nokia: Identifying and Seizing a Global Opportunity

 Jorma Jaakko Ollila was born in Seinäjoki, Finland, on August 15, 1950, and is the Chairman (since 1999), and former Chief Executive Officer, of Nokia Corporation (1992–2006). As of June 1, 2006 he became the Non-Executive Chairman of Royal Dutch Shell and Non-Executive Chairman of Nokia.

Prior to joining Nokia in 1985, Jorma Ollila worked for eight years in corporate banking at Citibank's London and Helsinki offices, and when he joined Nokia his tasks involved international investment deals. A year later, in 1986, Ollila found himself as head of Finance during Nokia's renewal under the then-CEO Kari Kairamo. Kairamo, who suffered from manic depression and later committed suicide on December 11, 1988. Ollila's career at Nokia continued as he was appointed as chief of the mobile phones section in 1990, and CEO two years later in 1992. When Ollila first came

(Case Study continued)

(*Case Study continued*)

into power the company had suffered from internal disputes and had run into a financial crisis over a number of years.

As CEO of Nokia, Ollila has been the leader of the strategy that restructured the former industrial conglomerate into one of the major companies in the mobile phone and telecommunications infrastructure markets in the world.

He was CEO of the company from 1992, and the Chairman and CEO of Nokia from 1999 to 2006 although he still serves as a part-time Chairman. He was succeeded as CEO by Olli-Pekka Kallasvuo.

In 2007, Nokia had a total earning of 51.1 billion euros, and net profit after tax, of 7.2 billion euros. Nokia Group employed worldwide some 112,262 employees. Nokia's total Research and Development spending amounted to 5.647 billion euros. Nokia's share price peaked at € 64.88 on June 21, 2000, declined sharply to € 9.67 on August 25, 2004, and has since almost doubled to € 18.06 in mid-August, 2008.

Here, in Ollila's own words, is how his insight into the implications of the Fall of the Berlin Wall led directly to Nokia's success.[1]

Question: In business schools, the "Ollila teleology (cause-and-effect)" is taught. In November, 1989, you were vacationing with your family in southern France. You watched the fall of the Berlin Wall on television on November 9. You built the following chain of reasoning:

- The fall of the Wall will quickly cause the two Germany's to unite.
- This, in turn, will hasten European unification, and the single European Market.
- In turn, the European Single Market will need, above all, communication.
- Communication will require mobile phones, because of difficulties in integrating national land-line systems.

Based on this reasoning, you returned to Nokia and built Nokia Mobile.

Answer: This is true. Except, I was made head of Nokia Mobile earlier, before the vacation in France (though I did not yet know it).

We made the right bets in the 1990s. It was not a matter of luck. When I returned from France, we divested all our businesses, except the

(*Case Study continued*)

---

[1] Based on a presentation by Jorma Ollila to a group of Israeli managers at Nokia headquarters, Espoo, Finland, July 2007.

(*Case Study continued*)

young mobile business. This was an enormous risk. But it was vital to our success.

We looked at the mobile handset industry. We took a different point of view from our competitors. We made two basic assumptions. They differed from the conventional wisdom.

1. The mobile handset is the NEXT BIG THING. But it is not an executive toy (as it was then); EVERYONE will eventually carry one, perhaps more than one. (At the time, no competitor made that assumption, not until 1998–1999. We were far ahead.)
2. A much less obvious challenge to conventional wisdom: The winner in the mobile handset market will be decided not in the United States, not in Japan but—in Asia!

We assumed that the ticket to being number one lies in the emerging markets. The winner there will rule the world.

Both these assumptions are fundamentally important to our ultimate success. Both were made in 1993 and 1994. We began to work in China in 1994. So we have been there already for 14 years. I have made 53 trips to China since 1988. And we did not have a private jet until 1999. So those trips were mainly made on commercial flights. In 1997, I went to India. We find now that this assumption and these visits have greatly paid off.

Our grasp of globalization was a key success factor.

TELEOLOGY: GLOBAL CAUSE-AND-EFFECT

Ollila made use of a powerful tool known as teleology.

Definition: Tel-e-ol-o-gy. n. Gr. Telos, an end; -logia, study of; the quality of being directed toward a definite end, or of having an ultimate purpose.
—Webster's New World Dictionary

Global managers think in terms of teleologies—cause-and-effect. They think like chess grandmasters, plotting their strategies several moves in advance. This is what Ollila did. He saw that the unification of Germany would lead to a European single market, which would need communication, which could only be provided by cellular phones.

Teleological cause-and-effect thinking is both risky and essential. It is risky, because an error in any of the links that form the chain of logic totally undermines the final business conclusion (in Ollila's case: sell all Nokia's businesses and invest everything in building the Mobile division). It is essential, because without it, global events appear random and unconnected and the ability to anticipate pro-actively, rather than react passively, disappears. (see Figure 2.1).

FIGURE 2.1   Teleology Cause-and-Effect: From the Fall of the Berlin Wall to Nokia Mobile

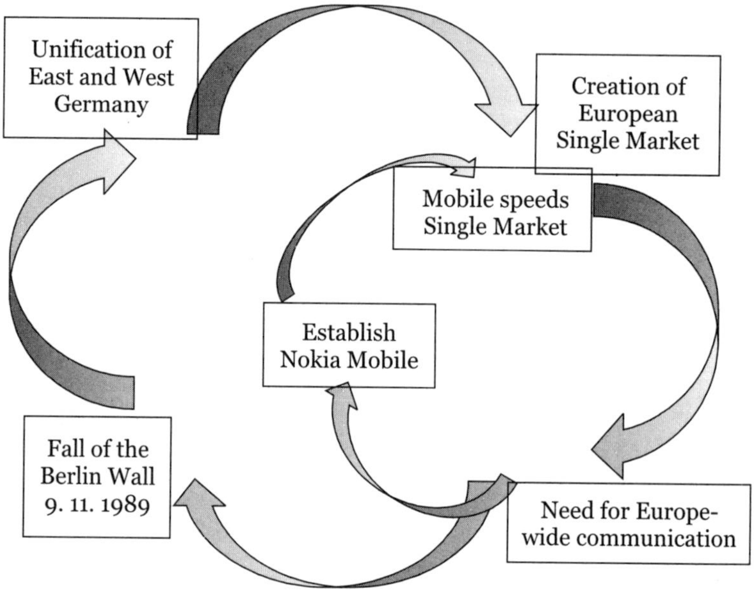

Unification of East and West Germany

Creation of European Single Market

Mobile speeds Single Market

Establish Nokia Mobile

Fall of the Berlin Wall 9. 11. 1989

Need for Europe-wide communication

Source: Authors.

WHAT IS YOUR STORY?

Readers will discern, in Ollila's remarkable business teleology that in the simplest possible terms, he created a powerful narrative—a story, composed of a sequence of events, that seemed plausible and that led to a sweeping business strategy.

So, reader, what is *your* story? What global story do you see unfolding, out of the confusing kaleidoscope of events, crises, changes and conflicts present in today's global markets? Does your story lead to a business strategy? It is important to note that perhaps 90 percent of Nokia's success arose *not* from Ollila's teleology, as wonderful as it was, but rather the excellence in Nokia's *implementation* of the story. It was Formulation: 10 percent and Implementation: 90 percent. Nokia's bold gamble in selling most of its assets and divisions, to raise sufficient resources to support the cash-hungry new Mobile division, was crucial; had the new business been underfunded, it would have doubtless failed.

Is there a tool that can help global managers build future-oriented powerful narratives, one that is able to drive new businesses like Nokia to growth and profit? We offer the reader the GELT tool. After explaining it, an action learning exercise follows.

GELT—GEOPOLITICS, ECONOMICS, LIFESTYLE, TECHNOLOGY

A basic principle of management is that risk and return are linked, positively co-related; generally achieving higher returns requires accepting higher risk. The issue is, does the added return justify the higher risk? Skilled investors seek *bargains*—higher returns that do not entail significantly higher risk.

This is true of global deployment as well. Higher-growth markets are also higher-risk markets. Skilled global managers find growth opportunities without accepting unreasonably high risks. The question is, how to do this?

We propose a simple methodology known as GELT, an acronym that stands for four key inter-related dimensions global managers must track.

- G: Geopolitics: Instabilities and changes resulting from political trends in various regions and countries in the world. For example, the Iranian *Ayatollahs*, Venezuela's President Hugo Chavez, the new French President, the American 2008 Presidential elections.
- E: Economics: Economic trends, including exchange rates, economic growth, trade, exports, finance, interest rates, capital flows.
- L: Lifestyle: Sociology, the way people live, social trends, cohort effects (differing values across age groups). I-pod and I-phone are lifestyle products.
- T: technology: Technology trends, new technologies, new basic science that can lead to new technologies (new ways to produce semi-conductors, new ways to test and evaluate them, new technologies for increasing transistor density on microprocessors, etc.)

These four areas are not independent; they are related. Lifestyle, for instance, can drive technologies (the need for mobility can generate technologies that support it, for example, Centrino; the ageing of society leads to higher healthcare spending, leading to Intel's mobile clinical assistant (MCA); etc.

There are global trends: Major changes in the four GELT categories that need to be tracked. Then there are industry trends: specific trends that impact mainly the semiconductor industry, or the Printed Circuit Board (PCB) or the Flat Panel Display (FPD) sub-industries, for example. A zoom-in approach can be used: begin with the *broad canvas*, zoom in on the specific sub-industries. This helps to avoid missing opportunities arising in *adjacent* industries.

A visual methodology for translating GELT global trend analysis into business opportunities, and action plans is based upon the mind-mapping technique. A mind-map is a diagram used to represent words, ideas, tasks, or other items linked to, and arranged around, a central key word or idea. It is used to generate, visualize, structure, and classify ideas. Our GELT version places the central idea not at the center of the mind-map, but at the end of a causal chain constructed as a narrative linking politics, economics, sociology, and technology.

What follows is a step-by-step method that can help global managers build innovative narratives. It is often helpful to apply this tool in small teams or groups.

THE 8-STEP GELT METHOD

Step 1: The shopping list

List the major trends, over the coming 3–5 years that you believe will impact the world. Put them down quickly. Each individual should take 10 minutes to write a *shopping* list. The team should then together build a single list based on the lists of its members. Write down the key trends regardless of their GELT category, on a flip chart page.

Step 2: Categorize

Beside each trend, write a letter: G, E, L, or T, depending on its category. Some trends may be hard to categorize: if so, write down two letters, such as, G and T.

Step 3: Prioritize

Of the entire list, select the major trends that the team believes will be most important for your organization. There should be 10–20 of them.

Step 4: Quantify

For each trend, assign two numbers, on a scale of 1 to 10. First, IMPACT: the impact of the trend on the industry, from 1 (very low) to 10 (very high). Second: TIMING: WHEN the trend will be fully felt, in *years from now*.

Step 5: Roadmap—diagram

Plot each trend, as a point on an X, Y graph: The X axis is TIME, the Y axis is IMPACT. Use four different colors: G: green; E: red; L: blue; T: black.

Step 6: Teleology *causality* and *narrative*

Connect the dots in a coherent narrative. Link trends, where possible, showing causal connections. Use for your model, the narrative constructed by Jorma Ollila (see Figure 2.2). Have you created a powerful plausible business story?

Step 7: Business opportunities

Identify a major business opportunity, the final destination of your GELT narrative.

Step 8: Action

Construct a business plan that will enable you and your organization to implement your GELT narrative.

FIGURE 2.2   The "GELT" Narrative that Created Nokia Mobile

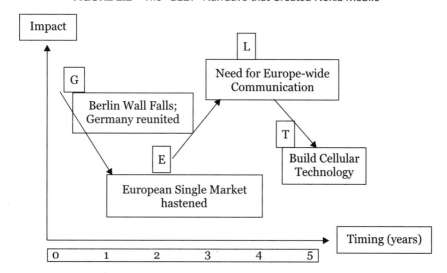

Source: Authors.

Several key implications derive from the GELT model.

- First, it is almost always true that it is not T, or technology, that drives sweeping global change, but rather Geopolitics, Economics and Lifestyle. Technology is an enabler. Technology helps bridge the gap between what is needed, and what is currently existing (for example, cellular technology). It is therefore often the last of the four GELT causal stations, rather than the first. Technology is in general pulled by the other three drivers, rather than pushing them.
- Second, most sweeping global trends, and business opportunities, involve a combination of all four drivers or forces. This is why one key hallmark of a global manager, and *a global perspective*, is the ability to track not only business and economics (E), but the other three drivers as well. Geopolitics is especially important. In today's global markets, shifting alliances, allegiances and conflicts among nation-states can be powerful creators and destroyers of global risk and global opportunity. This is in part why former U.S. Secretary of State, Henry Kissinger (who served under President Richard Nixon), has found great success with his consulting firm Kissinger Associates, which supplies geopolitical consulting services to leading global firms. It is of course legitimate to hire such companies, but vital for global managers to bolster their own geopolitical skills and insights.
- Third, an important determinant of success in using the GELT tool lies in the narrative, or story. Simply identifying global trends, without a story, and without causal links, is of little value, and rarely leads to business insights.
- Fourth, in almost all successful global innovations, all four elements of the GELT portfolio are present. The key lies in fitting them together into a seamless powerful business model, based on a persuasive narrative. Sometimes, the narrative may be quite wrong. But if it makes sense, sometimes it can be created rather than fulfilled. In other words, markets may be educated in order to create it, rather than exploited to fulfill it.

ACTION LEARNING

Identify the Key GELT Trends that Lead to Business Success

 Choose one of the following globally successful products: iPod, iPhone, PlayStation, High-definition television (HD TV), Wireless Fidelity (WiFi), Personal Computers (PC's), radio, hybrid cars. Identify the key GELT trends that led to business success. Link these trends in a simple narrative.

ACTION LEARNING

The Next Big Thing: What is Your Story?

Build a global narrative, linking geopolitics, lifestyle, economics, and technology, that tells the story of the *next big thing*—the next major global business innovation success.

TOOL # 2

Feedback Loops

Feedback is a "mechanism, process and signal that is looped back to control a system within itself".[2] The resulting loop is called a feedback loop. A control system usually has input and output to the system; when the output of the system is fed back into the system as part of its input, it is called the *feedback*.

Many global processes are feedback systems. There are positive and negative loops. Positive feedback exists, for instance, when stock prices rise, attracting more investor money, creating demand for stocks, in turn leading to even higher stock prices. Negative feedback occurs when the room temperature rises, causing the air conditioner to operate, which reduces the temperature. Positive feedback creates explosive growth. Negative feedback can preserve stability (for instance, more or less constant room temperature). Global managers know how to distinguish between negative self-regulating feedback loops that lead to equilibrium, and positive growth loops, which lead to explosive growth or implosive contraction, and above all, they can tell when situations shift from stable loops to explosive or implosive ones.

In electrical engineering, a common diagram looks like this (see Diagram below):

DIAGRAM   A Typical Electrical-Circuit Feedback Loop

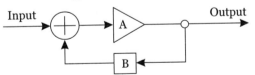

Here, A causes B, which in turn causes A, which in turn strengthens B, and so on. Readers will have experienced the *squeal* such a loop creates in a sound-amplifying system. This is a positive feedback loop.

---

[2] Source: Feedback,Wikipedia-The Free Encyclopedia. http://en.wikipedia.org/wiki/Feedback. (accessed January 26, 2010).

In Figure 2.1, discerning readers will notice that at the center of the diagram, there is a recurring self-reinforcing feedback loop. This loop works as follows: the more Nokia supplies convenient rapid and affordable mobile communication, the faster the Single Market evolves and develops; this in turn, creates more demand for mobile communication, which in turn accelerates the Single Market, and so on. This is known as a positive feedback loop, or a *growth spiral*. Great global businesses invariably have such feedback loops at their core. Great global managers are good at envisioning them, and then creating them.

Feedback loops are also vital for understanding and anticipating global risk. Figure 2.3 shows an example of a feedback loop that lies at the heart of the 2007–08 global liquidity crisis, which originated in the bursting of America's housing bubble and sub-prime and prime mortgage-backed securities collapse.

FIGURE 2.3   Feedback Loop Driving the Fall in US Housing Prices

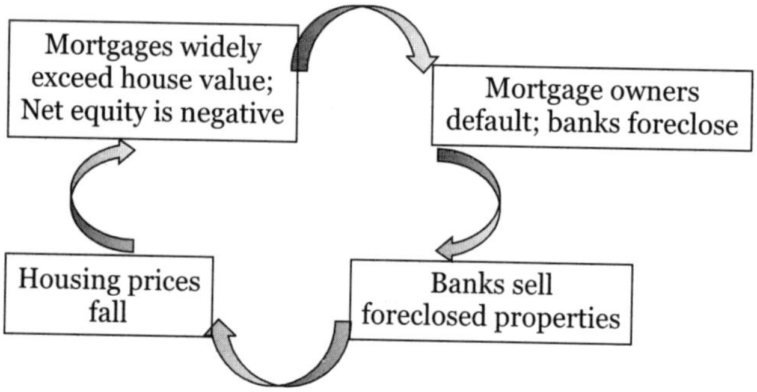

Mortgages widely exceed house value; Net equity is negative

Mortgage owners default; banks foreclose

Housing prices fall

Banks sell foreclosed properties

Source: Authors.

CASE STUDY

Why Did US Housing Prices Fall So Dramatically?

 Under American property law, in 26 of the largest American states along with the District of Columbia (Washington D.C.), the law provides for "non-recourse". This means that in those states, generally, when home-owners default on mortgage payments, and the holder of their mortgage (generally a bank) forecloses, the bank cannot pursue the defaulter for their financial losses.[3]

(*Case Study continued*)

---

[3] These states are West Virginia, Michigan, Minnesota, North Carolina, Rhode Island, South Dakota, Utah, Wyoming, Alaska, Arizona, Arkansas, California, Colorado, Georgia, Hawaii, Idaho, Mississippi, Missouri, Montana, Nevada, New Hampshire, Oregon, Tennessee, Texas, Virginia, Washington, along with District of Columbia (Washington DC).

(*Case Study continued*)

This law does not exist in Europe or in Japan. In Japan, when the housing bubble burst in 1990, Japanese households were left with mortgage debts hugely greater than the value of their underlying assets. But the option of default did not exist, because they had co-signers, usually their children or relatives, and the banks were free to pursue these co-signers if the original mortgage owner defaulted. As a result, Japan's property bubble created some 15 years of recession, and economic stagnation, as Japanese struggled to pay their debts. In America, the housing crisis began when interest rates rose and so-called sub-prime mortgage holders (those with low income, who probably should not have qualified for a mortgage in the first place) began to default, slashing the value of the securities that were backed by such mortgages, and causing large financial losses.

But the crisis grew and deepened, when even those *able* to pay their monthly mortgage payments began to default, simply because it was not worth their while—the underlying asset (house) was worth far less on the market than the debt they were paying. The non-recourse clause meant that banks could not pursue the mortgage holders for compensation for any financial losses incurred by the bank. All the banks could do was to place the foreclosed properties on the market for sale. This supply of houses led to further fall in housing prices—and to more defaults.

This created a powerful feedback loop, known as a *death spiral*, in which a negative trend is reinforced and strengthened (see Figure 2.3).

Could this death spiral have been anticipated? Note that in order to anticipate it, managers would have to be familiar with intricate details of mortgage law in the U.S., compared to other countries; for example, the *non-recourse* clause.

Here is a challenging action learning exercise for the reader:

ACTION LEARNING

The Teleology of US Financial Crisis and Dollar Decline in 2007–2008

In 2007–2008, the U.S. dollar declined steeply against the euro, yen, and other currencies. Can the reader link, in a coherent teleology, the decisions taken at Hotel Mt. Washington, in Bretton Woods, New Hampshire, between July 1–20, 1944, with the U.S. financial crisis and dollar decline in 2007–2008? (A more or less complete answer is given in the next page).

(*Action Learning continued*)

(*Action Learning continued*)

Readers may be familiar with displays of dominos—teams place dominos in sequence, so that one domino topples another—and the falling dominos unfold over long distances in a display of precision and planning. In many ways this is a powerful metaphor for global risk. As one country (domino) topples, it knocks over another country (domino), in an almost unending teleological chain that can continue, like ripples in a pond, almost forever.

Can we understand global risk better, by using the metaphor of dominos, along with the tools of feedback loops and teleology (causality)?

Here is a brief vest–pocket history of global crises, going back to the defining moment of global markets, the Bretton Woods conference, July 1–20, 1944. It shows how, in global markets, one crisis in one country inevitably spreads to other countries, in ways that are sometimes surprising, but often, predictable and understandable.

CASE STUDY

How to get from Hotel Mt. Washington, 1944, to Wall Street, 2008?

Or

Flying on Global Risk Airlines: A 64-year-long Journey[4]

 Flight attendant: "Welcome aboard. This is Global Risk Airlines Flight 001. Our route is from Bretton Woods, NH, in America's lovely New England White Mountains, to Wall Street. We will pass through Mexico and Argentina, with intermediate stops in Washington,

(*Case Study continued*)

---

[4] For a riveting visual account of the global crash, 1994–99, readers are urged to view *Frontline. The Great Crash.* (PBS Public Television: 1999). http://www.pbs.org/wgbh/americanexperience/crash (accessed on January 18, 2010).

(*Case Study continued*)

Thailand, Indonesia, Malaysia, Singapore, Russia, Grand Cayman Islands, and Brazil."

Expected flight time: About 64 years.

Please fasten your seat belts. We expect VERY rough weather along the way, in fact, for the entire journey. Indeed, we have no guarantee this flight will make it intact to its destination. We hope all our passengers have good paid-up life insurance policies and strong nerves. A few of our passengers will find this flight enjoyable and even profitable. Most of you will simply be bewildered by it all.

Thank you for flying Global Risk Airlines. We hope you'll fly with us again. In fact, we KNOW you will...because you have no choice. Because... It is baked into the cake. Meanwhile, here is our detailed itinerary. It is rather long and tedious, but merits careful study, especially for those of you passengers who aspire to become global managers with sharp global mindsets and perspectives.

- July 1–20, 1944: The world has been ravaged by war. Three weeks earlier, the D-Day invasion began and fierce fighting rages in France. Only the American economy has doubled twice, while Europe and Asia lie in ruins. America and Britain together convene a gathering of experts at a resort, Hotel Mt. Washington, in Bretton Woods, NH, USA, 90 minutes north of Boston. Around 40 countries, representing all the Allies, attended the convention. Leading the U.S. delegation is a Treasury official, Harry Dexter White. Leading the British delegation is the world's most distinguished economist, John Maynard Keynes, author of the pioneering 1936 book The General Theory of Employment, Interest and Money.

  White has a vision of a new world economy, built on free markets. He believes that economic democracy—free markets—requires political democracy. He argues that countries with both economic and political democracy will be friends of the U.S., and foes of the socialist U.S.S.R. (as the Hot War nears its end, the Cold War begins). The world's monetary system will be a *dollar standard*, with dollars replacing gold as reserves and backing for national moneys. Since dollars convert to gold at a fixed exchange rate, USD 35 per ounce, the system, America believes, will resemble the gold standard that worked so well in the 19th century.

  Keynes has a different vision. He envisions a world central bank, issuing a world currency to be known as *bancor*, backed by dollars,

(*Case Study continued*)

(*Case Study continued*)

gold and other currencies, and issued just as national Central Banks issue currency, in amounts sufficient to support global growth, trade and capital flows, but not excessive as to cause inflation.

America wins, Keynes loses. *The result will ultimately cause heavy damage to world markets 64 years later.*

- Mexico, 1994: America's vision, to now, has worked beautifully. The Berlin Wall falls on November 9, 1989. Europe unites. Soon three billion capitalists in Asia join the global system. World trade grows twice as fast as world GDP. Asian economies expand at rates previously unimagined. The gap between rich and poor nations closes, not because the rich countries decline but because the *emerging* economies (Wall Street jargon for developing nations) grow rapidly. America, which held 75 percent of world GDP in 1944, now comprises only about 22 percent. Recovery in Europe and in Asia has been miraculous, aided by generous Marshall Plan aid extended by America to Europe—perhaps the first time the victorious nation in war has paid large resources to the vanquished nations.

But there are deep underlying flaws in the global system. They are revealed in the first major crisis with global implications: Mexico.

Mexico heavily borrows US capital to support its growth and investment. US investors, fearing currency risk, demand dollar-denominated bonds; Mexican banks and companies incur large dollar liabilities. Rapid growth causes some inflation. An impending election keeps the incumbent Mexican President from devaluing the Mexican peso; he delays devaluation until after the election. The speculators do not wait. In December, 1994, there is a flight of capital, first by Mexicans sending their money to safe havens, and quickly followed, by foreigners and speculators. The peso collapses from 3.50 per USD to 7.00. Mexico asks President Clinton for emergency aid. Clinton sanctions this aid, without approval of Congress: a USD 50 billion loan on generous terms, fearing influx of millions of unemployed Mexican workers across the US border.

Mexico's economy goes into a deep dive, but because the emergency loan is not accompanied by draconian IMF terms, recovers as rapidly as it sank (see Figure 2.4). But as the Mexican domino falls and then is picked up, a new domino is about to be knocked over.

- Washington, 1994–1995: Federal Reserve Chair Alan Greenspan, who has held this office since September, 1987, acts to raise US interest

(*Case Study continued*)

(*Case Study continued*)

FIGURE 2.4   Mexico National Accounts, Gross Domestic Product

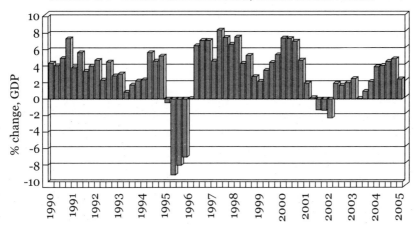

Source: Organization for Economic Cooperation and Development (OECD).

Note: Mexico's GDP shows deep decline for a year, then rapid recovery, as America-sponsored emergency loans enable its economy to restore growth, built on exports driven in turn by the devalued Mexican peso.

rates (see Figure 2.6), in order to strengthen the dollar and weaken the yen (see Figure 2.5). Higher interest rates cause investors to sell yen and buy dollars, to open high-interest deposits in New York. This was done, in order to help Japan emerge from its deep recession caused by collapse of Japanese property prices, and ensuing stock market collapse in 1990. This *good Samaritan* act, rather uncharacteristic of the US, has unexpected consequences. Thailand pays the price. Thailand is the domino.

The U.S. dollar strengthens in world markets by some 60 percent, between 1995 and 2001, when it peaks, as shown in Figure 2.5.

- 1997: Thailand has linked its currency, the baht, to the US dollar, in a fixed exchange rate of 25 baht per dollar, to eliminate currency risk for US investors, and attract inward foreign investment. The rise in the US dollar—engineered in order to help Japan—drags the baht up along with it. As the baht appreciates, relative to the Japanese yen (Japan is a major investor in Thailand), this causes Thai exports to decline, and generates a large trade deficit (see Figure 2.7). The trade

(*Case Study continued*)

(Case Study continued)

FIGURE 2.5   US Dollar, Trade-Weighted, 1985–2008

Financial- vs. Trade-Weighted Dollar Indices

Through July 2008 (ShadowStats.com, FRB, BIS)

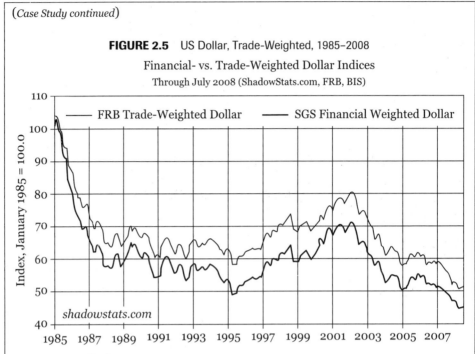

Source: www.shadowstats.com

FIGURE 2.6   US Short Term Interest Rates, 1993–1996

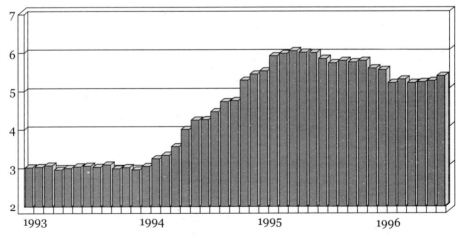

Transformation: Level

Source: Federal Reserve Board.

(Case Study continued)

(*Case Study continued*)

FIGURE 2.7   Thailand's Trade Balance and GDP: Portrait of a Crisis

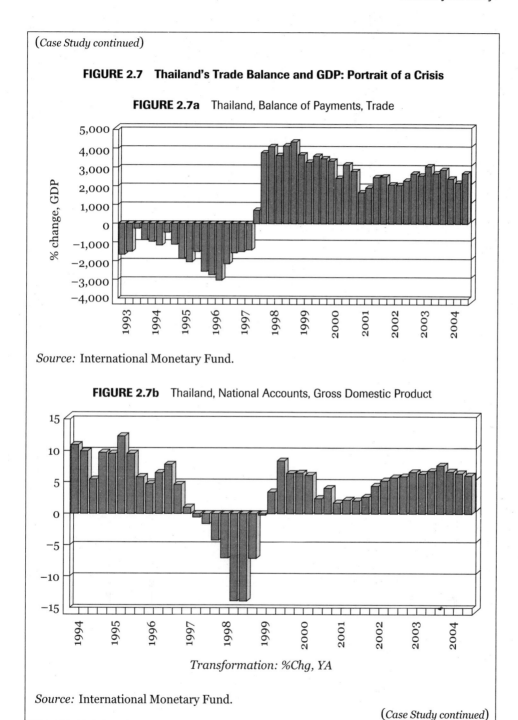

FIGURE 2.7a   Thailand, Balance of Payments, Trade

Source: International Monetary Fund.

FIGURE 2.7b   Thailand, National Accounts, Gross Domestic Product

Transformation: %Chg, YA

Source: International Monetary Fund.

(*Case Study continued*)

(Case Study continued)

deficit *telegraphs* a looming crisis well in advance, and signals that Thailand may be the next domino. But foreign investors blithely ignore the signals. However, speculators do not. The growing trade deficit results in speculation against the baht. On July 2, 1997, after pouring billions of dollars of foreign exchange reserves into the markets in a futile effort to defend the exchange rate, the Thai Central Bank and Government give up, and let the baht float. It drops quickly to 50 baht per dollar, as panicky investors *rush for the door*, and sell their baht investments. IMF emergency aid is needed; such aid comes with very stringent conditions. The Thai economy drops like a stone (see Figures 2.7[a] and 2.7[b]).

- 1998: The Asian Contagion: Panicky investors pull their money out of Indonesia, Malaysia, then Korea, and to some extent Taiwan, Hong Kong, and Singapore, even though the latter three countries are fiscally sound and stable. Indonesia's rupiah collapses to nearly 15,000 per dollar before recovering somewhat (see Figure 2.8). Asian economies go into recession. And they, in turn, topple the next domino: Russia.

FIGURE 2.8   Indonesia's Rupiah Exchange Rate, 1990–2006

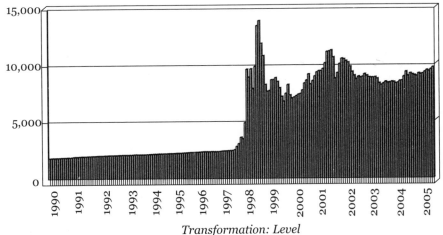

Transformation: Level

Source: International Monetary Fund.

(Case Study continued)

(*Case Study continued*)

- Russia, 1998: The Asian recession diminishes demand for crude oil, causing the price of oil to plummet. Russia, whose government earned most of its income from oil royalties (because it never did succeed in building a modern tax system), resorts to high-interest short-term borrowing (Gosudarstvennoe Kratkosrochnoe Obyazateltvo (GKO) bonds [short-term zero coupon Russian Government Treasury Bills issued by the state since February 1993]) to make ends meet when oil royalties decline. It rolls over old debt by issuing and selling new debt. In August, 1998, an emergency Indian Monetary Fund (IMF) loan to Russia, USD 4 billion, is stolen; Russia's Central Bank sends the funds to a numbered account in a Swiss bank. On August 28, President Boris Yeltsin announces Russia cannot, and will not pay its GKO foreign debtors. The ruble collapses. The shortfall for Russia was only USD 15 billion (see Figure 2.9). The ensuing damage to global markets and investors is many times that sum. The Russian domino falls heavily, and topples Brazil.

FIGURE 2.9   Russian Rubles per US Dollar, 1993–2003

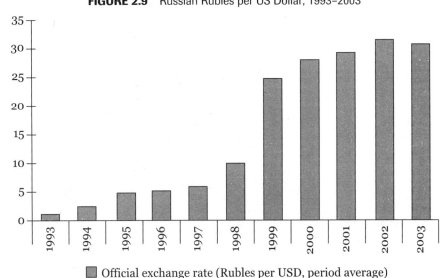

■ Official exchange rate (Rubles per USD, period average)

Source: Based on data in World Development Indicators, World Bank, 2009.

(*Case Study continued*)

(*Case Study continued*)

- Brazil, 1999: Investors worldwide panic, again, having assumed Russia, a nuclear power, would certainly be bailed out (it wasn't). They pull money out of countries regarded as *risky*, and Brazil is foremost among them, with its large short-term dollar debt. On January 15, 1999, Brazil's President flees journalists, takes refuge in a bathroom, pulls out his cell phone, and orders the Central Bank of Brazil to float the real (until then, fixed about one-to-one relative to the US Dollar). The Brazilian currency, the real, quickly falls to 2 real per dollar (see Figure 2.10), doubling (in terms of real) Brazil's dollar-denominated debt, necessitating an IMF rescue bailout and emergency loan with the usual stringent conditions (balance the budget, cut government spending, raise interest rates, raise taxes). IMF executive director, Stanley Fisher, breaks the world record for frequent flier miles and consumption of aspirin.

  Brazil topples its neighbor Argentina, joined with Brazil in a four-country *Mercosur* free-trade organization.

FIGURE 2.10   Brazil's Exchange Rate: Real per US Dollar, 1997–2006

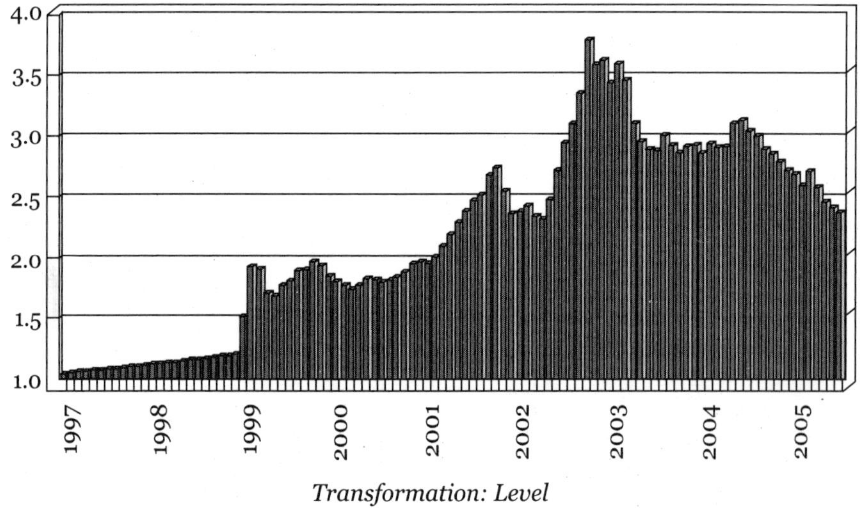

Transformation: Level

Source: Federal Reserve Board.

(*Case Study continued*)

(*Case Study continued*)

- 2001–02: Argentina: A major trading partner with Brazil, and member of the four-country Mercosur (Argentina, Paraguay, Brazil, Uruguay), Argentina suffers a sharp decline in its exports when Brazil's devaluation makes Brazil's dollar prices half those of Argentina. Argentina borrows heavily on world markets, accumulating enormous dollar-denominated debts (in the form of international bonds). Argentina's GDP drops sharply in 1999, recovers, and then drops sharply again in 2001. Argentina changes Presidents four times in two months, in a futile effort to stave off collapse. Argentina throws into jail Domingo Cavallo, the finance minister who saved Argentina from its hyperinflation in the 1990s, but is now unable to do so. Argentina abandons the fixed one peso per dollar exchange rate, and the rate rapidly rises to 3.50 pesos per dollar, more than tripling the peso value of Argentinean debt. IMF offers of emergency loans are rejected by Argentina, on the grounds that the terms are too severe. As a result, Argentina's economy collapses (see Figures 2.11[a] and 2.11[b]). Argentina's banks close, because they cannot service their dollar-denominated debt. Argentineans throng to the banks, hammer on the doors haplessly, but inside, there is no money. Neighboring

FIGURE 2.11   Argentina: Exchange Rate and GDP, 1996–2005

FIGURE 2.11a   Argentina, Finance, Exchange Rate, Argentine Pesos per US Dollar

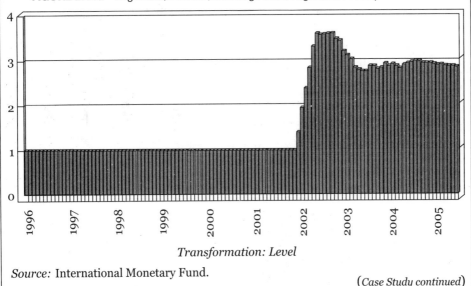

Transformation: Level

Source: International Monetary Fund.

(*Case Study continued*)

(*Case Study continued*)

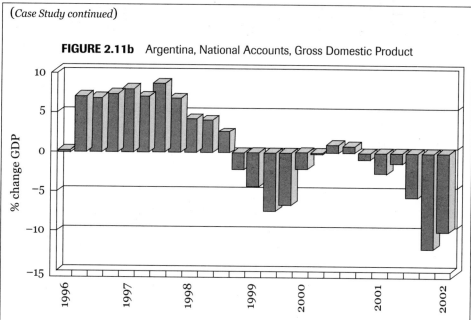

FIGURE 2.11b   Argentina, National Accounts, Gross Domestic Product

Source: International Monetary Fund.

Uruguay almost becomes the next domino, as Argentineans race across the border to pull savings out of Uruguayan banks. New President Nelson Kirchner restores some fiscal order. Finally in 2004, Argentina reaches agreement with the IMF on debt restructuring, and repays some of its debt. In 2005 the Argentinean economy grows strongly. But enormous damage has been done. As in Russia, the savings of the middle class have been wiped out.

It was now clear to all that there would be another domino, that the global system was inherently unstable. But who would it be? Which country? Might it be America?

- America, July, 2007: Before describing America's housing bubble crisis that began in July, 2007, let us first ask: Could global managers with a true global perspective, using simple tools, have foreseen that America was due to become the next toppled domino? Consider Figures 2.12(a) and 2.12(b) showing America's twin deficits (trade and budget). The trade deficit is defined as *net exports*, or exports minus imports. The budget deficit is the gap between government revenue and government expenditure.

(*Case Study continued*)

(Case Study continued)

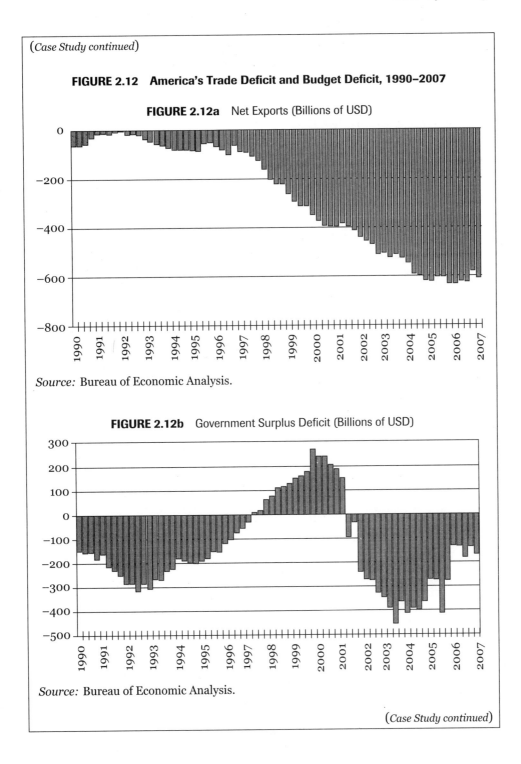

FIGURE 2.12   **America's Trade Deficit and Budget Deficit, 1990–2007**

FIGURE 2.12a   Net Exports (Billions of USD)

Source: Bureau of Economic Analysis.

FIGURE 2.12b   Government Surplus Deficit (Billions of USD)

Source: Bureau of Economic Analysis.

(Case Study continued)

(*Case Study continued*)

Had managers been closely tracking these two charts, they would have understood that for many years, America had been living beyond its means, spending its income, borrowing heavily from abroad, and buying more from foreign countries than it sold. The flip side of this coin was the fact that American dollars, and dollar-denominated securities were flooding into the world. Inevitably, a huge supply of dollars in the world, creating a kind of overhang, must result in a decline in the price of the asset whose supply has been excessive. This is precisely what happened. America was long overdue to become the next domino to be toppled. That it was predictable is clear; the precise timing, however, was far less easy to foresee.

As interest rates rose in the US, in the face of global inflation, mortgage payments for variable-interest-rate mortgages rose. Many who held such mortgages could no longer afford to meet the monthly payments. It suddenly became evident that many mortgage-backed securities, in which financial institutions and banks from the US and abroad, had invested heavily for their high return, were now worth far less than their face value. No one knew for certain what they were worth, because the *mix* of mortgages comprising them was complex. As mortgage holders defaulted, banks foreclosed, and dumped the properties on the market, causing home prices to fall. Major financial institutions revealed huge losses. America's fifth-largest investment bank, Bear Stearns, was bankrupt, and had to be bailed out by the US Federal Reserve, which assumed much of its debts, and arranged for its sale to J.P. Morgan for a small fraction of its previous market value. Fannie Mae and Freddie Mac—government-sponsored publicly-held institutions that bought mortgages, and used them as collateral for selling mortgage-backed securities—revealed huge losses, and they too needed Fed backing.[5] New York University economist Nouriel Roubini, who had foretold this crisis, estimated that total financial losses in the crisis could amount to over USD 1 trillion—a very large proportion of the USD 1.3 trillion total capital of the financial sector.

As the US economy sank into recession, European economies too declined, with Germany and France slowing, and Asian economies showing

(*Case Study continued*)

---

[5] Fannie Mae and Freddie Mac were former government financial institutions, later privatized, whose mission was to buy mortgages from banks, then use them as collateral to back their own bonds sold in capital markets to institutional investors like pension funds. This enabled such investors to invest in high-yield assets related to real estate, when otherwise they could not owing to regulations and laws.

(Case Study continued)

far slower growth than the previous decade's average. As banks revealed ever-larger losses on their balance sheets, they slashed lending in order to shore up crumbling balance sheets, and improve their capital ratios. Tight credit led to economic contraction worldwide.

More dominos were likely to fall. The question was, which ones?

Flight Attendant: *We hope you enjoyed your flight on Global Risk Airline. We're sorry we went from 30,000 feet to almost sea level, and back up again, on at least seven different occasions. Remember, flying Global Risk Airline is only for those with strong stomachs (and hearts). We are proud to serve so many resilient, brilliant global managers. Please fly with us again—we know you will, because, well, you have no choice.*

ACTION LEARNING

The Next Domino?

When will the next global crisis occur? What will be its nature? In which country will it originate? What opportunities will it offer for global managers? Develop several scenarios, and estimate the likelihood of each.

CASE STUDY

Long-Term Capital Management[6]

A minor and now nearly forgotten footnote to the above teleology almost destroyed the economy of the entire world. Most people have forgotten this episode. The world was saved only by the prompt decisive action of Alan Greenspan, Chairman of US Federal Reserve, acting well beyond his authority (because the protagonist, LTCM, Long-Term Capital Management, Hedge Fund, was registered in the Cayman Islands and not in the US).

(Case Study continued)

---

[6] Based on Roger Lowenstein's, *When Genius Failed: The Rise and Fall of Long-Term Capital Management* (New York: Random House, 2000). See also: Frontline, The Trillion Dollar Bet (PBS video, US). http://www.pbs.org/wgbh/nova/listseason/27.html. (accessed January 18, 2010).

(*Case Study continued*)

LTCM was founded by John Meriweather (leading Salomon Brothers bond trader), Professor Myron Scholes and Professor Robert Merton; the latter two, Nobel Prize winners in Economics for discovery of the Black-Scholes option pricing equation. They built a sophisticated mathematical model for arbitrage trading globally, hedging risk by operating in many different markets all over the world. They made enormous profits initially: some 25–40 percent returns annually. In 1998, losses mounted, when markets (rattled by the Russian default) departed from historical patterns on which the LTCM mathematical models were based. LTCM was heavily leveraged. Its liabilities at one point exceeded its capital by a ratio of 100:1. Competitors began imitating its models and narrowed its profitability. Losses mounted. At one point, global markets became totally illiquid, all over the world. This *liquidity risk* was not taken into account by LTCM models. A press report said LTCM debts amounted to as much as USD 1.25 trillion! Bankruptcy was imminent. Had LTCM gone bankrupt, it would have caused bankruptcy among some of the world's largest banks. The consequences would have been catastrophic.

Fed Chair Alan Greenspan called a meeting of the banks who had lent billions to LTCM. He pressed the banks to provide a bailout loan, realizing the disastrous consequences of failing to do so. Under pressure from Greenspan, the banks reluctantly agreed. A USD 3.5 billion loan was made to LTCM. This loan prevented immediate bankruptcy, and allowed LTCM to *unwind* some of its losing positions, gradually, as global capital markets recovered. LTCM closed its doors after its steep losses undermined its basic investment strategy and appeal to investors; some of its investors lost their money. Lately, LTCM has resumed operation under a different name, though Scholes and Merton are no longer associated with it. Alan Greenspan, it is widely agreed, saved the world from an enormous financial crisis that loomed large as a consequence of LTCM's imminent bankruptcy.

It is estimated that at its low point, LTCM's financial obligations amounted to more than a trillion dollars.

CLOSING THE CIRCLE: LINKING 2008 TO 1944

What was the causal connection between the Bretton Woods conference in 1944, and the global liquidity crisis in 2008, some 64 years later?

The answer is straightforward. America is the only nation with the sovereign right to issue dollars. Its money supply and interest rates are set by its Central Bank, the

Federal Reserve System, in order to stabilize and let the US economy grow. This is the main role of the dollar.

However, the dollar has another role—it is the primary currency for transactions in the world's capital and goods markets. Some 80 percent of global foreign exchange transactions involve, on one side, American dollars.

What happens when America's credit and monetary policy, designed to serve America's interests, becomes misaligned (or in direct conflict) with the interests of global markets? The answer: America will act according to its own interests. This is what has happened repeatedly, and it is the fundamental flaw in the current global ecosystem. And it will lead to repeated crises.

In the 1950s and early 1960s, there was a dollar shortage. America sold more abroad than it bought. Dollars poured into the US Credit abroad was scarce. Everyone spoke of the dollar scarcity. The world economy was damaged by it.

Beginning in the late 1960s, the dollar shortage turned into a dollar glut. This was equally damaging. America created far too many dollars. This was perceived to serve its interests. But ultimately it led to financial collapse which spread to all parts of the world.

To Keynes, this fundamental problem was evident in 1944. But only lately is it dawning on America, and the world, that the dollar cannot play the dual role of America's national currency and the world's global currency. Only a world central bank, with a world currency, managed like a national central bank, can resolve this basic error in the global financial architecture.

This is the lesson of the 2007–2008 crisis.

GLOBAL RISK: TAXONOMY OR ECOLOGY?

There are two distinct approaches to understanding, estimating, and forecasting global risk.

One approach is that of taxonomy—a systematic list or categorization of different kinds of risks. For example, inflation risk, deflation risk, default risk, liquidity risk, credit risk, political risk, recession risk, and many more.

The list, of course, is nearly endless. And lists of this sort provide very little help to global managers seeking their way through the thick murky fog of global events.

A second approach, one embraced in this book, is to gain an understanding of the global ecosystem, taking a systems approach. In this approach, global managers use the tools of teleology, feedback, and the *domino* approach to understand the dynamics of the entire global system, and above all, identify weak points, crisis nodes, and risks in their formative stage. Ultimately, global markets collapse when a combination of various risks converges, interacting and reinforcing one another. Moreover, the end of one crisis—and its various policies and *solutions*—invariably creates the seeds of the following one. For instance, as America struggles to revise its failed regulatory system that allowed the housing crisis to occur, it will doubtless create the nucleus of the next crisis, just as financial deregulation in the 1980s, a response to previous economic slowdowns, generated the Savings and Loan crisis when the deregulated banking sector allowed thousands of banks to spring up, many of them created and led by those with no banking experience, whose risk management skills were zero, and ultimately led to the collapse of the whole system.

In the end, global crisis always results from the failure to estimate and manage risk. The 2007–2008 crisis was caused by the failure of highly sophisticated, and highly-paid, risk managers to understand and prepare for the collapse of US housing prices. This failure, in turn, generally appears related to the inability to understand the dynamics of complex systems, and the inherent risks arising from those dynamics. We hope that using the tools described in this chapter will contribute to reducing such failures or making them less likely.

In the next chapter, we zero in on specific countries, after zooming out in this chapter on the global system as a whole. We examine the use of national accounts— Gross Domestic Product and its components—as kinds of profit-and-loss statements for nations, and argue that managers can understand country risk by examining countries as if they were businesses.

Chapter 3

Risk management with telescopes and microscopes

LEARNING OBJECTIVES

- After reading this chapter, you should understand why excellence in risk management requires a unique type of vision, able, with one eye, to zoom out on the global marketplace (*telescope*) and, with one eye, to zoom in on the business DNA of the organization you lead or manage (*microscope*).
- You should understand the reason for the failure of conventional risk-assessment models, such as *value-at-risk*.
- You should be able to employ telescopic vision to assess systemic risk, while at the same time focussing with microscopic vision on risks related to your organization, its internal operations, and its business environment.
- You should know how three very different segments of society—Wall Street (financial services), Main Street (ordinary consumers and investors), and Massachusetts Avenue (government and regulators)—all combined to create the global crisis of 2007–2009.

Tool # 3

Zoom Out, Zoom In with Telescope and Microscope

 Microscope: Zooms in on the business, products, and clients.
Telescope: Zooms out on the global business environment.
When joined together—*The Telemicroscope*.

A supplementary tool is that of feedback loops, used in the chapter to show how *bubbles* and crashes can develop, and how bubbles can become crashes very quickly.

...a persistent tension between those who assert that the best decisions are based on quantification and numbers, determined by the patterns of the past, and those who base their decisions on more subjective degrees of belief about the uncertain future. This is a controversy that has never been resolved.

—Peter Bernstein[1]

INTRODUCTION

By definition, a management tool is nearly always quantitative, concrete, and tangible. Management, we teach, begins with measurement. Nearly all the tools offered to global managers in this book are of this nature.

But the tool discussed in this chapter is somewhat different from the rest—it is abstract, and perhaps, even vague. Yet we believe it may be among the most important of all tools that global managers need, in order to measure and manage global risks and opportunities. Tool # 3 is about global managers' eyesight.

We believe that global managers need a peculiar type of vision—one that enables them, with one eye to zoom out on global events, and to look into the future, tracking minds markets and money all over the world, and with another eye to zoom in, on their own organizations, businesses, products, and clients (see Box 3.1). In other words, they need a *zoom out* lens, for one eye, and a *zoom in* lens, for the second. And, hardest of all, they need the ability to use both eyes simultaneously, while coordinating and integrating the information from each. They need something science has not yet invented: A *telemicroscope*.

BOX 3.1   Forty Powers of 10—Zoom out, Zoom in

In their eight-minute film Powers of 10, *made for IBM, Charles and Ray Eames explore the meaning of telescopic and microscopic distance. They begin with an innocent scene—a family picnicking on a blanket in a park in Chicago, a scene one meter-by-one meter. They zoom out 10 meters (10^1 m), then 100 meters (10^2 m), and continue, to the edge of the universe—a distance equal to 10^{24} m.*

Then they zoom back in, onto the hand of the person on the blanket, and shrink the distance every few seconds by 10^{-1}, from 1 meter to 1 centimeter, and so on, **traveling** *through the DNA of a cell, in its nucleus, until they reach the inside of the nucleus of a carbon atom, or 10^{-16}. The greatest distance in the universe, then, is 40 powers of 10.*

Forty powers of 10 serves as a powerful metaphor for risk managers. Except, in the film, zoom out, then zoom in, is serially done one after the other. First, zoom out to the

(Box 3.1 continued)

---

[1] Peter Bernstein, *Against the Gods: The Remarkable Story of Risk* (Wiley: New York, 1998).

> (*Box 3.1 continued*)
>
> *edge of the universe. Then, zoom in, to the nucleus of an atom. In life, risk managers must do both simultaneously—zoom out on the world and global markets, zoom in on their own particular world—an immensely difficult task.*

Global managers need both a telescope and a microscope. Each, in itself, is insufficient. *Only when they are joined together can a robust strategic risk management system emerge, that is able to seize, define, and capture opportunities.* We discussed an aspect of this issue briefly in Chapter One, in the section about "Analyst? Or strategist?" or "short-term vs. long-term horizons." Global risk managers must know how to zoom in on the near term, while zooming out to the long-term horizon. This is a special type of vision related to time. We now choose to return to this key issue in greater depth, in relation to *space*—geography, global markets and nations, big-picture thinking, along with organizational small-picture thinking.

Moreover, there is a different time dimension risk managers need. We believe global risk managers who seek opportunities in risk must know *where to point their telescopes*. They must point them back, in time and in history, to learn what they can from the past, and at the same time, point them forward, to the future, to pierce through the fog of uncertainty, and try to build best-case, worst-case and most-likely-case scenarios for global markets.

Only this rare and remarkable type of double vision can enable responsible risk management together with bold entrepreneurial seizing of opportunities.

ACTION LEARNING

Your Microscope? Your Telescope?

Microscope:

- On a scale of 1 to 10: How *sharp* is your zoom-in microscope (that is, How well do you understand the products, strategies, operations, and business design of your organization?) (1 is *poor*; 10 is *excellent* or superior).

1 —————————————— 5 —————————————— 10

Business design —————————————————————

Products —————————————————————

Operations —————————————————————

Strategies —————————————————————

Average score/10: X = ————

(*Action Learning continued*)

(*Action Learning continued*)

Telescope:

- On a scale of 1 to 10: How *sharp* is your zoom-out telescope (that is, How well do you track and understand global trends and markets?) (1 is *poor*; 10 is *excellent* or superior).

1 ———————————— 5 ———————————— 10

Global economics   _____

Global finance   _____

Global technology   _____

Global social trends _____

Average score/10: Y = _____

Place yourself in the 2 × 2 diagram below, by plotting the (X, Y) coordinate.

| Telescope |

10

1

1   10

Microscope

What action items emerge from this analysis? How can you increase the resolution of your microscope and of your telescope?

WHAT VALUE IS AT RISK?

Many organizations, especially those in banking and financial services, use a risk management methodology known as *value-at-risk* (VAR), first developed by the commercial bank J.P. Morgan in 1993. This tool is largely a *microscope*. Though it has been much maligned lately, in the wake of its alleged failure in the global financial risk that began in 2007, it is, in fact, a powerful and productive tool when used properly.

We will explain the basic essentials of VAR, though not the mathematical details. Our key message will be: However powerful they may be, microeconomic *microscope* tools are dangerous and destructive, when not closely accompanied by global macroeconomic *telescope* tools.

CASE STUDY

Banker's Trust: When Value-at-Risk Risk Management Models Collapsed

Value-at-Risk (VAR) models are mathematical tools for risk management, aimed at projecting and evaluating worst-case scenarios for the performance of investment and other financial activities, and initiating appropriate and effective loss-limiting strategies. The essence of VAR models is the analysis of the left *tail* of the normal curve, where large losses accrue, and analysis of the quantitative exposure of the investor to such potential losses. The most dramatic failure of VAR was in the near bankruptcy of Long-Term Capital Management, a highly leveraged hedge fund founded by Nobel Prize winners in economics and seasoned Wall Street experts, and discussed in the previous chapter.

But other dramatic failures of VAR have occurred elsewhere, with perhaps surprising regularity. The once-leading investment bank, Banker's Trust, used VAR to manage financial exposures globally, and specifically in Asia. But a chain of events led to enormous losses following Thailand's decision to float the baht on July 2, 1997 (as discused in Chapter Two). In the case of Banker's Trust, the VAR model's *worst-case* scenario was in reality supplanted, in 1997 and 1998, by a *worse-than-worst-case* scenario, caused by sudden, dramatic, and unanticipated losses in market liquidity, that made the closing of risky positions impossible, and revealed losses to be more than 10 times larger than the prediction by the VAR model. (Note: for years, the worst case scenario was the one-day 22 percent collapse in American share prices, on October 19, 1987. In 2007–2009, it turned out that there was a far worse "worst-case" scenario.) The result led directly to the disappearance of Banker's Trust, purchased by Deutsche Bank. The scenario that VAR models often failed to adequately address was the simultaneous, dramatic disappearance of liquidity worldwide, as global capital markets *froze* and became *sellers only*. If worst-case scenario planning fails to address the true *worst case*, strategic disaster can result, as it did with Long-Term Capital Management, and with Banker's Trust. (See Appendix: The Value of "Value-at-Risk"—A Cautionary Tale of Risk in Faulty Management.)

VAR will inevitably fail unless joined with a telescope—a global big-picture view of minds, markets, and money. This tool, which we call *systems thinking*, zooms out and scans unfolding trends and events. The combination of big-picture systems thinking and small-picture VAR will not totally protect managers from deep losses during financial crises, but, as the case study

(*Case Study continued*)

> (*Case Study continued*)
>
> of the leading investment bank Goldman Sachs below shows, *it can help them perform far better than managers who rely solely on the telescope or the microscope.*

CASE STUDY

Goldman Sachs Heads for Harbor[2]

 In July 2007, and in the following months, Wall Street was in shock. As mortgage-backed securities' prices collapsed, in the wake of the collapse of the sub-prime mortgages that were their foundation, Wall Street firms piled up mounting losses that grew daily. One company largely avoided this: the venerable investment bank Goldman Sachs.

How? What was their risk management secret? Their version of the *telemicroscope.*

In December 2006, Goldman Sachs' risk indicators (including VAR and other models) began suggesting that something was wrong. "Not hugely wrong," as Nocera writes, but "wrong enough to warrant a closer look."

"Our mortgage business lost money for 10 days in a row," notes Chief Financial Officer David Viniar. "It wasn't a lot of money, but by the 10th day we thought that we should sit down and talk about it."

Goldman Sachs' custom was to examine their P&L's (profit and loss statements) daily. Some 15 people took part in the meeting on mortgages, including risk managers and senior traders. A thick report was examined that included every trading position Goldman Sachs had (the *microscope*). They also talked about "how the mortgage-backed securities market 'felt' (the *telescope*)."

"Our guys said that it felt like it was going to get worse before it got better," Viniar recalls. A decision was made: Get closer to home. In trading jargon, that means reducing the risk exposure. This is done either by selling mortgage-backed securities or hedging them, so that if their value declines, the hedges generate financial gains that offset and negate the losses. Goldman Sachs both reduced their mortgage-backed securities positions,

(*Case Study continued*)

[2] This case study is based on Joe Nocera, "Risk Mismanagement," *New York Times Magazine,* January 4, 2009, referenced at www.nyt.com, http://www.nytimes.com/2009/01/04/magazine/04risk-t.html?cp=1&sg=Risk%20Management,%20JOE&st=cse (accessed January 18, 2010), and Charles D. Ellis, *The Partnership: The Making of Goldman Sachs* (USA: Penguin, 2008), 729.

(*Case Study continued*)

and hedged the remaining ones. They avoided the huge losses that later led to the collapse of the 5th largest investment bank Bear Stearns (taken over by J.P. Morgan), and the bankruptcy of Lehman Brothers.

Goldman Sachs has not escaped losses. With nearly all asset prices plummeting, there is no possible way it could. Its share price has plunged from a high of USD 260 down to USD 78 in January, 2009. And it has been forced, like other investment banks (including Morgan Stanley), to transform itself into a bank holding company.

But Goldman Sachs is alive and well, and its P&L will recover. It remains almost alone among its old Wall Street peer companies as a solvent, independent going concern. And it has the distinction of gaining a USD 5 billion cash infusion from legendary investor Warren Buffett and his Berkshire Hathaway company. Other companies, whose microscopes and telescopes were flawed and did not communicate, are gone, including the 165-year-old Lehman Brothers.

What, we must ask, drove the decision to "get closer to home?" Was it the microscope (VAR)? Or the telescope (a group of wise experienced leaders who set aside their quantitative models, and made their decisions based on *subjective beliefs about an uncertain future*)?

It was, of course, both. It was both *think* and *blink*.

BLINK: THINKING WITHOUT THINKING

We may well travel to the moon. But that is not very far. The greatest distance we have to travel lies within us.

—Charles de Gaulle, former President of France[3]

Those scholars who write about and study risk management would have given much to attend the meeting at Goldman Sachs called by its Chief Financial Officer since May 1999, David Viniar. Had we been there, we might have seen in action a powerful combination of *Think and Blink*.

Think is the process through which decisions are made by careful analytic processes, integrating data, mathematics, models, and decision criteria. *Blink* is the process through which our unconscious mind, our *gut feeling*, constantly active, and gathering data, sends quiet signals to our conscious mind (thinking without thinking), provided our conscious mind is willing, and able to listen. The longtime CEO of General Electric, Jack Welch, wrote a book titled *Jack: Straight*

---

[3] *Time Magazine*, Monday January 5, 1959. http://www.time.com/time/magazine/article/0,9171,810797,00.html

from the Gut. The book makes it clear that Welch used at least equal measures of *think* and *blink*.

In his book *Blink: The Power of Thinking without Thinking*,[4] Malcolm Gladwell discusses the risk management skills of the legendary hedge fund investor, George Soros, who single-handedly trashed the British pound sterling in September, 1992. Gladwell quotes Soros' son: "My father will sit down and give you theories to explain why he does this or that. But...at least half of this is bull.... You know the reason he changes his position on the market or whatever, is because his back starts killing him. He literally goes into a spasm, and it's this early warning sign."

Soros' back spasm does not always work. He reportedly lost large sums during the collapse of the Thai baht in 1997, and again in Russia a year later. This is not the point. The point is that Soros integrates both think and blink, in proportions that have made him extremely wealthy.

What the risk managers at Goldman Sachs showed is that *think* alone is vulnerable to strategic surprise. *Blink*—the subconscious process that integrates telescopic information with microscopic data, in mysterious ways we do not fully understand and perhaps never will—can be literally lifesaving in risk management. As de Gaulle noted, the distances within ourselves are large, and the intuitive wisdom about risks buried deep inside is often not allowed to cover the distance to our conscious mind, to join in the risk evaluation process. Sometimes, paradoxically, in order to see very far, with our telescope, we must learn to look deeply into ourselves, and listen to our inner voices (see Box 3.2).

BOX 3.2   Is Your Mind a Spin Bowler? Or a Batsman?

In cricket, there are bowlers, and there are batsmen. We usually conceive of our conscious mind as a bowler. For creative persons, the conscious mind initiates and *throws* ideas. And like bowlers, we can train our mind, it is thought, to throw ever-better ideas.

Now, comes some research from two brilliant neuroscientists, Joydeep Bhattacharya (London), and Bhavin Sheth (University of Houston), showing that the conscious mind is *not* a bowler—but rather, a batsman. It awaits idea *balls*. But from where? Where are the ideas thrown *from*?

From our unconscious minds—our *intuition* where our brain works on problems without our being aware of it. Their work is summarized in the April 16, 2009 issue of *The Economist*.[5] Here is their lovely experiment.

(Box 3.2 continued)

---

[4] Malcolm Gladwell, *Blink: The Power of Thinking without Thinking* (New York and Boston: Little, Brown & Co., 2005), 51–52.

[5] *The Economist*, "Conscious and Unconscious Thought: Incognito," April 18, 2009. www. economist.com, http://www.economist.com/sciencetechnology/displaystory.cfm?story_id=E1_TPQRJSNN (accessed January 18, 2010).

(*Box 3.2 continued*)

Subjects were given this problem.

There are 3 light switches on the wall of the ground floor of a 3-storey house. Two of the switches do nothing. One turns on a bulb on the second floor. When you begin, the bulb is off. You can make only one trip to the second floor. How do you work out which is the one that turns on the light?

Subjects were wired with EEG caps—electro-encephalograph machines that detect the magnitude and location of brain activity. Their key finding—The EEG machine *predicted which subject would get the answer, up to eight seconds before they actually solved the problem!* Subjects who cracked the problem had an increase in high-frequency gamma waves from the right frontal cortex before they solved it. They themselves were not aware they had solved it for several seconds.

"Conscious thought does not solve problems," summarizes *The Economist.* "Instead unconscious processing delivers the answer to consciousness once it has been arrived at."

Conclusion: Think hard about a problem, hard enough to get your subconscious, or intuition, or *third eye*, interested. Then forget about it—and wait for it to *pitch* the solution to your conscious mind. But be ready! Listen hard. And be sure to exercise your intuition, not just your conscious thought processes.[6]

ACTION LEARNING

Your Blink? Your Think?

Do you make decisions mainly based on conscious careful analysis (*think*)? Or do you make decisions mainly based on unconscious intuition (*blink*)? Or, are you able to listen to your inner *blink* voice while also weighing analytical thinking and evidence?

Which of the two aspects of decision-making should you strengthen? How can you better integrate these two essential dimensions of wise risk management and decision-making?

SYSTEMIC RISK: HARNESSING SYSTEMS THINKING

The magnitude of the financial losses incurred in the 2007–2009 global financial crisis are staggering and continue to mount. According to New York University economist

---

[6] Here is the answer to the problem: Turn on switch #2 and then turn it off. Turn on switch #3 and leave it. Go up to the second floor. If the bulb is on, it is switch #3. If the bulb is off, but is warm, it is #2. If the bulb is off and is cold, it is #1.

Nouriel Roubini, who predicted the crisis, US losses alone totaled a staggering USD 3.6 trillion, fully a quarter of America's annual Gross Domestic Product (GDP). Half of that came from US banks and brokerages, which Roubini says became essentially insolvent. (The reason: Their net capital was estimated at USD 1.2 trillion, substantially below the estimated financial losses. Losses elsewhere in the world may match that USD 3.6 trillion sum.[7])

According to *The Economist*, in 2008, stock market indexes in some 60 countries declined by between 30 percent (Switzerland, usually the gold standard of conservative finance) and 72.4 percent (Russia, which always enjoys a front row seat in any financial crisis). Who is to blame? What is to blame?

It is not easy to trace the primal cause (see Box 3.3), but responsibility for the secondary effects—risk managers who failed to *head for home* in time, as Goldman Sachs did—are clear. Such managers probably used only microscopes. They doubtless classified, quantified, sliced and diced many individual types of risk: inflation risk, deflation risk, default risk, interest-rate risk, principal risk, country risk, portfolio risk, hedging risk, political risk, bankruptcy risk; the list is endless. It is possible to chop risk into many tiny pieces, and for each piece, to build a quantitative model for evaluating it. In normal times, risk managers can get away with this type of blindness. But in abnormal times, it is fatal. A key principle of risk management is that the total risk related to an asset, loan, or financial position is never the sum of the individual types of risk that comprise it.

BOX 3.3   Who and What Caused the Crash of 2007–2009?[8]

The three Streets: Wall Street, Main Street, Massachusetts Avenue

Wall Street:

- Exotic securities that were complex, risky, and largely unregulated;
- Compensation: Bonus systems that encouraged bankers and traders to accept undue risks, because rewards were based on returns but not on risk;
- Leverage: Investment banks got the American Securities Exchange Commission to relax their capital requirements, and vastly increase leverage (ratio of debt to capital).

Main Street:

- (Ordinary people) Americans lived well beyond their means, overspent, and over-borrowed;
- Small and mid-sized banks over-lent to builders;
- Greedy homeowners used inflated home prices to borrow and spend.

(Box 3.3 continued)

---

[7] Nouriel Roubini addressing the World Economic Forum, Davos, Switzerland, January 29, 2009.

[8] *Fortune Magazine*, October 27, 2008: 14.

(*Box 3.3 continued*)

Massachusetts Avenue (Federal government):

- Gramm-Leach Bliley Act let commercial, investment banks recombine;
- Alan Greenspan (Fed Chair) lowered interest rates drastically, and excessively, fueling the housing bubble;
- Community Reinvestment Act: forced lending to people with bad or no credit rating.

J.M. Keynes once defined a sound banker as "one who, when he is ruined, is ruined in a conventional and orthodox way."[9] In 2007–2009, many bankers were ruined in highly unconventional ways. They were ruined by assets they failed to understand fully, and risks they failed to perceive fully. The reason: their inability to grasp telescopically the entire global financial system, and its vulnerabilities and dangers. Perhaps if more of them had practiced the kind of teleological reasoning we described in Chapters One and Two, they might have managed their risks better.

HOW BUBBLES AND BOOMS TURN INTO BUSTS AND COLLAPSE

In the 1950s, legendary business leader Alfred P. Sloan, who put together an industrial giant he called General Motors by buying many small car manufacturers (Chevrolet, Cadillac, Oldsmobile, Pontiac, Buick) donated USD 10 million to the science and technology university MIT (Massachusetts Institute of Technology), in Cambridge, MA.

"Let us try an experiment," Sloan said. "Let us put a business school right in the center of a major engineering university." It was named the M.I.T. Sloan School of Management, and opened in the building that once housed the detergent and soap company Lever Brothers, in a dingy industrial part of the city, on 50 Memorial Drive.

The experiment succeeded. In the early 1990s, the Sloan School was ranked the world's number 1 business school.

One of its earliest professors was named Jay Forrester. Forrester, an electrical engineer, had pioneered key inventions in computers, including matrix memory (data storage such that each cell has an x, y or row/column address). He had helped design the computers for the Sage early warning system, which despite being built with vacuum tubes had almost zero down time. Forrester chose to migrate, leaving his office in Electrical Engineering and moving to the new business school.

At Sloan, he invented a new discipline known as systems dynamics. Essentially, it was an attempt to build a wiring diagram for systems—businesses, economies, societies, or schools—showing feedback and interconnectedness. This was his

---

[9] Joe Nocera, "Risk Mismanagement," *New York Times Magazine*, January 4, 2009 (referenced at www.nyt.com). Quoted in Nocera, op. cit., p. 15.

answer to the question: What does an electrical engineer know, that can contribute to the understanding of business? It was an outstanding example of how an *outsider* with no specific knowledge of a discipline can, by bringing new perspectives, make breakthrough contributions.

His first effort was an attempt to model America's cities, which in the 1960s were troubled by poverty, social unrest, slums, and unemployment. Forrester used his new tool to diagnose the problem and propose a solution.[10] In a series of feedback loops, Forrester showed that the *solution* implemented at the time—construction of massive public housing in city centers—was in fact the root of the problem. Such housing pulled poor people into the city, while driving jobs and industry out, thus deepening and perpetuating the problem. This created a *doom loop*—a downward spiral of poverty and unemployment. The way to create a positive feedback loop, he showed, was through not public housing but by creating jobs, and bringing industry back to the cities. He was vilified by left-wing social reformers for daring to speak against public housing. But he was ultimately proven correct. Systems dynamics has since proven a powerful tool for big-picture thinking.

How would Forrester and his systems experts model the global financial crisis? Perhaps, in the following manner (see Figure 3.1:)

- The Leveraging Boom: Initially, as asset prices rise, people, businesses, and banks borrow money to buy assets; as asset prices rise, more borrowing (and leverage) becomes possible, and even desirable; as demand for financial assets rises, financial profits grow, borrowing and leverage both rise, and a positive feedback loop develops. As a result, asset prices come to exceed their true underlying value, based on the stable long-term income those assets generate. (Left-hand diagram, Figure 3.1a).
- The Deleveraging Bust: At some point, the *leveraging spiral* grinds to a halt and reverses direction. This happens, often, when a critical mass of *insiders* (those closest to capital markets and daily trading) realize that a bubble has developed, and that it is likely to burst. They begin selling, and de-leveraging (that is, liquidating old debt by selling old assets rather than incurring new debt to buy new assets). Those in the outer circles of capital markets take notice, and they too begin de-leveraging, selling assets to reduce debt. This process drives asset prices down, creating balance-sheet erosion and making de-leveraging even more urgent (because while assets fall in value, many liabilities and debts do not, greatly eroding net worth, capital or shareholders' equity and even leading to the threat of bankruptcy). (Right-hand diagram, Figure 3.1b.)

---

[10] Jay W. Forrester, *Urban Dynamics*, Riverside, CA: Pegasus Communications Inc., 1969).

FIGURE 3.1   How Financial Booms and Bubbles Quickly Evolve into Collapse

FIGURE 3.1a Increased Leveraging Spiral   **FIGURE 3.1b** Increased De-leveraging Spiral

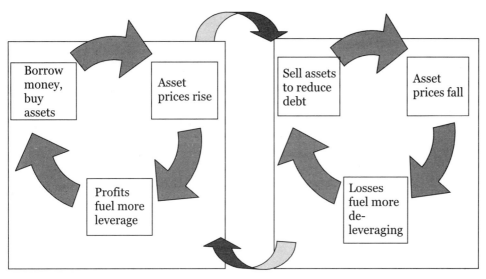

Source: Authors.

When does the *bust* end? When the de-leveraging cycle plays itself out, and investors return to asset markets, and begin buying and leveraging again.

How can risk managers anticipate the transition from leveraging to deleveraging, and then back to leveraging? A proper answer would require many books, and besides, if we had such an answer, we might not want or need to write books and educate managers. The key, and obvious point, though, is that those who manage risk—not only financial risk, but all types of risk—must constantly monitor the leverage big-picture and try to build scenarios in which there is a transition, often rapid. Even if they miss the transition, they must recognize it when it happens—many risk managers were in utter denial, and perhaps to this day remain in this dangerous state—and act swiftly to minimize their losses.

ACTION LEARNING

Timing the Market

1. What *early warning indicators* would you use, in order to anticipate a shift in capital market sentiment, from leveraging to de-leveraging? Since capital markets fluctuate, and are often

(*Action Learning continued*)

(*Action Learning continued*)

volatile—and such volatility has increased in recent years, in general—how can you distinguish between a random fluctuation, and a structural shift?

2. Research shows that in the United States, in a downturn, after stock prices reach bottom [measured by the Standard & Poor's (S&P) 500–stock index], they rise by 30 percent within 40 days. At the same time, both the S&P and Dow Jones stock indices fell by record amounts in the month of January 2009, dropping by between 8 and 8.5 per cent. This suggests that great importance (and profit) attach to detecting when boom turns to bust, and equally, when bust again turns to boom.

- What are the early warning indicators that you use, to spot the shift from *leveraging* to *de-leveraging* spirals (asset prices peak and begin to fall)? How can you best avoid waiting too long to liquidate assets, while avoiding selling them prematurely during temporary fluctuations?

- What are the early warning indicators that you use, to detect the shift from *de-leveraging* to *leveraging* spirals (asset prices reach bottom and begin to rise)? How can you capitalize on low equity and debt asset prices, without incurring the risk of buying low, and seeing asset prices fall even lower, much lower?

LEARNING SYSTEMS THINKING FROM LEONARDO DA VINCI

Perhaps the most creative and inventive human being who ever walked the face of the earth is the Italian Leonardo da Vinci, born some 557 years ago, on April 15, 1452, and died on May 2, 1519. Da Vinci invented and sketched the modern helicopter, airplane, tank, parachute, submarine, and a host of other things, centuries before their time. What can someone who lived so many centuries ago teach today's modern risk managers?

Among his many secrets of creativity, a key one was Leonardo's principle of "*connessione*," or "interconnectedness," in Italian. Leonardo closely observed patterns and connections in the world around him, and then wrote:

> The stone where it strikes the surface of the water, causes circles around it which spread out until they are lost; and in the same manner the air, struck by a voice or a noise, also has a circular motion, so he who is most distant cannot hear it.[11]

---

[11] Michael Gelb, *How to Think Like Leonardo da Vinci* (New York: Random House, 1998), 221.

Author Michael Gelb notes that many of us have encountered some version of the provocative question: If a butterly flaps its wings in a Brazilian rain forest, will it affect the weather in Siberia? Da Vinci anticipated it. He noted, according to Gelb, that "the earth is moved from its position by the weight of a tiny bird resting upon it."[12]

Connessione, interconnectedness, or systems thinking, is a skill that can be learnt and sharpened. Risk managers must practice it constantly. One approach is to regress in age, and become, again, a five-year-old. Young children learn enormous amounts in a very short time, and they do so by constantly asking, "Why?" Try the method of the Seven Whys. Very few puzzles or anomalies refuse to reveal their underlying secrets and causes, if we can successfully and successively ask "Why?" seven times, and get good answers. At the end of this process, a *teleology*, or cause-and-effect mechanism, will emerge, that will reveal very deep layers of *connessione*, or interconnectedness (see Box 3.4).

BOX 3.4   *Connessione*: The Crash of Black Monday, October 19, 1987[13]

Black Monday refers to Monday, October 19, 1987, when stock markets around the world crashed, with stock prices falling steeply in a very short time. The crash was the biggest single-day decline in American stock prices. It began in Hong Kong, spread west through international time zones to Europe, hitting the United States after other markets had already declined by a significant margin. The Dow Jones Industrial Average (DJIA) dropped by 508 points to 1,739 (22.6 percent). By the end of October, stock markets in Hong Kong had fallen to 45.8 percent, Australia 41.8 percent, Spain 31 percent, the United Kingdom 26.4 percent, the United States 22.68 percent, and Canada 22.5 percent.

Why? This collapse is still something of a mystery. It seems to be a result of *connessione*. Futures were traded in Chicago. Spot trades took place in New York.[14] A feedback loop developed. When spot stock prices fell in New York, this triggered futures selling in Chicago. But when futures prices fell, this in turn triggered spot sales. Because the two markets were physically separated, it was difficult for Chicago and New York stock exchange officials to coordinate policy or act together. Trading based on computer programs—so-called programmed trading—generated rapid selling pressure in both markets.

It was widely anticipated that the sharp decline would lead to a global recession. But this was wrong. Markets recovered and recession was averted, for then. America's next recession did not develop until 1991–1992.

---

[12] Op. cit., p. 222.

[13] Mark A. Carlson, "A Brief History of the 1987 Stock Market Crash with a Discussion of the Federal Reserve Response" (working paper, no. 2007–13. Federal Reserve Board of Governors, April 2007, Finance and Economics Discussion Series, FEDS).

[14] *Spot* trades are trades made for immediate delivery, or transfer of ownership. *Future* trades are trades made for delivery at some future date, in for instance, three, six, nine, or 12 months.

CONCLUSION

A common metaphoric expression speaks of those who miss seeing the forest for the trees. This is a common affliction in risk management. The more risk managers focus on their *trees*—the specific situation and parameters of their portfolio, investments, or organizations—the less-able they are to sense systemic risk, or weaknesses, and potential risks in the entire global system of markets.

This is why the *telemicroscope*—the combination of zoom-out vision and zoom-in vision—is so vital. A key lesson drawn from the 2007–2009 global crisis is precisely this—a great many clues existed, showing why the global market system was unstable and about to collapse, but a great many highly experienced, intelligent experts and managers simply did not see them. The same *double vision* skill that can sense looming risk can also sense impending recovery. It is far too late to take pre-emptive action before the market crash. But it is just the right time to use big-picture thinking to sense when markets will make a sustained recovery, and navigate the difficult transition from decline to growth. Those who cultivate this skill will be richly rewarded.

APPENDIX: THE VALUE OF "VALUE-AT-RISK"—A CAUTIONARY TALE OF RISK IN FAULTY MANAGEMENT[15]

I used to sleep easy at night with my VAR model.

—Alan Wheat, former CEO of Credit Suisse First Boston[16]

[Value-at-Risk] creates a false sense of security...it is like an air bag that works all the time, except when you have a car accident.

—Nassim Nicholas Taleb, author of The Black Swan [17]

---

[15] David Berray and Shlomo Maital, "Risk Management as a Critical Success Factor in Performance: A Cautionary Tale of a Global Financial Institution," unpublished case study, MIT Sloan School of Management, 2000. The hypothetical *RMIC Bank* is a fictitious composite based upon amalgamated financial and anecdotal information from several different, but real, financial institutions. This case was written in the year 2000. At the end there is a warning about a global financial earthquake that, unfortunately, proved clairvoyant.

[16] Sourced from the article "'Perfect Storms'—Beautiful & True Lies in Risk Management". http://www.wilmott.com/blogs/satyajitdas/enclosures/perfectstorms (May 2007)1.pdf (accessed January 26, 2010).

[17] Accessed from the article "Risk Management." http://www.nytimes.com/ 2009/01/04/ magazine/04risk-t.html (accessed January 26, 2010).

Introduction

This case study describes the variant of the Value-at-Risk (VAR) risk-management model used by a global financial institution we shall call *RMIC* (Risk Management is Critical), to manage financial exposures globally, and specifically in Asia, and the chain of events that led to significant losses throughout the region following Thailand's decision to float the baht on July 2, 1997. In the case of *RMIC Inc.*, the VAR model's *worst-case* scenario was supplanted in reality, in 1997 and 1998, by a *worse-than-worst-case* scenario, caused by sudden, dramatic, and unanticipated losses in market liquidity that made the closing of risky positions impossible, and revealed losses to be more than 10 times larger than the VAR model predicted. The result was a serious blow not only to RMIC's performance but to its very existence.

The objective of this case study is to review the development of RMIC Inc.'s VAR methodology and system and to identify the shortcomings in design and implementation which led to their systemic failure in the face of the Asian Economic Crisis. Our focus is not specifically on the VAR technique, but on the philosophy of risk management—microscopic portfolio risk management versus telescopic big-picture systemic risk management.

Background

Once, there was a global financial institution, venerable and profitable, that we will call RMIC Inc. RMIC calls to mind the old Hebrew saying, "Wise people avoid pitfalls smart people can extricate themselves from." At first, RMIC was merely smart. It piled up large losses on Third World debt in the 1980s, but offset them with large profits on its proprietary trading accounts. Then, it got wise.

Beginning in the 1970s, RMIC began to implement one of the most advanced VAR models in existence. RMIC thrived. Pre-tax earnings of RMIC for 1995 and 1996 were approximately USD 300 million, and USD 800 million, respectively. By every measure of performance evaluation and risk management, RMIC excelled. RMIC's risk management had careful loss limits, and allocated risk capital for its Asian portfolio of about USD 200 million, in line with a 99 percent (that is, worst 1 percent case) scenario.

In 1997, foreseeing a potential crisis, management reduced its Asian risk positions, and the VAR model indicated that less than USD 100 million of the allocated capital was at risk on July 2, 1997, when Thailand's baht collapsed.

Yet, despite sophisticated risk management implemented by a brilliant team, in 1998 risk exposures ultimately grew to a *full order of magnitude larger* than the VAR models previously predicted, and more than 10 times larger than the limits set by management. By the end of the year RMIC had isolated approximately USD 3 billion in liquidity, or credit-impaired financial exposures arising from Asian operations. Losses recognized through December 1998 on these exposures exceeded USD 400 million. Due to cost accounting conventions for investments, and *securities held for sale* these reported losses did not come close to accounting fully for the depressed value of the *impaired* portfolio. If the portfolio had been liquidated at that time, at market prices, *losses would certainly have exceeded USD 1 billion.*[18] It may never be clear how much of RMIC's shareholders' equity was erased by the Asian crash.

This is a cautionary tale, worth careful study by every financial institution and global enterprise. Today's global capital markets are an accident—or serious earthquake—waiting to happen. If and when it does, conventional risk measures and risk management will in hindsight prove remarkably naive, as they did for RMIC, and conventional performance measures will seem woefully inadequate.

Here are the lessons that RMIC's senior managers, shareholders, and regulators learned.

Asian crisis

On July 2, 1997, the Bank of Thailand—the nation's Central Bank—surrendered to speculative market pressure, and allowed the Thai baht to float freely. The baht lost approximately 20 percent of its value relative to the US dollar on that single-day alone, and depreciated by over 50 percent by the first quarter of 1998. Similar devaluations in Malaysia, the Philippines, and Korea soon followed. Most dramatically, the Indonesian rupiah, which was released from a managed trading band on August 14, 1997, would lose 80 percent of its value versus the dollar by the end of 1997. Regional stock markets also swooned and the *Asian Miracle* of economic growth came to a crashing halt as the flow of foreign investment capital which had fueled it, dried up, and fled the region.

No one claims to have predicted the depth and severity of the Asian economic crisis. Yet many, including the traders, investment bankers, management and even risk management officials at *RMIC Inc.*, detected the warning signs of mounting current account deficits, declining and jittery equity markets, and building pressures on artificially pegged or managed currency rates. Many salespeople and credit officers even warned their clients to reduce exposures.

RMIC Inc. had invested over 100 million dollars since the late 1970s to develop a leading edge VAR-based risk management system and process. In fact

---

[18] That huge loss is dwarfed by the record *quarterly* loss of AIG in the 4th quarter of 2008. A Reuter's news agency report noted: "American International Group Inc. posted a USD 61.7 billion fourth-quarter loss—the biggest quarterly loss in corporate history." Reuter's News Agency and Associated Press, Press Release, March 2, 2009.

RMIC Inc. was universally recognized as an innovator and leader in the area of managing financial market risk. Nonetheless, RMIC Inc. lost several hundred million dollars in the Asian conflagration. These losses far exceeded both the VAR projected by the VAR system, and the limits for acceptable risk of loss set by senior management and corporate policy. There was small comfort in knowing that virtually the same scenario was replicated at every one of RMIC Inc.'s peers and competitors in the region.

The development of the VAR system at RMIC Inc.

In the late 1970s, RMIC Inc.'s future Chairman, Simon Foster, was challenged by the difficulty in gauging, and comparing the performance of various divisions and activities throughout the bank. Profits from market-based and proprietary activities including the trading and sales of foreign exchange, corporate and government bonds, and related derivative products had been growing impressively, and were accounting for an increasing share of RMIC Inc.'s earnings. As a result, RMIC Inc. had been allocating additional resources, including capital, to these growth areas of the firm. Yet senior management realized that these growing returns were not being achieved without some risk. Especially, managers of areas within the bank which took far less risk, such as, the Transaction Processing and Financial Advisory divisions began to complain that their contributions to the firm's earnings were not being valued on a fair basis, with respect to risk. Also, though Simon could not at that time point to empirical evidence, he suspected that the analysts and investors who most influenced the price of RMIC Inc. shares, were translating RMIC's profits into overly-low expected share prices, because of RMIC's riskier market activities.

Simon was looking for a way to level the playing field for evaluating returns from various activities or divisions with differing risk characteristics. In capital markets, one can always achieve higher returns by taking on higher risk. In order to compare returns on assets with different degrees of risk, it is necessary to adjust for that risk. But how, Simon asked? The result was the internal development of a VAR model.

The first development and applications of the VAR model addressed market risk (the risk of decline in assets' market price). Later, the model and methodology were expanded to incorporate, first, credit risk (failure to repay loans), and later *all other*, or *operational* risk. With all three major risk components accounted for, RMIC Inc. had a remarkably powerful tool for measuring, managing, and describing its overall risk profile. Not surprisingly, RMIC Inc. received growing interest from various regulatory agencies concerned with monitoring the health of financial institutions, including the US Federal Reserve Bank, The Bank of England, and the Bank for International Settlements. An example of a typical VAR calculation is shown in Box 3.5.

BOX 3.5   Example of a Simple VAR Calculation

Assume an investment in a single share of a fictional MIT.com stock. The current price of a MIT.com share is USD 100.00. The historical weekly volatility (standard deviation of the weekly rate of return on the stock) has been 5 percent. What is the VAR for this investment, that is, the amount of money that will be lost if a worst-case scenario develops, with a probability of 1 percent (one time out of a 100)?

Value-at-Risk = Quantity × Price × Weekly Volatility × (Square Root of 52) × 2.33 Standard Deviations × (1-tax rate) ...
$$= 1 \times 100.00 \times .05 \times 7.21 \times 2.33 \times (1-0.39) = USD\ 51.23$$

Explanation—Quantity: 1 share. Price: USD 100. Weekly volatility (standard deviation): 5 percent. 7.21 is the square root of 52, required to convert weekly volatility to annual volatility; 2.33 is the number of standard deviations from the mean of a normal curve distribution, to reach the 1 percent area of the normal curve *tail*; and 39 percent is the effective tax rate for RMIC Inc. (since 39 percent of the loss is a tax expense deductible from future profits, the total loss is 1−0.39).

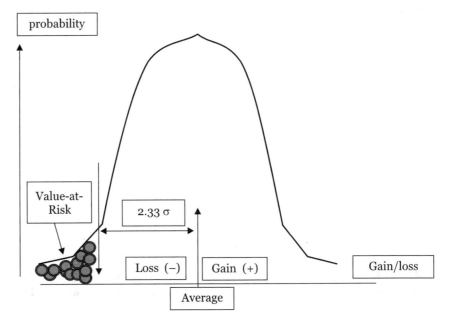

The distribution of gains and losses from an asset is assumed to be distributed according to a normal statistical distribution (the bell-shaped curve). The distance of 2.33 σ (where σ is the symbol for standard deviation) is the distance from the mean that brings us to a point on the normal curve where the probability of the loss is 1 percent. The area (the filled little circles), after adjustment for tax credits, is the VAR the loss incurred if the worst-case 1 percent scenario occurs.

This, of course, all took time, and developing the models and systems was only the first—and easiest—stage. Having built the basic system, RMIC Inc. senior management spent enormous amounts of time and effort to convince people throughout the firm that they were serious about managing economic returns on risk. Only when key incentive-driving systems such as capital allocation and bonus planning were directly linked to the VAR system did the message begin to stick. But stick it did, and by the time of the 1987 US stock market crash, VAR had become an integral and critical component of RMIC Inc.'s culture and management processes. This was a tremendous accomplishment, and it served management, shareholders and regulators alike well during the crash. In the decade between 1987 and 1997 management continued to develop and refine the VAR model and process, regularly investing in more computing power, more Ph.D.s, and more sophisticated modeling techniques.

In principle, the VAR system simply performs this calculation thousands of times for the various instruments in its portfolios and aggregates the risk, adjusting for correlation.

Systemic risk: The Asian contagion

When borrowed money is artificially cheap and financial risks become distorted by government guarantees, investment hurdle rates fall and unproductive projects get funded. To borrow another phrase from Krugman, with risks obfuscated, all potential investments take on "Pangloss Values." (From Voltaire's Candide: Dr Pangloss felt that all is for the best, "in this the best of all possible worlds).") The implication is that with the downside artificially truncated, any particular investment will be valued at only its potential upside value, in "this the best of all possible worlds." In a sense, this is what happened throughout Asia as more and more money chased increasingly risky and unprofitable projects and investments. Combined with a flood of new money availability into relatively small economies, the predictable result was asset inflation (both real and financial assets), and ultimately a bubble. Real estate, equity, and other real asset prices all soared to levels entirely unjustified by earnings or productivity gains.

Economic data signaled the danger of a growing bubble, and these indications were not opaque to RMIC Inc.'s traders, management, and risk management team in 1997. The prospect of a significant market correction was apparent to many. In fact credit officers and salespeople were actively working with many clients to sell hedging products, and/or reduce foreign borrowing exposures ahead of the potential storm. So why did the VAR model and overall risk management process allow for so much risk to remain on RMIC Inc.'s books?

The first answer lies in the interpretation of volatility. The model looked backward for three years in order to "forecast" potential volatility over the coming one year. Yet the previous three years of economic history in South East Asia painted a consistent picture of steadily rising economic growth. After all, that is why people called it the Asian Miracle! Even worse, historic volatility was predicated on pegged or managed exchange rates. The past movements of a pegged rate are certainly no predictor of what may happen when the peg breaks. Second, and equally important, the model—and RMIC Inc.'s risk managers—had been observing steady and impressive growth in liquidity in the Asian foreign exchange, interest rate, and equity markets. The wave of foreign investment, and overall banking activity of the 1990s had by definition meant more buyers and sellers. This growth in liquidity was an obvious phenomenon to those who were close to their markets. But many of them appear to have misunderstood the ephemeral nature of this liquidity. As noted previously, most of the money flowing into the region was provided by institutional fund managers, the so-called *hot money*. When times are good there may be lots of it; when things go bad, it can dry up and flee with alarming velocity. In a sense the growth in real liquidity was an illusion.

The bubble bursts

On July 2, 1997, while Hong Kong-based international bankers were still celebrating the return of Hong Kong to China by the British after 150 years of colonial rule, the Bank of Thailand surrendered to speculative market pressures, abandoned its managed target rate for the Thai baht, and allowed the currency to float. The baht immediately fell by 20 percent, and ultimately lost 50 percent of its value as traders and investors scrambled to get out of long positions in baht. After the break in Thailand, other markets too began to look vulnerable, and pressure grew on the Indonesian rupiah, the Malaysian ringit, and the Korean won. On August 14, the rupiah broke as well and quickly depreciated.

The implications for corporate earnings and economic growth were clearly negative, and regional equity markets swooned in sympathy with the currency markets. The price of foreign debt repayments exploded in terms of local currency costs, and these debts had to be repaid from local earnings as most borrowers had scant sources of dollar income. The ability of borrowers to repay was clearly in jeopardy, and as a result, banks froze nearly all new lending, and quickly scrambled to call in what loans they could. Simply put: everyone was a seller, no one a buyer, and liquidity fled the market.

Consequently, the value of trading positions, outstanding loans, and related derivative products on the books of RMIC Inc. declined steeply in value. Worse, even those positions—like dollar-denominated loans—which were theoretically still valuable became less likely to be repaid. Finally, derivative contracts based upon the relationship between local and foreign interest rates gyrated hugely in value, reflecting their leveraged, non-linear nature. In constructing these derivative deals, RMIC Inc. would typically strike a deal with a local borrower and then offset the deal with a hedge contracted with another financial institution. RMIC Inc. and others were caught in a whipsaw when the amounts owed on the contracts ballooned dramatically. Local borrowers were unable to pay, but RMIC Inc. was still required to pay on the other side of the deal. As markets caved, there was a realization that there was no theoretical limit as to how big some of these individual exposures could grow. RMIC Inc. quite suddenly discovered that the amount it was owed by certain derivatives clients was growing exponentially at the very same time as these clients' ability to meet their financial obligations was rapidly decaying. In total the exposures were soon a full order of magnitude greater than either the value-at-risk previously predicted by the VAR model or the limits set by management.

By the end of 1998, RMIC Inc. had isolated over USD 2.5 billion in liquidity or credit impaired financial exposures arising from Asian operations. Losses recognized through December, 1998 on these exposures approached USD 500 million. Due to financial accounting and reporting rules for investments and *securities held for sale* these reported losses failed to fully account for the depressed value in the *impaired* portfolio. If the portfolio had been forced to liquidation at that time and at market prices, losses for RMIC would undoubtedly have exceeded USD 1 billion. *By way of comparison, losses for each of the previous two years were in the area of only USD 500 million.* It may never be clear how much of RMIC Inc.'s shareholders equity was erased by the Asian crash. Less than 18 months after the devaluation of the baht, RMIC Inc. agreed to be acquired by another firm which its managers had once looked down upon as a second-tier, *would-be* competitor (see Epilogue).

The RMIC Inc. risk management process had established loss limits, and allocated a risk capital limit for the Asian portfolio in the area of USD 250 million. This was meant to be a 99 percent *worst-case* scenario figure, based upon its sophisticated assumptions. Because management had foreseen a potential crisis and had somewhat reduced Asian risk positions, the model indicated that less than USD 100 million of the allocated capital was actually at risk on July 2, 1997.

Picking up the pieces—What are the lessons?

The first and absolutely critical lesson of the Asian debacle at RMIC Inc. is deceptively simple. A model is only a model, not reality! In many ways RMIC Inc. was a victim of its own success. The risk-management function had prided itself on developing the most sophisticated risk model anywhere in the industry. The team had continuously refined and improved the model, tested it against real market events, and considered and incorporated feedback from traders and regulators alike. Moreover, senior management and the risk management function had labored incessantly to embed the VAR methodology into the culture of the firm. And they had succeeded. The VAR model—together with its underlying assumptions—had truly become part of the day-to-day language and culture at RMIC Inc. In short, it had come to be taken for granted. Traders would turn to their assistants and ask, "Hey Joe, what's the risk on that position?" Joe would punch a few keys and answer, "2 (million) dollars." And everyone knew that USD 2 was "the number." Little room was left for, "Why is it 2? Why isn't it 4?" or even "What if...?"

In retrospect, the events of the Asian crisis—and arguably the behavior of financial markets in general—do not fit the model perfectly. Expected returns aren't normal; the curve tails are fat and long. Discontinuous events happen. Liquidity cannot be taken for granted. It's only a model. Based upon the historical volatility of the Thai baht and Indonesian rupiah, upon which RMIC Inc.'s VAR system relied, the exchange rate moves in the latter half of 1997 represented variances of 3 and 4 standard deviations, respectively. Under the assumptions of the normal curve, these are *once in several millennia* events. Yet we see market disruptions of large magnitudes with much greater frequency. The US equity market crash of 1987, the Mexican debt crisis of the 1980s, the global bond market crash of 1994—each resulted in multiple standard deviation moves in financial markets.

More subtly, RMIC Inc. management may have forgotten the original design purpose for the VAR system. The original gestation of VAR was a desire to compare the relative performance of various risk-taking activities to one another across the firm, and allocate the firm capital accordingly to estimate EVA (Economic Value Added) for particular divisions.[19] As a comparative and allocational tool the VAR model is indeed as sound as any arbitrary standard. However, it was a short trip from this original intent to using the model to estimate or forecast the risk of future losses. This is not to say that VAR is not a powerful tool for this obvious application, but that it is essential to recognize the limitations of the application.

Two other fundamental lessons arise from this experience. First, a strong and independent risk management function, policy, and process are powerful and essential tools in the management of a modern financial institution. However, it is absolutely critical that front line traders, sales people, and their managers not be permitted to abdicate their risk responsibilities to a control function. Risk control functions exist to establish and monitor norms and limits and to provide management information and objective advice. But the responsibility for managing risk must reside with the front line. No trader at RMIC Inc. would have abdicated this responsibility in the

---

[19] Economic Value Added is defined as: Net income after taxes, minus the opportunity cost of shareholders' equity (the risk-adjusted rate of return on equity multiplied by the value of shareholders' equity, as listed in the balance-sheet).

area of market risk. Each knew absolutely that he *owned* his own position. However, in the area of credit risk, the accountability was far less clear. Traders and sales people up to the most senior levels of the firm (including two of four Vice-Chairmen) could, and did, claim that the credit losses from the Asian crash were the responsibility of the credit officers (a control function) who had approved their deals. In the end, market and credit risk turned out to be more closely intertwined than many had recognized, and RMIC Inc. paid dearly for this lapse.

Second, in any business, front line people and their managers must constantly ask themselves, "What business are we in, and what risks are appropriate to that business?" And more subtly, they must be prepared to ask that question about their clients. "What business is my client in? Is the risk of the deal I am proposing to him appropriate to his business and strategy? Does he understand this risk?" In the end, the model will give you a number. If you think you are in the stationery business, but your CFO is taking multi-million dollar bets with your shareholders' money on the direction of interest rates, you may have a problem. If it is your client who is in this position, you still have a problem!

The fact that state-of-the-art risk management can lead to losses on an order of magnitude larger than worst-case predictions, in the wake of a financial *earthquake*, troubles the sleep of some managers, and should probably trouble the sleep of all of them.

Finally, all businesses and organizations, not only financial ones, must constantly challenge the basic (often unstated or unspoken) assumptions on which their businesses rest. We can identify four assumptions made at RMIC that all proved wrong, and ultimately, fatal:

- There will always be a buyer on the other side of a transaction. In crises, markets become *sellers only*.
- Bad times in one part of the world are offset by good times in another part. In crises, capital markets are unsettled *everywhere*.
- Political risk is accurately assessed. Politicians march to different drummers than investors. With only slight hyperbole, hedge fund manager Warren Mosler says about Russia's bond default: "Nobody in the history of the world has ever done anything this foolish."[20]
- There will never be a *perfect storm* in global markets, that is, when everything, but everything, goes wrong.

  In fact, there was a perfect storm. It took a decade to arrive.

---

[20] Peter Coy and Suzanne Woolley, with Leah Nathans Spiro and William Glasgall, "Failed Wizards of Wall Street, Can you Devise Surefire ways to Beat the Markets? The Rocket Scientists thought they could. Boy, were they ever Wrong," in New York and Bureau Reports, *Business Week* (September 21, 1998), 116.

Are *you* prepared for a financial earthquake?

In many ways, RMIC Inc. and other global financial institutions could learn from insurance companies that insure property loss. In August 1999, a catastrophic earthquake struck Turkey, causing tens of thousands deaths and injuries, and billions in property losses. In September, 1999, an earthquake struck Athens (not far from this spot), again, with over a hundred dead. Geologists claim that the fault line that runs through Izmet, Turkey is geologically identical to the San Andreas Fault that runs through Los Angeles.

Realizing that a catastrophic earthquake in California—of the sort that struck Turkey—could cause unimaginable damage, insurance companies have begun to consult with geophysicists, to try to estimate the probability of such an event. They struggle with a very difficult mathematical problem.

Expected loss is equal to: "p," the probability of a severe earthquake (7.5 or more on the Richter scale) multiplied by the dollar value of the damage it would cause, "V":

$$\text{Expected Loss} = p \times V$$

where "p" is very small and its standard deviation (a measure of uncertainty) is very large. "V" is very large, and its standard deviation, too, is very large. The degree of uncertainty associated with Expected Loss is therefore exceedingly large. This is precisely parallel to the fundamental problem with VAR models in finance. $p \times V$ is the equivalent of the left tail of the distribution of returns.

While property insurance companies consult with geophysicists and plate tectonic experts, global financial institutions consult with, and employ, economists. Geophysicists insist that while they can state with near-certainty that a catastrophic earthquake WILL occur along the San Andreas Fault, at present they cannot state WHEN. *Economists, too—at least some of them—predict that a major financial crash will occur in world markets (because all of the fundamental underlying causes that led to the 1997–98 Asian crisis still exist, and have not been corrected)—but cannot say WHEN. Nor can they say WHERE.* One of the most worrisome aspects of this uncertainty is that even countries with impeccable economic policies in place—Singapore, or Taiwan—are subject to severe damage from quakes in nearby countries. In today's global capital markets, it is not enough to be blameless or without sin.

Questions for discussion

- Why did seasoned capital market players fail to recognize the flaws in VAR?
- Should VAR models be discarded, or can they still be useful tools when applied with appropriate circumspection?

- How can VAR and macroeconomic tools be used to spot signals of impending capital-market crisis in sufficient time to avoid major losses?
- Why should risk management be regarded as a critical success factor in performance evaluation?

EPILOGUE

RMIC is based in part on what was once Wall Street's most innovative investment bank, Banker's Trust (BT), where the late David Morrison Berray was employed. The bank suffered major losses in the summer of 1998. While Russia's default was officially blamed for them, many insiders realized then that a new, high risky stance in lending spearheaded by the BT CEO was a root cause of the bank's demise.

Deutsche Bank, Germany's largest commercial bank, bought BT in November, 1998. Shortly before this, BT pleaded guilty to institutional fraud. Rather than turn over to the states money from dormant customer accounts, and un-cashed dividend and interest checks as required by law, some of the bank's senior executives credited this money as income, and moved this money to BT's operating account.

In November, 1998, Deutsche Bank agreed to purchase BT for USD 9.8 billion; the purchase was finalized on June 4, 1999. BT then became an orphan, passed from one *parent* to another. In Australia, BT was acquired by Westpac from Principal Group, who had purchased it three years earlier from Deutsche Bank. This organization now uses the name BT Financial Group. The Trust and Custody business that Deutsche Bank acquired from BT was sold to State Street two years later.

Chapter 4

A country is a business

LEARNING OBJECTIVES

After reading this chapter, managers should be able to read a country's basic Gross Domestic Product (GDP) data, and draw strategic conclusions about the country's market size, saving and investment, growth orientation, and future prospects, useful for guiding business decisions related to country risk and exploration of new markets. You should understand why a country resembles a business—and ways it does not—and how to read a country's "Profit and Loss" statement, known as the GDP and its components. You should know how to deduce important insights about the country from its GDP data. You should be able and willing to delve into the GDP numbers, well beyond the sketchy press reports published quarterly, that announce the latest GDP growth rate. You should know how to use the GDP and its five components to carry out a quick analysis of the country's growth drivers—which part of GDP demand is generating the country's economic growth? You should know how to build two or three scenarios about how the country's economy will perform in the near term.

The reader should be able to answer the following questions, for any country:

- How is a country's output measured? What is GDP?
- Why is a GDP table similar to a company's income statement?
- Where do country's resources come from and who uses them?
- How can you measure whether a country is future-oriented?
- What is the difference between net investment and gross investment?
- Why a country's economic depreciation often is underestimated? How can it be estimated?
- Why is the difference between output that is produced (GDP) and output that is sold (final sales) very important?
- What are a country's *growth drivers* and what do they reveal about a market?

Tool # 4

 Gross Domestic Product (GDP)

The future still looks good, and you've got time to rectify.... All the things that you should
... Do what you want to do, and go where you're going to.... Think for yourself!

— Song by The Beatles from their 1965 album Rubber Soul[1]

INTRODUCTION

A quick Google search on *economic forecasting* reveals 54 organizations that sell economic predictions. Many of these organizations are led by top economists with stellar credentials, and doctorates from the world's leading universities.

Their crystal-ball gazing can be very expensive. The price tag for such forecasts may reach six figures (in dollars) or more.

Caveat emptor (buyer beware!). For many years, our message to managers and students of management has been one already stressed in Chapter One, and found in the 1965 Beatles song: Think for yourself! If you do your own forecasting, you may still be wrong, but you have as good, or better, a chance to predict near-term economic activity as professional economists. Their record is dismal.

The reason? Countries are businesses, in a very real sense. Their economies are comprised of small, medium, and large-sized businesses. Managers are trained to analyze businesses. *Why not, then, use the same approach to analyzing countries?* This is the theme of this chapter.

We will argue that by understanding some basic principles of the conventions of national accounting (the so-called GDP, and its components), and merging them with keen observations of clients, markets and daily business, managers can do no worse in their forecasts than economists, and often, far better. They can gain the skill of answering two key questions, for the major markets in which they operate:

- What is the current state of the country's economy and its inherent risks?
- Based on that analysis, what is its most likely near-term scenario?

We will seek to show that basic understanding of GDP can help managers X-ray a nation's national accounts, track country risk, and even construct a respectable, independent near-term forecast.

---

[1] http://www.mp3lyrics.org/t/the-beatles/think/diff-1-html (accessed January 26, 2010).

THE FAILURE OF ECONOMIC FORECASTS

Here is some evidence about what economists themselves accept as the poor results of their forecasting prowess. *Financial Times* economist Tim Harford notes:

> Back in 1995, the economist and FT [*The Financial Times*] columnist John Kay examined the record of 34 British forecasters from 1987 to 1994, and he concluded that they were birds of a feather. They tended to make similar forecasts, and then the economy disobligingly did something else, with economic growth usually falling outside the range of all 34 forecasters.

> Nor has the forecasters' record improved since.

> I repeated Kay's exercise with forecasts for economic growth for the UK, US and Eurozone over the years 2002–2008, diligently collected at the end of each previous year by Consensus Economics. The results are an eerie echo of Kay's.

> ...Recent US forecasters have done a little better: the spread of forecasts is tighter and the outcome sometimes falls within that spread. Still, five out of six were too pessimistic about 2003, almost everyone was too pessimistic about 2002; three-quarters were too optimistic about 2005 and nearly nine-tenths too optimistic about 2006. Perversely, the most accurate forecasts were made about 2007, despite the fact that the credit crunch was a surprise to many. In the Eurozone, forecasting over the past few years has been so wayward that it is kindest to say no more.

> ...The new data seem to confirm Kay's original finding that economic forecasters all tend to be wrong in the same way. Their incentives to flock together are obvious enough. What is less clear is why the *flight of the flock* is so often thought to augur much—but then, some astrologers are also profitably employed.[2]

If those who study and predict economic trends as their full-time profession fail, what can hapless managers do, faced with the need to plan budgets and strategies for the coming three to five years, yet struggling with extreme uncertainty surrounding national and world economies?

We urge managers and students of management to read this chapter carefully, then track what experts say, but apply the proverbial grain of salt, while using simple versions' of the experts' own tools combined with sharp observations in the field to build their own estimates. Think for yourself! Avoid the flight of the flock.

---

[2] Tim Harford, "Never Trust an Economic Forecast," *The Financial Times*. August 9, 2008. http://www.ft.com/cms/s/2/867c0148-6353-11dd-9fd0-0000779fd2ac.html (accessed January 18, 2010).

Let us begin our quest to learn to use and apply economists' basic macroeconomic GDP tool by examining a press report. We will refer to this report later in this chapter, to show managers how the basic macroeconomic GDP tool can provide insights beyond what ordinary readers may glean from a typical newspaper report.

US GDP SHRINKS

U.S. GDP Shrank 3.8 percent Last Quarter, Most Since 1982[3]

by Timothy R. Homan

Jan. 30 [2009] (Bloomberg)—The U.S. economy shrank the most since 1982 in the fourth quarter [of 2008] as consumer spending recorded the worst slide in the postwar era, a trajectory that's likely to continue in coming months.

The 3.8 percent annual pace of contraction in the final three months of last year was less than forecast, with a buildup of unsold goods cushioning the blow. Without the jump in inventories, the decline would have been 5.1 percent, the Commerce Department said today in Washington.

What is GDP? How is it measured? What does the *jump in inventories* mean? In this chapter, we will focus mainly on the United States economy, largest in the world, comprising fully one-fourth of world GDP, the source of the 2007–2009 global crisis and perhaps, the eventual engine of world recovery. After reading the chapter, we hope readers will find far deeper insights into press reports like Homan's written for Bloomberg.

But first, let us look at the big-picture—the world's dozen largest economies, comprising 71 percent of total world production and income. Before zooming in on the United States, we zoom out on the global economy.

World GDP

At this point, it suffices to state that Gross Domestic Product (GDP) is a measure of both the total output of goods and services in an economy, and the total income. (The World Bank, for instance, uses the term GDI, or Gross Domestic Income.) Later we will provide a more precise, detailed definition.

Table 4.1 shows GDP for the world as a whole, and for the dozen largest economies, ranked in order. It shows that world GDP for the year 2007 was some USD

---

[3] Timothy R. Homan, "U.S. GDP shrank 3.8% last quarter, most since 1982 (updated)", *Bloomberg News Service*. http://www.bloomberg.com/apps/news?pid=206011087&refer= home&sid=aN1OnWuR4C4k (accessed January 18, 2010).

TABLE 4.1   World Gross Domestic Product: 13 Largest Economies, 2007

Rank	Country	GDP (USD million)	Percentage of World GDP
	World	54,347,038	
1.	United States	13,811,200	25.4
	Eurozone	12,179,250	22.4
2.	Japan	4,376,705	8.1
3.	Germany	3,297,233	6.1
4.	China (PRC)	3,280,053	6.0
5.	United Kingdom	2,727,806	5.0
6.	France	2,562,288	4.7
7.	Italy	2,107,481	3.9
8.	Spain	1,429,226	2.6
9.	Canada	1,326,376	2.4
10.	Brazil	1,314,170	2.4
11.	Russia	1,291,011	2.4
12.	India	1,170,968	2.2
Total: 12 Largest economies		38,694,517	71.2

Source: World Bank, World Development Indicators 2009. www.worldbank.org (accessed February 1, 2010).

Note: EU or Eurozone is also considered as a country.

54,300 billion. (For 2008, world GDP was about 3 percent higher, or 56,000 billion.) Together, America and the Euro zone make up 48 percent of the world economy, or about half.

The American economy comprised a quarter of the world economy, or about USD 13,811 billion, while the Eurozone (for which the euro is their currency) comprised 22.4 percent.[4]

Table 4.2 shows world GDP for the year 1990 (the year that followed the collapse of the Berlin Wall and the ensuing integration of the former USSR and Asia into world markets), and the years 2004 and 2007 (just before the onset of the global crisis).

It shows the remarkable, and unprecedented, growth of world GDP, which rose by 90 percent in a decade (1990–1999), and by 136 percent between 1990 and 2007. In less than a single generation, world per capita GDP has doubled—unprecedented

TABLE 4.2   World Gross Domestic Product, Population and GDP per capita: 1990, 2004, 2007

	1990	2004	2007
Total (USD billion)	$21,736	$41,290	$54,347
Population (million)	5,256	6,365	6,606
GDP per capita: (USD)	$4,067	$6,487	$8,227

Source: World Bank, World Development Indicators, 2006, 2008.

---

[4] There are currently 27 nations that comprise the European Union, but 11 of them have not yet switched from their local currency to the euro; 16 nations of the 27 have adopted the euro, first created in 1999.

in human history. Even as world GDP growth slows in 2009 and 2010, the remarkable boom during 1990–2007 will remain noteworthy and remarkable. The growth in GDP was accompanied by even more remarkable growth in global financial assets. (see Box 4.1). Later, we will explore the drivers of this remarkable growth, led by fast-growing economies in Asia.

BOX 4.1   Global Wealth Creation, 1980–2006

A study by McKinsey Global Institute (see Figure 4.1) shows that from the birth of the modern global free-market system in 1990, some USD 124,000 billion in new financial wealth was created, comprised of bank deposits, stocks, and bonds. World Bank Chief Economist Justin Lin estimates that in 2007–09 global losses in stocks and bonds totaled USD 30 trillion.[5] Even if this is true, these losses comprise just one-fourth of the total capital gains since 1990.

FIGURE 4.1   Global Wealth Creation, 1980–2006[1]

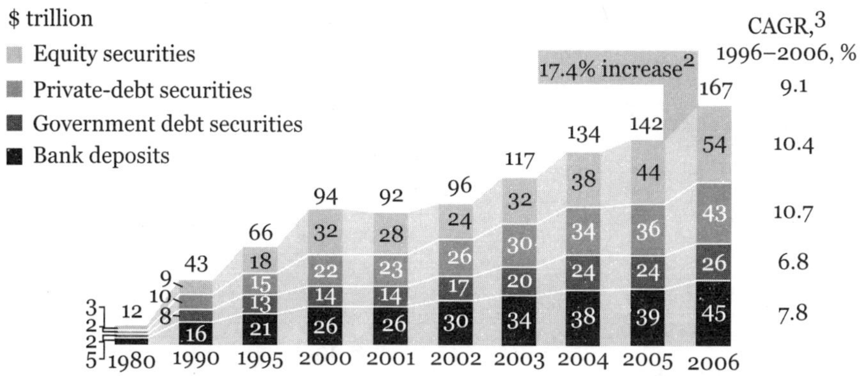

$ trillion

- Equity securities
- Private-debt securities
- Government debt securities
- Bank deposits

17.4% increase[2]

CAGR,[3] 1996–2006, %

Stacked bar chart values by year:

Category	1980	1990	1995	2000	2001	2002	2003	2004	2005	2006	CAGR 1996–2006, %
Total		43	66	94	92	96	117	134	142	167	9.1
Equity securities	3	9	18	32	28	24	32	38	44	54	10.4
Private-debt securities	2	10	15	22	23	26	30	34	36	43	10.7
Government debt securities	2	8	13	14	14	17	20	24	24	26	6.8
Bank deposits	5 / 12	16	21	26	26	30	34	38	39	45	7.8

	1980	1990	1995	2000	2001	2002	2003	2004	2005	2006	CAGR
Nominal GDP $ trillion	10.1	21.5	29.4	31.7	31.6	32.8	36.9	41.6	44.8	48.3	5.7
Financial depth, % of GDP	201	201	223	294	290	292	315	318	317	346	

Source: McKinsey Global Institute global-financial-stock database.

Notes: [1] Figure may not sum to totals, because of rounding.

[2] $5.9 trillion of increase in 2006 (from 2005) was caused by depreciation of US dollar against other currencies. Even at constant exchange rates, growth in 2006 was faster than average from 1995 to 2005.

[3] Compound annual growth rate.

---

[5] Agence France-Presse, "Nations must work together," *Sydney Morning Herald*, February 5, 2009. www.smh.com.au. http://www.smh.com/news/world/nations-must-work-together/2009/02/05/1233423318601.html (accessed January 18, 2010).

Measuring GDP

There are three ways that Gross Domestic Product is measured:

- By adding up all the incomes earned in the economy;
- By adding up all the spending and purchases on final goods and services bought for consumption;
- And finally, by adding all the added value (the difference between the value of goods or services at market prices and the cost of the materials and components that were used to make them).

Each method should in principle arrive at the same figure for GDP. We begin with the least used of the three: value added, because it corresponds nicely to the concept of the firm's income statement.

CASE STUDY

U.S.A. Inc.

 Managers are accustomed to analyzing their own companies and their competitors by studying profit-and-loss statements. The same approach can be applied to whole countries. What does the United States' P&L (profit and loss, or income) statement tell us about America? And what do similar national accounts show about other markets?[6] (see Table 4.3).

America is the world's biggest business. The US economy made about USD 14,000 billion worth of goods and services (at annual rate) in the fourth quarter of 2008. This number is an annual rate—it is the quarterly figure multiplied by four. This includes goods and services produced by governments at all levels, all businesses—both incorporated and unincorporated—and farms.

Businesses, individuals, and governments at all levels in America sold an estimated total of USD 27,000 billion worth of products and services (at an annual rate) in the third quarter of 2008 (that is, the quarterly value of goods

(Case Study continued)

---

[6] An enterprising Harvard economics undergraduate, Meredith Bagby, had the creative idea of drawing up "The First Annual Report of the United States of America" and published it herself. Harper Business published it in 1994, and a Ross Perot (business leader and one-time Presidential candidate) endorsement helped it sell well.

(Case Study continued)

TABLE 4.3   Profit and Loss Statement, U.S.A. Inc.

3rd Quarter 2008: USD Billion, at Annual Rate	
Gross sales	$27,000
Minus: cost of materials*	12,579
Equals: gross value added (GDP)	*14,421*
Minus: capital consumption	1,900
Equals: net value added (NDP)	*12,521*
Minus: Indirect Business taxes	628
Minus: compensation of workers	8,083
Equals: net operating surplus	*3,810*
Minus: interest, misc.	1,519
Equals: net income before tax	*2,291*
Minus: corp. profits tax	831
Equals: net after tax profits	*1,460*
Minus: dividend payments	999
Equals: retained earnings	*461*

Source: Based on US Economic Report of the President, 2008 (February, 2009),
  Table B–14, p. 302.
Note: * Authors' estimate.

and services sold, multiplied by four). Some of those goods and services
were *final goods* bought directly by consumers, but others were so-called
intermediate goods or *materials*—components and products used in making
other goods by other companies—an estimated USD 12,579 billion. We need
to eliminate this sum, in order to prevent *double counting*—adding in the
same products twice. The difference between total sales, and components
and materials is USD14,421 billion. This is known as gross value added. It
represents the *value added* to material components, by applying labor and
capital to them. It is also known as the *gross domestic product* (GDP) of
America. It is *gross* because it includes goods produced to replace worn-out
capital assets (capital consumption); those goods are not directly available
for our use.

DEFINITION

 Gross Domestic Product is the sum of all the added value, added to
materials and components, by a country's businesses, individuals and
governments, for a given period of time (quarter, or year). It is
measured by the market value of the total production of goods and services.

Note: When economic depreciation or capital consumption (see Box 4.2), is
subtracted from GDP, we get Net Domestic Product. This is a better measure

---

BOX 4.2   GDP... or GNP?

Some older readers may recall that the *D* in GDP was once an *N*, standing for GNP or Gross National Product. What is the difference? And why have we shifted from GNP to GDP?

GDP is the most widely used measure of a nation's economic size: the amount of goods and services produced within a country's borders. It is *Gross*, because it includes goods and services used to replace worn out capital (*depreciation*, or capital consumption). It is *Domestic* because it refers to all those goods and services produced within a country's geographical borders by anyone, whether a citizen, resident, or foreigner.

The shift to a geographical basis for measuring national income and output rather than one based on nationality, was motivated by practical considerations—it proved difficult to measure accurately, for instance, the sums Egyptian school teachers earn in Dubai and send home to their families in envelopes. The output of the Honda factory in Illinois is part of America's GDP, not Japan's; Mercedes-Benz's output of sports utility vehicles in Tuscaloosa, Alabama, is part of America's GDP, not Germany's; Motorola's production of pagers in Malaysia belongs to Malaysia's GDP, not America's. Nonetheless, some countries, like, the Philippines, Egypt, and Turkey earn significant parts of their national income from money sent home by their citizens working abroad. *It is thus well to learn what GNP is, as well as GDP.*

---

of a nation's output of goods and services, because it represents goods and services available for use (rather than used to replenish worn-out capital), but is little used, because of the inherent difficulty in measuring capital consumption.

DEFINITION

GNP, or Gross National Product, measures output or income *generated by the citizens of a country*, including those working abroad, and including net income generated by capital invested abroad, but excluding income earned by foreign residents in the country.

America's GNP in third quarter 2008 USD 11,809.6 billion (measured in prices of year 2000), compared to GDP of USD 11,712. 3 billion. This means that Americans working abroad sent home about USD 97 billion more income than foreigners working in America sent home.

Value added is a better measure of a nation's production than sales, because it eliminates double counting. If we add the sales of a lumber yard and the sales of a furniture company that buys its wood from the lumber yard, we would be adding the lumber twice. To measure GDP, we add up the value of the lumber yard's wood, and the net value the furniture firm adds to that wood when it produces and sells a table. General Electric, for instance, sold goods and services worth some USD 176.7 billion in 2007, but bought some USD 22 billion worth of materials and components. Therefore, its value added, or contribution to world GDP, was USD 154.7 billion. Since General Electric is a global company, and produces goods and services in many sites around the world, only about half of its value added was produced in the US, and is therefore part of America's GDP; the other half was produced in other countries.

Because every dollar of value added ultimately goes to some person, either as payment for labor or payment for the services of capital, GDP *is also a measure of national income*. But at least two parts of GDP never reach individual citizens' pockets:

1. economic depreciation, or *capital consumption*, that part of a nation's resources needed to replace capital that either wears out or becomes obsolete; and
2. indirect business taxes, such as sales taxes paid to state and local governments.

DEFINITION

Capital Consumption, also termed *economic depreciation,* is the value of a nation's capital goods (fixed assets) that either wear out or become obsolete during a period of time, and thus require replacement.

Deducting capital consumption from GDP leaves Net Domestic Product (NDP); deducting from that indirect business taxes (such as state sales taxes) yields Net Domestic Income (NDI). Of that sum, about two-thirds to three-fourths goes to workers and managers as *compensation of employees* (gross wages and salaries). This includes benefits like health insurance. After subtracting wages from NDI, we get profit before taxes, or USD 2,291 billion.

Corporations and other businesses paid USD 831 billion in taxes (about 36 percent); after deducting profit tax we get net profit of USD 1,460 billion. Of that sum, USD 999 billion was paid out in dividends. This leaves retained earnings (undistributed profits) of about USD 461 billion. These retained earnings are business saving and are used by companies for renewing and expanding their physical capital.

Should you buy shares of U.S.A. Inc.?

What can we learn from the P&L of U.S.A. Inc.? Suppose we compare U.S.A. Inc. to a profitable well-run corporation General Electric (GE)? (see Table 4.4 for GE's income statement).

TABLE 4.4   Profit and Loss Statement, General Electric Co., 2007 (USD billion)

Total Sales	*$176.7*
(of which: sales outside the USD 88.0)	
Minus Cost of materials	22.0
Equals: Gross Value Added	*154.7*
Minus Capital Consumption	10.3
Equals: Net Value Added	*144.4*
Minus Employees compensation*	71.2
Minus Other costs (taxes, etc.)	51.0
Equals: Net After-Tax Profits	*22.2*
Minus: Divided Payments	11.7
Equals: Retained Earnings	*10.5*

Source: General Electric Annual Report, 2007.

Note: *Authors' estimates.

- GE is America's sixth-largest company, measured by sales, and second-largest measured by net profits, in 2007. As a result, the market value of GE stock was USD 365.6 billion on March 28, 2007, second only to Exxon-Mobil, a huge global oil company. In the 2007–09 market downturn, GE's share price fell sharply and GE's market value dived to only USD 107.6 billion on February 17, 2009.
- GE saves half its net profits and reinvests them. (The paucity of saving in the US will be discussed and measured in the next chapter.) By generating large profits and by reinvesting them in innovation, GE constantly innovates, and creates new products that boost sales. This gave GE 5.0 percent growth rates in sales and 6.6 percent growth in profits, in 2007.

Would you buy stock in U.S.A. Inc.? Would you put U.S.A Inc. in the top-10 best-managed firms? One way to find out is to compare America's income statement and it's GDP with those of other countries. This is our next task.

GDP as a financial statement

Countries differ in many ways from businesses. Economist Paul Krugman argues that while individual businesses can expand their sales and employment by boosting their exports, "the ability of the US economy to increase exports or roll back imports has essentially nothing to do with its success in creating jobs."[7] Krugman argues that, "the constraint on the number of jobs in the United States is not the

---

[7] Paul Krugman, "A Country is Not a Company", *Harvard Business Review*, (January–February, 1996), 41.

US economy's ability to generate demand, from exports or any other source, but the level of unemployment that the Fed [America's Federal Reserve System, as its Central Bank is known] thinks the economy needs in order to keep inflation under control." The 2007–2009 economic crisis has featured unprecedented job losses, casting fundamental doubt on the viability of America's global competitive advantage and on the Fed's ability to manage unemployment.

Nonetheless, in many ways successful growing businesses are quite similar to successful growing countries.

- Both countries and businesses seek to invest in the future by setting aside ample resources;
- Both achieve success by being innovative, energetic, and hard-working. Like successful companies, successful countries' labor, knowledge, land, and capital are efficient and productive. And because many of the same accounting tools used in analyzing businesses apply to analyzing countries and global markets as well, most managers, perhaps unknowingly, already have the tools to be good macroeconomists. *In a very real sense, the GDP and its components are a kind of cash flow statement, showing where the nation's resources come from, and where they go, just as the cash flow statement for a business shows, "where does the money come from, and where does it go?"* This is the function of the Sources and Uses of Resources table, which we now address and explain.

SOURCES AND USES OF RESOURCES

A good way to understand GDP and the national accounts is through asking two questions:

- Where does a country get the goods and services (resources) that it uses?
- How does it use those goods and services?

The answer to these two questions comprises a table known as Sources and Uses of Resources. Because this and all the other tools described in this chapter are accounting definitions, we pause for a moment to explain the mathematical difference between an equation and an identity:

DEFINITION

Equality and Identity. The symbol $\equiv$ means, in mathematics, *identically equal to*, or *is defined as*. An example of an equation is: $x^2 = 4$. If x is +2 or −2, the equation holds; if x is equal to anything else, it does not.

In contrast, $(x - 2)(x + 2) \equiv x^2 - 4$. This is an identity, true by definition, and holds for all values of x. Throughout this chapter, we use not equations (where right and left-hand sides can for some values of the variables NOT be equal) but definitions or identities, where right and left hand sides are ALWAYS equal because they are defined to be so. This is an important point, because equality ($=$) and identity ($\equiv$) have very different meanings. Because of measurement errors, right and left sides of GDP identities do not always match. In the absence of such errors, however, they always do.

DEFINITION

Sources and Uses of Resources

 Sources of resources: Where a nation gets the goods and services that it uses. It consists of:

1. Imports of goods and services (what other nations make, and sell to it, as imports), and
2. GDP, what the nation makes itself, within its borders.

Every dollar of goods and services that a country uses comes from either of two sources: goods made "at home" (within the borders of the country itself) or goods made abroad and imported. Goods and services produced at home comprise the nation's Gross Domestic Product (GDP). Goods and services produced outside a country's borders and shipped in (or bought abroad and used by the country's citizens) are Imports. It is, therefore, true by definition that:

Sources of resources $\equiv$ Imports plus GDP

Uses of resources: How a nation uses the goods and services that it has. It consists of:

(*a*) What individuals and families purchase for their daily existence (personal consumption);
(*b*) What governments purchase to supply public goods and services, such as defense, and some types of education (public consumption);
(*c*) What businesses buy in order to expand their stock of productive capital (gross domestic capital formation, or gross investment); and
(*d*) What other nations purchase (exports).

Uses of resources $\equiv$ Personal consumption + Public Consumption
+ Gross Capital Formation + Exports

In this identity, each of the terms on the right side of the identity is elaborated in the following:

- Personal consumption is what households spend on their current standard of living, including food, clothing, transportation, health care, education, etc.
- Public consumption is purchase and production by government of *social* goods and services, such as education, law and order, and national defense, by state, local, and federal governments. This is not the same thing as *government spending*, which includes *transfer payments*—spending NOT for real goods and services, but for purposes of transferring income from one group (perhaps, middle-class taxpayers) to another (the poor, unemployed, aged, and infirm). For this reason government spending is much larger than government consumption.
- Gross domestic capital formation, or gross investment, is goods and services used to replace worn out machinery and buildings, and to add new machinery and buildings to the existing capital stock. Net domestic capital formation is the net addition to a country's productive capital, and is equal to gross investment minus capital consumption or economic depreciation (i.e., the value of capital that wears out, or becomes obsolete).
- Capital consumption, or economic depreciation, defined earlier, is the decline in the value of capital through wear and tear, and obsolescence. Note that economic depreciation is quite different from accounting depreciation, which reflects what tax laws allow companies to treat as a deductible expense, rather than the true decline in value of buildings and equipment due to wear and tear, and obsolescence.
- Exports—the value of goods and services sold to citizens of other countries, valued "free on board" (fob).

Like the financial accounts of a business, GDP measurement is based on double-entry book-keeping. Every dollar listed as *spending* (costs) is in principle listed somewhere else in the general GDP ledger as a dollar of *income* (sales).

This does not mean, of course, that the GDP accounts always balance—some countries list fairly large *statistical discrepancies* when the two sides, income and spending, do not add up. Country national accounts, unlike company accounts, do not have a single ledger for all transactions.

THE LAW OF CONSERVATION OF RESOURCES

In physics, the law of conservation of energy states that the total amount of energy in a system is constant, because energy cannot be created or destroyed.

In economics, there is a comparable law, the law of conservation of resources, which states that the sources of resources are identically equal to their uses, because all the resources available for our use are in fact used in some fashion. Every dollar, or resources, has to be used by someone. Hence, the Source of Resources (GDP and Imports) must be identically equal to the Uses of Resources. The balancing item is the change in inventories, which is a part of gross domestic capital formation. Goods produced but not sold in a given quarter or year become an addition to inventory, hence are included in gross capital formation.

Since Sources and Uses of Resources are equal, we have:

$$\text{Imports plus GDP} \equiv \text{Personal consumption} + \text{Public Consumption} \\ + \text{Gross Capital Formation} + \text{Exports}$$

If we subtract Imports from both sides of the above identity, we obtain one of the definitions of GDP:

$$\text{GDP} \equiv \text{Personal consumption} + \text{Public Consumption} \\ + \text{Gross Capital Formation} + \text{Exports} - \text{Imports}$$

Table 4.5 shows Sources and Uses of Resources for the United States, 4th quarter 2008.

TABLE 4.5   Sources and Uses of Resources, US 4th Quarter 2008 (USD billion), Annualised Data

Sources	Uses			
GDP + Imports	Personal Consumption + Public Consumption + Gross Investment + Exports			
14,421 + 2,678	10,170 + 2,944 + 2,014 + 1,971			
17,099	17,099			

Source: Economic Report of the President, 2008 (Council of Economic Advisors, Washington, DC, February, 2009).

Knowing those six numbers for a country (GDP and its five components), how they change, how they stand in relation to one another, and above all how they look when benchmarked against other countries, is a powerful tool for country risk management. They can reveal a surprising amount of information about a country's underlying *personality*, prospects and markets.[8]

---

[8] Readers who are comfortable with math and symbols are invited to read the Appendix, which provides GDP definitions and tools in mathematical shorthand.

Here is a partial checklist:

- Is the country an open one, engaging in foreign trade, or relatively closed?
- Are its citizens future-oriented, and use resources for future-oriented, rather than present-oriented, purposes?
- How important is household spending (personal consumption)?
- How important is the public sector (public consumption)?
- Is the country growing its stock of productive capital (physical assets that help it produce more GDP in future years)? Is its investment significant?
- Is the country earning more from its exports than it pays out for its imports (and hence is acquiring foreign assets), or is it importing more than it exports, and therefore is going into debt by paying for at least part of its domestic capital formation with foreign capital?

When GDP data are compiled and compared for several countries, and the above *checklist* is done relative to other nations, the results are especially insightful.

CASE STUDY

The Origins of GDP and National Accounts

 Like many powerful management tools, the idea to compile data on a nation's Sources and Uses of Resources was born, not out of a professor's theory but out of a dire practical need—in this case, the need to manage Britain's meager resources in the desperate early stages of World War II. And the origins of the earliest GDP data are found in a rather unusual place: In a series of three articles published by economist John Maynard Keynes, in *The Times of London*, November, 1939. Later, Keynes published these articles as a short book in 1940.[9] In it, Keynes noted that in World War I, excessive money creation stemming from defense-spending led to inflation, which greatly hurt the working classes. "Can we avoid this in World War II?", asked Keynes. We can. But how? First, by calculating "the maximum current output we are capable of organizing from our resources", (that is, GDP).[10] Next, "by estimating how fast we can safely draw on our foreign reserves by importing more

(Case Study continued)

---

[9] J.M. Keynes, "How to Pay for the War: A Radical Plan for the Chancellor of the Exchequer", (London: Macmillan, 1940), 88.

[10] Ibid., 13.

(Case Study continued)

than we export", (that is, Imports minus Exports). Next, "by estimating the minimum necessary capital formation needed to maintain plant and buildings" (Gross Capital Formation). Next, "by estimating how much will be required by our war effort" (Public Defense Consumption). What is left is "the size of the cake which will be left for civilian consumption" [that is, both personal and public]. Keynes recommended using taxation and compulsory saving to ensure that consumption spending did not exceed that *cake*, so that demand-pull inflation should not emerge.

His little book provided some initial estimates for Britain, 1940.

GDP = £ 4,850 million, equals Personal and Public Consumption plus Imports minus Exports (£ 4,140 million) plus Gross Investment (£ 710 million).

Partly as a result of Keynes' influence, Britain *did* finance World War II with relatively little inflation, far less than in World War I.

CASE STUDY

Benchmarking America vs. Other Nations

 US GDP cannot be directly compared to Japan's or China's; they are in different currencies, and are adjusted for inflation using different base years (see Table 4.6). [These obstacles to cross-country comparisons will be overcome later.] Nonetheless, by studying and comparing the *percentage composition* of GDP for each country, much valuable information can be gleaned.

TABLE 4.6   Structure of GDP: US, Germany, China, 2005

Country	Personal Consumption	Public Consumption	Gross Capital Formation	Exports	Imports	Total
US	70.5%	16.0%	19.3%	10.5%	−16.3%	100.0%
Germany	58.9	18.7	17.1	40.7	−35.5	100.0
China	36.1	14.5	43.9	37.3	−31.7	100.0

Source: US GDP data are from Economic Report of the President 2007 (Council of Economic Advisors, US Govt. Printing Office, Washington DC, February 2007), Table B-2, Real Gross Domestic Product, 1959–2006, p. 230.

Note: Imports are always deducted from GDP, hence the minus sign.

Even a quick glance at this table shows striking differences among the US, Germany, and China—differences sufficiently large to sound alarm bells long before the onset of the global crisis. America, the world's largest economy and among its wealthiest, is a *grasshopper*. China is an *ant* (see Box 4.3). This is the crux of the problem.

BOX 4.3　The Ant and the Grasshopper

In a field, one summer's day, a Grasshopper was hopping about, chirping and singing to its heart's content. An Ant walked by, grunting as he carried a plump kernel of corn.

"Where are you off to with that heavy thing?" asked the Grasshopper.

Without stopping, the Ant replied, "To our ant hill. This is the third kernel I've delivered today."

"Why not come and sing with me," said the Grasshopper, "instead of working so hard?"

"I am helping to store food for the winter," said the Ant, "and think you should do the same."

"Why bother about winter?" said the Grasshopper; "we have plenty of food right now."

But the Ant went on its way and continued its work.

The weather soon turned cold. All the food lying in the field was covered with a thick white blanket of snow that even the grasshopper could not dig through. Soon the Grasshopper found itself dying of hunger.

He staggered to the ants' hill and saw them handing out corn from the stores they had collected in the summer.

Then the Grasshopper knew: It is best to prepare for the days of necessity.

America, the quintessential Grasshopper, uses 86.5 percent of its GDP for personal and public consumption (see Table 4.6; 70.5 + 16.0 = 86.5). In contrast, for China, the perennial Ant, the proportion is slightly more than half. America uses up most of its resources in the present. China sets them aside for future generations. China's gross capital formation—the part of GDP invested in building new capital assets—is larger than its personal consumption! In America, gross capital formation is barely enough to cover capital consumption. As a result, America, a rich nation, must borrow from China, a poor one. America imports far more than it exports. This implies that Americans live beyond their means, and hence must ask foreigners to lend them money—just as an individual who spends more than he or she earns must borrow to fill the gap between earnings and expenditure. The people of China save extraordinary amounts, sufficient both to fund their unprecedented high level of capital formation at home, and lend resources to Americans. We see this in the fact that China's exports exceed its imports by nearly 6 percent of its GDP—precisely the opposite for America. Moreover, this situation has existed for a very long time (see Figure 4.2). In the United States, personal saving as a percentage of personal disposable (after-tax) income, has been steadily declining for over two decades, eventually reaching close to zero. A global economy in which the poor lend to the rich is obviously not sustainable. Yet many behaved as if America's *party* would last forever.

FIGURE 4.2   Personal Saving as Percentage of Personal Disposable Income, US 1980–2007

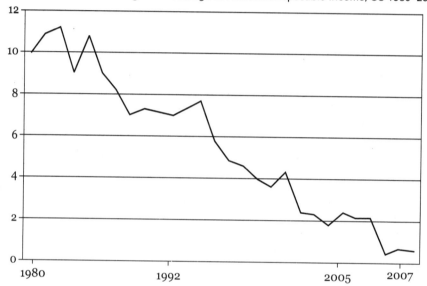

Source: Based on data in World Bank, World Development Indicators, 2009 (Washington, DC 2009).

Germany is somewhere between an Ant and a Grasshopper, consuming proportionately less than America, though far more than China, and saving more than America, though less than China. China and America are, in a sense, bookends, bracketing extremes of present and future orientation. Like the Grasshopper, America now finds that winter has come, and that it can no longer survive as it has in the past, because the external economic environment has changed, leaving it with massive debts, and little to live on.

The degree to which countries use up their resources in the present, or set them aside for the future, is very important. It tells us whether domestic, and foreign investment dominate, or whether personal and government consumption are of primary importance. This in turn helps reveal which product markets are booming: housing and construction (investment), for example, or automobiles and TV's (personal consumption).

PRESENT-ORIENTED OR FUTURE-ORIENTED?

The GDP financial statement can be used to measure the extent to which countries are future-oriented ants or present-oriented grasshoppers. Here is how.

PRESENT-FUTURE ORIENTATION

Divide the components of GDP spending into two parts:

- Spending focussed on present enjoyment, that is, personal and public consumption.
- Spending focused on building assets for future uses, i.e., gross capital formation and net exports (exports minus imports). Note that net exports, like investment, also build future assets—goods are sold to foreigners for dollars, rather than used up at home, and those dollars are available for the use of future generations. (For instance, China's persistent export surpluses have generated over USD 2,000 billion in foreign exchange reserves).

Comparing the percent of GDP allocated to the future we learn:

- China devotes a far larger proportion of their resources (GDP) to such future-oriented components as Investment and Net Exports than Germany or the US.
- In contrast, the United States is one of the world's most present-oriented societies, using up over 80 percent of its GDP in personal and public consumption.

Goods versus services

Another type of GDP data may help shed light on the Ant–Grasshopper dilemma—data on the composition of GDP between goods and services.

Table 4.7 shows the *Sources of GDP* for the United States, divided among goods and services, and within goods, among agriculture, mining, and construction and manufacturing.

Table 4.7 reveals that agriculture produces only 1.2 percent of America's GDP; in 1959, it generated over 4 percent, and a century ago, over half. Some 30 years ago, manufacturing comprised more than fifth of GDP; today, just under 12 percent. There has been a massive shift toward services in the US economy, now comprising 81 percent of GDP (the sum of private services, 68.4 percent, and government services, 12.6 percent) compared with about 69.3 percent in 1976.

TABLE 4.7   Sources of GDP: United States, 2007

| | As Percent of GDP | | | | |
| | Private Goods-Producing Industries | | | Private | |
Government	Agriculture	Mining & Constr.	Manufacturing	Services	Total
1976 14.7%	2.7%	6.8%	21.2%	54.6%	100.0%
2007 12.6	1.2	6.1	11.7	68.4	100.0

Source: Economic Report of the President, 2009, Table B-12.

America is a major exporter of services, exporting more than it imports. However, in general, world trade is conducted in goods. In 2007, world merchandise trade (total exports of goods) equaled USD 13,570 billion. In contrast, world exports of commercial services totaled only USD 3,260 billion, comprised of transport (USD 740 billion), travel (USD 860 billion) and other (1,650 billion). By shifting its manufacturing abroad, as Table 4.5 indicates, America has opted out of the technological and productivity advances inherent in factories. And now that America faces the need to boost goods exports to reduce foreign borrowing, it finds that this is difficult, because many American companies have transferred their production facilities offshore.

GDP: WHAT IS PRODUCED; FINAL SALES: WHAT IS SOLD

DEFINITION
GDP and Final Sales

GDP is what a country produces. Final Sales measures how much of a country's output is actually sold. The difference between GDP and Final Sales is the change in inventories: How much is added to warehouse shelves and car lots.

The stock of finished goods held by a company, and the stock of goods in process and raw materials, are a part of a company's capital and hence are part of a nation's capital. A change in inventories thus comprises a change in the nation's capital, and hence a part of investment or capital formation. An increase in inventories is an addition to gross investment; a decline in inventories is a decrease in investment. This suggests a second illuminating way to split up *gross investment* into its component parts:

1.   That part of investment that goes toward *fixed investment*—machinery, buildings, equipment, plus
2.   That part that comprises the *change in inventories*.

Definition

 Gross Investment $\equiv$ Gross fixed investment + Inventory Change

Inventory change is always a very small part of gross investment. However, its strategic importance is very great. The reason: When doing short-term tracking of an economy, it is often important to know whether GDP has grown because:

1. Sales (that is, demand) grew, or
2. Because companies made goods that piled up in warehouses, and on car lots.

GDP measures the amount of goods and services produced. Some of those goods may have gone into warehouses rather than into shopping carts. Inventory change tells us how much. Businesses that face unwanted build-up of inventory will, in future periods, cut back on production, and sell from their warehouses to reduce inventories. This in turn slows the economy, and may create unemployment. And this is precisely what occurred in the American economy in 2009.

For example: US GDP grew at a torrid 8 percent rate in 2nd Quarter of 2000, compared to the same period a year earlier, but final sales grew more slowly, at 6.4 percent. The explanation: parts of GDP was not sold, but put into inventory, so final sales grow more slowly than GDP. This was a signal that the economy was cooling, because in later quarters, firms will produce less to sell off excess inventory. This is directly comparable to what is known as "channel stuffing" for corporations—pushing stock into sales channels, far above true demand, to inflate revenue growth. This, in fact, is what actually happened.

Conclusion: Always read the fine print in the GDP announcements, and check whether final sales grew more slowly, or more quickly than GDP.

CASE STUDY

US Economy Slows

Referring again to a newspaper item cited earlier:

It looks like the economy carried a lot of negative momentum into the first quarter of 2009, former Federal Reserve Governor Laurence Meyer said in an interview with Bloomberg Television. The economy is likely to contract

(Case Study continued)

(*Case Study continued*)

further after retailers and manufacturers from Starbucks Corp. to Boeing Co. this week announced plans to slash payrolls and cut production to get rid of unwanted goods.[11]

Enlightened managers would thus read beyond the initial GDP negative growth figure of −3.8 percent, for 4th Quarter of 2008, and read that *final sales* declined far more, by 5.1 percent. This indicates that businesses sold less than they produced, generating unwanted inventory growth. (A substantial part of this unwanted inventory increase comprised unsold new cars and trucks.) This means, for both amateur and professional macroeconomists, that in future quarters, GDP will be less than it otherwise might have been, as businesses sell off their inventories rather than produce new goods. This is what the journalist calls *negative momentum*.

GROWTH DIVIDEND

The GDP statement can be transformed in yet another way, to calculate a *cash flow* or *growth dividend* account: the period-to-period change in GDP demand and the components of demand that contributed to that change. This useful statement helps us divide up the change in a country's GDP among its separate sources: demand from households, firms, governments, and foreign buyers.

DEFINITION

Growth Dividend

$$\Delta \text{ GDP} = \Delta \text{ Personal Consumption} + \Delta \text{ Public Consumption}$$
$$+ \Delta \text{ Gross Investment} + \Delta \text{ [Exports} - \text{Imports]}$$

Where Δ signifies *period-to-period* change—the absolute dollar change in GDP, and in each of its components between two periods, adjusted for inflation, for example, *current year value* minus *previous year value*.

Table 4.8 shows the Growth Dividend for the United States during the 1990–92 recession. The change in GDP is the *dividend*, on the left hand side of the identity, and the right hand side shows the five components that created that dividend.

---

[11] Timothy R. Homan, "U.S. GDP Shrank 3.8% Last Quarter, Most Since 1982 (Update2)", Bloomberg News Service, www.bloomberg.com. http://www.bloomberg.com/apps/news?pid=20601087 & refer=home&sid=aN1OnWuR4C4k (accessed January 18, 2010).

TABLE 4.8   US Growth Dividend and How it was Used: 1990–1992

USD Billion (year 2000 prices)

Year	GDP	Personal Consumption	Public Consumption	Gross Fixed Investment	Investment Inventory Change	Exports	Imports
1992	7,363.2	4,934.8	1,555.3	878.3	10.7	629.7	−645.6
1991	7,126.3	4,778.4	1,547.2	822.2	−6.9	589.1	−603.7
CHANGE	236.9	156.4	8.1	56.1	17.6	40.6	−41.9
1991	7,126.3	4,778.4	1,547.2	822.2	−6.9	589.1	−603.7
1990	7,149.6	4,770.3	1,530.3	895.1	8.5	552.5	−607.1
CHANGE	*−23.3*	*8.1*	*16.9*	*−72.9*	*−15.4*	*36.6*	*+3.4*

Source: Economic Report of the President, 2007 (Council of Economic Advisors, US Govt. Printing Office, Washington, DC, Feb. 2007), Table B-2, Real Gross Domestic Product, 1959–2006, p. 230.

For the United States, 1991 was a year of recession, while 1992 was a year of recovery. What caused the recession? And what drove the recovery?

What this table reveals is:

For 1990–91:

- The USD 23.3 billion decline in GDP was principally caused by a much larger drop in fixed investment (USD 72.9), and a shift from building up inventories in 1990 to selling off inventories in 1991, causing a further USD 15.4 billion drop in GDP. These declines were offset by a rise in exports (contributing USD 36.6 billion), a small decline in imports (contributing USD 3.4 billion), and increases in public consumption (USD 16.9 billion), and personal consumption (USD 8.1 billion).

In short: 1991 was a business investment recession. The causes of that are complex, and go beyond the needs of this chapter.

For 1991–1992:

- GDP grew strongly, by some USD 236.9 billion. About half of this GDP *grouth dividend* was driven by an increase of USD 156.4 billion in personal consumption. About a fifth was driven by the recovery in business investment, which contributed USD 56.1 billion. Rising exports were offset by rising imports. Finally, some of the GDP went toward building up inventories, ending the sell-off of inventories in 1991.

In short: The economic recovery encouraged people to spend, and encouraged businesses to invest, and of course, through the principle of feedback, was a result of them doing so.

The growth dividend tool is a valuable statement about the priorities of a country, as shown by the behavior of its government, business, and households. It shows where the increments of GDP are going, and helps managers better grasp the strategic direction of a nation. In times of recession, it shows what parts of demand are slowing; in times of growth, it shows what parts of demand are driving the growth.

BUILDING YOUR OWN FORECAST

It is now time to deliver on our promise to show how managers can construct their own macroeconomic forecast.

DEFINITION

Near-term Forecast

Δ GDP = Δ Personal Consumption + Δ Public Consumption + Δ Gross Investment + Δ [Exports − Imports]

This tool, of course, is simply the *Growth Dividend* tool in slightly different garb. Here, Δ represents the future year being predicted (say, 2010), minus the present year (2009). To build an independent forecast, managers need to estimate the predicted changes in the five components of GDP. Here is a short questionnaire to guide this process:

- Personal consumption: Do people have money? Do they have jobs? Are they worried about losing their job, or believe they will keep it? Is credit available? Are retail sales strengthening? Are people buying durable goods (appliances, cars)? What do industry associations predict and report? In shopping centers, are people just roaming around or are they buying?
- Public consumption: Are governments at all levels spending more, or are they slashing budgets, and trying to curtail deficits? What does the coming year's government budget look like? What will the defense budget be? Will taxes rise or fall?
- Gross Investment: Are factories riddled with excess capacity, making purchases of new machines unlikely, or are they working close to capacity? Are after-tax profits strong or weak (companies' investment is driven more by retained earnings than by borrowing). Do businesses expect demand to be strong, requiring new investment, or weak, meaning new investment will not be needed? At what stage in the technology cycle is industry (in terms of new types of machinery, software, information technology, computers, etc.)?

- Exports: Are foreign markets for the country's goods and services strong or weak? Will changes in the exchange rate relative to other currencies stimulate, or weaken, exports? Is the country's global competitive advantage growing stronger or weaker? Does the country sell goods and services other nations want to buy?
- Imports: Will outsourcing and off-shoring lead to higher imports? Will exchange rates encourage purchase of goods abroad rather than at home? Will prices abroad be attractive or expensive? Will consumer demand at home lead to higher imports?

By estimating each of the five components of Δ GDP, the change in GDP, managers can build their own independent forecast. It is advisable to calibrate this forecast against the predictions of professional forecasters—but only after constructing one's own. This approach can also be used for longer range forecasts. A key part of a good forecast is to identify the essential driver of GDP growth. For the US, it is personal consumption. No forecast for the US can be accurate if it fails to empathize with the American consumer, and predict their feelings and intentions. No forecast for China can be accurate if it fails to gauge accurately the climate for business investment, and for Chinese exports.

We have found it very useful, in building forecasts, to accompany the numerical estimates with a narrative or story. The *story* integrates the various elements of the forecast, makes the causalities comprehensible, and above all, makes it easier to communicate to others the meaning and essence of our prediction. For example, for the United States, in 2010, the story might read as follows:

> Desperate efforts by the U.S. Treasury, to stimulate the economy fiscally, and by the Federal Reserve, to inject credit and liquidity, finally paid off in 2010, as housing prices stopped falling and stock markets became stable. As retail sales picked up, businesses began contemplating new investment plans, to meet rising demand and replace equipment that became obsolete but had not been renewed for two to three years. Exports rose, and imports fell, as the value of the dollar declined 20 percent relative to other leading currencies, making imports more expensive and exports cheaper. Public consumption rose as state and local governments initiated infrastructure programs, rebuilding roads and bridges, funded by the federal government. Most of all, the leadership of a dynamic young president instilled hope.

With a slight mathematical manipulation, the growth dividend can help us partition (separate into its underlying components or *drivers*) the rate of a country's GDP growth, measured as a year-to-year percent, and learn precisely what is driving it. This is the subject of our next chapter, "Analyzing engines of growth".

CONCLUSION

As a concluding exercise, we invite readers to tackle the following action learning assignment:

ACTION LEARNING

A Country is a Business

- Use the data in Table 4.9 below to analyze, as a *business*, one or more of the following countries. Assess the overall country risk, in your analysis.
- For one of the countries, construct a near-term forecast, using the checklist method given in pages 146–47. You will probably need to gather additional information on the country, from websites.

TABLE 4.9   Comparable GDP Data for Selected Countries, 2005

| | | *(US $b. Year 2000 prices) 2005* | | | | |
Country	*GDP*	*Personal Consumption*	*Public Consumption*	*Gross Capital Formation*	*Exports*	*Imports*
United States	10,987	7,841	1,613	2,152	1,196	1,815
India	663	382	73	203	113	108
Brazil	733	456	143	111	107	83
Russian Federation	325	176	43	75	176	144
China	2,048	776	290	782	802	603
Japan	4,977	2,794	881	1,156	683	537
United Kingdom	1,626	1,085	321	290	484	555

Source: World Bank, *World Development Indicators 2008* (World Bank, Washington DC).

APPENDIX: FOR THOSE FOND OF MATHS AND SYMBOLS RATHER THAN WORDS

Definitions

Q: GDP, the value of goods and services produced in a country's borders, during a given period of time (usually one quarter or one year).

IM: Imports, the value of imports of goods and services, including customs, insurance, and freight (cif).

C: Personal consumption, what households spend on their current standard of living, including food, clothing, transportation, health care, education, etc.

G: Government consumption, purchase, and production by government of *social* goods and services, such as education, law and order, and national defense, by state, local, and federal governments.

Ig: Gross domestic capital formation (or in short: gross investment): goods and services used to replace worn out machinery and buildings, and to add new machinery and buildings to the existing capital stock. Net domestic capital formation is the net addition to a country's productive capital, and is equal to gross investment minus capital consumption or economic depreciation (that is, the value of capital that wears out or becomes obsolete).

CC: Capital consumption, or economic depreciation, is the decline in the value of capital through wear and tear, and obsolescence. Note that economic depreciation is quite different from accounting depreciation, which reflects what tax laws allow companies to treat as a deductible expense, rather than the true decline in value of buildings and equipment.

I_n: Net domestic capital formation, the addition to capital, or gross domestic capital formation less capital consumption.

INV: Inventories, the value of the stock of final goods and raw materials held by businesses.

I_{FIX}: Investment in fixed assets, the addition to capital comprising new machinery and buildings, or gross capital formation less the change in inventories.

X: Exports, the value of goods and services sold to citizens of other countries, valued *free on board* (fob).

FS: Final Sales, the value of goods and services actually purchased in a given year or quarter.

Δ: Year to Year absolute change, the value of, say, GDP in 2005, less the value of GDP in 2004.

[1] Sources of Resources: GDP + IM

Explanation: A nation's goods and services comprise what is produced at home (GDP) and what is produced abroad and purchased from other nations (IM).

[2] Uses of Resources: C + Ig + G + X

Explanation: Goods and services are bought by one of four entities: consumers (C), businesses (Ig), governments (G), or foreigners (X).

$$[3]\ GDP + IM \equiv C + Ig + G + X$$

Explanation: By the law of *conservation of goods and services*, the uses of resources add up exactly to their sources. Inventory change (see below) is the balancing item. Any part of GDP that is not sold is added to inventories, which are a part of investment.

$$[4]\ I_n \equiv Ig - CC$$

Explanation: Net capital formation (net investment) is equal to gross capital formation minus capital consumption, or economic depreciation.

$$[5]\ Ig \equiv I_{FIX} + \Delta INV$$

Explanation: Gross capital formation is by definition identically equal to gross fixed investment (in machines and structures) plus the change in inventories.

$$[6]\ Q \equiv FS + \Delta INV$$

Explanation: GDP is identically equal to final sales (the part of GDP that is sold) plus the change in inventories.

$$[7]\ \Delta Q \equiv \Delta C + \Delta G + \Delta Ig + \Delta X - \Delta IM$$

Explanation: The year-to-year absolute change in GDP is equal to the absolute year-to-year change in each of its five components.

Chapter 5

Analyzing engines of growth

LEARNING OBJECTIVES

After reading this chapter, readers should know how to measure, for any country, and any period, the underlying reasons in cases where the country enjoyed economic growth or suffered economic decline, measure the adequacy of a country's net saving and compute what parts of it are used for investment at home and abroad, and gauge how fast the country's capacity to produce GDP is growing.

They should be able to answer these questions:

- How can fast-growing high-potential markets be identified?
- How can the "engines" (i.e., drivers) of growth be determined and matched against your company's products and strengths?
- Why do some countries' economies grow faster than others?
- How can you determine the precise causes of rapid or slow economic growth?
- How are growth, saving, and investment related?
- Why do some countries invest abroad, while other countries have an influx of foreign investment?
- How can you calculate a country's "underlying" growth rate?
- How can the contributions of physical capital and human capital to productivity growth (the change in GDP per worker) be quantified?

TOOL # 5

 Engines of GDP Growth: Which GDP Components Drive Growth (or Decline)?

INTRODUCTION: GROW OR DIE

Why do some countries grow faster than others?
. . . National energy!
—W. Arthur Lewis, Nobel Laureate[1]

---

[1] Spoken in his famous Princeton University course on Economic Development, in which Maital was enrolled, in response to a question from students. http://www.jstor.org/pss/985935 (accessed January 31, 2010).

In 1996, CEOs of three leading global firms pursued different growth strategies.

- John Mack, president of the American investment bank Morgan Stanley was moving his company aggressively into the fast-growing Third World, or *emerging markets* as Wall Street dubbed them—skiing with Mexicans, joint-venturing in Beijing, privatizing Indonesia's telecom company, and investing heavily in India.[2]
- Michael Auld, chief of Ford Motor Co.'s export division, was trying to crack Korea's nearly-impenetrable car market.[3]
- General Electric's CEO Jack Welch was investing USD 10 billion in Europe—a market described by Morgan Stanley investment strategist Byron Wien as a likely "vast open-air museum in 20 years."[4]

More than a decade ago, each of these three CEOs had the same goal—to grow top-line revenues and bottom-line profits by tapping promising foreign markets. Each saw the world differently. "Europe is a relic," said Morgan Stanley, looking to Asia. "Asia makes the headlines, Europe makes the money," said a GE executive.

"High growth creates wealth", Morgan Stanley Chairman R.B. Fisher says, "and wealth is what generates business for us." John Mack added: *"It's grow or die."*

The three strategies were identical in one key way—all sought promising markets abroad. More and more businesses were looking abroad, beyond their home markets, for ways to grow—and a few independent-minded ones, like General Electric, were looking in places many others were not. Some 11 years later, all three strategies encountered country risk—the global downturn.

How can managers track distant markets, monitor their growth, dissect the causes of that growth, assess and manage country risk, and forecast those markets' future—all with a view to deciding whether they should do business in that country? How can they spot national energy? How can they assess country risk? This chapter provides some answers.

Readers are cautioned that this chapter is perhaps the most challenging in our book, containing numerous definitions and data tables, and a mathematical appendix.

---

[2] Leah Nathans Spiro, Sharon Moshavi, Michael Shari, Ian Katz, Heidi Dawley, Geri Smith, and Dave Lindorff, "Global Gamble," *Business Week* (February 12, 1996), 35. http://www.businessweek.com/archives/1996/b3462001.arc.htm

[3] Edward A. Robinson, "Ford cracks Korea's tough car market," *Fortune*, (October 28, 1996), 16. http://money.cnn.com/magazines/fortune/fortune_archive/1996/10/28/203923/index.htm

[4] Peter Koenig, "If Europe's dead, why is GE investing billions there?" *Fortune* (September 9, 1996), 114–118.

But we believe it may prove among the most useful. Seeking profitable growth in global markets is a mandate frequently assigned to managers, and the tools in this chapter that analyze growth engines are highly relevant for fulfilling this mandate.

At a time when the global economy is in a downturn, a focus on growth seems misguided. But it is not. Though the downturn of 2007–09 is indeed global, some markets are faring better than others, some markets will recover faster than others, and some American-based companies, for instance, are able to survive partly because of their operations abroad (for example, GM's Opel division, and Ford's European units), while others (such as, RBS—Royal Bank of Scotland) are in desperate trouble precisely because they expanded rapidly abroad.

Four basic macroeconomic ideas are enlisted: the role of saving and investment, the *underlying* growth of the capacity to produce GDP, and two different perspectives on how to decompose GDP growth into its underlying components, from the demand side and from the supply side.

We begin our journey with news reports from Japan and from America.

CASE STUDY

Japan and America—Two Headlines

- A headline story from the Los Angeles Times, February 16, 2009 reads:

  Japan's economy shrinks at fastest rate in 35 years in 4Q, battered by drop-off in exports

                                by Tomoko A. Hosaka, Associated Press Writer

TOKYO (AP)—Strangled by the collapse in global export demand, Japan's economy shrank at its fastest rate in 35 years in the fourth quarter and shows no signs of reversing course anytime soon. *Japan's gross domestic product contracted 3.3 percent from the previous quarter, or an annual pace of 12.7 percent,* in the October–December period, the government said on February 16.

That was worse than expected and the steepest slide for Japan since the oil shock in 1974. It is more than triple the 3.8 percent annualized contraction in the U.S. in the same quarter [later revised to 6.2 percent—see p. 154]. "There is no question that this is the worst economic crisis since the end of World War II," said Economy Minister Kaoru Yosano. "The outcome clearly shows that Japan's export-dependent economy has been severely hit." *Chief Cabinet Secretary Takeo Kawamura went further, calling the economic downturn a once-in-a-century calamity.*

(*Case Study continued*)

(Case Study continued)

And a headline from Bloomberg News Service reads:

U.S. Economy: GDP shrinks 6.2 percent, more than estimated

by Timothy R. Homan

February 27 (Bloomberg)—The U.S. economic contraction in the fourth quarter was deeper than the government first estimated, with other reports today signaling little prospect of relief until at least the middle of 2009. Gross domestic product shrank at a 6.2 percent annual pace from October through December, the most since 1982, the Commerce Department said today in Washington. Separate figures showed consumer sentiment and business activity dropped this month.

What caused Japan's and America's GDP to fall so drastically? And in general: How can managers track the drivers of GDP growth, during boom times, or, in recessions, track the causes of GDP decline? In particular, how can insights into the past create understanding of the future?

This chapter will provide tools to answer these questions. Our analysis will distinguish between two forms of capital: physical capital and human capital. Human capital is simply a synonym for labor, but the term emphasizes the fact that the productivity of labor can be enhanced by investment in education, just as physical capital can be enhanced and enlarged through investment in machinery and buildings. The tools in this chapter focus on how savings generate resources for investment, and how the two types of capital, human and physical, drive growth. Toward the end of the chapter, we will return to the Japanese and American economies to dissect their sharp 4th Quarter 2008 downturns with tools described in this chapter.

PHYSICAL AND HUMAN CAPITAL

Ultimately, the growth of a country's capacity to produce more goods and services, that is, higher GDP, depends on two forms of capital:

- Human capital (the skills and energy of its workers and managers), and
- Physical capital (the quality and quantity of its machinery and structures).

We begin our analysis with tools that enable us to measure and analyze a country's *saving* and *investment*, crucial for the formation of physical capital (machinery and buildings). Later, we will show how to measure the growth of productivity, and partition it into two components: that due to improvements in physical capital, and that due to improvements in human capital. In doing so, we will learn that even in countries like China, where saving rates are extraordinarily high, and physical capital formation is remarkably rapid, much of the economic growth is still driven by *human*, rather than *physical*, capital.

In order to fully understand how to address the question that began this chapter—what were the underlying causes of the sharpest quarterly fall in Japan's GDP since World War II and the sharp decline in America's GDP—we first must provide the reader with two tools related to saving and investment. Both are derived from the same GDP definition given in the previous chapter. From this single definition of GDP, two additional useful country-specific financial reports can be derived. They are:

- Investment and saving: Where does a nation find resources for its capital formation? and,
- Capacity growth: How fast is a country's *capacity* to produce goods and services (GDP) growing? The *capacity* to produce GDP represents a nation's ability to supply goods and services. GDP itself measures the actual demand for goods and services. Tracking global markets requires a deep understanding of both.

We begin with investment and saving.

GROSS AND NET INVESTMENT

In Chapter Four, we explained that the word *Gross* in Gross Domestic Product stems from a demand-side component, Gross Capital Formation, or Gross Investment, because it includes *capital consumption*, or economic depreciation, that is, the resources needed to replenish capital that wore out or became obsolete. Since the resources devoted to capital replenishment, needed to restore buildings and machinery to their initial state at the start of the year, are not really available for a nation's use, it would be better to remove them, and to focus on Net Domestic Product (NDP, or GDP less capital consumption). This is not done, even though for our purposes NDP is agreed to be a superior concept, because of the inherent difficulty in measuring capital consumption, and deducting it from Gross Investment to calculate Net Investment. To resolve this problem, we offer a definition and a rule of thumb.

DEFINITION

Net Gross Capital Formation (or Net Investment) is defined as: Gross Capital Formation (or Gross Investment) minus Capital Consumption.

 Some countries, such as the United States, do measure capital consumption, but we believe that even when it is calculated, official figures always understate it. This poses a dilemma for this chapter, because in order to estimate the rate of growth of a country's capacity to produce goods, it is essential to know what Net Investment is. Therefore, we propose a *rule of thumb* which nonetheless, in our experience, has proven useful.

RULE OF THUMB

Capital consumption is estimated at 15 percent of GDP.

Rationale: The underlying rationale is based on an assumption, and on a parameter.

 Assumption: Suppose we assume that the average lifetime of physical capital is 20 years. This is an average. Buildings last far longer. Machinery lasts for somewhat less. Computers live even shorter lives. A 20-year lifetime (which, incidentally, gives a *conservative* estimate of capital consumption, not an exaggerated one) implies that the annual rate at which capital is used up is 1/20 or 5 percent.

Parameter: Studies show that the ratio between capital and GDP (known as the capital–output ratio, or Capital/GDP) is approximately three; that is, it takes about three rupees of physical capital to generate a rupee of GDP.

It follows therefore, from the assumption and the parameter, that:

Capital Consumption equals $0.05 \times$ Capital =

$0.05 \times$ (Capital/GDP) $\times$ GDP = 0.05×3 GDP = $0.15 \times$ GDP

In other words, capital consumption is equal to about 15 percent of GDP.[5]

Net Investment = Gross Investment minus 0.15 times GDP

It is very important to understand the meaning of net investment: it is the addition to the total stock of physical capital (buildings and machinery) within the borders of the country; the full technical term is net *domestic capital formation*. We stress that investment is used in the economic sense, referring to physical capital, rather than to financial capital or financial assets, as in the statement "I invested in a 10-year Treasury Bond."

Table 5.1 shows gross and net investment as a proportion of GDP for seven countries, in 2004 and 2005, years of *normality* before the onset of the global downturn. Several important conclusions emerge.

---

[5] There are many nuances of this rule of thumb. It is possible to argue that for emerging countries, with newer factories, machines, and buildings, we should use a lower rate of capital consumption, perhaps, say, 12 percent of GDP. For simplicity, we retain the 15 percent rule of thumb, and note that using 12 percent makes very little difference to our overall analysis.

TABLE 5.1   Gross and Net Investment as Percentage of GDP, 2004 and 2005

		GDP $ million	Gross Inv.	Gross Inv./ GDP %	Net Inv.	Net Inv./GDP %
United States	2004	10,651,700	2,058,200	19.32	460,445	4.32
	2005	10,995,800	2,152,200	19.57	502,830	4.57
India	2004	589,668	170,527	28.92	82,077	13.92
	2005	644,107	202,667	31.46	106,051	16.46
Brazil	2004	717,346	107,288	14.96	−314	−0.04
	2005	738,166	111,145	15.06	420	0.06
Russia	2004	328,809	70,093	21.32	20,771	6.32
	2005	349,853	75,139	21.48	22,662	6.48
China	2004	1,715,000	700,930	40.87	443,680	25.87
	2005	1,893,360	782,240	41.31	498,236	26.31
Japan	2004	4,885,068	1,133,619	23.21	400,858	8.21
	2005	4,978,244	1,155,540	23.21	408,803	8.21
United Kingdom	2004	1,597,273	284,201	17.79	44,610	2.79
	2005	1,628,133	290,173	17.82	45,953	2.82

Source: World Bank, World Development Indicators 2008. Net Investment is calculated using the 0.15 × GDP *rule of thumb* to compute Capital Consumption as discussed earlier.

Analyzing national economies by examining their gross investment is highly misleading. For the US, gross investment for 2004–05 was 19–20 percent of GDP, which seems to be a respectable proportion. But when capital consumption is deducted, it emerges that net investment is a miniscule 4.3–4.6 percent of GDP—consistent with America's frayed shabby capital stock, crumbling bridges, crowded airports, snails pace *fast trains*, and non-existent public transportation. And in earlier years, net investment was often negative, falling short even of the capital consumption—resources needed to maintain the existing capital stock.

For Brazil, for example, Table 5.1 shows that net investment is essentially zero. (This has since changed—Brazil's investment rose in 2006–07, before again diminishing in the downturn.) In contrast, China's net investment is one-fourth of GDP, and India's is 13–16 percent. America's failure to invest has persisted for close to two decades. This table reveals an underlying structural weakness in the US economy that long preceded—and substantively contributed to—the sharp US downturn in 2007–09—the paucity of capital investment, and the financing of whatever little investment there was out of capital borrowed abroad instead of capital saved at home.

Since the logic of analyzing growth engines begins with capital investment, we will now proceed to show how nations fund their capital formation—whether from domestic savings or from resources imported from other countries. We will now build two additional, very useful tools. The first relates to how net investment is funded. The second relates to how net investment builds the capacity to produce GDP.

NET INVESTMENT AND DOMESTIC SAVING

Let us recall the basic GDP definition, which will form the basis of our analysis of net investment and saving, and modify it slightly to reflect net investment rather than gross investment, by replacing gross investment with *net investment plus capital consumption*:

DEFINITION

GDP ≡ Personal Consumption + Public Consumption + (Net Investment + Capital Consumption) + Exports − Imports

Rearrange the elements of this definition, to isolate net investment on the left hand side:

DEFINITION

- Net Investment ≡ Domestic Saving + Foreign Saving
- Domestic Saving ≡ GDP − Capital Consumption − Personal Consumption − Public Consumption (Domestic Saving is defined as the part of GDP that is *not* consumed)
- Foreign Saving ≡ Imports − Exports

Investment at home is, by definition, net investment. Investment abroad, or foreign investment, is equal to the difference between exports and imports. The reason for this will be more fully explained in Chapter Eight. It is sufficient at this stage to observe that *if a nation exports more than it imports, it is by definition acquiring other countries' debt and assets* (such as USD, Treasury Bills, etc.), and hence exporting capital. Because its dollar cash inflow exceeds its dollar cash outflow, it is by definition lending to other nations. If a nation *imports* more than it exports, it is incurring debt and importing capital, because when it imports more than it exports, this can be done only by borrowing from abroad, in the same way that when families spend more than they earn, they must borrow and incur debt.[6]

Therefore it follows that:

Net Investment ≡ Domestic Saving + (Imports − Exports)

This is a powerful tool. It shows how nations fund their net investment, through their own domestic savings, and through capital borrowed from other nations (*foreign saving*).

In the system of national accounting, saving is defined, and measured as *non consumption*. Resources are consumed in three ways: through capital consumption (obsolescence, and wear and tear), personal consumption (what individuals and families buy for their own daily needs), and public consumption (what governments buy and supply for collective use by citizens). Therefore, (net) domestic saving is simply GDP minus these three components of consumption. What is left is the resources available for future uses: investment at home and abroad.

We can expand the preceding tool, to account for two very different situations: nations that save and lend to other nations, and nations that undersave and borrow from other nations.

For countries that borrow from other countries (that is, imports exceed exports):

Net Investment ≡ Domestic Saving + Foreign Saving,
         Foreign Saving ≡ Imports − Exports

For countries that lend to other countries (that is, exports exceed imports):

Net Investment ≡ Domestic Saving − Foreign Investment
         Foreign Investment ≡ Exports − Imports

FOREIGN SAVING AND FOREIGN INVESTMENT

An import surplus—imports minus exports—has a dual personality: it measures both the excess of spending abroad over earnings abroad, and the amount lent by foreigners

---

[6] Astute readers may ask: Since the dollar is the key global currency, and since America can *create* dollars by actions of the Federal Reserve (see Chapters Six and Seven), cannot America import more than it exports simply by creating money (dollars), and paying for imports with them? This is true—but when foreigners hold dollars, the dollar itself is a kind of I.O.U. or *obligation to pay*, and hence represents US debt to foreigners. At some point foreigners who hold dollars can use them to acquire stocks, bonds, or goods.

to make this possible. When an individual spends less than she earns, the difference represents savings. When deposited in the bank, these savings are then loaned by the bank. Similarly, when a *country's* exports exceed imports, the resulting savings can be invested abroad in foreign countries, in many ways: purchase of bonds or equities, or property, or even acquisition of foreign companies.

Table 5.2 shows net investment, on the one hand, and domestic saving and foreign saving (or foreign investment) on the other, for seven key nations. What appears at first to be a rather dull, confusing jumble of numbers turns out to be a startling revelation of fundamental structural weakness in the world's largest economy, years before the US economic crisis began.

TABLE 5.2   Net Investment, Domestic Saving and Foreign Saving and Investment, Seven Nations, 2005 (USD billion)

		Net Inv. $ b.	Dom. Saving	Foreign Sav. (+)	Foreign Inv. (−)
United States	2005	502,830	−116,170	619,000	
India	2005	106,051	111,051		5,000
Brazil	2005	420	23,420		23,000
Russia	2005	22,662	54,662		32,000
China	2005	498,236	697,236		199,000
Japan	2005	408,803	554,803		146,000
United Kingdom	2005	45,953	−24,047	70,000	

Source: World Bank, World Development Indicators 2009, www.worldbank.org (accessed February 1, 2010).

FROM ANT TO GRASSHOPPER

What we learn at once from this tool is the extreme American (and to a lesser degree, UK) version of the parable of the ant and the grasshopper, discussed in Chapter Four. America, one of the world's wealthiest countries, once was an ant, with relatively high levels of domestic saving, which it used for:

1. domestic investment, and
2. foreign investment.

At some stage, in the early 1980s, almost three decades ago, America switched from being an ant to being a grasshopper. This required America, a wealthy nation, to borrow from poorer countries, as imports exceeded exports. The poorer countries were largely the high-saving thrifty nations of Asia (though Japan, not a poor country, also lent to America). These nations saved a remarkably high fraction of their GDP, using part of it to maintain high levels of domestic investment and part of it, to acquire debt and equities of America. The phenomenon of poorer countries lending massively and willingly to wealthy ones is unprecedented in history, and is a clear signal of high and growing global risk. The reason Asia lent to America is clear. By buying American dollar assets, Asian nations kept their own currencies from appreciating relative to the dollar. Increased demand for US dollars kept the value of the dollar relative to Asian currencies (yen, yuan) high. This in turn kept Asian export goods prices competitive (in dollars). Their lending was not altruistic. It was in support of these nations' fundamental business model. (see Box 5.1.)

BOX 5.1   Country Risk for Borrowers and Lenders

In Shakespeare's play *Hamlet*, Polonius cautions, "neither a borrower nor a lender be; for loan oft loses both itself and friend, and borrowing dulls the edge of husbandry."[7]

These words were written in 1603, four centuries ago. Yet no better description of global risk during 1980–2007 has ever been written. And they are a good summation of what America's investment and saving data seem to be telling us.

America has been borrowing and living beyond its means for decades. The result has been to create growing *country risk*—rising leverage and debt, among government, businesses, and individuals. Such borrowing dulled America's *edge of husbandry*. This trend was evident for at least a decade or more before the American financial crisis began, in July 2007. Many people assumed that, since this situation had continued already for so long (interrupted by not infrequent downturns, which fairly quickly reverted to normal growth), it could probably continue forever. But of course no business, individual, family, organization, or even country can continue to increase its indebtedness forever, even America. The collapse was inevitable.

A different kind of country risk exists for the high-saving nations, especially in Asia. Their business design is built on delayed gratification—very high levels of domestic saving, to support higher domestic investment as well as a strong export surplus, implying foreign investment. This means that while GDP grows rapidly, living standards do not, because much of the added GDP dividend is set aside for future purposes. At some stage, younger generations begin to become impatient, asking that their hard work and effort be translated into present, rather than future, gratification. This can lead to rising wages and lower saving, which may endanger the nation's business design, and create political instability. Asia's loans may not have *lost themselves*, in Polonius' words, but they do not seem to have made many friends in America, even though it is difficult to understand where America will find the lenders it still desperately needs, other than in Asia.

Both high-debt, and high-saving nations face country risk. Both require high levels of political wisdom and leadership.

---

[7] http://www.enotes.com/shakespeare-quotes/neither-borrower-nor-lender (accessed January 26, 2010).

The contrast between US saving and investment and that of China is striking.

American experts and policymakers continue to vilify China's economic policies. Yet the data for 2005 (close to the peak of the 2003–2007 boom) reveal that even though China's GDP is about one-sixth that of the US, the absolute value of China's net investment matches that of America! Moreover, China's enormous domestic savings are sufficient to fund China's high level of investment and at the same time lend massive resources to other countries, in particular America, not only to fund America's investment but also to fund its present-oriented personal consumption. Based on these data for 2005 alone, which country would, in the judgment of independent experts, comprise greater country risk? The answer is self-evident.

	Net Investment	Domestic Saving	Foreign Saving (+)	Foreign Investment (−)
United States	$504 b.	−$ 116 b.	+ $ 619 b.	
China	$498 b.	+ $ 697 b.		−$ 199 b.

Source: World Bank, World Bank Development Indicators 2009, www.worldbank.org (accessed February 1, 2010).

Note: Data relates to 2005.

CAPACITY GROWTH

GDP growth measures the rate at which *actual production* of goods and services grew. It is useful to know, in addition, how fast *the capacity* of a country to produce goods and services is growing. In other words, if GDP measures the demand for goods and services, and the rate of growth of GDP measures the growth in this demand, it is important to measure, in addition, the growth of the potential supply of GDP.

There is a useful rule of thumb for this.

DEFINITION

The rate of growth of the capacity to produce GDP measures the rate of growth of the ability of a nation to produce goods and services. Some of the capacity to produce GDP may not be utilized, if actual GDP grows slower than capacity GDP.

RULE OF THUMB

Capacity GDP Growth Rate = (Net Investment/GDP)/ICOR

where ICOR stands for *Incremental Capital-Output Ratio*, or the ratio between the increment to capital stock needed to produce an incremental dollar of GDP. (For the mathematical derivation of this rule of thumb, see Appendix, equations [5] to [7].)

If we suppose that the key resource that limits productive capacity is physical capital—as most countries have significant amounts of unemployed labor—then capacity growth will be related to net investment.

For wealthy industrial countries, the *ICOR* is usually assumed to be about three. We believe we can use this parameter value for emerging countries as well, since especially in Asia their growth has been highly capital intensive.

Table 5.3 uses the definition of Capacity GDP growth rate to compare this rate for seven leading countries in 2005. Capacity GDP growth is simply Net Investment as a proportion of GDP, divided by the ICOR (3.0).

TABLE 5.3   Rate of Growth in Capacity to Produce GDP, Five Nations, 2005

	Net Inv./GDP 2005 (%)	GDP Capacity Growth (%)
United States	4.6	1.52
India	16.5	5.49
Brazil	0.1	0.02
Russia	6.5	2.16
China	26.3	8.77

Source: World Bank, World Development Indicators, 2009, www.worldbank.org (accessed February 1, 2010).

Table 5.3 is consistent with the low level of saving by American businesses, households, and governments since 1973. In 2005, for the first time since the Depression of the 1930s, America's personal saving rate became negative. When Net Investment as a proportion of GDP is less than the import surplus (Imports minus Exports) as a proportion of GDP, the implication is that the country in question is using borrowed resources to fund, in part, not capital formation (assets that later will yield income that repay the debt) but personal consumption (resources used up today, leaving no assets for tomorrow to repay the debt). This situation has existed for two decades, at least. Managers tracking it would have been aware that a financial and economic crisis in America, and hence in the world, is imminent.

GLOBAL IMBALANCE

A direct result of the low level of saving and investment in the wealthy developed countries, and in contrast the high level of saving and investment in the developing countries, has been very large differences in the rate of GDP growth between the two nations. This, too, was a clear underlying source of global instability for decades. While world GDP grew by an unprecedented 4–5 percent in the early 2000s, this average concealed the imbalance between rapid growth in China, India, and other parts of Asia, and slow growth in the US and European Union (see Figure 5.1). It brings to mind the tale of the carpenter's shelves, which varied from 30 cm to 50 cm, but always averaged precisely 40 cms—and hence were of utterly no value. In 1984, world GDP growth was split 50/50 between developed and developing nations. In 2009, fully 80 percent of global GDP growth was generated by the developing economies (see Figure 5.1).

FIGURE 5.1   GDP Growth in Developed and Emerging Economies, 1984–2009

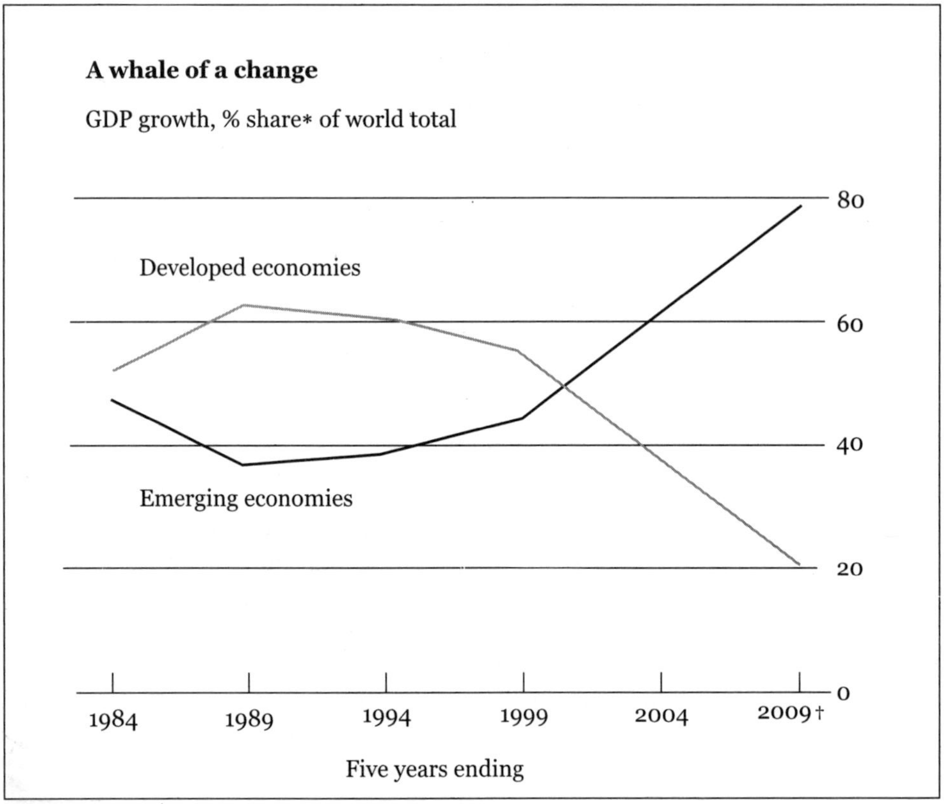

A whale of a change

GDP growth, % share* of world total

Developed economies

Emerging economies

1984   1989   1994   1999   2004   2009†

Five years ending

80
60
40
20
0

Source: The Economist, "Stumble or Fall? Will the Gloal Financial Crisis Halt the Rise of Emerging Economies?" January 10, 2009, p. 62.

Note: * At purchasing power parity.
          † Forecast.

CASE STUDY

Foreseeing the Perfect Storm: US, Japan, China

 Could managers who think globally and independently have used the tools described in this chapter, to foresee the looming financial and economic crises in the United States and the world, two decades before it happened? Hindsight, it is said, is always 20/20. Nonetheless, here is some macroeconomic analysis that could have been done in 1988. If it had, it would have caused America's political leadership, and indeed leaders and managers everywhere, some lost sleep.

United States, 1988

- Income: In 1988, the US had Net Domestic Product (NDP), or national income, of USD 4,989 billion (computed by taking GDP, equal USD 5,869 billion, and deducting capital consumption, equal to 15 percent of GDP, or USD 880 billion).
- Domestic saving: After subtracting USD 3,973 in personal consumption, and USD 995 billion in public consumption, from NDP of USD 4,989, that leaves only USD 21 billion in net domestic saving: (probably smaller than the error of measurement).
- Net investment: In 1988, it totaled only USD 135 billion (gross investment of USD 1,015 billion minus capital consumption, USD 879 billion).

That implied that USD 114 billion in foreign capital had to be obtained, equal to the difference between what Americans wanted to invest (USD 135 billion), and what American households, business and governments were willing to save: USD 21 billion.

This analysis shows that in 1988, the US had a very low level of net investment and essentially zero net domestic saving. Whatever personal savings were generated, most were swallowed by growing government budget deficits, that is, negative public saving. Hence, what little net investment there was had to be financed mainly by importing capital from abroad. Foreign capital was attracted to the US by relatively high real interest rates, caused in part by capital shortage as reflected by the low supply of capital (through savings) in proportion to the demand for it. This situation existed 20 years before the crisis began.

(*Case Study continued*)

(Case Study continued)

Japan, 1988

It is interesting to contrast the United States economy with that of Japan. Japan's investment and saving accounts tell a different story, and reveal a different kind of risk narrative. In 1988, Japan had a relatively high level of national saving, about 17 percent of GDP, and used it to fund a high level of net investment (16 percent of GDP, compared with only 2 percent of GDP in America) as well as substantial foreign investment.

These data suggested that post-1987, Japan would continue to grow faster than the US, as it is investing in future growth by expanding its capacity to produce goods and services. The fact that this did not happen shows how perilous and complex the task of country analysis is. Between 1985 and 1990, the price of land in Japan's six biggest cities tripled. Banks lent large sums of money backed by property-based collateral. Then the bubble burst. Land prices fell by more than 50 percent. Banks no longer had enough assets to back their liabilities. Credit was restricted. Interest rates rose. The Japanese economy contracted as spending was sharply reduced. The supply-side vigor of investment and growth crashed, as the financial crisis removed the ability of businesses and households to spend. Japan's fabled economic growth virtually came to a halt in 1992, and has not yet fully recovered.

For rapid growth, both supply and demand have to rise in step. America's risk was supply-side—insufficient investment. Japan's risk was demand side: Speculative property bubble that burst, causing large losses, leaving Japanese households with huge mortgage debts, in turn reducing their spending and demand.

China, 1994

China's net domestic saving was a remarkable 32 percent of GDP in 1994. This was enough to pay for China's high level of net investment, and to provide resources for a surplus of exports over imports (that is, investment abroad). What we learn from this is that China has for decades been funding its own rapid growth from its own saving, and also investing abroad—despite the press accounts of foreign money flowing into China, far more funds were flowing out. Businesses are rushing into China, but so far foreign investment is modest relative to the remarkable overall magnitude of investment and domestic saving in China. The saving behavior of ordinary Chinese workers is legendary.

Managers who seek to understand the threats and opportunities inherent in national economies are urged to study both the *supply* and the *demand* sides of the economy. One of the fatal errors made by economists, in the wake of the Great Depression of 1930–39, was to focus almost exclusively on the demand side, because that is where the Depression arose. But as Chapter Eight will show, economies have major supply-side problems as well.

We now proceed to analyze GDP *growth engines* from each of these two perspectives.

ANALYZING GROWTH ENGINES: SUPPLY SIDE

Why are some countries wealthier than others? There are two main answers. One of the answers came from Karl Marx. His epic work *Capital* said that countries grew wealthy when they saved, accumulated those savings and created capital. (He went on to add, with prescience, that the capital tended to concentrate in fewer and fewer hands, leading to a major crisis—more or less precisely what occurred in 2007.)

A second answer came from Professor Theodore Schultz, Nobel Laureate in 1979 (shared with W. Arthur Lewis). Schultz asked why Japan and Germany had achieved such rapid growth after World War II, when the United Kingdom grew far more slowly. It was their highly educated labor forces, he concluded, developing the notion of *educational capital* that evolved into *human capital*, or investments in education and improvements in *working smarter*, that is, brainpower rather than machine power.

Since capital and labor, or physical capital and human capital, are the only two primary factors of production, the improvements in the quality and quantity of capital, and of labor, must exhaustively explain GDP growth. But which of the two are most important?

Who was right—Marx or Schultz?

The definitive answer came from MIT Professor Robert Solow. He proceeded to construct a simple tool that provides a striking and conclusive answer. In 1957, Professor Solow invented the equation that partitioned the percentage change in GDP per worker into two components:

1. *Marx*, and
2. *Schultz* (see Box 5.2: Crunching the Numbers).

The mathematical construction of Solow's key equation is shown in the Appendix. Below, in the box, we provide a simpler version.

We choose to refer to component 2 as *Free Lunch Productivity* (FLP), because it represents ways of boosting GDP supply that *do not reflect immediate large capital investments*.[8] Of course, human capital is in part the result of investment in education in past years; but the fruits of that investment in, say, college education, are reaped decades later as the graduates emerge, and contribute to the economy.

Our calculations presented in Table 5.4 show that for 2004–05, while productivity growth due to FLP may not in all countries account for 87 percent of overall productivity growth (Solow's estimate for the United States; see Box 5.2), it still comprises on average 75 percent of overall productivity growth, for the seven countries studied, and as much as 99 percent for one of them (Brazil).

BOX 5.2   Crunching the Numbers: Partitioning Productivity Growth between Human Capital and Physical Capital

In his classic 1957 paper[9] Robert Solow addressed the core question: Why are some countries poor, and other countries rich? Solow felt the answer lay in the growth of labor productivity. Poor countries had stagnant productivity; rich ones had high and growing productivity. In his famous paper, which later won him a Nobel Prize in Economics, he showed how the change in a country's labor productivity was driven by two separate factors:

1. Capital deepening, that is, a rise in the amount of physical capital per unit of labor; and
2. What Solow called exogenous *technical change*, that is, improvements in knowledge, methods, etc., which later became known as investment in human capital.

Solow found, in his pioneering 1957 study, that: "...Over the 40 year period [1909–49] [for the United States], gross output per man hour doubled over the interval, with 87 percent of the increase attributable to technical change and the remaining 12 percent to increased use of capital" (p. 320). How did he compute this startling result?

(Box 5.2 continued)

---

[8] See Chapter 10 in our book *Innovation Management: Strategies, Concepts and Tools for Growth and Profit* (Response, 2007), for a fuller discussion of Free Lunch Productivity, in the context of individual businesses.

[9] Robert M. Solow, "Technical Change and the Aggregate Production Function," *The Review of Economics and Statistics*, 39 (August, 1957), 312–320.

TABLE 5.4 Growth of GDP per Worker (Productivity Growth) in Seven Nations, and the Part of Productivity Growth Generated by Free Lunch Productivity. 2005*

	Year	Labor Force [1]	GDP [2]	Gross Cap F. [3]	Net Cap F. [4]	Net Cap F/GDP	GDP/L [5]	% change GDP/L [6]	FLP Growth [7]	FLP/ProdGR [8]=[7]/[6]
United States	2004	153.8	10,651,700	2,058,200	460,445	4.32	69,235			
	2005	155.4	10,995,800	2,152,200	502,830	4.57	70,745	2.18	1.57	0.72
India	2004	422.8	589,668	170,527	82,077	13.92	1,395			
	2005	430.6	644,107	202,667	106,051	16.46	1,496	7.24	5.05	0.70
Brazil	2004	90.1	717,346	107,288	-314	-0.04	7,961			
	2005	91.7	738,166	111,145	420	0.06	8,051	1.13	1.13	0.99
Russia	2004	73.4	328,809	70,093	20,771	6.32	4,479			
	2005	73.4	349,853	75,139	22,662	6.48	4,766	6.41	5.54	0.87
China	2004	766.0	1,715,000	700,930	443,680	25.87	2,239			
	2005	774.1	1,893,360	782,240	498,236	26.31	2,446	9.25	5.75	0.62
Japan	2004	67.0	4,885,068	1,133,619	400,858	8.21	72,889			
	2005	66.7	4,978,244	1,155,540	408,803	8.21	74,659	2.43	1.33	0.55
United Kingdom	2004	30.4	1,597,273	284,201	44,610	2.79	52,615			
	2005	30.6	1,628,133	290,173	45,953	2.82	53,240	1.19	0.81	0.68

Source: World Bank, World Development Indicators, 2009, www.worldbank.org (accessed February 1, 2010).

Notes: * Labor force: number of people working or actively seeking work (millions); GDP: gross domestic product (USD millions); Gross Cap F.: gross capital formation (of real assets—buildings, machinery, equipment) (USD millions); Net Cap F.: gross capital formation minus economic depreciation (capital consumption) (USD millions); Net Cap F/GDP: net capital formation divided by GDP; GDP/L: GDP divided by the labor force (USD); percentage change GDP/L-year-to-year percentage change in GDP per worker; FLP growth—growth of GDP caused by Free Lunch Productivity; FLP/Prod GR-FLP divided by overall growth in GDP per worker (productivity growth).

(*Box 5.2 continued*)

While 2 could not be directly measured, it could be inferred as a residual, by subtracting the contribution of *capital deepening* from the overall change in labor productivity. This method was widely applied to analysis of countries and industries. It became known as *total factor productivity* (TFP), or, as we prefer to call it, Free Lunch Productivity (FLP).

1. Start with the conventional measure of productivity growth: the year-to-year percentage change in GDP per worker. This is found by dividing GDP by the labor force.
2. Subtract from this, the part of productivity growth caused by higher capital investment:
   SUBTRACT: 0.4 times the year-to-year percentage change in capital assets per employee.
3. The result is: year-to-year percentage change in FLP.

CASE STUDY

Singapore and Hong Kong: Lessons for Managers

 Singapore and Hong Kong are each city states, limited in their land areas and similar to successful businesses; each has achieved rapid growth, and high per capita GDP of around USD 25,000. But a study by economist Alwyn Young, using the FLP concept, reveals a surprising difference: If Singapore had shareholders, they would be exceedingly unhappy, while Hong Kong's *shareholders* would be in seventh heaven. The reason: Singapore's growth was achieved the expensive, hard way, with enormous capital investments, and with no *free lunch* FLP growth, hence very low capital profitability, while Hong Kong's growth was mainly of the free-lunch variety. According to Young's study, "fully 56% of the increase in output per worker in Hong Kong between 1971 and 1990 is attributable to FLP growth" [(that is, the *free lunch*)]; "in the case of Singapore FLP growth contributed minus 8%" [that is, there was absolutely no free lunch].[10]

ANALYZING GROWTH ENGINES: DEMAND SIDE

We can now respond to the question raised at the start of this chapter: Why did the Japanese economy contract drastically in the fourth quarter of 2008? And why did

---

[10] "A Tale of Two Cities: Factor Accumulation and Technical Change in Hong Kong and Singapore", *Alwyn Young NBER Macroeconomics Annual*, 7 (1992), 13–54.

the American economy similarly contract? Were the same forces at work? Or were they different?

Since GDP is comprised of five demand-side components, the overall year-to-year growth rate of GDP is clearly a weighted average of the growth rate of each component, with the weights reflecting the relative importance of that component in GDP. Each component's relative GDP weight, multiplied by its rate of growth, is called that component's *growth contribution*. The sum of the five growth contributions equals overall GDP growth. This comprises a powerful, insightful tool for analyzing growth engines (see Appendix for a formal mathematical derivation of this tool). Note that since imports are deducted from GDP (because they represent goods and services produced and bought from other countries, rather than produced at home), rising imports always *reduce* the rate of growth of GDP.

DEFINITION

Growth contribution: The growth contribution of each of the five components of GDP is defined by the proportion that component comprises in GDP, multiplied by the component's growth rate.

For instance, the contribution of personal consumption to GDP growth equals:

Personal Consumption/GDP × year-to-year growth rate of Personal Consumption

Adding up the five *growth contributions* [personal consumption, public consumption, gross investment, exports, and imports (with minus sign)] gives the GDP growth rate.

Supplementary Tool

Growth and its Engines

GDP Growth Rate = Sum of the Five Growth Contributions

We can now use this tool to address the issue raised at the start of the chapter: Why did the Japanese and American economies decline so rapidly in the last quarter of 2008? The causes for each economy are very different, and are revealed in Tables 5.5a and 5.5b. They show:

TABLE 5.5a   Drivers of Japan's 3.51 Percent Decline in GDP in Q4 2008

Yen Billion, constant prices

	GDP	Personal Cons.	Public Cons.	Gross Inv.	Exports	Imports	SUM
'08 Q4	540,392	308,237	98,489	117,646	79,255	63,235	
'08 Q3	559,381	309,506	97,311	121,994	92,035	61,465	
% change	−3.51	−0.41	1.20	−3.70	−16.13	2.80	
Weight		0.570	0.182	0.218	0.147	0.117	1.000
Growth contribution		−0.23	0.22	−0.80	−2.36	−0.33	−3.51

Source: World Bank, World Development Indicators 2009, www.worldbank.org (accessed February 1, 2010).

TABLE 5.5b   Drivers of America's 1.73 Percent Decline in GDP in Q4 2008

USD Billion, constant prices

	GDP	Personal Cons.	Public Cons.	Gross Inv.	Exports	Imports	SUM
'08 Q4	11,500.7	8,169.9	2,096.3	1,607.3	1,454.8	1,827.6	
'08 Q3	11,700.1	8,260.6	2,088.8	1,703.7	1,556.1	1,909.1	
% change	−1.73	−1.11	0.36	−6.00	−6.96	−4.46	
Weight		0.710	0.182	0.140	0.126	−0.159	1.000
Growth contribution		−0.79	0.07	−0.84	−0.88	0.71	−1.73

Source: World Bank, World Development Indicators 2009, www.worldbank.org (accessed February 1, 2010).

For Japan

- 2.36 percent of Japan's GDP decline of 3.51 percent (or two-thirds) was caused by a drastic decline of 16.1 percent in exports (note: the weight of exports in Japan's GDP is about 0.15 or 15 percent; 0.15 x 16.1 = 2.36).
- All the other components of GDP reduced Japan's GDP growth—rising imports, and falling investment—except for public consumption, the only component of demand that grew in the fourth quarter.

For the United States

- Nearly half the GDP decline in 4th quarter 2008 was, expectedly, generated by personal consumption, which fell by 1.11 percent. With a weight of 0.71 in

GDP, the contribution of the decline in personal consumption to overall GDP growth was $-0.71 \times 1.11 = -0.79$.

- More than half the GDP decline came from the drastic 6.96 percent fall in exports; exports' *growth contribution* was thus its weight, $0.126 \times -6.96 = -0.88$ percent. Imports, however, also fell, and this offset much of the decline in exports.
- Capital investment fell by 6 percent, and when multiplied by its weight, 0.14, contributed -0.84 percent to the GDP decline, or about half.

Together, the two tables tell a sad tale.

In good times, the interconnected global economy generates positive growth feedback loops. Japan exports to America. The resulting income creates higher demand in Japan, higher growth, and hence higher imports. These imports become demand for other nations' goods (such as the US), and those economies grow in turn, creating even more demand for Japan's goods.

In bad times, the interconnected global economy generates negative growth feedback loops. When Japan's exports decline, incomes in Japan fall, and so do Japanese imports. This, in turn, causes economic slowdown in the countries with which Japan trades. They, in turn, face falling incomes, hence falling imports. So Japan's exports, and economy, slow. This, in turns, causes GDP growth to decline in other nations, and so on.

The Japanese and American narratives are somewhat different, because the structure of the two economies differs widely. But broadly, to paraphrase poet John Donne, no "nation" is an island. Global trade, a double-edged sword, spurs growth in good times and amplifies downturns in bad times.

ACTION LEARNING

Apply the *Growth Drivers* Tool

Using the data in Table 5.6, apply the *growth drivers* tool, to partition the causes of GDP growth among the five components of demand: personal consumption, public consumption, gross investment, exports and imports (which are of course negative, since they reduce demand and GDP growth), in one or more of these seven countries. What insights can you gain?

TABLE 5.6   GDP Data for Seven Nations, 2004–2005 (USD Billion, constant prices)

(USD Billion Year 2000 prices)   *2004, 2005*

Country		GDP	Personal Consumption	Public Consumption	Gross Capital Formation	Exports	Imports
United States	2005	10,987	7,841	1,613	2,152	1,196	1,815
	2004	10,641	7,577	1,597	2,058	1,120	1,711
India	2005	663	382	73	203	113	108
	2004	603	358	66	171	106	97
Brazil	2005	733	456	143	111	107	83
	2004	707	439	140	107	97	76
Russian Federation	2005	325	176	43	75	176	144
	2004	318	164	42	70	165	123
China	2005	2,048	776	290	782	802	603
	2004	1,780	715	260	701	646	541
Japan	2005	4,977	2,794	881	1,156	683	537
	2004	4,882	2,751	867	1,134	638	507
United Kingdom	2005	1,626	1,085	321	290	484	555
	2004	1,596	1,070	311	284	449	519

Source: World Bank, World Development Indicators 2009 (World Bank, Washington, DC).

CASE STUDY

A Vestpocket History of Global GDP Growth–National Energy

Since the end of World War II, world GDP doubled two-and-one-half times—an annual real growth rate of about 3.5 percent. While this pace of growth seems modest compared with, say, China's two-decades-long 10 percent growth rate, which doubles GDP every seven years, it is in fact without historical precedent. Probably never in recorded history has world income and output grown as fast as it has in the past half-century.

What engines drove this growth?

The engines of world growth in the post World War II period were the *national energy* of nations eager to recover from war and rebuild their lives and their economies, or to join the ranks of modern industrial countries, along with the enormous expansion of investment and world markets and trade. Consider these facts:

(Case Study continued)

(*Case Study continued*)

- In 2000, world GDP totaled about USD 38 trillion; of this world exports of goods amounted to USD 5.5 trillion, and exports of services exceeded USD 2 trillion. This made total world trade USD 7.5 trillion—as large as the America's GDP, and fully a fifth of world GDP.
- By 2001, global trade was close to 16 times what it was in 1950. Trade has grown at an annual rate of 5 percent, much faster than world GDP growth.

Countries have grown wealthy by expanding their productive capacity, boosting production, and by selling their goods in foreign markets, using the revenues in turn to buy goods from other countries. In other words, both the supply of GDP and the demand for GDP grew in a synchronized fashion. Each was essential. Eventually as a nation's wealth and productive power grows, its own market becomes large enough and prosperous enough to create internally self-sustaining growth and the need for foreign markets diminishes.

America played a key role in fostering this growth boom. America had three-fourths of the world's income and output in 1945. America's markets were virtually the only markets at that time. Had they been closed to imports, the rest of the world would likely have remained in poverty, at least for many decades.

It was indeed fortunate that America's markets were open. Even while World War II was raging in Europe and the Pacific, the US convened a conference of global financial and economic experts at Mt Washington Hotel in Bretton Woods, New Hampshire, in October, 1944. There, the US spelled out its post-war policy. It would be based on a *level playing field*—open global trade, on the same terms, for all countries. The US would open her markets to other countries' goods. This policy was not driven by America's altruism but by a one-line foreign policy: America believed that if other countries became wealthy, they would also likely become democratic, and thus be allies of the US—thus freedom would triumph over socialism. The USD 15 billion in Marshall Plan Aid sent from America to Europe between 1947 and 1953 (worth perhaps 60 billion today) also played a key role.

The Japanese, German, and to a lesser degree French, and British economic miracles after World War II came about in part because America was willing to buy their goods. Japan's and Germany's national energy would have been to no avail, had these countries not found markets in which to sell the growing supply of goods they produced.

(*Case Study continued*)

(Case Study continued)

The collapse of the Berlin Wall on November 9, 1989, marked the ultimate victory of this policy. The world became more prosperous overall as many other nations joined America in becoming prosperous and wealthy. One may view the 2007–2009 global decline either as a temporary interruption in the post-World War II global expansion, or as a permanent paradigm shift that will lead to utterly different business conditions and economic systems worldwide. Only time will tell.

BUILDING YOUR OWN FORECAST

We conclude this chapter with a brief suggestion for do-it-yourself near-term forecasts.

Supplementary Tool

 Do-it-Yourself GDP Growth Forecast

Take the preceding GDP *growth contribution* tool and apply it to a country of your choice:

- Calculate the relative weights of the five GDP components (that is, proportions of GDP): personal consumption, public consumption, gross investment, exports, imports, for the latest year.
- Estimate the most likely rate of change in each component, by answering these questions:
  - *Do people have money (income), and are they in the mood to spend it? (personal consumption)*
  - *Does the government (at all levels—federal, state, local) have plans to expand its consumption, or to restrict it? (public consumption)*
  - *Are businesses responding to growth by boosting their investment, or are their profits shrinking, leading to a decline in investment? (gross investment)*
  - *Are foreign markets upbeat, leading to higher exports, or contracting, leading to lower exports, and will changes in the country's exchange rate be favorable or unfavorable for exports?*

- *Are imports likely to rise, responding to higher consumption and GDP growth, or will they decline? By how much?*

Estimate each of the five *growth contributions* (*weight* times predicted rate of change), and sum them up. The result is the GDP growth forecast.

It is of course advisable to examine existing forecasts. But it is even more important to think independently, and based in part on them, to construct your own. Once this is done, it is important to link those forecasts to your company's own business, and business design.

LINKING MACRO TO MICRO

How can the tools described in this chapter that analyze engines of growth (or lack of growth), be applied to individual businesses?

Businesses that create value by producing capital goods will of course be interested more in nations whose growth engines are primarily investment.

Business that creates value by producing consumer goods will be more interested in nations whose growth engines are primarily consumption.

Businesses that specialize primarily in services will focus on nations where services are a major part of GDP, or where demand for services (such as telecommunications) is high.

This analysis is of course superficial. The *zoom in* analysis of specific businesses, when weighing global markets, must be done on the basis of the firm's competencies, products, vision, strategies, and innovative excellence. This goes well beyond the mandate of this book.

CONCLUSION

Be happy and live within your means—even if you have to borrow to do so.

—American humorist Artemis Ward

The purpose of a business, Peter Drucker once wrote, with his typical brilliance in simplifying, is to create a customer. And, he may have added, to continually *recreate* them. Ultimately, however complicated corporate strategy may be, it boils down to finding and creating customers.

In times of global growth, customers may often be found and created in distant markets by analyzing their GDP's growth engines. The tools provided in this chapter will hopefully help managers assess country risk at the same time as they track strategic opportunities.

In times of downturn, the very same tools can help managers isolate the weaknesses in distant markets, and the underlying causes of GDP decline. They can also help managers carry out what, to many, seems a daunting task: To construct their own near-term forecasts of GDP, to help understand when economic decline ends, and growth resumes, in order to be ready with strategic initiatives that help their company gain market share, and to benefit from the inevitable market reshuffle that follows downturns.

In the next two chapters, we explore the key roles played in every country by money and credit, and provide tools to help managers track them. To track risk and opportunities inherent in global markets and minds, the role of money turns out to be crucial.

APPENDIX: FOR THOSE FOND OF MATHS AND SYMBOLS RATHER THAN WORDS

Definitions

Q: GDP
Q_{CAP}: GDP as it would be if labor and capital were fully used (capacity GDP)
r_{QCAP}: Year-to-year change in Q_{CAP}
C: Personal consumption
G: Government consumption
Ig: Gross domestic capital formation
X: Exports of goods and services
IM: Imports
CC: Capital consumption
I_n: Net domestic capital formation
S_{DOM}: (Net) domestic saving
Δ: Year-to-year absolute change, the value of, say, GDP in current period less the value of GDP in the previous period = $(GDP_{09} - GDP_{08})$
r_i: Year-to-year percentage change, component "i"= $100* \{(Y_t - Y_{t-1})/Y_{t-1}\}$
w_i: Weight of component "i" in GDP *for current year*, for example, $w_C = C/Q$
L: Labor force
K: Stock of physical capital
α: Share of labor in national income (*wage share*)
$(1 - \alpha)$: Share of capital in national income (*interest, rent, profits, dividends*)

$$[1]\ CC \equiv 0.15* Q$$

Explanation: Capital consumption, or economic depreciation, is approximately equal to 15 percent of GDP, equal to 5 percent of capital, and with capital equal to three times GDP (capital to output ratio).

$$[2] \; S_{DOM} \equiv (Q - CC) - C - G$$

Explanation: Domestic saving is defined as net GDP minus personal and public consumption.

$$[3] \; I_n \equiv (Q - CC - C - G) + (IM - X)$$

Explanation: This is the definition of GDP, with Ig equal to $I_n + CC$.

$$[4] \; I_n \equiv S_{DOM} + (IM - X)$$

Explanation: Substitute [2] into [3].

Capacity growth:

$$[5] \; r_{QCAP} \equiv (I_n/Q_{CAP})/(I_n/\Delta Q_{CAP}) \equiv (\text{Net Investment}/\text{GDP})/ICOR$$

where $ICOR \equiv \Delta K/\Delta Q$

$$[6] \; \therefore \; r_{QCAP} \equiv [I_n/Q]/ \; ICOR$$

[7] Contribution of GDP component to overall GDP growth $\equiv w_i \, r_i,$ for $i = C, G, Ig, X$ and IM and $r_i \equiv \Delta Q/Q, \; Q \equiv GDP$

$$[8] \; r_Q \equiv \sum w_i \, r_i \equiv w_C \, r_C + w_G \, r_G + w_{Ig} \, r_{Ig} + w_X \, r_X - w_{IM} \, r_{IM}$$

Explanation: GDP growth equals the weighted average of growth rates of the five individual GDP components (where imports has a minus sign), multiplied by the weight of each component in GDP in the current year.

Free Lunch Productivity:

[9] $Q = A(t) \, L^{\alpha} K^{1-\alpha}$, where $A(t)$ represents the stock of human-capital "knowledge" at time "t"

Explanation: This is a so-called production function, showing how GDP (value added) is generated by labor and capital, with the latter weighted geometrically according to their contributions to GDP, with the weights equal to α and $(1-\alpha)$ respectively.

$$[10] \; Q/L = A(t) \, [K/L]^{1-\alpha}$$

Explanation: Divide both sides of [9] by L.

[11] dlog $(Q/L)/dt$ = dlog $A(t)/dt$ + $[1-\alpha]$ dlog$(K/L)/dt$, where dlog $(Q/L)/dt$ is the year-to-year percentage change in labor productivity.[11]

Explanation: Take the logarithm of each side of [10] and then, take the derivative with respect to time.

[12] percentage change in labor productivity = "FLP growth" + $[1 - \alpha]$ (Percentage change in capital per worker)

Explanation: the derivate with respect to time of log x is equal to $(dx/dt)/x$, which, when multiplied by 100, is interpreted as a year-to-year percentage change. "FLP growth" is the part of productivity growth that is residual, that is, *not* explained by increases in the stock of capital per worker, K/L.

[13] $\therefore$ "FLP growth" = Percentage change in labor productivity – $[1 - \alpha]$ (Percentage change in capital per worker)

[14] percentage change in capital per worker = $\Delta(K/L)/K/L = (I_n/Q)(Q/L)\ (L/K)$ = $\Delta(I_n/Q)(Q/L)\ (L/K) = (I_n/Q)(Q/K)$

[15] since $Q/K = 1/3$ (1/"capital–output ratio"),

[16] $\Delta(K/L)/K/L = 3^* (I_n/Q)$

[17] $\therefore$ "FLP growth" = Percentage change in labor productivity – $[1 - \alpha](3\ \Delta(I_n/Q))$

---

[11] Note that dlogx/dt = $(dx/dt)/x$ = percentage change in x over time (when multiplied by 100).

Chapter 6

Money talks—Interest rates listen

LEARNING OBJECTIVES

After reading this chapter, readers should understand what money is, how the Central Bank controls the supply of money, how money, and the rate at which it changes hands (velocity), determine economic momentum (GDP), and why velocity of money (the rate at which money changes hands) is a crucial and often-overlooked variable. They should also understand how Central Banks control interest rates by buying and selling bonds, and why tracking nominal (not adjusted for inflation) interest rates can be disastrously misleading. Readers should grasp how the markets for goods and for capital are interconnected. They should understand the importance of theory and models, and why managers can, and should think like scientists, while acting as practitioners.

They should be able to answer these questions:

- What is money? How has the nature of money changed in the US (and elsewhere in the world) and why?
- How does money affect output, income, growth, and employment?
- What is economic momentum, and why is the velocity of money a crucial—and often overlooked—variable?
- How do Central Banks control the supply of money and the rate of interest?
- How are money, interest, and inflation related? Why are interest rates today the most important single macro variable in the US, Europe, and many other countries?
- How can managers track interest rates globally? Why should they?
- How do interest rates affect the economy?
- How do Central Banks influence interest rates? Which rates can they determine?
- How did George Soros use macro ecology to make about USD 2 billion in one week?

Tool # **6**

Economic Momentum
Supplemental tool: Real (Inflation-adjusted) Interest Rates

...money is not the slightest use whatever. But, all the same,.... you will find it a devil of a business not to have any.

—J.M. Keynes, 1942[1]

INTRODUCTION

"Money talks," a century-old American saying goes. It means, roughly: Those who hold the pot (of money) call the shots.

In the global crisis of 2007–09, money played a crucial role, as a primary cause—the collapse of global money and capital markets—and as a major policy lever for finding a solution.

Money has spoken, but managers often find it difficult to interpret what it is saying. The objective of this chapter is to enable managers and students of management to listen to what money is saying, and to what the money *numbers* are saying, on an ongoing global basis, as part of their daily routine for evaluating systemic risk. Forcing money to speak understandably is vital for managers, for whom deep and logical insight into the mysteries of money, and interest rates, is crucial for the quality of their decisions and hence, for the sustained well being of the organizations they guide.

Our focus will be on the United States and its Central Bank. Most of the money and interest mechanisms there are generic, and apply to Europe and Asia as well, with some local differences. The dramatic events in the US provide superlative, if often tragic, material for X-raying the role money plays in driving economic activity. Because the global financial crisis of 2007–2009 originated there, America's Central Bank policies generate fascinating case studies, as a real-world laboratory in which money speaks in clear short sentences.

In this chapter, we first examine what money is, how Central Banks control the quantity of money and credit, and how money is linked to the rate of interest. We then dissect how money is linked to economic activity, using the concept of economic momentum. Finally we show how management decisions based on interest rates not adjusted for inflation can be dangerous.

We begin by asking a deceptively simple question: What is money?

---

[1] Cited in Peter Kennedy, "Macroeconomic Essentials for Media Interpretation," Cambridge, (MA: MIT Press, 1998), 121.

WHAT IS MONEY?

If money is to speak clearly to us, we must first know what it is. Strangely, defining money is not simple. Ordinary people tend to regard money as cash—coins and notes. But coins and notes comprise only a small part of what economists define as money.

Assets are economic resources: money, land, buildings, machinery, and other property or property rights that generate a stream of income. Financial assets are assets bought and sold in capital markets. Money is the part of financial assets that is *liquid*, that is, widely acceptable as payment for goods, services, and debts. Measuring the amount of money, therefore, involves separating financial assets into two groups: those that are *liquid* and *widely acceptable as payment* and those that are *illiquid* and *not widely acceptable*. Since *liquidity* is a matter of degree, there are at least three definitions of money, ranging from highly liquid assets (cash) to less liquid ones (time deposits with limited checking privileges).

DEFINITION

Money is a liquid asset, a store of value that exchanges for goods and services. There are essentially three definitions of money: *currency*, *narrow*, and *broad*. Currency is coins and notes (M0). *Narrow* money is called M1, and *broad* money is called M2.

$$M0 = \text{coins and paper currency}$$

M1 = M0 plus travellers' checks and demand deposits at commercial banks.
M2 = M1 plus savings deposits, time deposits (less than USD 100,000) and money market mutual funds (MMMF).[2]

Figure 6.1 provides snapshot data for each of the three definitions of *money* for the United States, as of March 31, 2009. In this figure, we see clearly that while ordinary people interpret money as cash, in fact, currency is only about 10 percent of broadly-defined money; the rest is comprised of bank accounts against which checks can be written. This is important, because we will see later that money is *created* not by printing notes but rather by enabling creation of checking deposits through bank lending and credit. It is interesting that fully half of America's USD 844 billion in currency is held abroad, outside the United States.

---

[2] Money market mutual funds are funds that invest only in short-term money market assets; they pay interest, but at the same time provide limited checking privileges, combining liquidity with interest-earning capability.

FIGURE 6.1   Snapshot Data for Each of the Three Definitions of "Money" for the United States, as of March 31, 2009

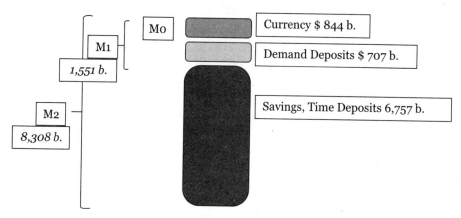

Source: Economic Report of the President 2009 (US Government Printing Office, Washington D.C., January 2009), Table B-69 (p. 35), "Money, Stock and Debt Measures."

WHAT IS INTEREST?

Interest rates are the price of money—the cost of borrowing and the return for lending money. Generally, though not always, the longer the term of the loan, the higher is the rate of interest. Interest rates reflect the degree of risk in the loan (that is, the probability that the loan will not be repaid). This default risk is reflected in a risk premium, the difference between risk-free and risky interest rates. Interest rates also reflect the price of time—the fact that those who lend the money will not be able to use it for the period of the loan and therefore receive compensation for *deferring gratification*. Interest rates are like all prices—they are generally set by the forces of supply and demand. The supply of money and the demand for it determines the cost of money, interest rates.

There are several varieties of interest rates. A key short-term interest rate is the so-called Federal Funds rate. Other interest rates in the US and abroad are influenced by this rate, and tend to change when it changes. The main types of interest rates along with their definitions and values on March 19, 2003 are shown below:

DEFINITIONS

Varieties of interest rates

- Federal Funds: Money lent overnight among commercial banks, in amounts of USD 1 million or more. Such lending is often done

to meet reserve requirements of the Federal Reserve (see below), hence its name.
- Prime Rate: Base rate on corporate loans charged by the 30 biggest banks in the US.
- Certificates of Deposit: Rate paid by major New York banks on large-denomination CDs (Certificates of Deposit).
- London Interbank Offered Rates (LIBOR): Average of offered rates for dollar deposits in London, among banks.
- Treasury bills: Yield of 90-day US Government Treasury bills. Under one-year maturities. Treasury *bonds* have longer maturities.

FINANCIAL DEREGULATION AND THE CHANGING NATURE OF MONEY

Understanding what money is, and how it is defined, requires a historical perspective. We shall therefore survey briefly the history of financial deregulation in the US and abroad because it fundamentally changed what money is and how it is created.

Financial deregulation began in the US in the 1980s during the Reagan administration. It culminated in a dramatic all-night negotiating session between the Clinton administration and Congressional Republicans on October 22, 1999. The resulting agreement set the stage for passage of the most sweeping banking deregulation bill in American history, lifting virtually all restraints on the operation of giant US commercial and investment banks, in the Financial Services Modernization Act. This act removed restrictions on the integration of banking, insurance, and stock trading, imposed by the Glass-Steagall Act of 1933, one of the central pillars of Roosevelt's New Deal in the 1930s. Under this law, banks, brokerages, and insurance companies were effectively barred from entering each others' industries, and investment banking and commercial banking were separated by a Chinese Wall. This Act was designed to correct the excesses that led to the collapse of the stock market bubble in 1929. The new law removed those restrictions. Many believe that this sweeping deregulation sowed the seeds for the bubble and resulting global collapse of 2007–09 by fostering excessive risk-taking, and conflict of interest between those who lent money to clients, and those who advised the same clients how to invest their money. Perhaps history does repeat itself.

The process of financial deregulation in the US later spread to the UK and elsewhere. It led to many new financial assets, as regulators took the wraps off what banks were allowed to do. Some of these new assets were very close substitutes for *widely acceptable means of payment*, such as: Negotiable order of withdrawal (NOW) accounts-interest bearing checkable accounts; savings accounts with automatic transfer (ATS) to checking deposits; and money market mutual funds (MMMF) with checking privileges. From a simple definition of money (M1), the new financial assets created new ever broader definitions of money. As businesses and households shifted their assets back and forth from one asset to another—for instance, moving money from a checking account into a money market mutual fund (MMMF)—in search of higher rates of return or lower risk, money supply became harder to control, as it was no longer clear which definition of money should be used. Each time a dollar moved from a checking account into an MMMF, for instance, M1 declined (though M2 remained stable). The components of money became volatile and unstable. In stable times, when assets more or less remain where they are, this is not a problem. But in times of rapid financial change, when assets (aided by modern computers and information technology, and the profit-driven innovation of financial engineers) shift rapidly, *any* definition of money becomes inherently unstable.

Central banks have been in a perpetual race to broaden the definition of money, trying to trap ever-shifting financial assets in a huge *bin*, moving from M1 to M2, M3, and even M4 (M3 and M4 include less-liquid money assets not included in M2). In the 1960s and 1970s, M1 was the choice. When financial deregulation destabilized M1, the Fed moved to a broader definition: M2. But M2's velocity, too, became unstable. Other countries like Germany look to M3 and even M4. Britain for a time focussed even on M0 (currency and cash). Today most Central Banks compromise, and track and control both M1 and M2, while focussing on M2 as the primary target of control.

America's Central Bank is known as the Federal Reserve System, or *Fed* for short. It was established by an Act of Congress in 1913 (see Box 6.1).

BOX 6.1   America's Central Bank: The *Fed*

The United States's Central Bank is known as the Federal Reserve System—known as the *Fed*, for short, and *reserve*, because it regulates the reserves held by commercial banks, that underpin the banks' lending activities, and actually holds those reserves as commercial bank deposits. It was first established by an Act of Congress in 1913 by President Woodrow Wilson. Monetary policy—which controls both the quantity of money and credit, and the rate of interest—is set by a 12-person committee, known as the Federal Reserve Open Market Committee (FOMC), which meets every six weeks. The chairperson of this committee—officially known as Chairman of the Federal Reserve Board of Governors—was Alan Greenspan, first appointed in 1987; he served for nearly 20 years. He was succeeded by the current Chair, Ben Bernanke, a former Princeton University economics professor, in February, 2006. The appointment is for four years, renewable. Bernanke has a counterpart in every major country—generally known as the Governor of the Central Bank. In Europe, it is the ECB (European Central Bank); in England, the Bank of England; in Japan, the Bank of Japan; and in India, the Reserve Bank of India.

(*Box 6.1 continued*)

(*Box 6.1 continued*)

There are seven members of the Federal Reserve Board of Governors, appointed by the President to seven-year terms. These governors are all members of the FOMC, along with a rotating board of five Federal Reserve Bank Presidents drawn from the 12 regional Fed banks. A large staff of economists at the Federal Reserve Board of Governors headquarters in Washington, D.C. generates data, economic analysis, and position papers to assist the FOMC members and its Chair. In addition, the 12 regional Fed Banks supply reports on regional conditions—the so-called Beige Books—on a regular basis.

The Federal Reserve System in US differs in structure and operation from those in most other countries. Congress positioned Federal Reserve Banks in twelve leading US cities[3] rather than locate a single Central Bank in the nation's capital as in other countries. The objective was to disperse information-gathering and decision-making.

Long in advance of the FOMC meetings, markets churn in expectation of possible interest changes. Minutes of these meetings, once long delayed, are now published soon afterward. Experts who track interest-rate policy read FOMC meetings' protocols carefully.

The elegant room in which the FOMC meets, in Washington, D.C., has a long oval-shaped wooden table, and high ceilings. In 1940, it was the only large room in Washington, D.C. with air conditioning. As a result, the FOMC was evicted, and replaced by the Armed Forces Joint Chiefs of Staff for the war's duration. Perhaps it is symbolic that in America, both war and peace were directed from the same oval table.

HOW CENTRAL BANKS CREATE MONEY AND LOWER INTEREST RATES

Tuesday, January 22, 2008 was a dramatic day in the US and world central bank history. Headlines screamed, "Fed Lowers Interest Rates in Surprising Move." Front-page articles explained that:

> ...the Federal Reserve (Fed) lowered the Fed Funds Rate today by 3/4 point to 3.5 percent, in the biggest cut in 18 years. It was a surprising move in that the group is scheduled to meet next week, when they were widely anticipated to lower rates. However, over worldwide fears that the United States is heading into or possibly already in a recession, the Fed got a jump on things and took this key interest rate down this morning in an effort to stimulate the economy.[4]

What precisely happened, that brought interest rates down and increased the supply of money and credit, in the wake of that dramatic Fed decision on January 22, 2008?

---

[3] Boston, Buffalo, Cleveland, Dallas, New York, Richmond, San Francisco, Chicago, St. Louis, Miami, Atlanta, and Minneapolis.

[4] Source: blog.quizzle.com http://blog.quizzle.com/2008/01/fed-lowers-interest-rates-in-surprising-move/(accessed January 18, 2010).

The key to understanding the events of January 22, and in general to hearing what money is saying, lies in understanding *how to read the balance sheets of both commercial banks and the Federal Reserve*.[5] Stylized highly-simplified versions are shown below. The initial balance sheets, on January 21, 2008, could be:

(USD billion)			
Commercial Banks		Federal Reserve	
Assets	Liabilities	Assets	Liabilities
Reserves USD 1,000	Deposits USD 10,000	Bonds USD 2,000	Currency USD 1,000
Loans 7,000			Reserves 1,000
Bonds 1,000			
S. Equity 1,000			

There are two key facts embodied in these balance sheets.

1. Banks make money by lending money. Loans are their principal assets. Deposits are their principal liabilities. Loans are made when bank managers lend money to clients, in the course of which *deposit accounts are created*. In this sense, money is not printed (except for a relatively small amount of paper currency), but *created*, when banks make loans.
2. Banks, however, *cannot lend money without limit*. They are limited by reserve requirements—the need to hold money to *back* the loans they make. These reserves are held as deposits in the Central Bank (Fed). Reserve requirements are always a fraction of deposit liabilities. In the example above, reserves are 10 percent of deposits. The commercial banks whose balance-sheet is shown above cannot increase lending, because to do so would expand deposits beyond what their USD 1,000 in reserves permit.

Central banks lower interest rates and expand credit and loans, by influencing the so-called monetary base, which is the amount of reserves held by commercial banks. They do this by what is known as open market operations—buying and selling bonds in bond markets.

Let us now track the events of January 22, 2008, blow-by-blow, to fully understand the financial engineering of credit expansion and interest-rate reduction.

---

[5] Prof. Bernanke gave a speech on April 3, 2009, in Richmond, VA, in which he began by saying: "The Federal Reserve's Balance-Sheet might not be considered a *grabber* (that is, grabber of attention and interest) but ... a guided tour of our balance-sheet might be an instructive way to discuss the Fed's policy." It is indeed.

Blow-by-blow

An extraordinary January 22, 2008, meeting of the FOMC, is held, a week in advance of the regularly-scheduled one. The reason: the very gloomy economic data emerging, indicating a looming recession. The FOMC decides to lower interest rates drastically, from 4.25 percent to 3.75 percent, a fall of 0.75 percent, or 75 basis points, the largest single interest-rate cut in 18 years.

But how is this decision implemented? Here is what happens:

1. The secretary of the FOMC calls the New York Fed, at 33 Liberty Street, in Manhattan, close to Wall Street in lower Manhattan. The New York Fed is the operational arm of the Fed, and runs a very large bond trading room. The secretary informs the head trader of the FOMC's decision.
2. The New York Fed buys USD 100 billion bonds from commercial banks in the open market. Banks deposit the New York Fed check in their Fed reserve accounts.

Here is how the two balance sheets look immediately after this transaction, on, say, January 23:

IMMEDIATELY AFTER (JANUARY 23):

(USD billion)

Commercial Banks		Federal Reserve	
Assets	Liabilities	Assets	Liabilities
Reserves USD 1,100	Deposits USD 10,000	Bonds USD 2,100	Currency USD 1,000
Loans 7,000			Reserves USD 1,100
Bonds 900			
S. Equity 1,000			

Note: The Commercial Banks have "excess reserves"—reserves are USD 1,100 billion, while they are required to hold only USD 1,000 billion, or 10 percent of deposits.

Bank managers thus call their clients, saying: "Sir, or madam, you recall calling me last month and asking for a loan?" And I replied: "Sorry, I cannot, we are loaned up to our reserve limit at present? Well, today, I'm happy to say, I can make that loan. Please drop in to my office at your earliest convenience." These new loans simply create money, when bank managers give borrowers passbooks with the amount of the loan written in them as the new bank balance—the borrower's asset and the bank's liability, offset by the value of the loan, on the asset side. This credit creation is limited by the constraints of available reserves.

This credit expansion, when it is fully played out, will boost deposits by USD 1,000 billion (10 times USD 100 billion) and will boost loans by the same amount, USD 1,000 billion. The new balance sheets will become (by, say, January 30):

ONE WEEK LATER (JANUARY 30):

(USD billion)			
Commercial Banks		**Federal Reserve**	
Assets	Liabilities	Assets	Liabilities
Reserves USD 1,100	Deposits USD 11,000	Bonds USD 2,100	Currency USD 1,000
Loans 8,000			Reserves USD 1,100
Bonds 900			
S. Equity 1,000			

The money supply has risen by USD 1,000 billion as a result of the FOMC's decision and the operations of its operational arm, the New York Fed. Money has not been "printed"—it has been created by bank managers, but only to the extent permitted by law, in accordance with the available bank reserves (see Figure 6.2).

As a result of money being more plentiful, and more credit being supplied to markets, by the law of supply and demand the price of money (interest rates) will decline. This is known as the *credit multiplier*: a dollar of reserves can support, say, 10 dollars of new deposits and loans. The New York Fed will continue its *open market operations* until interest rates decline to the target rate. The New York Fed may also lend money in the Federal Funds market to directly lower interest rates by boosting the supply of offered credit.

(For a mathematical description of this "credit multiplier", see the appendix to this chapter.)

THEORY AND PRACTICE

What was described to this point was the theory of fractional-reserve banking, and credit expansion. Under this theory, Central Banks expand credit, lending, and the money supply, to stimulate the economy, by injecting bank reserves through bond purchases.

But in extraordinary times, like those we live in now, the process fails. Here is an example. We call it the paradox of the Monetary Ancient Mariner. To paraphrase Coleridge's famous poem "The Rime of the Ancient Mariner"—Money, money everywhere, not any rupee/dollar/euro/yuan/yen to borrow.

FIGURE 6.2   Money and Credit Expansion

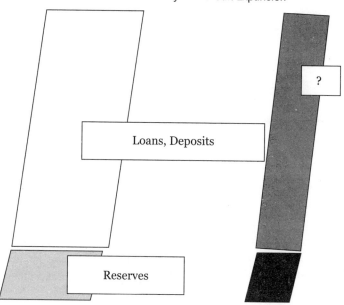

Source: Authors.

Note: When Central Banks expand reserves (the black rectangle on the right bottom), by buying bonds, commercial banks "may" then expand loans and deposits (money) by a multiple of the additional reserves (the dark shaded rectangle on the right block). The question mark beside the dark shaded rectangle block emphasizes the word "may"—banks are not compelled to lend, and may for various reasons choose instead to hold the reserves rather than lend them. This in fact is what has occurred.

Everywhere, in America, Asia, and Europe, the media speaks of a credit crunch, liquidity crisis and shortage of money. Businesses fail when cash flow turns negative, and credit is unavailable.

- Almost everywhere, the supply of money has grown dramatically. China's money supply was 25.5 percent higher in March, 2009 than a year earlier. In the United States, from August, 2008 through February, 2009, the *narrow* definition of money grew at an annual rate of 24 percent, and the *broad* definition of money grew at an annual rate of 15 percent. (*Broad* and *narrow* definitions of money were defined earlier in this chapter.)
- At the same time, families, businesses, and even huge global concerns like General Motors complained of the *credit squeeze*, and lack of credit and lending. And according to Stephen King, chief economist of the global bank HSBC, as

rich-country governments embark on a round of *capital market protectionism* (keeping scarce credit for their own businesses), developing countries face the threat of a financial drought.[6]

Why?

The explanation is relatively simple. Central Banks, like the Fed, can provide commercial banks with added reserves, even in massive amounts. But—they cannot *force* those banks to make loans. What if the commercial banks need the reserves more than they need the lending? What if commercial banks' balance sheets have been ravaged, by deep losses in mortgage-backed securities and other *toxic* or *troubled* assets? What if these losses have created huge craters in bank balance-sheet assets, greatly reducing bank capital (shareholders' equity)? In this case, the banks will want to hold on to the cash rather than lend it, especially if economic conditions are so bad that they fear default on the loans they make, even to seemingly-solid clients.

The Table below shows the remarkable shift in the American commercial banks' reserve position between August, 2008 (just before the collapse of the leading investment bank Lehman Brothers, on September 15, 2008), and April 8, 2009:

Reserves of Commercial Banks, US, Aug. 2008, April 2009

	USD billion		
	Total Reserves	*Required Reserves*	*Excess Reserves*
August 2008	USD 44,565	USD 42,571	USD 1,993
April 2009	USD 861,537	USD 56,733	USD 804,805

In the wake of the financial crisis following September 15, 2008, the Fed has clearly injected massive amounts of bank reserves, to support the commercial banks, expand liquidity and credit, and deal with the collapse of asset prices. *Yet those reserves were largely held by the commercial banks*, rather than used and lent—had they been lent and used to create new loans, and demand deposits, the *required reserves* would have expanded equally dramatically. Yet as the Table shows, they barely rose at all. The question mark, in Figure 6.2, is dramatically present. The Fed expanded the reserve base, but the banks have not expanded lending and credit.

This phenomenon is known colloquially as *pushing on a string*. The Fed, and Central Banks everywhere, can expand reserves. But they cannot *force* banks to lend, nor force companies to borrow, nor force individuals to spend their deposits.

---

[6] See Heather Stewart, Economics Editor, *The Observer*, Sunday, January 4, 2009. www.guardian.co.uk, http://www.guardian.co.uk/business/2009/jan/04/interest-rates-bank-of-england1 (accessed January 18, 2010).

This is proving a major, severe limitation on the use of money and interest-rate policy to moderate the deep recession in the United States and elsewhere.

CASE STUDY

China

 China has been widely criticized for its lack of democracy. But its partial command economy may have some advantages in times of crisis. China's major banks are largely state-owned or state-controlled. According to Reuter's, "the government has said it wants banks to lend at least 5 trillion yuan (about USD 658 billion) over all of 2009 to support economic growth." Banks, of course, comply. "New yuan loans in March (2009) hit a record high of 1.89 trillion yuan (USD 248 billion), 29.8 percent higher than a year earlier."[7]

We now turn to the issue of how the supply of money and credit is related to the level of real economic activity in the economy (GDP). We introduce this topic by describing a puzzle—why has the Central Bank policy described above, pumping reserves into the banking system, not created inflation (rising prices)?

MUCH MONEY, BUT NO INFLATION

Not long ago, there were fears of rising world inflation, in the wake of growing amounts of US dollars flooding into the world. One expert commented a little over a decade ago: "The most serious threat to the further advance of the market system would be the re-emergence of high inflation.... Is the long-term downward trend of world inflation secure?"[8]

As noted above, the supply of money has risen rapidly in major countries. This generally ignited fears of inflation. Yet the world's problem has become not *inflation* but the opposite, *deflation* (declining prices), as noted in this report:

> Global concern about inflation, which was widespread just a few months ago, has given way to worries about an opposite and potentially more dangerous problem: deflation. In the United States, the Consumer Price Index (CPI) took a rare nose dive, plunging by 1 percent

---

[7] Source: Reuters, "China loan growth hits record high," April 11, 2009 (Reuters website).

[8] Hamish McRae, *The World in 2020* (Boston, MA: Harvard Business School Press, 1995), 159–160.

in October, the Labor Department said Wednesday. That's the largest fall in a single month since 1938. October saw one of only seven monthly drops in the core Consumer Price Index since 1947 ... most economists are forecasting that 2009 will see the kind of broad and persistent price declines that helped make the Great Depression so severe.[9]

Why? Why has the booming money supply not eased credit, created more bank lending, and generated inflation? How does money *speak* to GDP?

CASE STUDY

"Helicopter Money"

 The G-20 is a forum of Central Bank governors and finance ministers of 19 leading countries: Argentina, Australia, Brazil, Canada, China, France, Germany, India, Indonesia, Italy, Japan, Mexico, Russia, Saudi Arabia, South Africa, South Korea, Turkey, United Kingdom, and United States. The 20th member is the European Union.

In early April, 2009 presidents and prime ministers of the G-20 countries met in London. US President Obama pressed for a decision supporting a massive money stimulus of USD 750 billion to battle the global downturn, through the International Monetary Fund. The European Union's response, led by the European Central Bank (ECB), was blistering criticism. Said Jurgen Stark, the ECB's chief economist, "this is helicopter money for the globe!", "pure cash creation" outside the normal mechanisms of control.[10]

Helicopter money refers to a term invented by Nobel Laureate Professor Milton Friedman. Friedman addressed a largely theoretical issue: What if interest rates were so low, they could not be lowered further, and what if the economy were still in recession? His response: Helicopter money. Inject money directly into the economy, metaphorically *dropping money on people from a helicopter.* Elsewhere, Friedman uses the helicopter metaphor to show that creation and distribution of new money, as if dropped from

(Case Study continued)

[9] Mark Trumbull, "Deflation risk grows," *The Christian Science Monitor*, November 20, 2008 (web edition).

[10] Ambrose Evans-Pritchard, "ECB attacks G20 plan to boost IMF drawing rights to pump cash into global economy," April 7, 2009. http://www.telegraph.co.uk/finance/financetopics/recession/5119671/ECB-attacks-G20-plans-to-use-IMF-to-pump-cash-into-global-economy.html (accessed January 26, 2010).

(Case Study continued)

a helicopter, simply causes higher prices, but no growth of real output. The issue of *helicopter money* has now metamorphosed from a highly theoretical debate to a highly practical one, with US interest rates near zero and the economy still in a deep slump.[11] Will America's helicopter money reduce unemployment and spur growth? Or will it simply generate inflation?

HOW MONEY "SPEAKS" TO THE ECONOMY—AND TO GDP

"Pull over!" the traffic cop said to the 10-dollar banknote.

"But officer," said the Note. "I was not speeding. I was barely doing 10 km per hour (6 mph)."

"Sure," said the officer. He was tough and grizzled and had heard it all. "That's exactly the problem, buddy. You were going too slow!"

"Too slow?!" said the Note.

The stunned Note fell silent, then recovered.

"Officer, believe me. I want to be a Ferrari. But these bankers, these people. They turn me into a turtle. They hang on to me. They used to spend and lend me like there was no tomorrow. Now? I can sit in a pocket or a vault for days! Weeks! I can't get no ... momentum!"

In physics, high school students learn that the momentum of a moving body is the product of its mass (M) times its velocity (V). Momentum equals M times V.

$$\text{Momentum equals Mass times Velocity, or } M \times V$$

High momentum can result either from having a heavy body move slowly or a light body move rapidly. According to Einstein's special theory of relativity, a tiny elementary particle like an electron gets heavier and heavier (higher and higher mass), theoretically, as it speeds up and approaches the speed of light. By the same token, in cricket the ball can vary in weight, legally, from 5.5 to 5.75 ounces. So a 5.5 ounce ball bowled by a pace bowler at 100 mph (the fastest ever recorded) has the same momentum as a 5.75 ounce ball thrown by a spin bowler at only 95.7 mph.

The same relationship holds true in economics. This theory is one of the oldest in the history of economics, dating back to David Hume's famous 1748 essay,[12] and before that, even to Nicholas Copernicus. This theory states that the economic momentum

---

[11] Source: Milton Friedman, *Money Mischief: Episodes in Monetary History* (New York: Harcourt Brace, 1994).

[12] David Hume (1748), "Of Interest," Indianapolis, Liberty Fund, Inc., Edinburgh, 1752.

of a nation, measured by its Gross Domestic Product, is the product of its money (M) times the velocity of money (V), or the number of times a unit of money changes hands during a year. This is definitional, or tautological, because velocity is identically equal to (defined as) GDP divided by Money. But it is also a behavioral theory, because perceptions, psychology and *minds* determine how fast money turns over.

Tool # 6

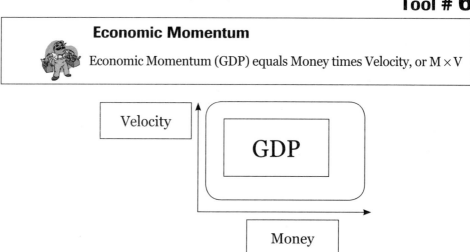

Economic Momentum

Economic Momentum (GDP) equals Money times Velocity, or M × V

This tool explains why Central Banks everywhere are struggling to combat the ongoing economic downturn. If they could, they would legislate a minimum speed limit for money. But they cannot. M is rising. But V is often falling even faster than the rate at which M is rising. So the product of M times V is falling. (See Appendix for a more precise mathematical statement of this theory.) This is why we see, in several major countries, seemingly inflationary growth in money but falling prices.

In his book on the Great Depression, *The Great Contraction, 1929–1933*, University of Chicago Professor Milton Friedman notes that between 1929 and 1933, the stock of money in America fell by a third, as many banks closed their doors. But, he notes, the velocity of money also fell by almost a third. As a result, America's GDP declined by more than half. Apparently history does repeat itself. This has occurred again, at the end of 2008. Central Banks have learned from the 1930s how to prevent bank failures and the collapse of the money supply. But they have not yet found the secret for overcoming the slowing of money velocity, which greatly blunts the positive impact of more money.

CASE STUDY

Sharp US GDP Decline, 2008 4th Quarter

 Real gross domestic product—the output of goods and services produced by labor and property located in the United States—decreased at an annual rate of 6.3 percent in the fourth quarter of 2008 (that is, from the third quarter to the fourth quarter).

—*Bureau of Economic Analysis, US Dept of Commerce.*[13]

Why did GDP fall so sharply in the United States at the end of 2008, even though the Fed was pumping money into the system incredibly aggressively?

Note: Between the 3rd and 4th quarters of 2008, the supply of money in the United States expanded rapidly, as the US Central Bank acted aggressively to inject liquidity after asset prices plummeted. The money supply known as M1 grew from USD 1,452 billion to USD 1,595 billion, an increase of almost 10 percent—an extraordinarily rapid growth of money in just three months. But the rate at which existing money changed hands (velocity) decreased even more, from 9.9 to 8.9. The result was that economic momentum declined—the rate at which money changed hands slowed by even more than the rate at which actual amount of money grew. Real (inflation-adjusted) GDP declined by some 6.3 percent (at an annual rate) in the 4th Quarter of 2008 (see Table below and Figures 6.3 and 6.4).

	2008-III	2008-IV (USD billion)
Real GDP (Q)	11,712	11,522
Price Index (P)	1.23	1.23
Q × P	14,413	14,200
Money (M)	1,452	1,595
Velocity (V)	9.9	8.9
M × V	14,413	14,200

Note: Real GDP: inflation-adjusted GDP; Price Index: GDP measured in current prices divided by GDP measured in 2000 prices; Money = M1; Velocity = Q × P/M1.

Economic momentum declined sharply at the end of 2008, despite a large increase in the supply of money, because the rate at which money changed hands (velocity) fell from 10.3 in the 2nd quarter of 2008 to 8.9 in the final (4th) quarter, a drop of 14 percent in just six months!

---

[13] Staff of Econedlink.org. http://www.econedlink.org/real_gdp/(accessed March 10, 2010).

FIGURE 6.3 Velocity of Money (GDP/M1), United States, 2007–2008

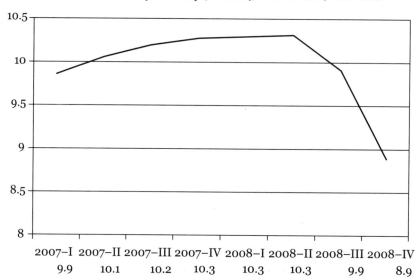

10.5
10
9.5
9
8.5
8
2007–I 2007–II 2007–III 2007–IV 2008–I 2008–II 2008–III 2008–IV
9.9 10.1 10.2 10.3 10.3 10.3 9.9 8.9

Source: Based on data in the Economic Report of the President, Tables B-1 and B-69, pp. 328 and 411, respectively (Council of Economic Advisors: US Govt, Printing Office, Washington D.C., February 2010).

FIGURE 6.4 Sharp Decline in Economic Momentum of US at the End of 2008

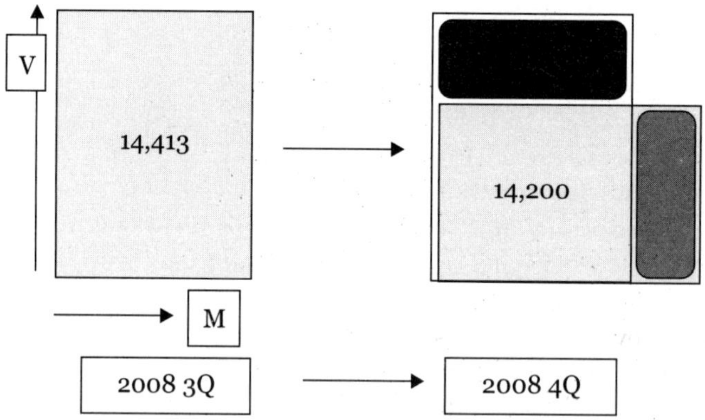

V
14,413
14,200
M
2008 3Q
2008 4Q

Source: Based on data in the Economic Report of the President, Tables B-1 and B-69, pp. 328 and 411, respectively (Council of Economic Advisors: US Govt Printing Office, Washington, D.C., February 2010).

Note: Even though the money supply rose sharply in the United States in the fourth quarter of 2008, causing higher economic momentum (the dark shaded rectangle), the rate at which money changed hands (velocity) fell by much more, leading to a decline in economic momentum (GDP) during that quarter (the black rectangle), and a net fall in GDP (dark rectangle minus the shaded rectangle).

The reason for this was partly psychological—fear of banks to lend money, lest the loans not be repaid when borrowers got into trouble, and fear of individuals to spend, in the face of the declining economy, falling asset prices and rising unemployment. This episode explains and motivates the phrase in the subtitle of our book: *Minds, Markets & Money*; it is not an accident that *minds* comes first.

Yale Professor Robert Shiller first invented the term *irrational exuberance* (to describe the bubble psychology). He has said that "it's really psychology that drives the stock market—and increasingly, the market for homes as well."[14] He might have added "...and in fact, drives the entire economy, through people's willingness to spend the money they hold, or cling on to it."

CASE STUDY

Money and Inflation: Israel 2008–2009

A headline in Israel's business daily *The Marker* reads: "Money supply jumps 41% in a year." A subhead asks: "What do the numbers mean? Has inflation returned?"[15] The author, Moti Bassok, notes, "The total rise in the M1 money supply over the past 12 months through March, 2009 was 40.6%, according to the Bank of Israel ... in 2007 and 2008, the money supply rose 17.4% each year, and only 8.3% in 2006." Clearly, more money means more inflation? The answer to those questions is, no, inflation has not returned. A Reuters report noted that "Israel posted an inflation rate of 3.8 percent in 2008 but prices are poised to slide this year as the domestic economy slows sharply." The only explanation for this is that despite the combined boom in money supply and declining prices, there must have been an even larger fall in the velocity of money—the rate at which money changes hands: in Israel, in such times, like in America, businesses and people hang on to their money rather than spend it. The deflationary psychology means that if prices do not rise, people feel secure in holding money rather than spending it, because money holds its value even when it sits in our pockets and bank accounts. If prices are expected to be cheaper tomorrow than today, why buy now, why not wait? The result is that this deflationary psychology postpones spending and slows money velocity.

---

[14] Source: Robert Shiller, interview by Rik Kirkland, March 2009, taped at Yale University, transcript, *McKinsey Quarterly*.

[15] Haaretz, *The Marker*, (April 17, 2009), A 10.

If wages are the price of labor, then interest is the price of money. Like all prices, interest is determined by forces of supply and demand. How, then, do the supply of, and demand for money act to determine interest rates? This is the subject to which we now turn our attention.

LINKING MONEY WITH INTEREST RATES

The paradox of low and High interest rates

Even though Central Banks in the United States, Europe, and Asia have drastically reduced Central Bank interest rates, in some cases to the lowest rates in history, businesses complain that the interest they pay remains very high. What, in general, is the link between the supply of money and interest rates? How can we explain the paradox of simultaneous low and high interest rates?

Figure 6.5 shows short-term Federal Funds (see below) interest rates for over five decades. This figure shows how America's Central Bank has used interest-rate policy aggressively to battle the double-digit inflation of 1980–82 (raising rates to 19 percent), and to battle the deflationary effects of the dot.com bubble (lowering rates from 6 percent in 2001 to 1 percent in 2004). It also shows how today's Fed,

FIGURE 6.5   Very Short-term "Federal Funds" Interest Rates, US 1952–2009

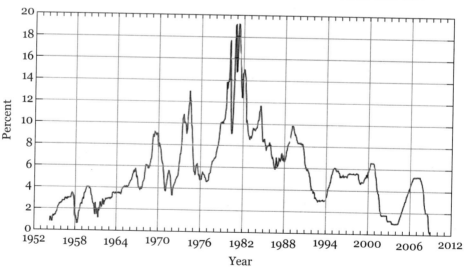

Source: http://www.moneycafe.com/library/fedfundsratehistory.htm (accessed March 10, 2010).

under Ben Bernanke, lowered the Federal Funds rate to a historical record-low level of zero to 0.25 percent on December 16, 2008.

Why, then, do businesses claim they are still paying high-interest rates? There are two answers to this puzzle. One is simple. The second is rather complex.

The first relates to what is known as the *term structure of interest rates* or the *yield curve*. The second relates to the difference between nominal ("not-adjusted-for-inflation") and real (adjusted-for-inflation) interest rates.

DEFINITION

Term Structure of Interest Rates (yield curve): The rate of interest (yield) for notes, bills and bonds, according to the amount of time left until the asset matures and is redeemed; from a day or two, to 30 years (see Figure 6.6).

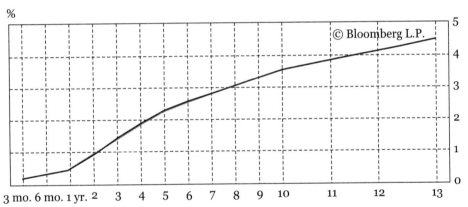

FIGURE 6.6   Yield Curve: Interest Rates for US Treasury Notes, Bills, and Bonds, 3 months to 30 years

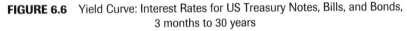

Source: Bloomberg.com, http://www.bloomberg.com/markets/rates/indexm.html (accessed February 3, 2010).

Figure 6.6 shows that America's Central Bank has been effective in lowering *the very short-term rate of interest, the Federal Funds rate, for borrowing and lending for only a few days.* The Fed has tugged downward on the left end of the *interest rate string*, because it is here that the Fed can intervene and influence rates most quickly and powerfully. Businesses, however, borrow for much longer than just a few days. The Fed's policy, causing historically record-low short-term interest rates, has been far less powerful in affecting longer-term rates, which remain quite high, at close to 4 percent.

This is why Central Banks in the US, Israel, and elsewhere have intervened aggressively in bond markets, to buy not only Treasury bonds but also long-term corporate bonds. Buying such bonds raises the demand for them and, other things equal, thus raises their price. The higher the price of a bond, the lower its yield, or interest rate (see Box 6.2). This is partly why the Fed's Ben Bernanke has noted that the Federal Reserve's balance-sheet assets "have more than doubled, from roughly USD 870 billion before the crisis to more than USD 2,000 billion now."

BOX 6.2   Bond Prices and Bond Yields

There is a small, technical issue that is vital for understanding interest rates.

The yield, or rate of interest on a bond varies inversely with its price. Here is why. Suppose a bond's price is USD 100, and has a USD 5 annual interest coupon. Its yield, or interest rate, is therefore 5 percent ($5/100 \times 100$). Suppose, now, that the price of the bond rises (perhaps, because the Fed has intervened to buy such bonds, raising the demand and hence raising the price). Suppose the new price is USD 120. The bond yield is therefore 4.17 percent ($5/120 \times 100$). The higher the bond price, the lower its yield.

INTEREST RATES: "GET REAL"

The second reason regarding why businesses' complaints about high-interest rates is justified is more complex than the first. It relates to the difference between interest rates that are not adjusted for inflation (nominal), and those that are (real).

Tool # 6

Nominal and Real Interest Rates

Real interest rate $\cong$ *Nominal* interest rate minus the inflation rate

DEFINITION

Real and nominal interest rates.

Nominal rate of interest: The rate of interest not adjusted for inflation; rates of interest as published in the media (R). Real rate of interest: The nominal rate of interest adjusted for inflation (r).

The Appendix to this chapter shows two formulae useful for computing real interest rates.

For small values of R, and inflation, real interest rates can be approximated by simply subtracting the inflation rate from the nominal rate of interest.

If global capital markets are interconnected, and if money flows quickly and easily from one country to another, perhaps via instantaneous wire transfers, *why then should not risk-adjusted interest rates be exactly the same in every country? In fact, interest rates differ widely; ten-year government bond rates range from 7.25 percent in India, and 6.16 percent in Brazil, down to only 1.31 percent in Japan. Why?* (See Table below.)

Nominal and Real Interest Rates, Eight Countries, March 21, 2009

Country	Nominal Interest Rate*	Real Interest Rate*
US	2.53	3.13
Japan	1.31	2.11
China	3.21	3.41
Britain	3.11	2.11
Canada	2.86	2.36
Euro Area	3.22	2.62
India	7.25	1.85
Brazil	6.16	1.76

Source: The Economist, March 21, 2009, 102.

Notes: * Nominal: Interest rate on 10-year government bond; Real: Nominal rate less forecast inflation rate for 2009.

The answer lies in part in the difference between real and nominal. If you borrow 1,000 rupees in India today, at 5 percent interest, you pay them back a year hence with interest, the sum of 1,050 rupees. Because of inflation, the 1,050 rupees you repay are worth much less, only 1,050/(1+p), in real or purchasing-power terms, where p is the rate of inflation during the coming year. So the true, or inflation-adjusted interest rate, is approximately 5 percent–p percent. If inflation exceeds 5 percent, the *real* rate of interest is negative. This means that the lender is in fact paying *you* to borrow (though, possibly, unintentionally).

When these global 10-year bond interest rates are adjusted for inflation, a much more reasonable picture emerges: Differences in real interest rates across the eight countries are very similar, ranging from 2 to 3 percent (see the lower curve, Figure 6.7), with the differences accounted for largely by differences in country-risk premiums.

A good source of data for global interest rates, for some 50 countries, is found in *The Economist* weekly financial magazine, in the "Economic and financial indicators," the last two pages in every issue. But the interest rates listed there by countries

FIGURE 6.7   Nominal and Real Interest Rates, Selected Countries, March 21, 2009

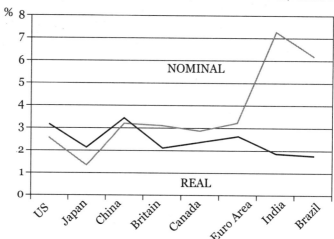

Source: *The Economist*. London, March 21, 2009, "Markets and Data." http://www.economist.com/markets/(accessed February 3, 2010).

are nominal. Managers need to become accustomed to adjusting them for inflation by themselves, by deducting the rate of inflation. It would probably be a good idea if *The Economist*, an outstanding publication, helped managers by providing real interest rates.

CASE STUDY

Free Money in Japan in 1997

 Most things in Japan are very expensive. Except for money. In Japan money is cheap. In fact, money there is free—and even subsidized. They pay YOU to borrow. According to Jesper Koll, an economist at J.P. Morgan Securities Asia Ltd, "here in Japan [in 1997] you are in an extraordinary situation, and that extraordinary fact is that money is free."[16] For a call loan (payable on demand), the annual rate of interest in early 1997 was 0.49 percent. Japan's rate of inflation was about 0.6 percent. This means that:

Real short-term interest rate = 0.49 percent minus
0.6 percent = −0.11 percent

(Case Study continued)

[16] *International Herald Tribune*, February 22–23, 1997, 1.

(*Case Study continued*)

No wonder then that many foreign investors are trying to borrow in Japan, where money is *free*, and lend money in America, where it is expensive. Some estimates suggest between 5 and 7 trillion yen are borrowed by foreigners each month in Japan. Why were yen free in Japan? In part because the Bank of Japan was trying to stimulate a flagging economy with low interest rates. The strong outflow of money hinders that policy by reducing Japanese money supply, and making credit more expensive. The money flowing out of Japan, and flowing in to the US, works in the US to *lower* interest rates. In this way capital flows among countries work to equalize real interest rates.

Over the years a so-called *carry trade* has developed—investors borrow at low rates in Japan, and invest at higher rates elsewhere (in the US or the euro zone). This can be risky, because if the value of Japanese yen in terms of dollars or euros falls, when investors have to pay back their yen loans by cashing in their dollars or euros, what they lose on the exchange rate transaction may be even greater than the higher interest rates they enjoyed abroad. In August, 2007 a journalist wrote, "the end of the yen carry trade could be devastating for capital markets throughout the world." Experts estimate that there are several hundred billion dollars of positions in the carry trade to be unwound. David Bloom, currency analyst at HSBC, says that it has pervaded "every single instrument imaginable," so that when it comes to an end later this year it's going to be "ugly."[17] It did come to an end ... and it was indeed *ugly*. The end was inevitable, because when the price of yen relative to dollars or euros rises sharply, as it did at the end of 2008 (from 6.2 euros to 7.5 euros per 1,000 yen), carry-trade speculators lose heavily when they repay their yen loans—and the *game* comes to an unhappy end.

WHY MANAGERS MUST "GET REAL" IN JUDGING INTEREST RATES

Figure 6.8 shows both nominal and real 10-year bond rates for the United States, for the period 1970–94. This graph shows the pitfalls awaiting unwary managers who tracked nominal interest rates, and make debt and borrowing decisions based on them rather than based on inflation-adjusted rates.

---

[17] Chris Sholto Heaton, "What is the carry trade?" August 24, 2007. www.moneyweek. com http://www.moneyweek.com/investments/why-is-the-carry-trade-so-dangerous.aspx (accessed January 18, 2010).

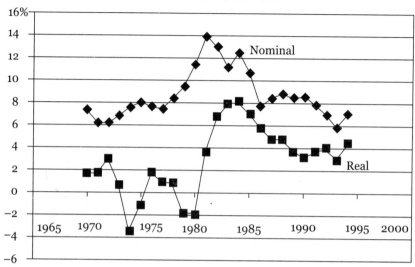

FIGURE 6.8   Nominal (10-Year Bond Rate) vs. Real (Inflation-Adjusted)
Interest Rates, US, 1970–1994

Source: Based on data drawn from Economic Report of the President, 2009 (US Govt Printing
Office, Washington D.C., Jan. 2009), Tables B-73 (p. 370) and B-64 (p. 358).

- In the period 1972–1974 nominal interest rates were rising, but real interest rates were falling; managers tracking only rates unadjusted for inflation would have been misled that the price of credit was rising, when in fact it was falling. This was because the rate of inflation was rising faster than nominal interest rates during the 1972–1974 cost-push inflation, discussed in the next chapter.
- In the period 1981–1983, nominal rates were falling, but real interest rates were rising steeply, making credit more expensive (because inflation fell faster than interest rates). Managers deceived into thinking the cost of credit was falling based on nominal rates quickly found that their organizations' debt was increasingly burdensome as real rates rose.
- In 1985–1987, nominal rates changed direction, and began to rise; but as inflation accelerated, real rates declined. Again, the divergence could lead to faulty decisions regarding borrowing, leverage, and asset–liability management.

In statistical data tables, virtually all key variables, such as GDP, are adjusted for inflation. There are two key variables that almost never are. They are: interest rates, discussed in this chapter, and long-term stock market indexes, discussed in the next chapter. Wise managers do their own inflation adjustment, aware that failure to do so will lead to decisions based on wrong or misleading information.

So far, we have discussed money, its creation, and its price—interest rates—as well as the link between money and economic momentum (GDP). In other words, we have examined two key markets: the market for money and credit, and the market for goods and services, and the links between them. It is now time to generalize our thinking, to take a more systemic view of the system. Managers capable of global analysis are strong in such big-picture systemic ecological thinking.

EVERY ECONOMY IS AN ECOLOGY: THE FOUR-MARKETS MODEL

Every economy is an ecology. The global economy is an ecology, comprised of highly interdependent national economies that interact through trade and capital flows. No single fact is more important in understanding the world economy.

Economy and ecology have the same Greek root, *oikos*, meaning *house*. Economy deals with managing a *household*, or small or large group of people; ecology deals with the *science of* households—how people and other living organisms interact with their environment.

Every economy is composed of four major markets. Each of those markets is defined by a quantity and price—what is being sold and bought, and how much of it, and at what price. Understanding the four markets and how they interact is one of our key objectives.

The four key macro markets are:

- Services and goods: The market for services and goods matches producers of goods with buyers. Demand and supply are balanced by market prices, tracked either through the Consumer Price Index, or the so-called GDP Deflator. (The GDP Deflator is a weighted average price index, reflecting prices of the goods and services comprising the GDP, with weights determined by the proportion of each type of good and service: personal consumption, public consumption, investment, exports and imports.)
- Labor: The labor market brings those who want to supply labor together with employers who need it, at agreed-upon wages.
- Capital: The capital market matches those with capital to lend with those who want to borrow it, with interest rates as the cost, or prices, of capital. Key *products* are cash, notes, bills, bonds, stocks, certificates of deposit, money market deposit accounts, mutual funds, and so on. The cost of capital is affected by the degree of risk inherent in each transaction.
- Foreign exchange: Yen, yuan, rupee, or euros, etc.—the price of foreign exchange is the rate at which currencies exchange for dollars.

To fully understand what is happening in a national economy, and in global economies, *how each market interacts with the other three must be understood.* Those interactions are often crucial, because, it is they that drive economic change, and underlie strategic managerial decisions.

Viewing economies as ecologies characterizes modern economic thinking. Managers encounter it as the *systems approach* to organizations. Countries, like businesses, can be understood fully only through a systems approach, because countries, like businesses, are intricate systems in which complex interaction among their parts drives change, growth, and decline. The four-markets' macro ecology model is shown schematically in Figure 6.9.

FIGURE 6.9   The Four-Market Ecology Model

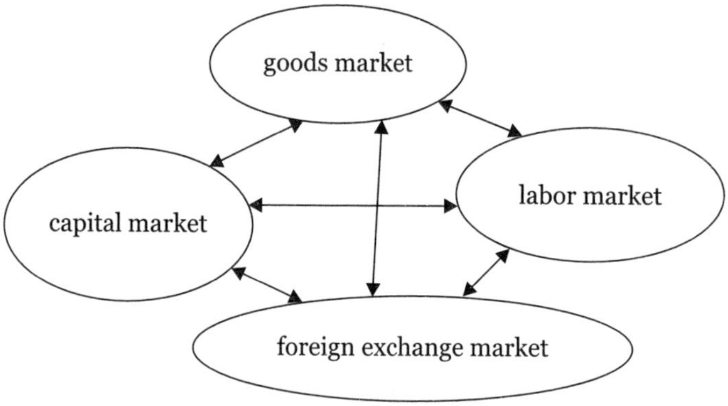

Source: Authors.

BOX 6.3   Are Managers Scientists?

The first author once invited Professor Jay Forrester, MIT Sloan professor and distinguished inventor of matrix memory and the discipline of System Dynamics, to speak to a group of his graduate management students, mostly scientists and engineers.

"How many of you make decisions by using 'models'?" he asked. No one raised their hand.

"Every one of you uses models," he said. "The question is: Are your models inexact, vague, unclear, imprecise. Or are they explicit, well thought out, susceptible of testing, falsifiable, easy to confront with data, and hence easy to improve."

Every manager has, in his or her head, some sort of model of the global economy. A *model* is simply:

(Box 6.3 continued)

(*Box 6.3 continued*)

1. A set of definitions, stating what we mean by terms like *GDP*, *interest* and *money*;
2. A set of assumptions about what forces are important, and which can be ignored; and
3. A number of *theories* or hypotheses about how things work, and how one thing leads to another.

This is the so-called *scientific method*. When applied to what is going on in the world, the scientific method asks us to develop hypotheses through keen observation, toss out ideas that do not work, buttress ones that do, and above all, *to adapt thinking to the rapid changes now occurring in the world*. It is a version of *continuous improvement*—a way to learn and improve our understanding.

By clarifying their assumptions and continually testing their hypotheses against ever-changing reality, managers stay abreast with change, and build accurate world-views.

The basis of learning about the global economy is to think ahead, to err, to trace the source of the error and correct it—and to try again. Good managers who have global mindsets think like scientists, while acting as practitioners.

Scientists have no monopoly on the scientific method. Smart managers use it as well. For interest rates specifically, by spotlighting the key interactions among such variables as interest rates, inflation, money, exchange rates, unemployment and GDP, stating how they work, and then testing whether they work in the way we think they do, the quality of managers' understanding of global markets can be consistently improved.

ACTION LEARNING

What is *Your* Model?

 By clarifying their assumptions, and continually testing their hypothesis against ever-changing reality, managers stay abreast with change and build accurate world views.

Take a sheet of paper. Draw on it Figure 6.9. There are six arrows, linking the four markets pair-wise, with six distinct interactions. Tracking an economy is done by, building a basic understanding of those six interactions, and finding a set of indicators that help managers track them.

1. Take each arrow in turn, and examine your understanding of how it works—state how you think the two markets the arrow connects are linked to one another, in important ways. Simplify—list only the essence of what you believe are the key links.
2. How will you test your theory, or model? What evidence might lead you to modify it?

(*Action Learning continued*)

(*Action Learning continued*)

      The basis of learning about the global economy is to think ahead, to err, to trace the source of the error and correct it—and to try again. Moreover, global markets are always in flux, in a constant state of change, demanding that we constantly update, and revise our theories and models. To fully understand what is happening in national and global economies, *how* each market interacts with the other three must be understood. Those interactions are often crucial, because it is they that drive economic change, and underlie strategic managerial decisions.

  3. How has the global crisis of 2007–2009 altered *your* mental model of the global economy? How? Why? What is your evidence?

We now continue our examination of how markets for credit and goods interact, with a startling case study showing how a deep understanding of the four-market ecology and systemic risk can generate huge profits.

THE MARKET FOR GOODS AND THE MARKET FOR MONEY

Higher interest rates affect the demand for goods and services in two main ways.

- When interest rates rise, "numerous investment projects are set aside until costs of financing seem more favorable."[18]
- Moreover, the cost to households of buying on credit rises. Monthly installment payments go up, and the ability and desire of households to buy large-ticket items (including houses) falls. Thus, the overall demand for goods and services declines, as interest rates rise.[19]

It follows, therefore, that interest rates are determined in the capital market, but influence demand and supply for goods. In turn, the demand and supply of goods affect the demand for money, and hence interest rates. This particular ecology has great importance for managers—especially in the way they measure interest rates, and use those measures for strategic decision-making about borrowing and debt.

---

[18] Arthur Burns, 1949, cited in Alfred L. Malabre Jr., *Lost Prophets* (Boston, MA: Harvard Business School Press, 1994), 57. Burns was a former Fed Chair and Columbia University economics professor. He was a Chairman of the Council of Economic Advisors from 1953 to 1956, and later a close advisor of Richard Nixon.

[19] For example, the Economic Report of the President notes: "the high real interest rates that resulted from the burgeoning deficits and tight money of the early 1980's...[caused] private fixed investment net of depreciation [to fall] from about 8 percent to about 5 percent of GDP." Economic Report of the President, 1996: US Govt. Printing Office, Washington D.C., p. 44.

Here is an interesting case study showing how a legendary hedge fund investor, George Soros, founder of the Quantum Fund, made a profit of USD 2 billion in a few days, by a deep understanding of macroeconomic ecology—how capital and goods markets interact.

CASE STUDY

Soros' USD 2 billion

In 1992, Britain's economy was seriously lagging. Unemployment was high and rising, demand was flagging, and a recession was in the works.

Background: At this time, Germany was rapidly integrating East Germany with the West, by exchanging each Eastern mark for one Western mark—far above the true value of Eastern marks. The result was inflationary. Hence Germany's central bank raised its interest rates.

Britain was committed by legally-binding Exchange Rate Mechanism (ERM) agreements not to let the pound sterling fall below 2.95 DM per pound. The British began to regret joining ERM in 1990 because it chained them to a strong currency, the mark, and to high German interest rates. Why should Britain not try lowering interest rates? This could be done by expanding the supply of money, a standard approach to stimulating a sluggish economy, done many times by the United States, for example. But there was a catch. If British interest rates fell, while German rates remained steady, *investors would naturally prefer shifting their funds from London to Frankfurt.* A 0.25 percent interest rate difference on USD 100 million amounts to USD 250,000 over one year. To shift money from Britain to Germany, investors sell British pounds, and buy German marks. But when large amounts of pounds are dumped on the market, the price of those pounds must fall. The laws of supply and demand say when the product in excess supply falls in price, the product in excess demand appreciates.

The result: if interest rates in Britain fell, England's Central Bank, the Bank of England, would have to step in to currency markets, and supply large amounts of marks, buying large amounts of pounds. This would shrink the money supply—pounds disappearing into the coffers of the Bank of England by definition cease to be part of the money supply circulating within Britain—and boost interest rates again. The hemorrhage of money out of Britain would continue as long as British interest rates significantly diverged from Germany's. (The ecology of foreign exchange rates is discussed in Chapter Eight.)

(Case Study continued)

(*Case Study continued*)

In short, the sequence would be:

- Britain expands the money supply and lowers interest rates.
- Money flows out of pound sterling into Deutschemarks, away from low British interest rates and toward higher German interest rates. The price of pounds, in terms of DM, drops.
- The Bank of England is forced to buy pounds to support their value.
- The purchase of pounds shrinks the money supply (as those pounds disappear into Bank of England vaults and cease to be circulating money), and push interest rates back up again.

Full circle—an exercise in futility.

The bitter conclusion: Britain, by joining the ERM, had made its monetary policy, and perhaps entire economy, a prisoner to decisions made in Frankfurt, at the Bundesbank's 13th floor. It had given up its interest-rate policy. With fiscal policy not an option, it had surrendered independent economic policy altogether.

Would Britain remain a prisoner? Would the market break the Bank of England? Or would Britain, and its central bank break its ERM bonds?

Stanley Druckenmiller, manager of George Soros' Quantum Fund, a hedge fund that invests globally, consulted with Soros. Soros' advice: Sell British pounds, betting that the value of the pound would fall. Double your bet, he counseled.

They did and made USD 2 billion in profit. Here is what Druckenmiller and Soros did.

1. In the days before September 15, 1992: Buy USD 10 billion, in US funds, at USD 1.75 per pound, in return for 5.71 billion pounds. (Disguise your buying carefully; once it is known, you will have imitators, and the opportunity will be lost.) This huge *bet* may have been substantially greater than the value of the Quantum Fund, implying very high leverage, and hence high risk, should the bet go wrong and lead to losses rather than gains.
2. Britain announces it is leaving the ERM. It devalues its currency, by 15 percent. The pound is now worth only USD 1.50 per pound.
3. Soon after: Sell USD 10 billion, at USD 1.50 per Pound: receive in return 6.67 billion pounds (USD 10 billion divided by USD 1.50).

(*Case Study continued*)

(*Case Study continued*)

4. The net profit for Soros and the Quantum Fun: 6.67 – 5.71 billion pounds = 0.96 billion pounds, or, in dollars: USD 1.44 billion US dollars. Together with speculation in other currencies, Soros is said to have pocketed about USD 2 billion.

Who lost? Robert Frost once advised: "Take care to sell your horse before he dies. The art of life is passing losses on." The Bank of England probably lost heavily, trying to support the pound before it gave up. Those who sold the sterling horse, before it died, passed large losses on to unwary companies, Central Banks—and taxpayers.

Source: Robert Slater, *Soros: The Life, Times and Trading Secrets of the World's Greatest Investor* (Burr Ridge, IL: Irwin Professional Publishing, 1995).

CONCLUSION

In a 1942 radio broadcast, economist John Maynard Keynes recounts a conversation with an eminent architect, Sir John, who is deeply concerned about financing the post-World War II rebuilding of war-ravaged London:[20]

Architect: Where's the money to come from?
Keynes: "The money? But surely, Sir John, you don't build houses with money! Do you mean that there won't be enough bricks and mortar and steel and cement?"
Architect: "Oh, no, of course there will be plenty of all that."
Keynes: "Do you mean that there won't be enough labor? For what will the builders be doing if not building houses?"
Architect: "Oh, no, that's all right".
Keynes: "Then there is only one conclusion. You must be meaning, Sir John, that there won't be enough architects." (The rather impudent Keynes admits he is "passing the boundaries of politeness", and hurries to add) "If there are bricks and mortar and steel and concrete and labor and architects, why not assemble all this good material into houses?"
Architect: "What I want to know is, where is the money coming from!"
Keynes: "The same place it is coming from now [defense spending by the government]."
Added Keynes: "'The architect might have added, 'Of course I know that money is not the slightest use whatever. But, all the same, my dear sir, you will find it a devil of a business not to have any.'"

---

[20] Peter Kennedy, *Macroeconomic Essentials for Media Interpretation* (Cambridge, MA: MIT Press, 1998), 121.

Keynes' point is that if there are unused resources (labor and capital, bricks and mortar), as expected after World War II, when the British army is demobilized, and defense spending plummets, the least prickly problem is for the government to supply the money that will enable houses to be built, because labor is plentiful, and so are bricks and mortar. Supplying that money is not only non-inflationary; it creates jobs, spending, income, and growth.

In the global crisis of 2007–2009, the world faces similar difficulties—plentiful labor, with growing unemployment, and endemic contractions in spending and in demand, causing GDP to contract. Supplying the needed amounts of money should, in Keynes' words, be the least of our problems. But it turns out to be far more difficult and complex, as we have seen in this chapter.

In the next chapter, we will examine the causes of business cycles—including the global downturn now afflicting the world—and the underlying causes of inflation (rising prices), and deflation (falling prices). The theories of J.M. Keynes will play a prominent role, as they make a comeback after being rejected during the bubble era. We will also seek to link the business cycle with the stock market, and seek to understand how markets for goods and services, and for common stock are interconnected.

APPENDIX: THE CREDIT MULTIPLIER

Definitions

R = reserves
L = loans
D = demand deposits
e = required reserve ratio (the fraction of deposits held as bank reserves)
Δ = change

1. L + R = D (bank assets are L + R, and equal bank liabilities, D)
2. ΔL + ΔR = ΔD (the change in loans plus the change in reserves equals the change in deposits)
3. R = e D (reserves are e percent of demand deposits)
4. Thus ΔD = (1/e) ΔR
    For e = 10 percent (0.10), demand deposits rise by 10 times (1/0.1) the addition to reserves.

Economic Momentum

Definitions

M = money supply
V = velocity of money
Q = real GDP
P = price index
100 m = percentage change in M, 100 v = percentage change in V, 100 q = percentage change in Q, 100 p = percentage change in P

1. Economic momentum = *nominal* GDP = Q × P
2. Velocity ≡ (Q × P)/M
3. Economic momentum = Q × P ≡ M × V
4. Percentage change in economic momentum = q + p + pq = m + v + m v[21]
5. For small percentage changes:
   Percentage change in economic momentum ≅ q + p = m + v
   Percentage change in real GDP = q ≅ m + v − p

Real and Nominal Interest Rates

100 R = nominal interest rate (not adjusted for inflation) (percent)
100 r = real interest rate (adjusted for inflation) (percent)
100 p = annual rate of change in price index (inflation rate) (percent)

1. Exact formula:

$$r = (1 + R)/(1 + p) − 1$$

Explanation: 1 + R is what an investor receives, after lending USD 1 at the start of the year, and receiving USD 1 + R at the end of the year. But during the year, prices have risen, by 100 percent; so the real purchasing power of the money received by the investor is actually USD (1 + R)/(1 + p). The real inflation-adjusted interest rate is amount the investor receives, less the original dollar (the principal):

$$(1 + R)/(1 + p) − 1$$

2. Approximate formula (for small R and small p):

$$r = R − p$$

---

[21] Explanation: The percentage change in Q × P is equal to 100[(1 + q) (1+p) − 1] = 100[q + p + pq]. The same reasoning applies to calculating the change in M × V.

Chapter 7

Tracking booms and busts

LEARNING OBJECTIVES

After reading this chapter, readers should understand the basic forces that drive business cycles (periods of boom and bust). They should understand the link between demand components and recession (including consumer spending, public consumption, investment, and net exports), and the key role played by two key deficits—the trade deficit and the budget deficit—and how they interact. They should be able to use the twin-deficit tool to help anticipate future economic cycles and track current cycles. They should be able to explain the 2007–09 global downturn, and link prices of common stock with changes in the real economy. They should be able to use basic supply–demand analysis to distinguish between cost-push and demand-pull inflation (and deflation), in order to gauge future stock market performance. They should know how to use price-earnings ratios to judge when common stock prices are inflated, reaching *bubble* levels.

They should be able to answer these questions:

- What are the main economic theories that explain business cycles? Which one is most correct?
- In what ways are business cycles similar, and in what ways is each unique?
- How do trade deficits and budget deficits impact the real economy, and how are these two deficits inter-related?
- What are the underlying causes of inflation, of deflation? How do they impact the real economy? What are the two fundamentally different causes of inflation and deflation?
- Why do asset prices—specifically, the prices of common stock—tend to rise above sustainable values (that is, *bubbles*), and how can managers know when this occurs?

Tool # 7

Twin Deficits: Budget and Trade Deficits
Supplemental Tool: *Real* (inflation-adjusted) Common Stock Prices

INTRODUCTION

The 2007–2009 global financial and economic crisis was severe, far more so than experts predicted. Even so, it should not be regarded by managers as an aberration or even as a strategic surprise. Using a metaphor from astronomy, the global crisis is not a supernova (exploding star, a rare event hard to predict) but rather more like sunspots (a regular 11-year cycle of electromagnetic activity on the sun's surface).[1] Business booms and busts are not nearly as predictable as sunspots, in their frequency and amplitude, but they are certainly a permanent part of our global economy, and will doubtless remain so. Even as the 2007–2009 global downturn reaches bottom and global recovery begins, *the seeds of the next downturn have probably already been sowed.*

This chapter focuses on business cycles, their causes and effects, and how they are linked with equity markets, specifically, with common share (stock) prices.

DEFINITION

Common stock: A document giving its owner a share of the ownership of the company, a share in its profits, and a share in the voting rights.

 Preferred stock: Stock to which dividends are paid before they are paid to owners of common stock.

Shareholders' equity: On the company's balance-sheet, the difference between what the company owns (assets), and what the company owes (liabilities). It is the *book value* (that is, value as listed on the balance-sheet) of the company's net assets, or what shareholders own after paying off the debts.

Market capitalization: The total market value of a company's shares, at a given point in time.

There are two main reasons why the prices of company common stock (or shares) are of vital importance for global managers. First, share prices are a measure of managers' success, they determine a company's ability to raise capital, and they measure in general how capital markets assess the health and prospects of the manager's organization. It is therefore vitally important that managers know how to track economic booms and busts, and link them to share prices, using some simple but powerful tools of macroeconomics. Supplying these tools is the objective of this chapter.

---

[1] The British economist William Jevons (1835–1882) proposed that the business cycle is linked to the regular occurrence of sunspots. Both, he thought, had 11-year cycles.

Second, share prices are a *leading indicator*—that is, they tend to decline well in advance of a general economic decline, and rise in advance of economic recovery. For instance, US stock prices fell sharply in October, 1929 (the so-called Great Crash) well before the economy itself declined. This is not a hard and fast law. On October 19, 1987, US stock prices fell 20 percent in a single day. A recession was widely expected to follow, but in fact, partly due to decisive action taken by the newly-appointed head of the US Federal Reserve system, Alan Greenspan, who slashed interest rates and expanded liquidity, the US economy continued to grow strongly for another four years. This unusual episode may be an exception to the rule.[2]

The size of the world stock market (that is, the total market capitalization of shares, worldwide) was estimated at about USD 36,600 billion at the beginning of October, 2008, or nearly 60 percent of annual world GDP. The *total* world derivatives market (linked closely to equity markets) has been estimated at about USD 791,000 billion; 12 times the size of the entire world economy. Clearly, these markets are huge, and must be carefully studied in relation to boom-bust cycles.

The logic of this chapter is as follows. We first examine various theories explaining the boom–bust cycles and propose our own eclectic one, focussing on what J.M. Keynes called *animal spirits*. We then link boom–bust cycles in demand for, and supply of goods and services (GDP) with cycles in share prices, and again, propose a simple theory for understanding why share prices are highly volatile. We propose two useful tools for tracking markets for goods and services, and markets for common stock—the *twin deficit* tool, and the *real (inflation-adjusted) stock price* tool—and illustrate their use.

Let us begin our journey with some clarifying definitions, to dispel confusion surrounding many of the loosely-used terms that describe boom–bust cycles.

DEFINITIONS

Business cycles are short-term fluctuations in GDP and unemployment—cycles of recession, recovery, growth, and again recession, around a long-term growth trend, over periods of about four to eight years. They involve shifts between periods of relatively rapid growth (expansion, or boom), and periods of relative stagnation or decline (contraction, recession, or bust).

---

[2] There were special circumstances that caused this collapse. Computerized trading created an out-of-control feedback loop; a small decline in the price of stocks triggered computer-generated *sell* orders for futures and options for that stock, causing their market price to fall, triggering further *sell* orders for stock, and this automatic mechanism rapidly amplified before it could be stopped. Today so-called *circuit breaker* provisions exist that are designed to prevent a recurrence.

Trends are long-term movements in GDP, prices, income, and employment, with consistent direction and nature, over the course of a decade or more.

Recession: Once defined as "two consecutive quarters of decline in real GDP," the most recent authoritative definition is: "A significant decline in economic activity spread across the economy, lasting more than a few months, normally visible in real GDP, real income, employment, industrial production, and wholesale-retail sales."[3]

Downturn: Loosely-used phrase referring to the contraction phase of the boom-bust cycle. A downturn can mean either an actual decline in real GDP (as occurred in the US, Europe, and Japan, in 2009), or a significant slowdown in the rate of growth of GDP (as occurred in China, in 2009).

Depression: A prolonged severe economic contraction that lasts longer than a typical recession, and that afflicts economies in many parts of the world; a global economic contraction.

Inflation: A general and progressive increase in prices, often occurring during the *boom* part of the business cycle.

Deflation: A general and progressive decrease in prices, often occurring during the *bust* part of the cycle.

Trends and cycles always occur together. Cycles are superimposed on top of long-term trends. Knowing how to separate out the part of economic activity that represents a cyclical fluctuation from the long-term trend is a major challenge—much like listening to a piece of Bach and the Beatles at the same time, at full volume, and hearing both clearly.

It is a depression

How should we define the 2007–2009 global economic events—Downturn; Recession; Depression? As we write these words, the world is still in the midst of the economic decline, making it hard to define precisely. However, economist Barry Eichengreen has shown conclusively that "it is a depression, all right!"[4]

For three key indicators—world industrial production, world stock prices, and world trade—Eichengreen and O'Rourke find that the month-by-month decline from the peak of economic activity in April, 2008 has been sharper than the decline from the peak in June, 1929. The fall in stock prices has been particularly steep. See Figure 7.1 for the comparative decline in global stock prices, 1929 and 2008.

---

[3] National Bureau of Economic Research, www.nber.org.

[4] Barry Eichengreen and Kevin H. O'Rourke, "A Tale of Two Depressions." www.voxeu.org, (accessed February 3, 2010).

FIGURE 7.1   World Stock Markets, 1929 and 2008

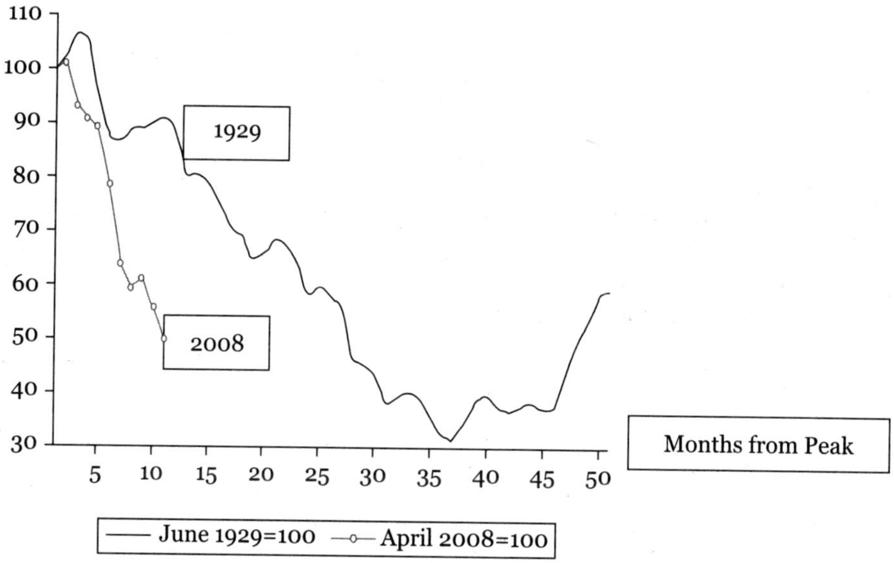

Source: "A Tale of Two Depressions," Barry Eichengreen and Kevin H. O'Rourke, http://www. voxeu.org/index.php?q=node/4225 (accessed January 18, 2010).

Why did the 2007–2009 downturn take so many knowledgeable experts by surprise, both in its magnitude and its relatively lengthy duration? Consider the American economy. Data on business cycles in the United States over 150 years, compiled by researchers at America's National Bureau for Economic Research, (see Table 7.1) show that since 1854, there have been 32 boom–bust cycles. In recent years, the duration of *boom* periods has lengthened. The boom period from the trough in November, 2001 to the peak in December, 2007 lasted 73 months, or more than six years. (A *trough* is the point in time when the recession is at its worst, and when

TABLE 7.1   Number and Duration of US Business Cycles, 1854–2007

Period	Number of Business Cycles	Average Duration (months)*
1854–1919	16	49
1919–1945	6	53
1945–2001	10	67
1854–2001	32	55
March 2001–December 2007	0	—

Source: National Bureau of Economic Research. www.nber.org/cycles.html (accessed January 18, 2010).

Note: * Duration: Number of months to peak of economic activity from the previous peak.

economic recovery begins. A *peak* is a point in time when the boom reaches its height and the economy begins to decline.) The previous boom period lasted 120 months, or 10 years, from March 1991 to March 2001.

Both the recessions of July, 1990–March 1991 and March 2001–November 2001 were short, and very mild. Hence, until December 2007 most managers had experienced only mild, and infrequent recessions for a large proportion of their working lives. It is perhaps not surprising that many of them were not mentally prepared for the severity and duration of the 2007–2009 Depression. "Those who forget the past," the philosopher Santayana once said, "are condemned to repeat it."[5] Perhaps, he might have added, those who *remember* the past may be strategically surprised by the future, when it turns out to be radically different from the past.

It seems clear from Table 7.1 that boom–bust cycles are endemic in the United States. They are also endemic in Europe and Latin America, and now have begun to afflict emerging economies. The 1997–98 Asian crisis has now been followed by the 2007–09 global downturn that has seen economic growth rates decline sharply in Japan, China, India, and other leading Asian economies.

But why? Why do these cycles recur? To anticipate them, managers need to understand their root causes.

WHAT CAUSES BOOMS AND BUSTS?

Face the brutal facts is a well-known axiom for good management, stated forcefully by management guru James Collins. It means that however painful it may be, one must always manage based on truth and hard facts. It is an advice economists should have heeded, but failed to.

Despite powerful evidence on the ground to the contrary, conventional economics taught, from about the year 1800 onward, that economic downturns accompanied by severe, involuntary unemployment cannot occur. A *law* formulated by French economist Jean Baptiste Say (1767–1832), dominated economic thinking for over a century. Say's Law states essentially that "production (supply) creates its own demand."[6] This, even though Europe experienced a deep Depression after Waterloo in 1815, when prices collapsed; even though there were eight global depressions between 1815 and 1929; and even though the United States experienced a severe

[5] "Those who forget George Santayanas dictum." http://justoneminute.typepad.com/main/2009/01/those-who-forget-george-santayanas-dictum.html (accessed January 26, 2010).

[6] Says Law, http://www.amosweb.com/cgi-bin/awb_nav.pl?s=wpd&c=dsp&k=Say's+law (accessed January 26, 2010).

23-year financial collapse and Depression, worse than in the 1930s, from 1873–1896. It is an enigma why macroeconomics—the study of national economies, including boom-bust cycles—did not truly exist until the mid-1930s, despite the need to explain and understand frequent, deep business cycles that persisted for over a century.

According to Say's Law, the production of goods provides the means for the producers to purchase what is produced, and hence, demand will grow as supply grows. If, for instance, a manufacturer in Shenzhen, China, makes a 10-yuan tie, then, it is argued, the market value of the tie is identically equal to the income the tie creates—the cost of the fabric (3 yuan), wages to the workers (3 yuan), and profit for the plant's owners (say, 4 yuan). So by definition, *there is never inadequate income in the economic system.* There is always enough income to buy what is produced. Here is what Say argued, in 1803, in his own words:

> It is worthwhile to remark that a product is no sooner created than it, from that instant, affords a market for other products to the full extent of its own value. When the producer has put the finishing hand to his product, he is most anxious to sell it immediately, lest its value should diminish in his hands. Nor is he less anxious to dispose of the money he may get for it; for the value of money is also perishable. But the only way of getting rid of money is in the purchase of some product or other. Thus *the mere circumstance of creation of one product immediately opens a vent for other products.*[7]

This *law* dominated economic thinking until the 1930s, when the global Great Depression contravened Say's Law decisively, and could no longer be ignored. In 1936, British economist John Maynard Keynes formulated as theory what was self-evident in reality—people may have sufficient *income*, but:

1. If they restrain their *spending* and save more (because of fear and uncertainty about the future, perhaps sparked by a stock market decline), and
2. If businesses do not take up the added saving to fund higher investment, aggregate demand will decline.[8]

This will create unemployment, declines in wages and incomes, and further falls in aggregate demand. The end result is a downward spiral that can create a decade-long Depression, until and unless governments intervene by injecting massive amounts

---

[7] J.B. Say, *A Treatise on Political Economy, or the Production, Distribution and Consumption of Wealth*, Trans. (Philadelphia: Lippincott, Grambo & Co., 1803 [1855]), 138–139.

[8] See J.M. Keynes, *The General Theory of Employment, Interest and Money* (New York: Harcourt Brace, 1936).

of purchasing power, which Keynes powerfully advocated. (We discuss his ideas at length later in the chapter.)

It is always and everywhere true that measured gross domestic product (supply) is identically equal to gross national income. It is *not* always true, however, that what businesses *produce* is identically equal to what people want to buy. Readers will recall that this point was discussed in Chapter Four, "A Country is a Business," where it was shown that gross domestic product (what is produced) is equal to final sales (what is actually purchased) plus inventory change (what is produced but not sold, and hence is added to inventory). When people buy less than what firms produce, and expect to sell, inventories rise. Since addition to inventories are part of business investment, this leads to unplanned investment. The result is that in the following period of time, businesses slash their current production in order to sell off goods held in inventory. This leads to unemployment, lower income, lower spending—and a recessionary spiral. This inventory effect is the proximate, though not necessarily the underlying, cause of many mild recessions. *The real question is, of course, what causes people and businesses to reduce their spending and refrain from purchasing all that is produced, causing inventories to grow?*

A wide variety of theories exists, each seeking to explain the underlying cause of the boom–bust cycle. A brief summary is provided below. Managers can easily be confused by this blinding variety of theories. We provide brief capsule descriptions (see Box 7.1) of a variety of business-cycle theories. There are elements of truth in each of them; each of these theories can point to supporting evidence in the 2007–09 crisis.

BOX 7.1   Varieties of Business Cycle Theories

A great many theories exist to explain boom–bust cycles. Here is a brief summary of the main models:

- Government policy: It is sometimes argued that government policy itself exacerbates, or even causes, rather than mitigates, business cycles. In what has been called the stop-go cycle, promulgated especially by critics of Britain's economic policies in the 1950s and 1960s, it was argued that Britain's monetary and fiscal policy braked, or stimulated, the economy, very vigorously, but always too late. This made the business cycle worse than it would have been in the absence of any policy, braking the economy when it was already slowing, or stimulating it when it had begun to grow.[9]

(Box 7.1 continued)

---

[9] Oxford Economic Dictionary, OUP. www.enotes.com (accessed January 18, 2010).

(*Box 7.1 continued*)

- Politics: Related to stop-go is the so-called *political cycle*. Democracies have elections every four years or so. In the two years prior to the election, governments stimulate the economy, creating a boom, in order to be elected or re-elected. In the two years after it, they brake the economy, creating a bust, to resolve the problems created during the boom. This so-called political cycle has been documented in nearly every democracy. One researcher noted, "U.S. Presidential elections every four years have a profound impact on the economy and the stock market. Wars, recessions and bear markets tend to start or occur in the first half of the term and bull markets, in the latter half."[10] Another study found that, "... from 1941 through 2000, (U.S.) stock market lows have occurred surprisingly close to mid-year congressional elections, or approximately two years before presidential elections."[11]
- Cyclical responses to initial shocks: This theory, due to J.M. Keynes and expanded by MIT Professor Paul Samuelson, shows how the complex interaction between consumers (personal consumption), and businesses (investment) can create cycles. Each added dollar of consumer-spending multiplies into three or four dollars of added spending, as spending creates successive *rounds* of spending, output, added employment, higher income, more spending, and so on. This is known as the *multiplier* (discussed below). For businesses, booming sales—perhaps caused by the *multiplier*— lead to higher investment, in turn creating higher output, income, and spending, leading to higher investment spending to expand productive capacity. This mechanism is known as the *accelerator*. The multiplier and accelerator interact to create boom– bust cycles. When both spending and investment become *excessive*, consumers and businesses brake their demands, leading to economic decline, amplified by *reverse* multiplier and accelerator effects. For instance, in a downturn, businesses have excess productive capacity, and so may cease buying new assets completely (rather than simply reduce investment spending by 5 or 10 percent). This implies that investment is a highly volatile component of GDP, more so than other components.
- Real business cycles: External *innovation* shocks occur, as new technologies replace old ones, and economies decline, then boom, as investment pauses, and then accelerates. In this theory, business cycles are not a sign of inefficiency or market failure, but rather a sign of rejuvenation, implying that governments should not try to intervene or *smooth* the cycle. If they do, they just make things worse. In the 2007–2009 crisis, it is evident that the world has not yet discovered the next huge consumer appliance

(*Box 7.1 continued*)

---

[10] Yale Hirsch and Jeffrey Hirsch, *The Stock Trader's Almanac 2004* (Hoboken, NJ: John Wiley and Sons, 2004), 127.

[11] Marshall D. Nickles, "Presidential Elections and Stock Market Cycles: Can you Profit from the Relationship?" (Working Paper, *Graziadio Business Report*, 7, no. 3, Pepperdine University 2004). http://gbr.pepperdine.edu/043/stocks.html (accessed January 18, 2010).

(*Box 7.1 continued*)

> fad; radios, TVs, computers and cell phones in turn drove waves of expansion, but their successor has, many believe, not yet made its appearance. However, it will. TV was invented in the 1930s. And personal computers were born during the 1977–1979 and 1980–1982 stagflation (falling GDP, or stagnation, accompanied by rising prices, or inflation), and recession periods.
>
> - Marx: Capital accumulation causes profit rates to fall, leading businesses to merge and create monopolies, to reduce wages, leading to economic crisis.
> - Credit cycles: In boom times, banks overlend, businesses and people over-borrow, as interest rates fall, and real (inflation-adjusted) rates may become negative. When borrowing halts, as a result of over-leverage, investment slows, asset prices decline, and the economy dives into recession.

In the face of so many different theories, we clearly need an eclectic one that adapts and integrates the most valid parts of other theories. We now proceed to construct one.

TOWARD A GROUNDED THEORY OF BOOM–BUST CYCLES

In thinking independently about boom–bust cycles, and trying to track them, managers would do well to avoid the fierce theory wars of economists, and to simplify, by focussing on four key market-based questions that drive boom–bust cycles, and that underlie all of the business-cycle theories listed in Box 7.1.

- Do people have money and are they optimistic and keen to spend it? Or are they concerned about debt and pessimistic about losing their jobs?
- Are businesses making profits and are they keen to reinvest them, in creating new assets (buildings, machineries, equipment, software)?
- Do governments have money and are they keen to spend it, beyond what they absorb in tax revenues?
- Are businesses selling more abroad to other nations than is being bought from abroad, that is, do exports exceed (or fall short of) imports, and is the gap widening or shrinking?

The first two questions require managers to track the underlying sentiment that drives personal consumption and business investment. The latter two questions require that we track, (and perhaps forecast) two key deficits: The budget deficit, and the trade deficit. This, it emerges, generates a simple and powerful tool for tracking national economies.

ACTION LEARNING

Using the Four Question Framework

For the country in which you live or work, answer these four boom–bust questions. How can you find data that generate accurate answers? How can you supplement such data with your own observations, in stores, malls and workplaces? Do your answers lead you to conclusions that differ from those of the forecasting experts? Why? Above all, can you anticipate major shifts in consumption, investment, public spending, and trade?

THE CRUCIAL ROLE OF THE CONSUMER

For *grasshopper* Western economies, which emphasize spending over saving, the behavior of consumers and consumer spending play a key role. Any theory that seeks to explain business cycles must understand what drives consumer spending. This is vital, even for understanding Asian *ant* economies, because in large measure those economies too have been driven by Western consumer spending creating demand for their exports. A simple theory built by J.M. Keynes, known as the *multiplier*, explains why consumer demand is so important.

Over the past 59 years, American households spent an additional 71 cents on personal consumption out of every additional GDP dollar; the remaining 29 cents went to taxes, depreciation, and saving. The relationship between consumption (C) and GDP (Q) has been quite stable and linear:

$$\text{Personal Consumption} = \text{Constant} + 0.71\,\text{GDP}$$

Suppose, now, state governments rebuild crumbling public schools, or fill potholes on state highways, and spend an added USD 1 billion (without raising taxes). What will the effect of that USD 1 billion be? Assume that there is sufficient unused resources—labor (millions of unemployed), and capital (unused factories), available to satisfy demand. Initially, GDP grows by USD 1 billion. As a result, incomes rise, too. As incomes grow, personal consumption grows by about USD 0.71 billion, as the above equation shows. But that spending generates additional GDP as people demand more clothing, food, housing, entertainment, travel, etc. So GDP rises by USD 0.71 billion. As a result, personal consumption grows by 0.71 × 0.71 = USD 0.50 ..., and so on.

An infinite geometric series results:

USD 1 billion + 0.71 billion + .50 billion + 0.36 billion + 0.25 billion ... etc.

The formula for the sum of a geometric series is:

$$SUM = 1/(1 - a)$$

where "a" is the constant multiplicative factor in the geometric series. In the case of the Keynesian multiplier, this *factor* is the fraction of each dollar of GDP spent on personal consumption, termed by Keynes "the marginal propensity to consume." For the US it is 0.71, as noted.

In the above example, therefore, the USD 1 billion initial stimulus generates USD 3.448 billion in overall GDP growth:

$$SUM = (USD\ 1\ billion)\ [1/(1 - 0.71)] = USD\ 1\ billion\ times\ 3.448 = USD\ 3.448$$
billion.

As GDP grows, so does employment; in fact, Keynes and his associates termed this mechanism *the employment multiplier*. This *multiplier* theory shows that the stimulative role of personal consumption is powerful. In the nine-year expansionary period 1992–2000, in the US, and in the 1980–1989 period, consumer spending was the major engine of sustained growth for the US economy. From 1980–1996, American households saved 12 cents out of every dollar of spendable income in 1980. In 1996, they saved only 3.3 cents. And in 2007, they saved virtually nothing. In contrast, both Japanese and German households saved more than 12 percent of their disposable income in the same year. And over the 20 year period 1980–2000, Americans spent 109 percent of the increase in their spendable disposable income. They did this, because they believed they were indeed saving, as the value of their houses, and financial assets rose rapidly. Those capital gains turned out tragically to be ephemeral.

Is this high spending a problem? Or is it a solution? What is so wonderful about high saving anyway? Between 1982 and 1990, Americans spent their way to the longest economic expansion since World War II. The reason is clear. Ronald Reagan ran for President in the 1980 Presidential elections on a platform of promised tax cuts. His theory was that lower taxes would encourage saving, leading to higher investment and lower interest rates. When he became President, Reagan kept his promise, slashing income taxes substantially twice, in 1981 and again in 1987. But the American taxpayer behaved differently than Reagan's theory. Americans spent the tax cut rather than save it. The result was a Keynesian *multiplier* boom, not a savings–investment boom.

After recovery from the 1991 recession, the American economy again spent itself to another 10-year expansion. Japan, in contrast, is struggling to emerge from a zero GDP growth long recession that began in 1990.

Spending can occur either out of current income or through incurring debt. Debt, like inventories, is also a strong driver of business cycles, and growth trends. For cycles, *excessive* debt can cause consumers to slow their spending until debt is paid off or reduced. The growth trend of 1980–1997 in the US was powered in part by a remarkable rise of 25 percentage points in the ratio of household debt to household income, from 70 percent in 1980 to about 100 percent today. This means households owed fully a year's income at the end of the period. Current debt levels of households thus bear close watching. In the 2007–2009 crisis, American consumers have cut back spending in order to pay their heavy debts. Household debt in the United Kingdom is proportionately even heavier.

When households become nervous about this debt, especially in the face of higher interest rates and debt-service charges, spending contracts, and with it the economy. Credit card delinquencies are a good early-warning indicator; in the US they have been rising strongly since 1994, and as of March 2009, exceed 4 percent of outstanding loans, a record high. Many experts expect that credit card debt default will be the next US financial crisis.

CASE STUDY

Keynes and the Rains in Spain[12]

 There are cycles in fashionable economic theories, just as there are cycles in business. For many years, following the publication of Keynes' General Theory (1936), Keynesian theory was highly fashionable among economists. In the 1970s, it fell out of fashion, partly because the theory was misused and misinterpreted. Keynes focussed on the primary cause of the Great Depression of the 1930s lack of demand. But the primary cause of the Great Stagflation (falling GDP, or stagnation, accompanied by rising prices, or inflation) of the 1970s was not on the demand side, but on the supply side—cost-push (see the discussion on cost-push versus demand-pull inflation).

(*Case Study continued*)

---

[12] This case study is based on Paul Day, "Spain rearranges furniture as economy sinks," *Reuters*, May 27, 2009. http://www.reuters.com/article/idUSLQ6131620090527 (accessed January 18, 2010).

(*Case Study continued*)

Using Keynesian demand-stimulus remedies to cure a supply-side *illness* proved disastrous. Misuse of a treatment should not invalidate the treatment—but in this case, it apparently did. As two senior economists recently noted:

> The dominance of Keynesianism ended in the 1970s. Government spending and deficits ballooned, but the result was higher inflation, not lower unemployment. These events, and the rise in monetarism led by Milton Friedman, [strengthened the belief that] Keynesianism was flawed and its prescription of active fiscal intervention was misguided.[13]

In the global crisis of 2007–2009, Keynesian theory has made a powerful comeback—*it is fashionable again*. Spain is a case in point. Spain has had the worst economic downturn of any European Union country. Spain's unemployment rate is expected to hit a staggering 20.5 percent in 2010. Spain's socialist government has reacted by reviving Keynesian policies. As a result, there are (to paraphrase My Fair Lady): Keynes' *rains* (of money) in the plains of Spain. Journalist Paul Day writes:

> Moving a 17-meter high monument to Christopher Columbus 100 meters down the road is how the Spanish government is interpreting the advice of John Maynard Keynes. The economist once argued it would be preferable to pay workers to dig holes in the ground, and fill them in again, rather than allowing them to stand idle and deprive the economy of the multiplier effect of their wages. So Spain's government is paying for the return of the concrete-based monument, topped by a three-meter marble statue of the Italian explorer, to a roundabout in the middle of Madrid's Plaza Colon—exactly where it had stood for almost 100 years until 1973. Plan E (Spanish Plan for Economic Stimulus and Employment) is part of Spain's equivalent to the *New Deal* US President Franklin D. Roosevelt devised in response to The Great Depression, a plan partly drawn up by Keynes himself. Moving the Columbus monument will take 65 workers until the end of the year. For them, the project gives Spain a little time to find a longer-term solution to unemployment that is rising faster than in any other European Union country.[14]

(*Case Study continued*)

---

[13] Ike Brannan and Chris Edwards, "Barack Obama's Keynesian Mistake," *Exception Magazine*, February 2, 2009. http://www.exceptionmag.com/politics/government/000302/barack-obamas-keynesian-mistake (accessed January 18, 2010).

[14] Paul Day, "Spain rearranges furniture as economy sinks," *Reuters*, May 27, 2009. www.forexyard.com.

(*Case Study continued*)

Spain, like other countries struggling to create jobs in the face of the global depression, confronts a bitter dilemma: balancing short-term *hole-digging* make-work stopgaps with long-term strategic change.

"The question is how to balance the short term 'hole digging' approach with investments which may not provide so much bang for the buck in the short term, but are good for long-term productivity," said Eswar Prasad, Senior Professor of Trade Policy at Cornell University. "*Everyone, from China to the United States is grappling for that balance.*"[15]

Spain has gone from a budget surplus of 2.2 percent of GDP, in 2007, to an anticipated 10 percent deficit in 2010. The result has been for bond rating agencies to downgrade Spanish bonds, which raises the interest rates the Spanish government must pay on its bonds, in turn further boosting expenditures, and worsening the deficit. Ireland, too, faced similar capital market pressures after its deficit ballooned. Spain, Ireland, US, and other countries face a painful and bitter choice between *fiscal suicide* and *criminal complacency*.

FISCAL SUICIDE OR CRIMINAL COMPLACENCY?

"More than any other time in history, mankind faces a crossroads," comedian and film director Woody Allen once quipped. "One path leads to despair and utter hopelessness. The other, to total extinction. Let us pray we have the wisdom to choose correctly."[16]

It is no laughing matter. In today's global crisis, virtually every country in the world today faces a similar thorny choice. No nation, to our knowledge, has fully solved the problem. The hard choice, stated baldly, is this: Fiscal suicide? Or criminal complacency?

Fiscal suicide: Defined as excessive irresponsible government spending to stimulate collapsing economies, creating enormous debt burdens that cripple future generations and scare away foreign investors, driving stock prices down, but have little impact on current jobs and incomes. Ireland, for instance, climbed onto the fiscal suicide ledge, then stepped back. Journalist Eamon Quinn recently wrote in the International Herald Tribune: "...Asserting Ireland must restore international

---

[15] Day, Op. cit. www.northexasism.net

[16] C. Christopher Hook, "The Techno Sapiens Are Coming." http://www.christianitytoday.com/ct/2004/january/1.36.html (accessed January 26, 2010).

confidence in its debt-laden economy, Finance Minister Brian Lenihan announced an emergency budget plan [that included] higher taxes and lower government spending to bring the deficit in line."[17]

Consider the following article from *Time* magazine:

...last week in Washington ... [there] emerged a major agreement: Federal taxes must be jumped up. The [] deficit was pointing inevitably toward ... billion dollars ... into such a colossal hole the Treasury could no longer keep pouring bond issue after bond issue. More revenue was imperative to save the Government's good credit.[18]

This passage could have come from today's *Wall Street Journal*. It could describe the United States—with a near USD 300 billion deficit in 1992 or Germany trying to get its budget deficit down to 3 percent of GDP, to meet requirements for European Monetary Union, or France, Italy or Spain, or Japan. But it does not. *It is from the November 30, 1931 issue of Time magazine.* The "[]" refers to a USD 2 billion deficit in 1932. Over a year after the Great Depression got underway, both lay persons and experts alike still thought the core problem was growing budget deficits, and that the solution was to raise taxes. In his radio fireside chats, President Franklin Delano Roosevelt preached saving, not spending, as a cure for Depression. He was concerned about fiscal suicide, and downplayed criminal complacency.

Criminal complacency: Defined as obsessively trimming budget deficits, and slashing spending, in the face of declining tax revenues, to avoid future debts, and to curry favor with credit-rating agencies, thus failing to create jobs and allowing unemployment to reach levels above 10 percent of the workforce that destabilize society, and create enormous human suffering. For example, Nobel Laureate and *New York Times* columnist Paul Krugman claims that:

...people who think fiscal expansion today is bad for future generations have got it exactly wrong. The best course of action both for today's workers and for their children is to do whatever it takes to get this economy on the road to recovery.[19]

---

[17] Eamon Quinn, "Ireland's emergency budget includes help for banks," April 7, 2009. http://www.nytimes.com/2009/04/08/business/global/08irecon.htm (accessed January 26, 2010).

[18] *Time*, "TAXATION: Jumps & junket," Monday, November 30, 1931. www.time.com/time/magazine/article/0,9171,753132,00.html (accessed February 3, 2010).

[19] Paul Krugman, "Large fiscal expansion today is essential to save economy for future generations," December 1, 2008. http://thejakartaglobe.com/business/large-fiscal-expansion-today-is-essential-to-save-economy-for-future-generations/301557 (accessed January 26, 2010).

How can policymakers steer the ship of state between these two disastrous Woody-Allen-like reefs?

Somehow, countries all over the world, including the US must find creative ways to square the circle of maintaining fiscal health while engaging in massive job-creating government intervention. Despite deep uncertainty, they must act quickly, and decisively.

New thinking on deficits: A major change in public attitude toward budget deficits and spending was due in large measure to one man—J.M Keynes. Keynes (1883–1946) was a British-born economist who invented modern macroeconomics. He specifically tackled the question: What causes recessions and depressions, and what should governments do about it. Keynes himself had deep insight into the psychological forces that underlie fluctuations in aggregate demand. He gave these forces the rather unusual name of *animal spirits*. It is animal spirits that were largely responsible for driving down global asset prices and demand, and it is animal spirits that global managers must seek to understand and to track. This is a major reason why *minds* appears in our book's subtitle, along with money and markets. We now proceed to build an *animal spirit* theory of the business cycle.

ANIMAL SPIRITS

In Keynes' landmark 1936 book *The General Theory*, which struggled to explain the Great Depression then afflicting the major economies of the world, there is the following passage:

> ...There is instability due to the characteristic of human nature that a large proportion of our positive activities depend on spontaneous optimism rather than mathematical expectations. ... Our decisions to do something positive ... can only be taken as the result of animal spirits—a spontaneous urge to action rather than inaction....[20]

Expanding on this concept, economist Russell Fowler observed:

> The economy is solidly based on human nature. When things are going good, some human reactions occur: overconfidence, complacency, poor workmanship, greed, overexpansion, mistakes; all bad and leading to a downturn. Then, when things are going bad, there's a tendency to shape up and turn things around....[21]

---

[20] J.M. Keynes, *The General Theory of Employment, Interest and Money* (London: Macmillan, 1936), 161–162.

[21] Russell Fowler, cited in Alfred Malabre Jr., *Lost Prophets* (Harvard Business School Press, 1993), 232.

In other words, ultimately, every market is driven by psychology. Markets will continue to rise and fall with the animal spirits of human beings. Those spirits are the ultimate drivers of trends and cycles. And it is those spirits that explain why boom-bust cycles are a permanent part of the business landscape.

For managers, the key issue here is whether *animal spirits*—spontaneous urges to spend, buy or sell assets or houses, and engage in other economic activities—are rational and predictable, or whether they are essentially random. The title of a powerful best-selling book by Dan Ariely supplies the answer: Predictably Irrational.[22] Many elements of consumer behavior are what economists regard as *irrational*. Yet they are not random—they are predictable. As Ariely observes:

> What we've learned is that relying on standard economic theory alone as a guiding principle for building markets and institutions might, in fact, be dangerous. It has become tragically clear that the mistakes we all make are not at all random, but part and parcel of the human condition. Worse, our mistakes of judgment can aggregate in the market, sparking a scenario in which, much like an earthquake, no one has any idea what is happening.[23]

In recent years, the concept of *viral marketing* (employing social networks to create rapid communication from one person to many others, about products, brands, etc.) has become widely used. There may also exist something called *viral animal spirits*. Ariely cites research by Nicholas Christakis, a physician and sociologist at Harvard University. Using data from a study that tracked about 5,000 people over 20 years, Christakis found that happiness, like the flu, can spread from person to person:

> When people who are close to us, both in terms of social ties (friends or relatives) and physical proximity, become happier, we do too. For example, when a person who lives within a mile of a good friend becomes happier, the probability that this person's good friend will also become happier increases 15%. More surprising is that the effect can transcend direct links and reach a third degree of separation: when a friend of a friend becomes happier, we become happier, even when we don't know that third person directly.[24]

---

[22] Dan Ariely, *Predictably Irrational: The Hidden Forces that Shape our Decisions* (New York: Harper Collins, 2008).

[23] Source: Dan Ariely, Blog: "2008 was a good year for behavioral economics." www.predictablyirrational.com May 20, 2009, http://www.predictablyirrational.com/?page_id=17&paged=3 (accessed January 18, 2010).

[24] James H. Fowler and Nicholas A. Christakis, "Dynamic Spread of Happiness in a Large Social Network: Longitudinal Analysis Over 20 Years in the Framingham Heart Study," *British Medical Journal*, December 4, 2008. www.bmj.com/cgi/content/full/337/dec04_2/a2338 (accessed February 3, 2010).

We surmise that the *animal spirits* optimism that fuels consumer spending, and rising asset prices spreads virally, in the same way Christakis found that happiness spreads. The opposite, Christakis found, is less robust; sadness spreads more slowly than happiness—but nonetheless, it spreads. Political leaders sometimes try to manipulate this effect, by speaking optimistically when the economy is in a downturn. This rarely works, because instead of imbuing optimism, it breeds skepticism, cynicism and mistrust, which sometimes becomes pessimism.

Another key element of animal spirits is the effect of perceived uncertainty. When consumers and investors feel certain about the future, they are happier. When they are uncertain, they are unhappy. It turns out, according to research by Harvard psychologist Daniel Gilbert, that the unhappiness caused by the economic downturn in the US is not directly because people have less wealth and less income, but rather because they simply do not know what the future holds, and are troubled by this uncertainty. He observes:

> Our (America's) national gloom is real enough, but it isn't a matter of insufficient funds. Americans have been perfectly happy with far less wealth than most of us have now, and we could quickly become those Americans again—if only we knew we had to.[25]

What does this brief discussion of *animal spirits* imply for global managers? In a previous chapter, we discussed the rather vague notion of *national energy* as a key determinant of economic growth and dynamism. Here, we argue that *national mood* is a key determinant of booms and busts. Booms are characterized by optimism, perhaps excessive, and busts are characterized by pessimism, also frequently excessive. Optimism and pessimism spread rapidly, like influenza epidemics. The *bust* ends and becomes a boom, when optimism returns, when uncertainty dissipates, and when consumers and investors feel sufficiently confident and secure about the future to engage in new spending and investment.

This *animal spirits* theory is a cause for both optimism and pessimism among global managers—pessimism, because *national mood* is very hard to quantify and measure (see Box 7.2), and optimism, because managers who interact daily with workers and customers, *who diligently cultivate listening skills and who become skilled at hearing the national mood* can gain insights and can foresee developments even better than experts equipped with thousands of *hard* data sets (see Action Learning exercise on p. 235). The *soft stuff* (national mood) is, indeed, the hard stuff—both in terms of the difficulty entailed in gathering information, and in terms of its strong, real impact on the prices of assets, including common shares.

---

[25] Daniel Gilbert, "What you don't know makes you nervous," *New York Times*, May 20, 2009; see also his book *Stumbling on Happiness* (Alfred Knopf: New York, 2008).

BOX 7.2   Consumer Sentiment

One of the strongest attempts to assess animal spirits, and link national mood with consumer spending, is a measure known as the Index of Consumer Sentiment.

Such an index exists for the US and for major European countries. Two organizations in the US each measure consumer sentiment: University of Michigan, and The Conference Board, a non-profit consulting organization. The methods are the same—a brief questionnaire asks a monthly random sample of people whether they are better off now than six months ago, whether they expect to be better off in six months than they are now, and whether they plan to make a major purchase (car, house, appliance). As we write this, Reuters news agencies reports: "European shares gain on U.S. consumer confidence."[26] Reporter Brian Gorman writes that:

European shares gained on Tuesday, reversing earlier losses, after U.S. consumer sentiment readings came in stronger than expected. *U.S. consumer confidence soared in May to its highest level in eight months* as severe strains in the labor market showed some signs of easing, though the mood of Americans remained depressed by historical standards.

Because of the 5–7 hour time difference, European stock markets begin trading before markets open in the US, hence they react first to newly-announced American data.

ACTION LEARNING

Gauging Animal Spirits

Global managers constantly measure the pulse of business sentiment first-hand, by talking to clients, fellow workers and the *man or woman in the street*, as well as by tracking surveys of consumer sentiment and business sentiment.

Do you regularly engage in such informal conversations? Do you cross-check by matching survey data with your own observations? Can you acquire a sense of *animal spirits* through these conversations?

Some excellent sources of such data are: taxi drivers (taxis are sensitive to the business cycle, because people walk or take public transportation when their incomes decline); restaurants (also sensitive to business conditions); shopping malls (are they crowded, and are people carrying packages, or simply window-shopping?).

---

[26] Brian Gorman, "European shares gain on U.S. consumer confidence", May 26, 2009. http://www.reuters.com/article/idUSLQ10898020090526 (accessed January 18, 2010).

THE TWIN DEFICITS AS BOOM–BUST DRIVERS

Tool # 7

Twin Deficits: Tracking the Government Budget Deficit and the Trade Deficit

Recessions are caused by short-term declines in demand, arising from one or more of four possible sources: declines in consumer spending and business investment, decreases in budget deficits and increases in trade deficits. Earlier in this chapter, we listed four key questions that help track business cycles. The first two related to consumer spending, and business investment. The last two related to government budgets, and to trade. In what follows, we explain the link between the budget deficit and the trade deficit, and how this concept can become a powerful tool for tracking the course of the business cycle. Using it, we can develop useful scenarios regarding when the current global downturn will end—a topic surrounded by enormous doubt and uncertainty.

One way to track aggregate demand is to follow closely the path of the government budget deficit (the difference between what governments spend, and what they earn in tax revenues), and the trade deficit (the difference between what a country sells abroad, in exports, and what it buys abroad, as imports). Predicted changes in these two deficits can tell us much about whether the demand in an economy is expected to grow or to shrink. If you follow closely whether businesses, governments, households, and individuals have growing spendable incomes, and whether they are eager to spend them—you will know a lot about the future course of the economy.

To construct this tool, we recall the definition of GDP given in Chapter Four:

$$\text{GDP} \equiv \text{Personal Consumption} + \text{Public Consumption}$$
$$+ \text{Gross Capital Formation} - (\text{Imports} - \text{Exports})$$

We expand this definition slightly, to place *disposable income* on the left hand side of the definition rather than GDP. Disposable income is equal to GDP minus *net taxes* (taxes paid to the government less transfers received from the government). It is the amount of income people have to spend, or to save:

$$\text{GDP} \equiv \text{Disposal Income} + \text{Net Taxes}$$

(*Tool 7 continued*)

(*Tool 7 continued*)

Therefore it follows that:

Disposable Income ≡ Personal Consumption + Gross Capital Formation
+ (Public Consumption − Net Taxes) (*budget deficit*)
− (Imports − Exports) (*trade deficit*)

Public consumption less net taxes is the government budget deficit.[27] Imports less exports is the trade deficit. Note a key fact: *These deficits impact disposable income in opposite directions.* The budget deficit increases disposable income, by pumping demand into the system, both directly and indirectly through the Keynesian multiplier. The trade deficit reduces disposable income by diverting purchasing power from the domestic economic system, to foreign economies, through imports, by *leaking* spending and jobs to foreigners.

It follows from the above logic that when we hold personal consumption and gross capital formation constant:

Change in Disposal Income ≡ Change in the budget deficit
minus the change in the trade deficit

Hence, to track changes in the economy, we need to know whether the expected change in the budget deficit will be larger than the change in the trade deficit. When each of these two deficits is changing, the net impact on the economy can be analyzed by asking: Is the budget deficit shrinking faster than the trade deficit?

There are four possibilities:

1. Both deficits are growing. The impact on the economy will then depend on which is growing faster. If the budget deficit grows faster than the trade deficit, disposable income will rise; if it grows slower, disposable income will fall.
2. Both deficits are shrinking. The impact on the economy will then depend on which is shrinking faster. If the budget deficit declines

(*Tool 7 continued*)

---

[27] The budget deficit equals spending less taxes. Spending in turn equals public consumption plus transfer payments (payments that do not purchase real goods or services, but simply transfer money from one pocket to another; for example, unemployment insurance). It follows that the deficit equals public consumption plus transfers minus taxes, or public consumption minus net taxes.

(*Tool 7 continued*)

by more than the trade deficit, disposable income falls; if the budget deficit declines by less than the trade deficit, disposable income rises.

3. The budget deficit grows, the trade deficit shrinks; unequivocally, each change causes disposable income to grow.

4. The budget deficit shrinks, while the trade deficit grows: unequivocally, each change causes disposable income to decline.

Shrinking disposable income leads to "bust." Growing disposable income leads to "boom."

What is the connection between the twin-deficit tool and the business cycle? It is straightforward. Government policy seeks, in general, to smooth business cycles, to cool the economy when it is overheating, and stimulate it when it stagnates. To this end, policies operate directly through the budget (so-called *fiscal policy*) and indirectly, through the trade deficit (exchange rate policies, discussed in Chapter Eight).

But often, we find the opposite. Policy measures *aggravate or create* a business cycle. This can happen, for instance, because of multiple lags in time. Policymakers identify an economic slowdown months after it happens, take many more months to formulate the policy, then more months pass as the policy is implemented and its impact is felt—and by the time the policy affects the economy, the business cycle may be in the *boom* stage rather than *bust*, meaning that the policies achieve an effect opposite to that intended. For this reason, global managers who diligently track (and anticipate) business cycles must keep a close watch on the government budget, and on anti-cyclical policy. The *twin-deficit* approach is a good way to do this.

CASE STUDY

The American Albatross

 Two puzzling questions exist about the US economy. America's GDP growth was relatively strong during the 1980s and 1990s but weakened during the first decade of the 2000s:

Decade Average Annual	1980–89	1990–99	2000–09
GDP growth (Percentage)	3.07%	3.11%	1.79%

(*Case Study continued*)

(*Case Study continued*)

- Why did its growth during 2000–2009 lag behind the two previous decades (even before the 2007–2009 crisis)?
- And why have massive budget deficits not helped stimulate the economy after the 2007–2009 crisis?

The difference may seem small—only about 1.3 percent of GDP—but measured in terms of lost employment, lower wage gains and lost GDP, it is large (1.3 percent of America's annual GDP amounts, today, to USD 187 billion, more than the GDP of most countries; over a decade, it totals USD 1.87 trillion).

Why did this happen? The twin-deficit tool provides some answers (see Figure 7.2).

FIGURE 7.2   United States, 1987–2009: Budget Deficit for State, Local, and Federal Governments; and Trade Deficit (Imports minus Exports), USD Billions.

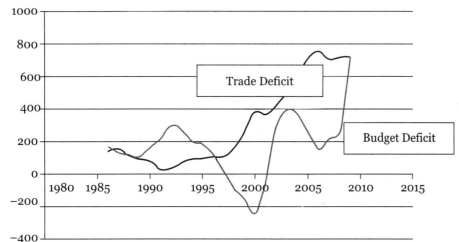

Source: Authors (based on data from Economic Report of the President 2009: Council of Economic Advisors, US Govt Printing Office: Washington, D.C., February 2009).

In Figure 7.2 we see that *from 1992 America has had an albatross around its economic neck*—the trade deficit.[28] Its trade deficit, which *reduces*

(*Case Study continued*)

----

[28] In Coleridge's famous poem, the Ancient Mariner shoots an albatross (an omen of bad luck) and is forced to wear it around his neck as punishment.

(*Case Study continued*)

disposable income, has been consistently larger than its budget deficit, which *increases* disposable income.

In 1992, the Budget Deficit Reduction Act passed Congress (very narrowly).

The result was dramatic—the deficit soon became a large and growing surplus. At the same time, the strengthening US dollar led to stronger imports, and a growing trade deficit. These two trends each operated strongly to slow the US economy, and eventually contributed to the 2001 economic recession.

In 2009–2010, the federal budget deficit is expected to amount to a staggering 13 percent of GDP. This should have a powerful impact on the American economy. But so far it has not. Figure 7.2 shows that with the trade deficit still large and growing—*virtually every dollar pumped in to the economy by the budget deficit is taken out of the economy again by the "leakage" caused by the excess of imports over exports.* Even the weaker dollar has not helped to spur exports, because America has shifted so much of its manufacturing offshore; it may now be cost-effective to produce in America, but few US factories exist that can exploit this to boost exports.

Is there a causal link between the budget deficit and the trade deficit? At this stage, it is sufficient to note that a budget deficit (government spending exceeds revenues) represents *negative government saving*. This means governments need to borrow, to finance the deficit. They can either borrow by selling bonds to individuals and businesses at home, in their own country, or abroad. If domestic saving is insufficient to fund government borrowing, as in the US, then government bonds must be sold abroad (importing capital). As Chapter Eight explains, a surplus of imports over exports necessarily implies that capital is imported from abroad. US sale of Treasury bonds abroad, to China and Japan, has been massive. Lacking domestic savings to finance its deficits, the US government has had to sell its bonds abroad.

BOOM-BUST CYCLES AND THE STOCK MARKET

For global managers who seek to track the boom–bust cycle, it is essential to track stock markets closely. The price of common stock has been shown to be a leading indicator of business downturns—that means, stock prices tend to fall in advance of the economic decline. During the current crisis, global economic activity reached a peak in April 2008. Within five months of that peak, global share prices fell by over

20 percent (see Figure 7.1), well before GDP began to decline significantly in most countries. Worldwide, share prices have now fallen by half. This was both a portend, and a cause, of the decline in real-world GDP.

There are two reasons why in theory stock prices should predict the economy:

- First, stock prices are an important *engine* driving the economy. For instance, when consumers' wealth in stocks rises, for each dollar in added wealth, spending rises by between two and seven cents. This is true, even when the capital gains are ephemeral, driven by what later turns out to be a *bubble* (discussed below). Indirectly, higher stock prices enable businesses to raise capital, and hence expand their investment. Lower stock prices globally *destroyed* enormous amounts of wealth, making consumers poorer, and ultimately leading them to slash their spending.
- Second, stock prices are *forward looking*, that is, they are determined by investors who look ahead, and buy or sell shares based on their expectations of future profits. To the extent that investors are good at forecasting, current stock prices will reflect future earnings, which in turn reflect the future state of the economy.

Empirical evidence shows that "the stock market does predict the economy."[29] The reverse is also true, through wealth effects—capital losses in the stock market make investors poorer, hence less likely to spend.

In many countries, as we noted in Chapter One, equity markets have grown faster than the economy, because of *asset monetization*—real businesses create new paper assets that reflect their value, by issuing debt (selling bonds), and by selling common shares to investors. A large and growing proportion of real productive assets, therefore, are backed by financial (paper) assets traded in capital markets.

Table 7.2 shows the relative size of the value of common stock (*market capitalization*) in August 2007, just at the onset of the global downturn, as a proportion of GDP, for 10 major nations. This table shows that for six of the 10 countries, the value of common stocks (that is, the market capitalization of companies' common stocks traded in that country's stock exchanges) in August, 2007 exceeded the annual value of GDP for 2007, and approximately equaled annual GDP for two nations (China and India). (Hong Kong, a part of China, is unique, because a major fraction of Chinese stocks trade there, hence its high market cap/GDP ratio.)

---

[29] Among many studies, see B. Comincioli, "The Stock Market as a Leading Indicator", *Univ. Avenue Undergraduate Journal of Economics* (1996); his study was for the US, 1970–94.

TABLE 7.2 Market Capitalization of Stocks and GDP, 10 Countries, August 2007

	Country	Market Cap $ b.	GDP $ b.	Market Cap/GDP %
1.	USA	17,923	13,841	129
2.	Japan	4,615	4,380	105
3.	United Kingdom	3,722	2,770	134
4.	China	3,059	3,242	94
5.	France	2,653	2,556	104
6.	Hong Kong	2,180	207	1053
7.	Germany	1,976	3,317	60
8.	Canada	1,620	1,426	114
9.	Switzerland	1,207	424	285
10.	India	1,090	1,135	96

Source: World Competitiveness Yearbook 2009, Table 3.3.10, "Stock Market Capitalization," p. 397 (Lausanne, Switzerland, IMD: June 2009).

Hence, the magnitude of the wealth embodied in common shares, and the weather-vane nature of the stock market, make it imperative that global managers track global share prices carefully and consistently.

One American in five now holds shares directly, compared with only four of every 100 in the 1950s. When indirect equity holdings (like pension funds) are considered, four Americans in 10 have an equity stake. In 1995, for the first time in American history, propelled by soaring stock prices, the value of family holdings of stock surpassed the value of home equity.[30] The stock-market bubble of the 1990s drove the value of common stocks well beyond the annual value of US GDP.

FROM BULL MARKET TO BEAR MARKET AND BACK TO BULL MARKET: 1955–2000

People love mysteries. Each year, many millions of mystery fiction books are bought, which challenge readers to figure out *who-dunnit*—who committed the murder?

There is a fascinating *who-dunnit* mystery involving share prices, too. For 15 years, from 1966–1981, something *murdered* equity prices. Who? Why?

- From the end of World War II until 1967, prices of common stocks soared in the United States and abroad. It was a consistent and strong *bull market*.
- But from 1967 through 1982, the price of common stocks stagnated, creating a 15-year *bear market*. The real value of equities fell by two-thirds.

---

[30] Study by James Poterba (MIT, and Andrew A. Samwick (Dartmouth), cited in "America's love affair with stocks," *Business Week*, June 3, 1996, 35–38.

- Then in the second week of August, 1982, the price of common stocks rose rapidly, and continued to rise until the dot.com bubble burst in March, 2000.
- Stocks then declined, then began to rise again until the global crisis began in 2007–2008. Since April, 2008 we have experienced another (global) *bear market*.

Table 7.3 shows the annual real (inflation-adjusted) returns on three types of assets: stocks, gold, and bonds, from 1871 through 2001, divided into three main periods. It is clear that the return on stocks, averaging a steady 7–10 percent since 1871, was disrupted during 1966–1981, becoming negative before recovering during 1982–2001 to a strong annual 10.5 percent.

TABLE 7.3   US: Annual Real Returns, Stocks, Gold, Bonds, 1870–2001

Period	Stocks	Gold	Bonds
1871–2001	6.8%	−0.1%	2.8%
1946–1965	10.0	−2.7	−1.2
1966–1981	−0.4	8.8	−4.2
1982–2001	10.5	−4.8	8.5

Source: Jeremy Siegel, *Stocks for the Long Run* (fourth edition: NY: McGraw-Hill, 2007).

CASE STUDY

Small Crisis Precedes a Larger One

Lord, please give me just one more bubble.
      –bumper sticker seen in Silicon Valley, March 2003[31]

 On March 10, 2000, the NASDAQ (National Association of Security Dealers Automated Quotations) composite stock index—an average of US stocks, mainly technology-based, traded electronically—reached an all-time high of 5,086 points. It then began a rapid decline of nearly 40 percent, recovered erratically until September, then declined again to about 1,800 in March 2001—a fall of 65 percent in 12 months. Other stock indexes declined less dramatically. Paper capital losses incurred by shareholders totaled trillions of dollars. The *new economy* bubble

(Case Study continued)

---

[31] Sam, "Always on venture summit West-Laissez le bons temps rouler!", December 6, 2007, http://conferenzablog.typepad.com/conferenza/startups/(accessed February 3, 2010).

(*Case Study continued*)

(soon dubbed *the dot.com bubble*, because so many Web-based companies with no real business substance or revenue model were established) had finally burst. As often happens, financial collapse heralded economic recession. Late in 2001 the US GDP contracted, though it would recover in 2002. In 2007–08, it emerged that the 2000–01 *bust* was a precursor to a far more serious *bust* that would begin only 6–7 years later. Many managers were misled into believing that the rapid emergence from the 2001 recession implied that a new decade-long *boom* was in the offing. But it was not.

Why? What explains these fluctuations in common stock prices? Is there a simple theory that managers can use to help track, and anticipate, stock market fluctuations? In order to anticipate future boom–bust cycles, we need to understand those in the past. This is our next task.

With this objective, we must introduce a supplementary tool, without which stock prices cannot be fully understood in their historical context.

COMMON STOCKS: GET REAL!

Supplementary Tool

Real Dow-Jones

Real Dow-Jones Index = Nominal Dow-Jones Index/Price Index

Almost every important economic variable is adjusted for inflation, when it is reported, to facilitate period-to-period comparisons. There are two major exceptions. One is interest rates (see discussion in Chapter Six). The other is common stock prices. Managers cannot properly place stock prices in historical perspective, without adjusting stock indexes for inflation. What follows explains how to do this, and reveals the insights that accrue when it is done. The mystery of the 1966–1981 Great Bear Market can be solved, only when stock prices are adjusted for inflation. Once this is done, everything falls into place.

In the discussion that follows, we will often refer to the Dow-Jones 30-Stock Industrial Average, a measure of overall share prices on the New York Stock Exchange.

DEFINITION

The Dow-Jones 30 Industrial Stock Average

The *Dow* in Dow-Jones comes from Charles Henry Dow, who founded the Dow-Jones & Co. in 1882. Dow started calculating an average of prices of stocks to track movements in individual stocks. He first published his average on July 3, 1884. It included 11 stocks. The first average comparable to today's 30 industrial stocks appeared on October 1, 1928.

The Dow-Jones *Average* is not really an average, but simply the sum of the prices of 30 stocks, continually adjusted for stock splits. The 30 Dow industrials are chosen to be representative of their industry, and the market, and comprise around 20 percent of the market value of all stocks, and about a fourth of the value of all stocks listed on the New York Stock Exchange. Only three of the original 30 stocks from 1928 remain. They are Exxon-Mobil (once Standard Oil of NJ), General Electric, and General Motors.

The list of 30 companies changes fairly frequently. In 2009 it was: 3M, Alcoa, American Express, AT&T, Bank of America, Boeing, Caterpillar, Chevron, Citigroup, Coca-Cola, DuPont, Exxon-Mobil, GE, GM, HP, IBM, Intel, Johnson & Johnson, JP Morgan Chase, Kraft, McDonald's, Merck, Microsoft, Pfizer, Procter & Gamble, Home Depot, United Technologies, Verizon, Wal-Mart, and Walt Disney.

Consider Figure 7.3, showing 80 years' history of the Dow-Jones Index. An unsuspecting manager might inspect it, and reason as follows. "Stock prices have risen strongly in the US, until the year 2000. They declined from around 11,000 to about 8,000, then recovered again until 2008, when they fell again from 14,000 down to below 8,000."

FIGURE 7.3   Dow-Jones 30-Stock Industrial Average, 1928–2009

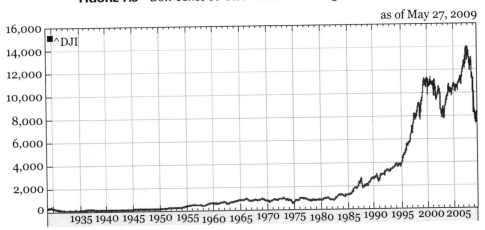

Source: Based on data from http://schwert.ssb.rochester.edu/volatility.htm (accessed February 3, 2010).

This is an accurate reading of the graph. But the graph itself is highly misleading. To understand why, consider an interesting meal enjoyed by the late BBC journalist Alistair Cooke, with a friend, in 1933.

Filet Mignon for USD 2.20: On March 6, 1933, the day President Franklin Delano Roosevelt shut America's banks for a whole week, journalist Alistair Cooke relates that he took a friend to dinner at a fine New York restaurant. The tab for two filet mignon and kirsch flambé: USD 2.20. Four years later, San Francisco's Golden Gate Bridge opened. The bill for that splendid structure: USD 27 million.

No one would dream of buying the same repast today for two bucks, or building the same bridge for USD 27 million. Today it takes a whole dollar to buy what you could get for a thin dime at the end of World War II. Everyone knows that 1933 dollars or 1937 dollars bought far more than 1995 dollars. *Why then do published reports ignore inflation when tracking stock prices?* For instance, why was the value of the Dow-Jones Index, 4,270, widely, and wrongly, heralded in April, 1995 as a new all-time high?

As the Dow-Jones 30-Stock Industrial Average (DJIA) soared a thousand points in 1996, to 4,800, headlines heralded *new records* and *new heights.* The fact is, at 4,750 the Dow—*corrected for inflation by measuring it in constant-purchasing-power dollars*—was only equal to the post-war peak it reached on January 19, 1966, almost 30 years ago.

How then should stock price averages be adjusted for inflation? The method is precisely the same as the one for adjusting GDP for inflation. Divide the DJIA by a Price Index, such as the Consumer Price Index (DJIA/CPI). For comparison purposes, the unadjusted, and adjusted stock price indexes are shown side-by-side (see Figure 7.4 below).

FIGURE 7.4 Dow-Jones 30-Stock Index, 1949–2009: Unadjusted and Adjusted for Inflation ("Real")

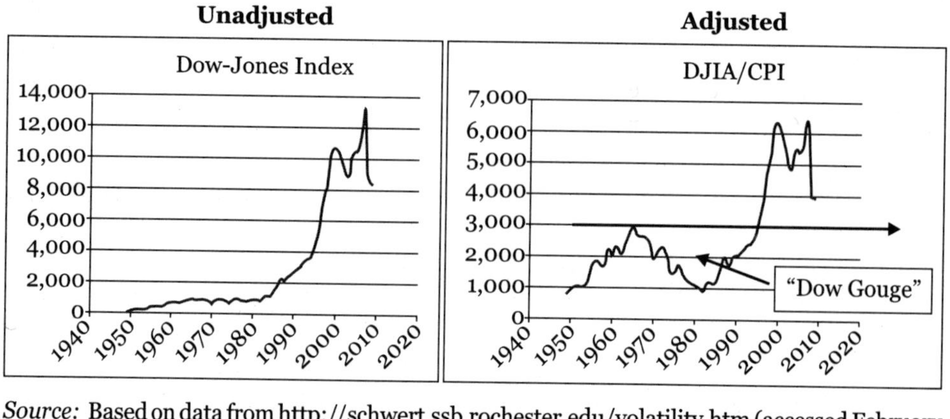

Source: Based on data from http://schwert.ssb.rochester.edu/volatility.htm (accessed February 3, 2010).

Charting the *real* Dow reveals a major mystery—a Grand Canyon of equity values: the Great Dow Gouge, 1966–82—a decline of 2/3 in the real value of share prices! The dimensions of the Gouge are extraordinarily large. Moreover, despite the sharp decline in the Dow-Jones, in real terms stocks are still two-thirds higher than they were at their peak during the previous *bull market* that ended in 1966. Share prices rose steadily since August 13, 1982 from about 800 to over 7,000 in early 1997. By April, 1995 headlines were proclaiming *record highs* for the 20 or more countries mentioned by the Wall Street Journal. *They were not record highs at all, because they failed to take into account, and adjust, for inflation.* Stock prices rose, but so did *other* prices.

A SHORT HISTORY OF STOCK PRICES

- The post-war Bull Market: Common stocks rose sharply after World War II, until January, 1966. The Real Dow-Jones index (adjusted for inflation) nearly tripled its value between 1950 and 1966. This yielded a return of over 7 percent annually on common stock investments, *after adjusting for inflation.*
- The 1970s Bear Market lasted from January 18, 1966, until Friday, August 13, 1982. During this period, the inflation-adjusted Dow slumped, until it hit rock-bottom, plummeting back down to its starting-point value 30 years earlier, in 1950!

The inflation-adjusted return to stocks during 1982–1997 was again over 7 percent—doubling stock portfolios every decade. However, in the wake of the 17-year decline in stocks, the real (inflation-adjusted) prices of stocks on the New York Stock Exchange did not achieve *record highs* in 1994, as the press reported, but in fact only returned to the (inflation-adjusted) levels prevailing in 1966, 28 years earlier. It took 14 years for real stock prices to climb back to their earlier highs in 1966. The bull market was then well underway. By 1997 the real DJIA was about 41 percent higher than its 1966 peak, and corporate after-tax profits, the key variable underlying stock prices, were 63 percent larger.

The *Dow Gouge* (the 1966–95 *valley* in Figure 7.4) caused serious structural dislocations. In 1982, equities were mired on average at their 1965 values. But prices were three times their 1965 levels. Result: you could buy stocks at 1965 prices with dollars worth only one-third what they were then—almost like buying filet mignon for USD 2.20. No wonder companies chose to buy up *existing* assets, through acquisition of stocks, rather than build *new* ones, even at the cost of incurring high-interest debt. Some of America's economic ills can be traced to this. Other economies built new productive assets, while America wasted time and energy shifting ownership of existing ones. For investors and managers, these remarkable three decades posed serious dilemmas.

The question is: *What caused the deep 15-year decline in real stock prices during 1966–1982? And what caused the 15-year (and counting) rise?* Knowing the answer is important, if managers and investors want to know whether the stock prices decline will continue, and want to judge when they may begin to rise.

MAY THE (TWO) FORCES BE WITH YOU

A superficial answer to the above question is this: The unadjusted DJIA fluctuated in the range of 800–1,000 for 15 long years. Meanwhile, inflation, like the Colorado River chewing out the Grand Canyon, gradually eroded the real value of the 800–1000 Dow. The consumer price index nearly tripled, from about 33 in 1966 to 97 in 1982.

But what *caused* the inflation? And why was inflation at times good for stocks (1945–1966, 1982–1997), and at times disastrous (1966–1982)? Why did equities not keep pace with inflation? How come equities were a great hedge for inflation in the 1950s and early 1960s—and stopped being so in 1965–1966?

Good and bad cholesterol: It is well known that there are two types of cholesterol in the human body. One is called *good cholesterol* (HDL, or high-density lipoprotein). It is good because it carries cholesterol in the blood stream back to the liver, thus getting rid of it. The second type of cholesterol is *bad cholesterol* (LDL, or low-density lipoprotein). It is bad because it can build up in the arteries, and eventually clog them, causing heart attacks. By the same token, there is *good* and *bad* inflation, and *good* and *bad* deflation. The key to solving the *who-dunnit* of the mysterious Bear Market, 1966–1981, lies in distinguishing between two types of inflation:

- Demand-pull: Rising prices owing to excess demand for goods and services, originating with expansions of demand, as businesses, households, and consumers choose to spend more. As household's disposable incomes, and willingness to spend them grow, demand curves shift upward and outward (see Figure 7.5). While prices rise, GDP increases. To produce more, more workers must be hired. Hence, in the case of demand-pull inflation, *higher inflation is accompanied by lower unemployment*. This inverse relation between inflation and unemployment is known as the Phillips Curve relation, and it did prevail in the US during the 1960s.
- Cost-push: Rising prices owing to rising costs of labor, capital, energy, and materials, originating with contraction in supply, higher unit costs and resulting increases in prices. Supply contracts when it costs producers more for each unit of output they make. This occurs when energy prices rise, wages increase, interest

rates rise, taxes rise—in general, when the unit costs of factors of production, and other business expenses increase. When unit costs rise, producers charge more for their products, and raise prices. This shifts the aggregate supply curve inward, and to the left (see Figure 7.5). The result is higher prices and at the same time, a lower level of GDP. Here unlike demand-pull, inflation is not at all a mixed evil; the level of economic activity *contracts* with inflation. As a result, output and profits also shrink.

Thus, two *very different* forces are capable of pushing up prices and causing inflation. One operates on the demand side of the economy. The other finds expression on the supply side. Both are at work, in varying degrees, at any point in time. *It is important to understand the nature of each, and to know which is dominant*, in every country where global managers operate or plan to operate (see Table 7.4).

TABLE 7.4   Two Inflationary Forces

Demand-Pull	*Cost-Push*
• higher disposable income	• slower productivity growth
• lower personal taxes	• higher wages and interest rates
• higher budget deficits	• higher food and energy costs
• baby boom	• wage-price spiral
• investment boom	• falling dollar

Source: Authors.

The periods 1945–1966 and 1982–1997 were episodes of demand-pull inflation. Demand-pull inflation implies *growth plus inflation*—generally favorable for profits, and hence for stock prices.

The period 1966–1982 was one of cost-push inflation. Higher unit costs began with rising food prices in the early 1970s. Then came the two energy crises in 1973–1974 and 1979–1980, followed by higher wages and interest rates. Higher costs mean resources are less productive. GDP stagnates or declines as a result. Thus cost-push inflation implies *GDP stagnation plus inflation. This is almost always unfavorable for profits and hence for stock prices.*

One of the main culprits was the collapse in productivity growth. Between 1948 and 1965 output per hour in the private business sector grew by more than 3 percent a year. From 1965 to 1973, it grew by only 2 percent a year, and from 1973–78, less than 1 percent a year.[32] The recovery of productivity growth to 2 percent a year in

---

[32] Albert Rees, "On Interpreting Productivity Change," in *Lagging Productivity Growth: Causes and Remedies*, S. Maital and N. Meltz (Cambridge, MA: Ballinger, 1980).

the 1980s has contributed a lot to price stability, by matching wage increases, and offsetting their effect on costs and prices. Since 1982, the US economy has been undergoing very moderate demand-pull inflation, with little or no cost pressures.

Demand-pull inflation is consistent with the behavior of the stock market in the 1950s and 1960s. Budget deficits were good for stocks because they were expansionary, raising GDP and economic activity, and with it profits. Inflation too was good for stock prices because it too signaled an increase in GDP and employment.

But the 1970s and 1980s were quite different. While prices rose, GDP contracted. This is known as stagflation: stagnation + inflation. The cause was cost-push: inflation caused by a contraction in supply rather than an expansion of demand.

Cost-push inflation can indeed explain the causalities of the 1970s and 1980s. If inflation is contractionary in its impact on the economy, then higher inflation will hurt stock prices. Higher monetary growth will be seen as inflationary and will result in lower bond prices as investors demand higher interest rates. Lower bond prices will attract investors to shift their money from common stocks—another reason why inflation might hurt stocks.

Cost-push inflation ended in 1982. In the 1980s and 1990s US firms invested unprecedented sums in information technology and computers. Those investments generated remarkable gains in productivity in 1995–2000.

TRACING THE FOOTPRINTS: KNOWING YOUR P's AND Q's

How can managers tell whether it is cost-push inflation, or demand-pull inflation, that is dominant?

One approach is to track the footprints of supply and demand—trace the price index against real GDP. By observing prices and GDP over time, we can grasp where the economy has been, and why, and perhaps where it and the stock market may be headed. When prices (P) rise and GDP (Q) falls—stagflation—it is cost-push. When prices rise and GDP rises, it is demand-pull (see Figure 7.5).

If the Q, P (quantity, price) point moves, for instance, northeast, from one year to the next, that suggests that the primary *driver* was an outward shift in demand, through higher spending by consumers, businesses, and governments. This is a demand-driven change, leading to demand-pull inflation and growth. The diagram shows the strong expansion in demand that occurred in the US from 1982 through 1990, propelled through tax cuts and higher consumer spending.

If the Q, P point moves, for instance, in a northwest direction, it suggests that on a stable demand curve, the supply curve contracted, moving leftward and upward (recall that supply curves are really cost curves—so rising wages without comparable increases in productivity could cause supply curves to shift inward, leading to higher

FIGURE 7.5 Cost-Push vs. Demand-Pull Inflation

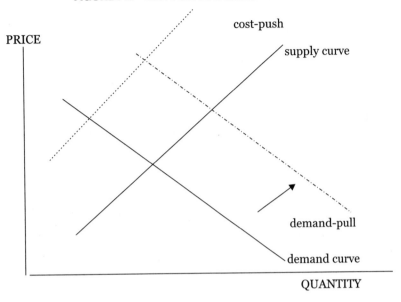

Source: Authors.

unit costs at each level of GDP). This occurred in 1981 and 1990—a phenomenon known as stagflation.

CASE STUDY

Mexico, Germany, and Japan

Mexico: Rising GDP and prices continued from 1980 through 1994, as Mexico gained from cross-border trade with the United States and Canada in NAFTA. In late 1994, Mexico faced a financial crisis, as the peso was devalued ultimately to half its former value relative to the dollar. The result: cost-push inflation as imported materials (and later wages) rose steeply. Mexico's real GDP fell 7 percent in 1995—a deep recession and stagflation. As the US supplied over USD 50 billion in emergency aid, Mexico's economy recovered, and seems again on a demand-pull growth path, according to OECD projections.

Germany: Reunification of the two Germany's in 1990–2001 added 17 million more people—and 12 percent higher GDP—to Western Germany,

(*Case Study continued*)

(Case Study continued)

but also cost-push inflation as rising wages met stagnant productivity. In 2001 Germany continued to struggle with its high wage structure and with Eastern Germany's crumbling infrastructure.

Japan: In 1992–1994, Japan's economy came to a screeching halt, marching on the spot as demand growth ceased. In this recession, real GDP simply stopped growing. The result was stagnation that contrasted sharply with three previous decades of rapid export-driven demand-pull growth. After some recovery in the late 1990s, Japan's economy again slid into deep recession during the 2007–2009 global depression. Japan is still in some ways like a boxcar waiting for a demand engine to pull it ahead, three decades after the property bubble burst.

Note that this good–bad inflation analysis applies to deflation as well. There is *good* deflation, driven by productivity gains that lowers costs and hence prices, while expanding GDP. There is *bad* deflation, driven by contractions in demand, leading to lower prices but also to lower GDP and rising unemployment. In the global crisis of 2007–2009, there has been widespread deflation driven by *demand-pull*. It has been an unmitigated evil: declining GDP along with rising unemployment. Many companies have responded to resulting falling profit margins by aggressively seeking to lower costs by raising productivity. If sufficiently widespread, this could lead to *good* cost-push deflation: declining prices, but accompanied by rising GDP, and rising employment.

TRACKING STOCKS THROUGH PRICE-EARNINGS MULTIPLES

A share of common stock entitles its owner to share in profits earned by the company, after it pays its workers, creditors, and taxes. There should thus be a long-run link between the price of a share, and the per-share earnings to which the share entitles its owner. The ratio between the price of common stock and earnings per share is known as the P/E ratio, or price-earnings ratio, or simply *the multiple*.

DEFINITION

Price-Earnings Ratio (P-E): the ratio between the price of common stock (what you pay for one share), and the net after-tax earnings per share, either for an individual stock or for a group of stocks (such as the Dow-Jones Index or the Standard and Poor 500 Index).

The crucial ratio between the price of common stock and earnings per share—*the P/E multiple*—has a long-term average value of about 25. When inverted, Price/Earnings becomes Earnings/Price; at 1/25, this reflects about a 4 percent rate of return. Since the long-term return on investment in equities is about 11 percent, this suggests that fully 7 percent of that return stems from the risk premium (stocks are riskier than bonds), and from expectations of earnings growth, while 4 percent reflects current earnings. We learn from this, how crucial a role expectations play in driving stock prices.

During bubble-like bull markets, it appears that price/earnings ratios have skyrocketed, and lost contact with the reality of their long-term averages. But closer analysis reveals: This is not in fact the case. It is not P/E ratios that get out of whack, but expectation of future earnings. When markets become wiser and sadder, and adjust future earnings expectation downward, stock prices fall.

The basic equation that helps us understand this is:

$$\frac{P_F}{E_F} = \frac{P_N}{E_N}$$

where P is stock price, E is earnings per share, subscript F signifies (expected) Future, and subscript N signifies (actual) Now.

This equation says that over the long haul, there is a constant ratio between the price of a share of common stock and earnings per share. Viewed from another perspective, the equation says: the expected change in stock prices varies directly and linearly with expected future earnings:

$$P_F/P_N = E_F/E_N$$

Figure 7.6 tracks the price-earnings ratio, on average, for a leading stock index, the Standard & Poor (S&P) 500 Stock Index, for a broad basket of US common shares. (The S&P index measures the share prices for 500 leading US companies; it is a more comprehensive index than the Dow-Jones.) The graph shows the average P-E ratio for the 500 leading companies. It shows that this average, since 1900, has fluctuated around about 14.5 (stock prices average about 15 times earnings per share), and that when the P-E ratio has gotten well above this average stock prices tend to fall to bring the price-earnings line back into its long run relation. This is especially evident for the 1982–2000 stock bubble, when talk about the *new economy* led many to believe that the price-earnings link had been permanently revised upward. Despite sharp falls in the price of stocks after March, 2000, the P-E ratio has only

FIGURE 7.6   Price-Earnings Ratio for Standard & Poor 500 Index (US) 1900–2009

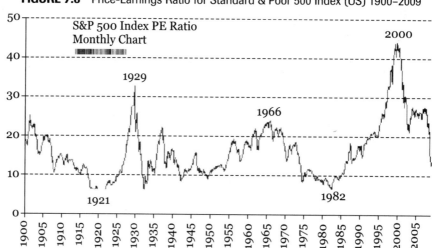

Source: www.bcg.com (accessed January 18, 2010).

recently declined to its historical average, and fell slightly below it. But the P-E ratio still remains above its trough levels in 1921 and 1982. This Figure also shows that stock prices tend to *overshoot*—that is, fall by more than underlying profits suggest they should, because of *animal spirits* effects.

Why then did the aggregate P/E value for US stock markets leap from under 10 in 1982, the year stock prices hit bottom, to over 40 in 2000, the year the dot.com bubble burst?

We believe the answer is this: Driven by optimism (*animal spirits*) regarding expected profits from new economy profits, in turn driven by higher productivity, E_F rose dramatically. This in turn generated a dramatic rise in P_F. It is the nature of capital markets that future developments are capitalized in current prices. Basically, P_F very quickly became P_N, as the consensus view developed that New Economy future profits would be large and growing. In hindsight, this is rather puzzling, because many of the companies whose stocks were highly touted during the 1996–2000 bubble had no *revenue*, let alone profits. We can see now, looking back, that this was an extreme *bubble*. Had managers posted this chart on their walls, and updated it frequently, surely alarm bells would have sounded long before the year 2000, when the bubble burst. Yet while the bubble was happening, it was not easy to grasp.

P-E and bubbles: There is a simple but persuasive *P-E* theory of financial bubbles. It is best understood by an example.

CASE STUDY

How Financial Bubbles Occur—ABC Ltd

 Consider a stock, ABC Ltd, selling for USD 50 (P = USD 50). Earnings per share are USD 2. Thus the P-E ratio is 50/2 = 25, close to the long-term average. Now suppose the economy is strong and growing, optimism runs high, and investors anticipate ABC's earnings will double in the medium term (E = USD 4). Based on this expectation, it becomes widely believed that the future price of the ABC stock will be P = USD 100 (P-E of 25, times E, or USD 4). This belief will create demand for the shares in the present, anticipating future profits. This demand, in turn, will increase the current price of the ABC stock to USD 100, if a critical mass of investors believe the optimistic forecast. By buying now at USD 50, investors can double their money when the stock price rises to USD 100. Note that not everyone has to believe this; just a sufficiently large fraction of the investing community. If the optimistic earnings forecast is well-founded, the USD 100 price is not a bubble. If it is not, then, a bubble exists.

Now, suppose that something impacts the animal spirits optimism—bad economic news, a political crisis, hurricane, etc. Earnings forecasts are adjusted downward. Not only are earnings not expected to grow, but the fear of an economic downturn implies that earnings will actually fall, to, say USD 1 per share. The result: Widespread sale of shares, often rapid and panicky, will cause the price of ABC shares to fall by 75 percent, to 25 (P-E of 25 times E, or USD 1). If the panic is widespread, panic selling will drive the share price even lower, as will a readjustment of P-E ratios themselves (the market may decide that 25 is too high, and adopt an implied risk-averse P-E ratio of, say, 15). This mechanism can easily transmit the fear of a downturn into a bursting of a financial bubble, and in turn, feed back into the real economy, making the downturn much worse.

Expectation premium: Boston Consulting Group has calculated the proportion of company value (market capitalization of its shares plus corporate debt) that reflects the *expectation premium*—the expectation of higher *future* profits, as opposed to the part of company value accounted for by current *actual* profitability, for the US, 1994–2000. Their results are shown in Figure 7.7.

This analysis shows that in 1994, when the stock prices were recovering from the 1991–1992 recession, only about 18 percent of company value came from *bubble*

FIGURE 7.7   Company Value (1994 = 100 percent): Fundamental Value and Expectation Premium, 1994 and 2000

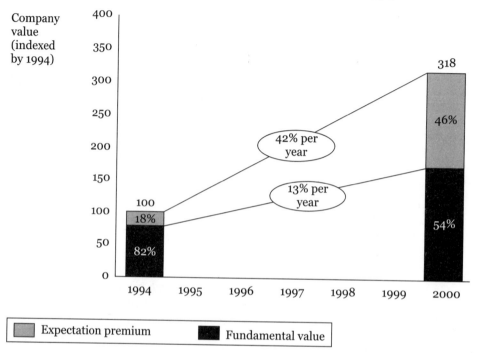

Source: Boston Consulting Group, www.bcg.com, based on a sample of 287 companies; company value = market capitalization plus debt.

expectations of future profits, while 82 percent came from *fundamental value* (that is, actual after-tax earnings). But as the economy grew, expectations strengthened, and dreams of future profits boomed. So, while fundamental value rose by only 13 percent annually, the expectation premium grew by an enormous 42 percent annually. At its peak in 2000, company value was almost half *bubble*, or expectations. When those expectations turned out to be overly rosy, it was natural that stock prices would plummet. By using the P/E approach described earlier, and by tracking the expectation premium, it is possible to identify *bubbles* as they form and grow, in time to avoid risk and loss when those bubbles burst, as they inevitably do.

CONCLUSION

The title of this book is *Global Risk/Global Opportunity*. This is not an empty phrase or a marketing ploy. We truly believe that every risk embodies within it a major business opportunity. However, transforming risk into opportunity requires wisdom, courage, insight, management skill, and leadership.

Nowhere is this more evident than in the risks inherent in the boom–bust business cycle. Major opportunities are hidden in the *bust* cycle, because while many organizations focus during downturns on mere survival, through cost-cutting, redundancies, layoffs and budget cuts, agile innovators can read the changing global map, and act boldly to identify new business opportunities; arising from new *rules of the game*—changing business paradigms.

Capturing these opportunities depends on achieving several ambitious goals. First, think differently—identify *bubbles* and *bubble psychology* while others are still caught up in them. Second, assess the timing—try to gauge when the bubble is likely to burst, and when *boom* shifts to *bust*. Third, catch the tide not only when it goes out, but also when it comes in—assess when the *bust* phase is likely to reach bottom, and the economy begins its recovery.

We have sought to provide several simple tools and concepts in this chapter, to assist global managers in this difficult task. Underlying all these tools is one simple, crucially important principle: Think independently. It is the nature of human society to think as others do. Nothing can be more dangerous for a global manager. Thinking as others do implies being caught up inevitably in asset bubbles, with all the risk that it entails. Thinking for yourself, using the simple tools of macroeconomics, can transform major business-cycle risk into global opportunities.

We now turn to world trade and foreign exchange. Since trade has been the key driver of global economic growth for over two decades, it is vital that global managers know how to track trade and global capital flows, know how to understand changes in foreign exchange rates, and understand how to read Balance of Payments data as a country's *dollar cash flow* statement. This is the objective of Chapter Eight.

Chapter 8
Tracking trade and forex

LEARNING OBJECTIVES

After reading this chapter, readers should understand how to analyze the crucial foreign-exchange cash flow performance of countries, using the Balance of Payments statement. They should know why official exchange rates may not reflect true currency value, how to gauge future changes in exchange rates, why exchange rates have become exceedingly volatile, and why global businesses need to carefully track and manage exchange-rate swings.

Readers should be able to answer these questions:

- What role does trade play in global economic growth?
- What is a country's Balance of Payments? Why is it often out of balance, and what does it reveal about a country's foreign debt and foreign-currency cash flow? What does a *deficit* in balance mean anyway?
- How did the rules of the global trading game change, dating from the Bretton Woods, NH conference of 1944?
- How has foreign investment changed? How is it measured?
- How can managers adapt global operations to short-term and long-term changes in currency values?
- Why have exchange rates become extremely volatile since 1971?
- How can you tell whether a country's currency is undervalued or overvalued relative to the US dollar, or whether the US dollar is wrongly valued?
- What drives short-term changes in a country's currency value?

Tool # **8**

Balance of Payments: Orderly account of transactions between people and businesses of one country with other countries.

 Supplementary Tool: Purchasing power parity (PPP) exchange rate (Big Mac rate)

In the global village, the temptation is great to move out of one's regional or national niche into a wider and therefore more unfamiliar environment. Even those companies that resist the temptation run the risk that the outside world will invade their home turf. Over time, as a result, fewer and fewer companies will live and work in an environment over which they have a lot of control.

—Arie de Geus, The Living Company[1]

INTRODUCTION

In Chapter Seven, we saw how global opportunities in the markets for common stock turned rapidly into global risks, as rising share prices soared above realistic values, and floated into *bubble* territory. In just 12 months, from April 2008, global stocks fell in value by half.

Normally, we regard world trade flows as more stable than volatile capital markets, because trade is driven by long-term fundamental forces of comparative advantage, and mutual gain, based on cost, price, quality, and market demands, and arranged through long-term contracts. This held true for decades. World trade was a powerful reliable engine of phenomenal global economic growth in GDP since the end of World War II—ever since the conference of 40 allied powers, July 1–20, 1944, at Bretton Woods, New Hampshire, US, laid the foundations for a new world economy based on free trade, through the General Agreement on Tariffs and Trade (GATT). The GATT agreement led to successive tariff-reduction negotiating rounds during six decades that sharply reduced most tariff restrictions on trade. The World Bank, International Monetary Fund, and other global institutions were also born there.

The Bretton Woods *architecture* was a phenomenal success. Figure 8.1 shows that except for the brief recession year of 2001, world trade has expanded at twice or more the growth rate of world GDP. This trend accelerated after the Berlin Wall collapsed, on November 9, 1989. At that time, in the words of trade expert, Clyde Prestowitz, "three billion new capitalists" were created (in Asia).[2] From 1990–2006, world exports grew on average twice as fast as GDP. Clearly, as de Geus notes, companies have moved into new, often distant markets and business environments, with profitable results but, at the same time, loss of control and increased risk.

With the onset of the 2007–2009 global crisis, world trade collapsed. As domestic economies slowed and incomes declined, imports fell sharply, and world trade declined. World trade has fallen much more rapidly in the 2007–2009 crisis than it

---

[1] Arie de Geus, *The Living Company* (Boston, MA: Harvard Business School Press, 2002), 199.

[2] Clyde Prestowitz, *Three Billion New Capitalists: The Great Shift of Wealth and Power to the East* (New York: Basic Books, 2005).

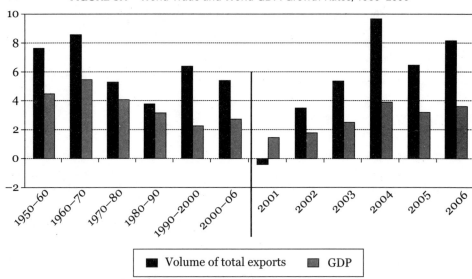

FIGURE 8.1   World Trade and World GDP: Growth Rates, 1950–2006

Source: World Trade Organization, 2009 Press Release; Press/554, March 23, 2009, "World Trade 2008, Prospects for 2009, Chart 3." http://www.wto.org/english/news e/ press09 e/pr554 e.htm (accessed January 31, 2010).

did in the Global Depression that began in 1929. From April 2008, the peak of the boom, world trade fell by 20 percent in just 10 months (see Figure 8.2). And in the first quarter of 2009, the pace of the decline in world trade actually accelerated, *as global trade fell by 40 percent compared to the same period a year earlier.*[3] As a result, the United Nations predicted world GDP would decline by an unprecedented 2.6 percent in 2009—far larger than the 0.5 percent decline forecasted only four months earlier—driven by a steep 11 percent fall in world trade, the largest such drop since 1929. In 2009, only seven countries, the United Nations predicts, will register per capita growth of 3 percent or higher (among them, China and India). Hence, in

---

[3] Edith Lederer, reporter for The Associated Press news service, reported on May 27, 2009: "According to the U.N., world trade has declined dramatically since the end of 2008, falling in the first quarter of the year at an annual rate of more than 40 percent," in an article "UN predicts 2009 economic decline of 2.6 percent." www.ap.org., http://nl.newsbank.com/nlsearch/ we/Archives?p_product=APAB&p_theme=apab&p_action=search&p_maxdocs=200&s_ dispstring=According%20to%20the%20U.N.,%20world%20trade%20has%20declined% 20dramatically%20since%20the%20end%20of%202008&p_ field_advanced=0=&p_text_ advanced0= ("According%20to%20the%20U.N.,%20world%20trade%20has%20declined %20dramatically%20since%20the%20end%20of%202008") &xcal_numdocs=20&p_ perpage=10&p_sort=YMD_date:D&xcal_useweights=no (accessed January 26, 2010).

FIGURE 8.2   World Trade: Decline from the Peak of Economic Activity:
June 1929 and April 2008

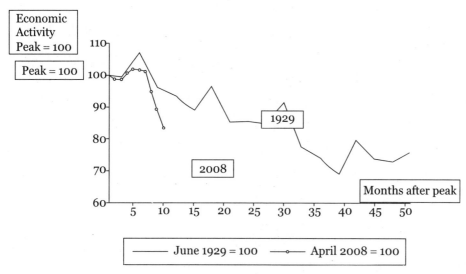

Source: Barry Eichengreen and Kevin H.O'Rourke, "A Tale of two depressions," 1 September
2009. www.voxeu.org (accessed January 31, 2010).

just a few months, world trade has been transformed from a powerful engine bringing
prosperity to countries able and willing to compete in global markets, to an equally
powerful brake that has brought the global economy to a halt. Underlying the
40 percent decline in global trade are sharply lower corporate revenues and earnings,
especially for global companies.

Why has this enormous turnabout in world trade occurred? Could this shift
have been anticipated? What are the risks and the opportunities inherent in today's
global trading and forex (foreign exchange) systems? Has the business model that
focuses on seeking large, growing foreign markets proved too risky? We address
these key questions in this chapter, and provide tools for global managers to help
answer them. Our journey will require analysis not only of trade but also of foreign
exchange. The market for foreign exchange is the largest single market in terms of
daily turnover, and is also among the most volatile. Since this market determines
the rates at which currencies exchange for one another—of crucial importance for
exporters, and for investors—we will offer a supplementary tool to help managers
gauge whether exchange rates are stable or are likely to become unstable.

A gentle warning is called for. *This chapter is a data-intensive zone. We hope to
show that a small investment in persistence and patience, to build skill in reading*

trade and forex numbers and tracking them consistently will provide important insights that generate a high rate of return in identifying opportunities and anticipating risks.

Our analysis will show that the collapse in world trade was inevitable—an accident waiting to happen, due to serious persistent imbalances in trade patterns. With intelligent use of simple tools, global managers could have anticipated the rising risk of this collapse in trade, years in advance.

COMPETITIVENESS, TRADE, AND WEALTH

In the post-World War II era, nations' path to prosperity was paved by success in competing in global markets and sharing in the new wealth created by trade. This can be shown empirically. Figure 8.3 plots, for 55 countries, a *world competitiveness* score, reflecting countries' ability to compete in world markets, against GDP per capita, for 2007–08. World competitiveness is measured each year by the Swiss business school I.M.D. For each of four key dimensions—economy, business efficiency, government efficiency, and infrastructure—countries are ranked and measured, using hundreds of variables which are compiled into an overall competitiveness score. It ranges from a low of 31.1 for Venezuela to 100 for the United States (2008). In Figure 8.3, this score is plotted against GDP per capita, measured in US dollars and calculated using *true* ("purchasing power parity" or PPP) exchange rates (see ahead for a discussion of PPP). The correlation is far from perfect. Many countries—notably, China and India—have per capita GDP far below what their competitiveness scores warrant. But in general, the trend line indicates that each *competitiveness* point (on a scale of 1 to 100) adds USD 100 to GDP per capita.

Global managers seeking opportunities in new markets may use Figure 8.3 to find *underperformers*—nations whose GDP per capita is much lower than its competitiveness score warrants. China and India are in this group. Luxembourg, strikingly, is an overperformer; it has GDP per capita, USD 77,187, the world's highest, far higher than its 84.4 competitiveness score warrants, owing to its particular circumstances—its half-million citizens benefit from high-paying jobs with European Union institutions located there, as well as from Luxembourg's role as a financial center.

We begin our discussion of trade and foreign exchange with the main tool discussed in this chapter—the Balance of Payments. We will show how the United States's Balance of Payments has been badly out of balance for decades, which ultimately led to the current global crisis. Global managers familiar with this tool would have known long ago that the world was headed for trouble.

FIGURE 8.3 55 Nations: GDP per capita (USD) vs. World Competitiveness, 2007–2008

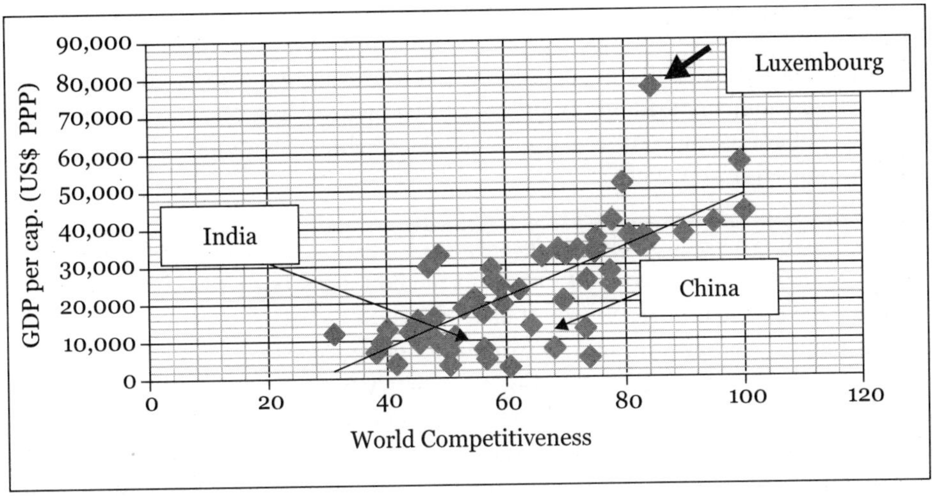

Luxembourg

India

China

GDP per cap. (US$ PPP)

World Competitiveness

Source: IMD, *World Competitiveness Yearbook*, 2008 (Lausanne, Switzerland: International Institute for Management Development, 2009).

A COUNTRY IS A BUSINESS: DOLLAR CASH FLOW

If indeed a country is a business, as Chapter Four argues, then it is vital to analyze the country's cash flow. GDP (Gross Domestic Product) was seen, in Chapter Four, as a kind of cash flow statement in local currency. Another key cash flow statement for a country is the cash flow *in US dollars*, which summarizes the transactions between citizens of the country and foreign citizens. This cash flow statement, known as the Balance of Payments, is vital, because it is an X-ray of how the country interacts with global markets. This in turn is of crucial importance, in the era of globalization, when the path to prosperity and growth lies not in building domestic markets but mainly in competing successfully in global markets. Managers can learn a great deal about a country, and about country risk, by examining its *foreign exchange cash flow*, or *Balance of Payments*.

Supplementary Tool

Balance of Payments

DEFINITION

Balance of Payments

A systematic listing of all transactions between citizens of the home country and citizens or residents of other countries, involving purchase, and sale of goods and services, and of assets, during a given period (usually a quarter or a year).

Unlike GDP, where the basis for measuring a country's output of goods and services is *geographical* (that is, production within the country's borders), the basis of the Balance of Payments is *nationality*—it lists transactions between a country's citizens and permanent residents, and those from other countries. These transactions could take place at home (for instance, foreign tourists who pay hotel bills in New York City), or abroad (for instance, sale of American Harley motorcycles to Qatar). Each of these transactions is listed as a US export.

Every transaction with a foreigner enters twice—similar to double-entry book-keeping. This is why the Balance of Payments always balances in principle, and in practice, *almost* balances (with small statistical errors).

Table 8.1 shows the Balance of Payments numbers for the United States for 2007. The Balance of Payments has a straightforward *vertical/horizontal* logic. It is divided vertically, between *dollar inflow* (items on the left) and *dollar outflow* (items on the right); and horizontally, between items related to goods and services (*above the line*) and items related to capital assets (*below the line*).

Left versus right: On the left hand side are listed transactions that generate positive cash flow—the inflow of dollars. On the right hand side (or, middle column) are transactions that generate negative cash flow—outflow of dollars (Balance of Payments data are generally measured in US dollars, because the dollar is the currency most widely used, by far, for global trade and investment). The far-right summary column lists the *net balance between the cash inflow and outflow*. Every dollar earned and used by a country's citizen goes somewhere—for each country, inflow of dollars must by definition equal outflow. That is why the Balance of Payments balances. Of course, a country *can* spend more dollars than it receives, provided it has either savings—reserves of foreign exchange—or if other nations are willing to lend it their savings.

Above and below the line: The Balance of Payments is split *horizontally* into two parts. *Above the line* is the so-called Current Account—a listing of transactions involving *purchase and sale of goods and services*, that is, exports and imports. This is parallel to the current *operations* part of a company's cash flow. Below the line is the Capital Account—all transactions involving *purchase and sale of assets*. This includes such transactions as sale of Treasury bills to foreigners, purchase of US firms

TABLE 8.1 Balance of Payments Summary: United States, 2007 (USD billion)

	CURRENT ACCOUNT		
	$ Inflow (+)	$ Outflow (–)	Net
Goods:			– $ 819
Exports	+ $1,149		
Imports		– $1,968	
Services:			+$119
Exports	+ $497		
Imports		– $ 378	
Balance on Goods and Services:			– $700
Other:*		– $31	
CURRENT ACCOUNT BALANCE:			– $731
	CAPITAL ACCOUNT		
U.S. Investment Abroad (Outflow)		–$1,290	
Foreign Investment in U.S. (Inflow)	+$2,064		
CAPITAL ACCOUNT BALANCE			+ $774
TOTAL DOLLAR INFLOW:**	+ $3,710		
TOTAL DOLLAR OUTFLOW:		– $3,667	
Statistical discrepancy:		$43 b.	

Source: Economic Report of the President 2009, Table B.103, (Washington: Council of Economic Advisors, Office of the President, February 2009), pp. 401–402.

Notes: * foreign aid, net interest on foreign investments, etc.
** Total dollar inflow is the total inflow of dollars from both current and capital accounts; similarly, total dollar outflow is the total outflow of dollars on both accounts. In theory they should always be equal.

by foreigners, or transfer of funds from New York to a Frankfurt Euro dollar account. The capital account is parallel to the part of a company's cash flow showing borrowing, stock issue, and asset sale or purchase. Note that this separation of current and capital accounts is precisely parallel to a company's net cash flow statement, split into:

1. *Operational cash flows*, received or spent as a result of the company's internal business activities, and
2. *Investment and financial cash flows*, cash received from, or spent on, sale or purchase of assets, from issue of debt and equity, payment of dividends and share repurchases.

The measured supply of, and demand for dollars must necessarily be equal. Dollars, like matter or energy, cannot be created from *nothing*. Hence total inflow of dollars listed in the Balance of Payments, above and below the line, must equal total outflow. It follows that if there is a Current Account deficit—for instance, a country may import more than it exports—*there must be an equal, offsetting Capital Account surplus.* In this sense, then, the balance of Payments always balances. Managers and non-economists may wonder, how can a balance account be in deficit, and what does the widely-used phrase *Balance of Payments deficit* mean? The answer is: the term Balance of Payments deficit is short for *a current account deficit in the Balance of Payments.* A Balance of Payments deficit indicates that the Balance of Payments balances in a manner that may be unstable in the long run. This has been true for the US for decades, as we will learn below.

ANATOMY OF AMERICA'S BALANCE OF PAYMENTS

Table 8.1 is a *snapshot*, at a point in time, of America's transactions with the rest of the world in 2007. It reveals an enormous imbalance. America, it shows, imported USD 819 billion more in goods than it exported—a direct result of global American corporations shifting their production offshore, mainly to Asia, to lower-cost sites. Most of the merchandise (goods) trade deficit was accounted for by autos and automobile parts, crude oil, and consumer electronics. It is indeed true that America has a surplus of services exports (tourism, software, TV programs, movies, etc.) amounting to USD 119 billion. But this surplus offsets only about one-seventh of the goods deficit. In general, overall world trade is predominantly goods, or merchandise, trade. It is likely true that no nation can enjoy stability if it seeks to offset goods imports solely through services exports.

America's large trade deficit proved a major boon for other nations, mainly Asian. If America buys more abroad than it sells, clearly other nations sell more than they buy. America's trade deficit provided massive amounts of demand for other nations' products. America's GDP decline, 2008–09, has greatly reduced America's demands for other nations' products, and has exported America's recession to the world.

If an individual or a family spends USD 731 more than they earn in a given month, they must borrow. The same holds for a country. In order for America to spend USD 731 billion more abroad than it sells in a year, it must borrow that amount. Note that this is true, even though the global currency is the US dollar and America, unlike any other nation, can *create* dollars (see Chapter Six). Even if America creates massive amounts of dollars to pay for its excess spending, other nations must be willing to accept and hold such dollars as payment for real goods and services. When those nations hold American dollars, they are essentially lending to America, because those dollars represent *I.O.U.'s*—debt owed by the US to other countries. The US dollars represent a claim on real goods and services in the future. The capital account of America's balance of payments (below the line) shows that the US invested USD 1,290 billion abroad in 2007, but foreigners invested USD 2,064 billion (by buying

American Treasury bonds, bills, notes, common shares, corporate bonds, options, real estate, and other assets). Net, this meant America borrowed USD 774 billion. Note, incidentally, that *the magnitude of capital flows to and from America dwarfs the value of trade* (imports and exports). This is true not only of the US but of the entire world. The creation of the global capital market has generated capital flows many times those representing trade.

Table 8.1 reveals why the global economy was so shaky in 2007. America, the nation whose currency supported global trade and investment, incurred enormous amounts of debt in 2007. Just as a business loses the confidence of investors when it borrows excessively, so does a country. Was this an aberration, an unusual year? It was not. US has been borrowing abroad since the late 1970s, or for almost 30 years! Figure 8.4 plots the difference between total exports and total imports, for the United States, since 1946. It shows that US trade deficits grew rapidly since 1993, tripling from about USD 31 billion in that year to USD 104 billion in 1996, (more than) tripling again to USD 365 billion in 2001, and then doubling once more in 2007 to USD 771 billion, a deficit 25 times larger than only 14 years earlier!

Had global managers been tracking America's Balance of Payments carefully every month, and perhaps pinned a graph like Figure 8.4 of America's current account deficit to their wall, they would have been aware of the alarming explosion in the US current account deficit, eroding confidence in the US dollar and thus undermining the foundations of the global trade and investment system, a decade before the global crisis erupted in 2007–2008. Had global managers noted in particular the gradient (slope) of Figure 8.4, they would have sensed growing global risk long before the crisis exploded in 2007–2008.

Many observers label the global crisis as originating with the US sub-prime mortgage crisis. But in fact, as Figure 8.4 shows, the roots are far deeper; they lie in US policies that endangered the world by excessive spending and debt. *What is remarkable is not that the crisis erupted in 2007–2008, but that it took so long to arrive.* It is also noteworthy that with globally integrated markets, dangerous and irresponsible policies in any major country (or even, at times, in a *minor* country, such as Thailand in 1997) ultimately wreak havoc in virtually every country. *The United States not only hurt its own citizens, with desperately bad economic policies, but citizens in virtually every country in the world.*

From whom has America been borrowing? In general, rich persons lend money to poorer ones and rich countries lend money to poorer countries. But since the early 1990s, the situation has been reversed. Much of low-saving America's borrowing has been from high-saving, but poorer, Asian nations. Table 8.2 shows the official foreign exchange reserves held by key Asian nations as of March 2009. These reserves represent the dollar assets acquired by those nations in the course of lending money to the United States. Worldwide, some 64 percent of nations' foreign exchange

FIGURE 8.4 US Goods and Services (Trade) Deficit: Exports Minus Imports, 1946–2008 (USD billion)

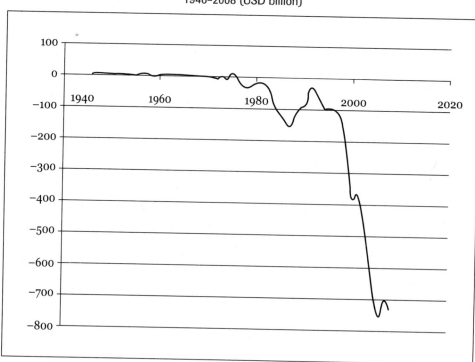

Source: Federal Reserve Bank of St. Louis, Economic Research Department; Trade Weighted Index of the US Dollar 1994–2010. http://research.stlouisfed.org/fred2/series/ TWEXB (accessed January 31, 2010).

reserves are held in dollars, while 26 percent are held in euros. Table 8.2 shows that Asian nations have accumulated a massive amount of American dollars, over USD 4 trillion worth. This sum amounts to about one-third of America's annual GDP.

Why did Asian nations find it worthwhile to lend over USD 4,000 billion to America, while America found it worthwhile to borrow to enjoy short-term consumption beyond what its long-term interests could justify? The answer is, Asian countries lent the US massive sums *in order to enable America to buy Asian exports*—much like General Motors used its General Motors Acceptance Corp. to lend car-buyers the money to buy GM cars. This can be seen in the data table, showing the complex network of world trade between continents. Asian countries also bought massive amounts of dollars, to keep the exchange rate between their currencies and the dollar from appreciating, and hence making their exports expensive and uncompetitive, an issue discussed later in this chapter.

TABLE 8.2   Official Foreign Exchange Reserves, Key Asian Countries, March 2009 (USD billion)

Country	Official Forex Reserves
China + Hong Kong	2,139
Japan	1,019
Taiwan	305
India	256
S. Korea	212
Singapore	166
Total	**4,097**

Source: International Monetary Fund. www.imf.org (accessed January 31, 2010).

WORLD TRADE NETWORK: WHO TRADES WITH WHOM?

Table 8.3 is a matrix that reveals who bought how much, from whom, for 2006, the year before the global crisis began. The rows and columns of the matrix are continents (except for the Commonwealth of Independent States, representing the nations that once comprised the USSR). The rows represent *exports*—total value of goods exports according to the continent of origin. The columns represent *imports*—the total value of goods imports according to the continent of destination. For instance, Asia exported USD 728 billion worth of goods to North America (US, Canada, Mexico) in 2006, out of its total exports of USD 3,278 billion.

What can we learn from this table? While not easy to read, it is highly revealing. It provides at least four key insights:

- World trade is quantitatively large. Goods trade, totaling USD 11,783 billion, comprised about one-fifth of total world GDP. Two decades earlier, the proportion was only one-tenth.
- Countries trade mainly with their neighbors. About half of Asia's total exports (USD 1,654 billion out of USD 3,278 billion) are made within Asia; and nearly three-fourths of the exports of the 27 European Union nations (USD 3,679 billion out of USD 4,963 billion) are made within Europe (see Box 8.1). There are two exceptions. There is very little trade within Africa. This reveals a major opportunity—by boosting trade among African countries, important new growth engines can be created. A second exception is the Mid-east, simply because most Mideast exports are oil.
- Overall, exports from Africa and from South and Central America to the world are relatively small. Few nations in these continents are truly globally competitive in world markets (Brazil is an exception). The path to economic growth and prosperity for Africa and South America lies through building capability to expand sales in foreign markets.

TABLE 8.3 World Merchandise Trade Network: Trade between Continents, by Origin and Destination, 2006 (USD billion)

	N. America	S., Centr. Am	Europe	C.I.S.	Africa	Mideast	Asia	WORLD
				IMPORTS: BOUGHT BY				
EXPORTS: SOLD BY								
N. America	906	107	279	8	22	42	314	1,678
S., Cen. Am.	134	117	88	6	11	8	66	430
Europe	450	77	3,679	142	120	129	366	4,963
CIS	24	8	248	81	6	13	46	426
Africa	82	13	150	4	35	6	73	363
Mid-east	72	4	103	3	21	7	435	645
Asia	728	90	624	70	90	20	1,656	3,278
WORLD	2,396	416	5,171	314	305	225	2,956	11,783

Source: World Trade Organization International Trade Statistics, 2009. Table A2. Network of Merchandise Trade, by Region, 2008–09. www.wto.org (accessed January 31, 2010).

Note: CIS (Commonwealth of Independent States) is not strictly a continent, but represents the grouping of nations formerly known as the USSR, including Russia.

- There are notable imbalances that clearly cannot be sustained. North America buys over USD 700 billion more from the world than it sells (mainly, the US). About 43 percent of this trade deficit (USD 414 billion out of USD 700 billion) comes from trade with Asia, and 57 percent, from the rest of the world. America's large and growing import surpluses were perceived by China, Japan, Taiwan, Singapore and other major exporting nations as beneficial, since they supplied enormous amounts of demand for those countries' products, generating high economic growth and prosperity for their citizens. The Mideast has an especially large trade surplus, through oil exports, amounting to USD 400 billion. Europe, too, has a trade deficit of some USD 200 billion, of which more than 100 percent stems from trade with Asia.

BOX 8.1   Trade and Peace

France and Germany fought three bitter bloody wars, in 1870, 1914–1918, and 1939–1945. At the end of World War II, a Frenchman named Jean Monnet asked, how can we ensure that a fourth such war does not recur? The answer: Nations that do business with one another, that grow wealthy together, and hence have much to lose from going to war,

(Box 8.1 continued)

(*Box 8.1 continued*)

are more likely to keep the peace. Monnet initiated a brilliant series of policies, driven by the vision of a single European market that began with a coal and steel community between Belgium, Luxembourg, and Holland, and culminated in the European Single Market and the euro. France and Germany today are each other's best customer. It is unthinkable that they would go to war. Moreover, trade within Europe comprises fully 42 percent of global merchandise trade. The trading system within Europe has clearly benefitted all the nations that participate in it. The European Union provides a powerful model for other groups of nations, some of which are in conflict with neighboring countries, for peace-making, in Asia, South America, and Africa.

A not implausible scenario for the medium term, 2015–25, is that Asian nations will replace lost American demand for their goods with internal Asian demand, by building an Asian Single Market, with an Asian currency. Similarly, a North and South American Single Market could be created, joining the economies of Canada, US, Mexico, and South American nations in a single trading bloc, using the US dollar. This scenario is a reasonable alternative to the so-called *The World Is Flat* global system that preceded the 2007–2009 crisis, in which goods could flow freely and unhampered among countries. African nations, whose borders were drawn almost randomly and irrationally by colonial powers, would do well, too, to emulate the European Union *pace through trade* model. Partial, though abortive, experiments, such as the East African Trading Union and the West African Trading Union, have been promising. South America's "Mercosur" trading group (Brazil, Argentina, Uruguay, Paraguay) is a similar, small-scale experiment that at least for a time brought major benefits to its participants.

IS INTERNATIONAL TRADE ALWAYS WIN-WIN?

Managers who have taken a standard Introductory Economics course—so-called Eco 101—will likely recall a basic truism taught universally, the Law of Comparative Advantage, dating back nearly two centuries, to economist David Ricardo, in 1817. This *law* states that when countries specialize in the goods they produce relatively most efficiently, and sell them to other nations in return for goods in which they are less efficient, all countries participating in such trade are better off. In Ricardo's famous example, England made cloth and bought wine from Portugal. England's climate makes it difficult and costly to produce wine, but its industrial prowess makes it efficient at producing cloth. Both England and Portugal gain, when Portugal sells wine to England in return for British cloth. According to this theorem, it must be true that all nations participating in the global trade network shown in Table 8.3 are better off than they would have been in the absence of such trade. Of course, within each country, there are winners (workers and capitalists in industries that export), and losers (workers and capitalists in industries whose goods are replaced by imports). But, it is argued, the overall gains of the winners far outweigh the overall losses of the losers. Without doubt, this is true for many countries that have leveraged booming exports to create jobs, income and wealth. Some economists have claimed that even America's gains from globalization are enormous.[4]

But recently, the dean of American economists, Nobel Laureate Paul Samuelson, cast doubt on whether America has indeed benefitted from the massive world trading system that it helped create in 1944. Trade, argued Samuelson, may not always work to the advantage of the American economy. "...sometimes free trade globalization can [mean that] a productivity gain in one country can benefit that country alone, while *permanently* hurting the other country by reducing the gains from trade that are possible between the two countries."[5]

What Samuelson means is that countries that shift their manufacturing to other countries may lose, when technological improvements and dynamic productivity gains occur primarily in manufacturing, and hence benefit only the countries engaged in it. And this is precisely what has occurred to the United States, we believe. The static *Law of Comparative Advantage* has been repealed, or at least, invalidated, when tested in an ongoing long-run setting.

If Samuelson's argument is true, it suggests not only that America has hurt its own interests in the short-run, by engaging in excessive borrowing that generated a global financial crisis, but also in the long run, by foregoing the productivity gains inherent in producing goods, and ceding those gains to other nations.

The decline in the value of the US dollar relative to other key currencies, (discussed in the next section) may reflect this fact.

INSIDE FOREIGN EXCHANGE

In the preceding chapter, we saw how the price of a company's shares reflects current, and mainly future, after-tax earnings. Similarly, for a country, its *share price* (the value of its currency, relative to other countries' currencies) should also reflect the country's success in global markets, in selling its products relative to the products

---

[4] For example, "The Peterson Institute calculates that the US economy was approximately $1 trillion richer in 2003 due to past globalization—the payoff both from technological innovation and from policy liberalization—and could gain another $500 billion annually from future policy liberalization ... Past gains amounted to about 9% of GDP in 2003, and potential future gains constitute another 4%.." G. Hufbauer, M. Adler, "Why large American gains from globalization are plausible." www.voxeu.org (accessed July 24, 2008).

[5] Paul Samuelson, "Where Ricardo and Mill Rebut and Confirm Arguments of Mainstream Economists Supporting Globalization," *Journal of Economic Perspectives* 18, no. 3. (Summer, 2004): 142.

it buys from other countries. We now proceed to examine the link between global trade and capital flows, and foreign exchange (forex) rates.

Figure 8.5 graphs the relative value of the US dollar in terms of other major countries' currencies, weighted by America's trade with those countries, since 1994. It tells an interesting story about the rise and fall of the dollar.

FIGURE 8.5   Rise and Fall of the American Dollar: Trade-Weighted Index of the Value of the US Dollar, 1994–2009

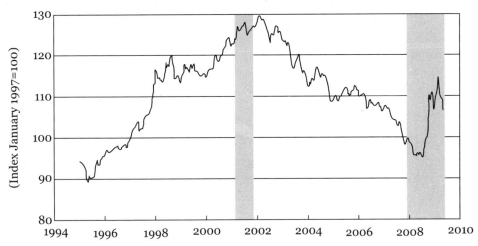

Source: Federal Reserve Bank of St. Louis, 2009. research.stlouisfed.org.
Note: Shaded areas indicate US recessions.

Here is a brief, highly stylized account of how and why, over a quarter century, the dollar rose and declined.

Background

Our story begins well before the start of the graph, in 1985. In that year, the governments of France, West Germany, Japan, UK, and US agreed to purposely lower the value of the dollar. The accord was signed at the Plaza Hotel in New York City, on September 22, 1985. The purpose of the agreement was in part, to boost America's economy, emerging from recession, but mainly, to reduce America's current account deficit, worrisome at the time not only to America but to the world (Why did the much larger, ballooning US trade deficits of the 1990s not worry either America or the world? This is a major mystery!). At the time, the dollar was priced very high in terms of other currencies, partly because very high US interest rates created to battle double-digit inflation in 1980–1982 drew large amounts of money into the US to benefit from those rates. This created demand for US dollars.

So, the fall of the dollar was engineered simply by having Central Banks in the participating nations sell dollars in the forex market. From 1985 to 1987, as a result, the value of the dollar relative to other major currencies fell by a massive 51 percent. America's trade deficit with Western Europe responded well and declined. However, its trade deficit with Japan did not, partly for *structural* reasons—Japan's competitive advantage was not primarily a result of the cheap yen prices, but mainly because of its manufacturing prowess relative to America's. This episode is important, because it does show that decades ago America did seek to actively remedy its trade deficits, albeit with partial success.

Good samaritan

In 1995, America took on the role of global Good Samaritan. Japan's economy was in deep trouble, after Japan's property bubble burst in 1990 and Japanese stocks fell by 75 percent. America decided to help Japan, since Japan's economy was the world's second largest, by strengthening the dollar, thus weakening the yen, and making Japanese exports more competitive, stimulating demand for Japanese goods. The dollar was strengthened in the same way that its value was increased in the early 1980s—through higher interest rates that attracted demand for US dollars. The dollar continued to rise until 2002. The rise in the dollar was steep—an increase of 44 percent, 1995–2002, relative to other major currencies. The dollar then declined. Demand for dollars fell, after US stocks declined, US interest rates fell, and dollars were sold by investors taking their money out of US markets. The decline from 2002–08 was 25 percent.

These swings are very large. They represent substantial risk for global businesses. For a foreign company that sells in America, a falling dollar reduces the value, in local currency, of sales in the US. For example, a car part made in Mexico may bring a USD 10 sale price in the US. At 3.50 pesos per dollar, it is worth 35 pesos. But at 3 pesos per dollar, it is worth 14.3 percent less, or 30 pesos. Similarly a rising dollar reduces the value of foreign revenues for American firms.

Since the end of 2008, the US dollar has strengthened overall by some 25 percent. This may puzzle observers, in light of the continuing weakness of the US economy. It may simply reflect that America's downturn began earlier than in other countries, hence observers anticipate the US recovery will begin sooner, and seek bargains in US asset markets.

Figure 8.5 should have sounded alarm bells years ago. The US dollar is the global marketplace's key currency and main reserve currency. Dollars finance world trade and investment. The world economy, like any domestic economy, requires a stable currency if it is to grow in a sustained and stable fashion. The dollar has been unstable for nearly three decades.

In 1973, US Treasury Secretary John Connolly was asked by foreign journalists about the US dollar, then (as now) in crisis. *"The dollar is our currency—and your (the world's) problem," Connolly said.*[6] This appears to have been America's attitude. US economic policy has focussed mainly on the American economy, but has powerful implications for the world economy, which have been for the most part ignored. Global instability arises, in part, from the fact that the world's currency is managed not according to the broad overall interests of the world, but according to the rather narrow interests of America—and even that, it emerges, was done badly. The dollar is, of course, *both* America's problem *and* the world's.

Exchange rates are determined by supply and demand operating in the world's largest single market—the market for foreign exchange. We now take a closer look at this remarkable, volatile market.

THE GLOBAL FOREIGN EXCHANGE MARKET: USD 1.6–USD 1.9 TRILLION A DAY

The global foreign exchange market is by far the world's largest single market, with daily turnover of an estimated USD 1.6–USD 1.9 trillion. A relatively small number of insiders participate in, and dominate the market. The forex market is entirely electronic and telephonic, built on trust, and on fiber-optic cable. The principal players are banks, oil companies, multinationals, Central Banks, the Sultan of Brunei, and other wealthy individuals. Major players have large foreign exchange trading rooms, often with 30 or more professional traders hunched over computer screens and telephones.

This is a market with no rules except one—if you make a deal, even if you lose your shirt or your job on it, you must pay up. All deals are verbal, made by telephone, with no more legal obligation than the trust binding all the players (many telephone conversations are tape-recorded—just in case).

The forex market is completely frictionless. Broker commissions are miniscule, bid-ask spreads [the difference between what the buyer pays, and what the seller receives, which is the commission taken by the forex broker] are very small, and

---

[6] Harold James, "The Dollar Wars Return." www.project-syndicate.org/commentary/granville10 (accessed January 26, 2010).

a massive amount of trading is carried on simply to get the *feel* of the market—to sense whether players are *long* or *short* on dollars, are tense or loose, whether USD 50 million or USD 100 million can *move the market*. There are no rules. There is no *insider trading*—what is *insider information* in foreign exchange? *Parking* funds with cooperative banks is commonplace, in order to hide a *position*. Traders more than once have floated false rumors to move exchange rates in the direction they want, including the rumor that President Reagan was shot.

The market never closes. When New York trading ceases, action moves to Los Angeles and San Francisco, then to Tokyo, Singapore, Australia, the Far East, the Mideast, then on to Frankfurt, Paris, and London, then back to new York, and so on, in an unending frenzy. Active traders who are running a *position* (holding large amounts of some currency) can literally not afford to sleep. A quick drop in the currency they are holding can bankrupt them while they sleep. Traders take portable Quotron machines (that supply currency rates) to the bathroom and on their daily jobs.

Most trades are done in US dollars, either for yen or Deutschemarks. There are some cross-trades (for example, yen for DM), but most deals are done for dollars. Some currencies are more volatile than others. The Australian and New Zealand dollars (*Aussie* and *Kiwi* are their nicknames) are especially unstable, as funds flow in and out of those countries in search of high-interest rates. Most activity is in *spot* trades, though there is a rapidly growing market in foreign-exchange-related derivatives (futures, options, etc.).

Successful trading in the forex market can generate huge profits. Banker's Trust made over USD 500 million in 1988 from its foreign exchange trading operation, enabling it to write off huge chunks of its uncollectible Latin American debt without foundering. Success in any market requires knowledge or skill that others lack. Successful traders develop a network of friends and acquaintances, who provide tips, opinions and money-parking places. The underlying trade of information is as important to the trader as the overlying trade of dollars.

Corporations with foreign exchange exposures run the risk of incurring large losses. This is a market for insiders and experts. It is not sufficient for a corporation to assign four of five people to manage their foreign exchange risk. The big banks trade heavily enough so that they can, if they wish, at times move the market. The practice of *frontrunning*—trading on the bank's own account before executing a buy order for a client, then selling, pocketing the profit and making the foreign exchange more expensive than need be for the client—is not unknown.

What created this enormous market and when was it born? Its birthday is December 17–18, 1971, the day the Smithsonian Agreements signed in Washington shifted the world from fixed to floating exchange rates. At Bretton Woods, it was agreed that exchange rates would be fixed, to facilitate stability and world trade. But US–Vietnam spending had spilled dollars into the world, and undermined the dollar's value. In December, 1971, and later, in March, 1973, the link between the dollar and gold was broken. Exchange rates were no longer fixed, but *floating*, determined by forces of demand and supply.

Under floating rates, currency values fluctuate. Anything that fluctuates can be a source of speculative profit. Such profits attract funds, which in turn cause increased fluctuations, and like a magnet pull in even more funds. The result: daily turnover has risen by an order of magnitude since 1980. Where currency values were once driven by trade flows, they are now driven by enormous short-term capital flows and interest rates. The tail of capital flows, which once served to finance and facilitate trade, now wags the dog of trade, as it is capital flows that have become dominant rather than exports and imports.

Exchange rates can powerfully impact companies and their financial results. With capital flows now driving exchange rates far more than real trade flows, global businesses may find that losses accrue not because of poor products, but simply because exchange rates have turned unfavorable. The following two case studies reflect this.

CASE STUDY

Harley Davidson Motorcycles

 Harley Davidson is an American motorcycle company, based in Milwaukee. Its long history began in 1901, when William Hartley drew up plans for a motorbike. The rise and fall of Harley parallels the rise and fall of the US dollar, and the US manufacturing sector, as this nutshell history shows.

During the 1950s, Harley Davidson was the market leader in the American motorcycle market. Its motorcycles were known affectionately as *Hogs*. In the 1960s, Japanese cycle manufacturers—Yamaha and Honda—vigorously invaded the US market, beginning with small low-priced bikes, and ultimately challenging Harley's more expensive ones. "I'd rather push a Harley than drive a Honda," read Harley bikers' T-shirts; and their motorcycles often obliged. Harley's US market share of super-heavyweight motorbikes fell from 78 percent in 1973 to less than 30 percent in 1981, as the world invaded their home turf. In that year, a team of 13 Harley executives led by Vaughn L. Beals bought the nearly-bankrupt company.

(Case Study continued)

(Case Study continued)

President Ronald Reagan said in 1980, that if elected he would

1. boost defense spending; and
2. cut taxes.

He was, and he did. The result was ballooning federal budget deficits—from USD 39 billion in 1979 to USD 238 billion in 1986. When the US government borrowed to pay for deficits, the demand for scarce capital raised interest rates. Higher interest rates attracted foreign money to America. This in turn raised the value of the dollar relative yen and marks. *The strong dollar made imports cheaper and exports expensive.* Thus America's trade deficit (difference between imports and exports) grew—and made it necessary to help Harley Davidson in its battle with imported Japanese motorcycles.

In 1983, Harley was given temporary five-year protection from imports, through a 45 percent tariff on Japanese motorcycles (with 700 cc engines or more), under the 1974 Trade Act. By 1986, Harley had sharply raised its market share, and become profitable. The falling US dollar helped by making imported cycles more costly—though Harley's principle success factors were improving quality, design, marketing, and cost efficiency. Harley was able to ask for removal of the high protective tariff well before it expired.

As Harley became more competitive and *Hogs* replaced imported Yamahas, Hondas, and Kawasakis, other US exporters, too, found success in world markets. America's merchandise (that is, goods) trade deficit (the difference between goods imports, and goods exports) fell by half. Meanwhile, back from the brink of bankruptcy, Harley Davidson's stock was listed on the New York Stock Exchange on July 1, 1987, as hordes of *Hog* enthusiasts revved their engines in celebration on Wall Street.

As of November 29, 2002, Harley's stock was worth USD 14.7 billion in market value, and its share price was USD 49, down 18 percent for the year (a smaller drop than the stock averages). Harley earned a high 26 percent return on equity (that is, net profits as a percentage of shareholder's equity). Harley's sales of heavyweight cycles exceed all its competitors combined. However fierce competition from Japanese and German firms eroded Harley's profit margins, and brought its overall motorcycle market share down sharply from its 71 percent high in 1991.

The ferocious ups and downs experienced by Harley Davidson reflect the huge challenges faced by American managers who seek to maintain manufacturing capability in their own country, and the huge risks created by fluctuations in the dollar and other currencies.

CASE STUDY

How Exchange Rate Fluctuations Impact Businesses

 Until 1971, the world's monetary system was based on a system of fixed prices for dollars in terms of pounds, yen, and deutschemarks (DM). For a whole generation, from the end of World War II to 1971, a dollar traded for about 360 yen, 3.5 DM, and about 0.4 British pounds—and USD 35 per ounce of gold. Managers could learn exchange rates *once each generation*. The system then changed radically, as the US dollar was no longer anchored to gold (see ahead: The Gold Standard). *Managers now, it emerged, had to learn exchange rates, not once in a generation but perhaps even once every hour.*

- A Nissan compact car made in Japan, with a 2.1 million. Yen price tag, sold for USD 15,000 in San Francisco in 1989. After the dollar plummeted in value relative to the yen (from 142 yen per dollar to 80) in 1995, the same car cost USD 26, 250 in April 1995—75 percent more—*when Nissan kept its yen price steady.* The Yen later fell to over 120 per dollar in 2001.

- An auto parts firm invests 100 million pesos (about USD 30 million) in a plant in Mexico in 1993, when the peso is about 3.5 per dollar. By Spring 1995 the value of that 100 million peso investment is worth half, as the peso is rapidly devalued from 3.5 per dollar to 7. The company is consoled, however, by the fact that an auto part made in Mexico for 1,000 pesos and sent north, now costs in dollars half what it did earlier: USD 142 rather than USD 285.

- GM's Opel division in Germany finds that a hundred million Deutschemarks (DM) in profit, when listed in GM's P&L in US dollars, is worth only USD 28.5 million in 1985, but as the value of the DM in terms of dollars more than doubles, is worth USD 66.7 million. in 1995. When the DM abruptly falls, the windfall gain turns to loss—100 million DM is worth only USD 58 million in 1997.

- Nissan, after struggling for years against the ravage of the soaring yen (and soaring costs and prices abroad), gets a respite, as the dollar strengthens 50 percent between 1995 and 1997, pricing its 2.1 million Yen compact car back at USD 16,800—almost closing the 1985–1995–1997 circle.

If exchange rate changes are a source of global risk, how can global managers track them, and anticipate future changes? These case studies direct us toward our next challenge—to use the concept of PPP to provide a useful tool for tracking exchange rates. We offer a useful tool for this purpose.

Supplementary Tool

 Purchasing power parity exchange rate (PPP): The big Mac rate.

CHINA'S BUSINESS MODEL: IN SEARCH OF THE TRUE RENMINBI

China's currency is known as the RMB or ren-min-bi, which means *money of the people* in Mandarin. It is also called the yuan, meaning *round* in Mandarin (pertaining to round coins). The *money of the people* holds the key to understanding China's remarkable business model, which has delivered double-digit GDP growth rates for two decades—a feat hard to sustain for a small company, let alone a nation with 1.2 billion people once mired in poverty. To understand how this was done, we need to employ a tool that helps measure the *real*, economic or purchasing power value of a currency, relative to the dollar. This is needed, because it is argued that the Chinese government has artificially maintained a highly undervalued exchange rate for RMB relative to dollars, by massive purchases of dollars.

Several years ago, the first author purchased a bright red genuine imitation-silk tie in Shanghai. The tie cost 10 yuan, or renminbi. At the time, the dollar-yuan exchange rate was 8 yuan per dollar. In dollars, therefore, the tie cost USD 1.25. The manufacturer of the tie, whom we will call *China Ties*, made a respectable profit. Few if any tie-makers outside of China could even begin to compete with that manufacturer.

What gave China Ties, and every other exporter in China, an enormous advantage, was the 8 yuan-per-dollar exchange rate. The true, economic, or *purchasing power* exchange rate, the exchange rate that would have prevailed had the forces of supply and demand operated freely and fully in foreign exchange markets, was 4 yuan per dollar (see Purchasing Power Parity tool). Had that exchange rate prevailed, the tie would have cost 10 yuan/4 = USD 2.50. And it would have prevailed, had the forces of supply and demand for yuan and dollars operated freely, without intervention.

Perhaps, just perhaps, foreign tie-makers in, say, Bolivia and Malaysia could have competed in world markets at that USD 2.50 price. But not at USD 1.25. The world's most powerful tie, apparently, is a result of one of the world's most powerful currency, the yuan, which enables foreigners to buy twice as much in China, with their own money, as they would if the exchange rate reflected true purchasing power.

China maintained the *undervalued* 8 yuan-per-dollar exchange rate for years, by massive purchases of US dollars, and dollar assets in foreign exchange markets. For over a entire decade, from 1996–2006, China maintained the 8.31 yuan per dollar rate. This process continues, despite the sharp drop in the value of the dollar, creating major capital losses for China, which holds some USD 2 trillion in dollar assets, and despite massive US pressure on China to allow its currency to appreciate, making its exports more expensive and reducing the export surplus in its trade with the US.

Where did China acquire its *undervalued yuan* business model? The answer is clear—it learned from Japan (see Box 8.2).

BOX 8.2   *Rocket Science* Sets the Yen–Dollar Rate

The exchange rate between the Japanese yen and the American dollar remained constant for a full generation, 25 years, from 1945 through 1970, at 360 yen per dollar. What miracles of economic rocket science were used to set this magical exchange rate—one that drove trade patterns and economic relations between the US and Japan for over two decades?

General Douglas MacArthur, head of the American military and civilian forces occupying (and running) Japan after World War II, asked the Japanese what their currency was called. The yen, they said. What does that mean? He asked.

It means, *roundlike*, a circle, they responded.

"Hmmm," mused MacArthur, "a circle...."

And then, in a flash of insight, he knew he had zeroed in on the appropriate exchange rate.

Circle—360. Three hundred and sixty degrees—and that was how the Yen got its 360-yen-per-dollar exchange rate. It proved fateful, and fortuitous, for Japan's economy and people. The true purchasing power of the Japanese yen was far greater than the 360-yen-per-dollar exchange rate indicated. Perhaps, what a dollar could buy, 180 yen could buy. *This gave Japanese goods a permanent "half-price sale"—their goods cost half, in dollars, than what they would have, if the exchange rate had been determined by relative buying power.* Years later, China simply copied this powerful business model, that created rapid export-driven growth.

PURCHASING POWER EXCHANGE RATES

How would we know what the PPP value of the renminbi, or yuan, is? How can we show, for instance, that the PPP rate is 3.53 yuan per dollar, in 2009, making the yuan far more valuable than the official exchange rate of 6.86? The answer is supplied by our supplementary tool, the PPP exchange rate.

The basic idea behind the method for judging the true value, or purchasing power, of a currency, relative to that of the American dollar, is appealingly simple.

Construct a shopping list

Take the list to New York and other US cities and buy everything on it. Make a note of what the products on the list cost—say, a total of USD 1,000. Now take the same list to Shanghai, Beijing, Nanjang, and Guangzhou. Buy everything on it. Say the same shopping list costs 3,530 yuan (RMB) to buy.

If USD 1,000 buys what 3,530 yuan buys—then USD 1 is equivalent in purchasing power to 3,530 yuan:

$$1,000 \text{ USD} = 3,530 \text{ Yuan}$$

Therefore:

$$\text{USD } 1 = 3.53 \text{ Yuan}$$

If your shopping list were a basket of items that enter into US–China trade, then your shopping expedition offers a clue about "underlying" or "true value" exchange rates between dollars and yen. This simple idea is known as purchasing power parity—and it says that *exchange rates should reflect underlying prices and costs in each country, and each unit of currency should buy roughly equal amounts of goods and services in the two countries.*

If the shopping basket wasn't too big and bulky one could *arbitrage* it. Arbitrage is the operation of buying low and selling high, to make a profit. If, say, the actual dollar–yuan exchange rate were 8 Yuan per dollar (a level it maintained for over a decade, until 2007) one could invest 3,530/8 = USD 441, buy the *basket* of goods in China for 3,530 yuan, take it to America, sell the goods for USD 1,000, and pocket the sizeable profit of USD 1,000–USD 441 = USD 559. A 56 percent profit—not bad for one trip. And, of course, *this is precisely what occurs*, though it is not called arbitrage and largely it happens when, for instance, the US retail chain Wal-Mart buys goods from its over 6,000 suppliers in Shanghai alone, then ships them to the US, and sells them in its huge stores.

Burgernomics

How can the purchasing power parity notion be implemented in practice? No one is going to travel the world weekly with shopping lists. In 1986, *The Economist* found an amusing and original way to compute true rates, known as *burgernomics* or the Big Mac exchange rate. Their idea was to use Big Macs, consistent in quality and weight, in place of the cumbersome *shopping list.*

"It is not a precise predictor of currencies," *The Economist* puns, "simply a tool to make exchange-rate theory a bit more digestible."[7] Big Macs, the largest-selling hamburger of the McDonald's hamburger chain, are sold in 80 countries around the world. (It is not sold in India due to the widespread taboo on eating beef, stemming from the Hindu religious belief. However, the Maharaja Burger in India is equivalent, and can be used for the same purpose.)

In each country, the Big Mac has a price, in local currency. For instance, in China a Big Mac cost 12.50 yuan in January, 2009. At the same time the average price of a Big Mac in New York, Chicago, San Francisco, and Atlanta was USD 3.54. Hence: What 12.50 Yuan buys in Beijing, USD 3.54 buys in the US.

The Big Mac Purchasing Power Parity exchange rate is simply the ratio of those two numbers: the ratio of the dollar price of a Big Mac, and the yuan price:

$$USD\ 3.54 = 12.50\ Yuan = ONE\ BIG\ MAC$$

Therefore:

$$USD\ 1.00 = 12.50\ Yuan/USD\ 3.54 = 3.53\ Yuan$$

The Big Mac exchange rate of the Yuan, when compared with the official exchange rate (6.84 Yuan per dollar on January 30, 2009) shows the Purchasing Power rate (3.53 Yuan per dollar) is only 52 percent of the official rate (6.84 yuan). In other words the Yuan is undervalued by about half. If Chinese goods were priced at the Big Mac exchange rate, rather than the official rate, they would cost twice as much in US dollars.

The Big Mac exchange rates are calculated at regular intervals, and published in *The Economist* (see Table 8.4). They reveal an interesting pattern. Like China, many countries purposely undervalue their currencies—that is, foster exchange rates relative to the dollar, so that dollars are very expensive in terms of local currency. Far more currencies in the world are undervalued (that is, the price of local currency in terms of US dollars is very cheap) than are overvalued. This is simply another way of saying that the American dollar is still overvalued (too expensive), despite its sharp decline.

JUDGING MARKET SIZE

In carrying out *due diligence* studies of possible new markets, global managers first want to know how large that market is. A preliminary measure is simply GDP. But comparing GDP values of different countries requires measuring them in a common currency, usually dollars, and this in turn means we need to choose an exchange rate, to convert GDP in local currency to GDP in dollars. Which exchange rate should be used for this purpose, market exchange rates or PPP rates?

---

[7] http://www.encyclopedia.com/doc/1G1-73409219.html (accessed January 26, 2010).

TABLE 8.4   Actual and "Big Mac" Exchange Rates (Number of Local Currency Units that One US Dollar Can Buy), January 30, 2009

Country	Actual Exchange Rate Local Money Per US$	Big Mac Exchange Rate Local Money Per US$	Big Mac/Actual (%)
Brazil	2.32	2.27	97.8
Britain	1.44	1.55	107.6
China	6.84	3.53	51.6
Hong Kong	7.75	3.76	48.5
Japan	89.8	81.9	91.2
Euro Zone	1.28	1.04	81.3
Switzerland	1.16	1.84	158.6
S. Korea	1,380	932	67.5
India	47	27.1	57.7

Source: "Big Mac Index," *The Economist*, London, UK, January 22, 2009. www.economist.com, (accessed January 31, 2010).

Table 8.5 shows GDP for a dozen major countries, in dollars, measured with both actual exchange rates and PPP exchange rates (note: this data come from the IMD World Competitiveness Yearbook, based on World Bank data, and use PPP rates that differ, often substantially, from the Big Mac rates shown above). The table reveals that when existing market exchange rates are used, China Mainland's economy is only fourth in size in the world. But measured at PPP rates, it is second. If China's GDP grows by 8 percent, while US GDP grows by only 2 percent annually, China's GDP (at PPP) will overtake America's in less than a decade. India leaps from

TABLE 8.5   GDP, at Market Exchange Rates, and at PPP Exchange Rates, 2007, 12 Countries, (USD Billion)

Country	GDP	Country	GDP (PPP)
US	13,841	US	13,453
Japan	4,380	China Mainland	6,786
Germany	3,317	Japan	4,167
China Mainland	3,242	India	2,978
UK	2,770	Germany	2,729
France	2,556	UK	2,064
Italy	2,102	Russia	2,020
Spain	1,437	France	1,997
Canada	1,426	Brazil	1,786
Brazil	1,314	Italy	1,735
Russia	1,290	Spain	1,312
India	1,135	Mexico	1,311

Source: World Competitiveness Yearbook, 2008 (Lausanne, Switzerland, IMD: 2009). GDP and GDP (PPP), p. 293.

12th to 4th, using PPP rates. Canada exits the table altogether, replaced by Mexico, when PPP is used.

Both measures are required. Use GDP at market rates to determine the actual market size. Use GDP at PPP rates to determine how large the market would be, if exchange rates were to change in the direction of the PPP rates—a change that in the medium to long term, is quite likely.

Can Big Mac exchange rates serve as a serious guide for managers to impending exchange rate changes? The answer appears to be yes—with reservations (see Case Study: PPP as a Crystal Ball).

CASE STUDY

PPP as a Crystal Ball

- On April 7, 1995, the Japanese yen soared to its all-time high of only 84 yen to the dollar, while the Big Mac yen-dollar PPP rate was 169 yen to the dollar—implying the yen was 100 percent overvalued. The source of this overvaluation was Japan's high prices stemming from its protected domestic market, insulated from the competition of foreign goods. The Big Mac yen-dollar rate hinted that the 84 yen per dollar exchange rate gave the yen an exaggerated value—and indeed, within weeks, the yen dropped, to over 100 yen per dollar. By April 1997, deflation within Japan, and changes in the yen-dollar exchange rates, had adjusted exchange rates close to their PPP value.

- Two major currencies remain out-of-line with underlying values. China maintains its policy of maintaining an undervalued yuan, thanks to continuing purchases of dollars. And the Swiss franc remains powerfully overvalued, making Swiss products expensive, because of ongoing strong demand for Swiss francs (as money flows into Switzerland, to their banks). China faces the cruel dilemma of continuing to acquire dollar assets, with inherent risk that a decline in the dollar will create large capital losses, or stop acquiring them, and see the yuan–dollar rate sink, endangering China's business model. Switzerland, a major exporting nation, struggles to maintain its competitive advantage despite the fact that buying Swiss goods (hence buying Swiss francs) is very expensive. We predict that both the overvalued Swiss franc, and undervalued Chinese yuan, will move toward their PPP rates in the future. To some degree, this has happened in the past two years with the yuan.

WHY DO THE VALUE OF CURRENCIES DEVIATE FROM PPP?

What is it that *causes* currencies to deviate from their purchasing-power values? A study of 14 countries by Robert Cumby notes that the average dollar prices of Big Macs differ substantially across countries owing to differences in taxes, labor costs, and rents. But once these deviations are taken into account, deviations from *Big Mac parity*—that is, exchange rates that make the price of a Big Mac the same in each country—are temporary, with a half-life of about a year (that is, half the deviation between the Big Mac rate and the actual rate vanishes in a year). More important, deviations from Big Mac parity provide useful information for forecasting exchange rates. Cumby finds "a 10 percent undervaluation according to the hamburger standard in one year is associated with a 3.5 percent appreciation over the following year."[8] In other words, undervalued currencies tend toward appreciation (rise in value relative to the dollar) over the next year, though *The Economist* itself notes, "studies have found that although [Purchasing Power Parity] does hold in the very long run, currencies can indeed deviate from the (PPP) equilibrium for lengthy periods." This is particularly true for China, which has used massive purchases of US dollars and dollar assets to maintain its export-favorable yuan exchange rate.

There are three powerful forces that affect market exchange rates. One is intervention—Central Banks buy and sell dollars to manipulate exchange rates in directions they believe are desirable. A second is *expectations* and the speculation they drive. The third is interest rates.

Expectations

In any volatile market with huge speculative activity, traders bet on future directions. A market driven by expectations is by definition unstable, because expectations are fickle and subject to rapid change. It tends to become a one-way market, when traders mostly agree, and hence *moves* are large and often overshoot. The behavior of the dollar relative to their currencies exhibits the behavior of an unstable feedback system, and has been so for about a decade. Two *Wall Street Journal* headlines in 1996 reveal how market expectations operate:

---

[8] Robert Cumby, "Forecasting Exchange Rate and Relative Prices with the Hamburger Standard: Is What You Want What You Get with McParity?" (Cambridge, MA, 1996) Working Paper #5675, NBER).

- "U.S. Trade Deficit Balloons to its Worst Level in Years":

  The U.S. in July posted its largest trade deficit in almost five years, an USD 11.68 billion gap that stunned economists. In a textbook example of everything going wrong that could, exports shrank—by USD 2.54 billion to USD 67.19 billion—and imports grew, by USD 953 million. It was America's worst monthly trade performance since January, 1992.... America's performance with all of its major trading partners was equally dismal ... the Trade gap with China continued to spiral, increasing to USD 3.82 billion from last month's USD 3.33 billion ... and with Japan, grew to USD 4.31 billion from USD 3.24 billion.... Economists said that slow growth in Western Europe accounted for that large deficit [with Western Europe]....

- "Dollar Tumbles into Gap Left by U.S. Trade Figures":

  The dollar plunged in a matter of minutes against the mark and yen in afternoon trading here on news the U.S. trade deficit widened surprisingly in July from June. At the same time the yen gained against most major currencies....[9]

The operative mechanism here driving exchange rates is *not* the fact that as the US imports more than it exports, excess supply of dollars drives the exchange rate down. Rather, the huge trillion-dollar market *reacts* to that news, and many other sorts of news, by selling dollars and driving down its value. The *expectation* of such a reaction to the news is sufficient to create the drop itself. Often, the dollar dives or soars on the whisper of rumors about impending data, which often turn out to be false or misguided.

Interest rates

Huge pools of capital exist that race from city to city, currency to currency, seeking fractionally higher interest rates and fractionally lower exchange risk or inflation. As this money travels the world, it bounces exchange rates up and down.

EXCHANGE RATES: FIXED OR FLOATING?

In December, 1971, we have observed, the link between the dollar and gold was broken. Exchange rates soon were *floating*, rather than fixed. In this new system, managers had to update their knowledge of exchange rates *hourly* or in crisis conditions each *minute*. Few changes in the global business environment were more sweeping, less predictable, or less understood.

---

[9] *Wall Street Journal* Europe, September 19, 1996, pp. 2, 20.

Suppose you earned a billion Italian lire in sales in July 1992. At that time, Italy was part of the so-called Exchange Rate Mechanism (ERM), which linked currencies to one another at fixed prices. The French franc, British pound, German mark, Italian lire, etc., were allowed to fluctuate against one another only within narrow 2.25 percent bands above and below central rates.

You might have felt safe in leaving your lire in Italy. After all, under the ERM Italy promised to keep its currency at close to the prevailing rate of 1,130 lire for one US dollar. At that exchange rate, a billion lire were worth USD 885,000. Moreover, interest rates in Italy were much higher than in the US So, why rush to buy dollars and bring home the Italian earnings? But in mid-September 1992, following massive speculative selling of pounds and lire, the United Kingdom dropped out of the ERM and Italy's *band* was widened; the pound and the lire plummeted as a result. Individuals and businesses with *unhedged* (that is, uninsured against changes in exchange rates) lire and pounds lost heavily. In July 1993, one US dollar cost 1,583 lire. Your billion Italian lire were worth on USD 632,000—30 percent fewer dollars than a year earlier. Had you failed to insure yourself against this risk, the loss would have been painful. For smaller businesses, it could even have been life-threatening. Hedging—buying *insurance* against currency risk—is not without pain. Like auto insurance, the cost rises as the roads get riskier. At times, it is prohibitively costly—Ciba Geigy, for instance, chose not to hedge in the late 1980s, despite the consequences.

The Gold Standard

In many ways, today's globalization is *déjà vu*. We had a far more global world in the 19th century, when governments were small, regulation was nonexistent, and a world trading system existed, organized and run by Britain and its empire. And we had a far more stable, clever monetary system, based on the gold standard.

For over a century and a half, currencies were defined in terms of fixed amounts of gold. For instance, in 1900, the US dollar was set at USD 20 per ounce of gold. That basic rate remained true, until the Great Depression, when the dollar was devalued to USD 35 per ounce.

When nations traded, countries that exported more than they imported gained gold. So their money supply increased. As a result prices rose, thus decreasing their export advantage, and making imports more worthwhile. This continued until the trade surplus disappeared.

Conversely, nations that had import surpluses lost gold. Their money supply contracted. As a result, prices fell, the economy contracted, incomes fell and people bought fewer imports—until the import surplus disappeared. *It was an automatic mechanism* that did not depend on the clever policy actions of national governments. And it worked for over 150 years (see Figure 8.6).

FIGURE 8.6   The Automatic Feedback Mechanism of the Gold Standard

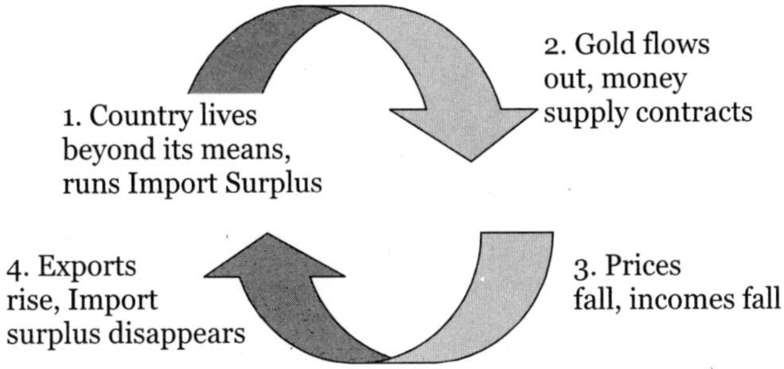

1. Country lives beyond its means, runs Import Surplus

2. Gold flows out, money supply contracts

3. Prices fall, incomes fall

4. Exports rise, Import surplus disappears

Source: Authors.

Some experts have recommended a return to the gold standard, as a way of stabilizing the world's monetary system. The flaw in this proposal is that if world trade again begins to grow rapidly, it will be necessary to expand the world's money supply to finance that growth—but if the gold standard prevails, linking domestic currencies to gold stocks, then world money can grow only as fast as the mining of new gold for monetary purposes. This may be inadequate. There is a better solution. It is one proposed by J.M. Keynes in 1944, at Bretton Woods. Had the world listened to Keynes and adopted it then, perhaps the successive crises, culminating with the 2007–2009 crisis, would not have occurred (see Box 8.3).

Box 8.3   Bretton Woods: Why *Bancor* was Still-born?

Two proposals were on the table at Bretton Woods, in 1944, for redesigning the world's monetary system. One proposal came from America's Harry Dexter White, a Treasury official. White proposed a *dollar standard*. Dollars are convertible into gold, White observed. So why not fix the price of dollars in terms of gold, and have countries hold dollars as their monetary reserves? The gold standard worked well. The dollar standard will work equally well.

British economist J.M. Keynes was unconvinced. Because the US can *create* dollars, it may create too many of them or, indeed, create too few. In any event, the amount of dollars created by America will be set by American, not world, interests. Why not establish a world central bank, Keynes proposed, with the power to create global money (money used only in international transactions, for trade and capital investment)? Just as major countries have central banks, so should the world have its own central bank, with money creation determined by the interests of the global trading system.

America rejected Keynes' plan. At the time, America dominated Bretton Woods. His plan made much sense. Had it been implemented, perhaps many of the crises described in this and the preceding chapters would not have occurred.

CONCLUSION

World trade has grown rapidly since World War II, providing the main fuel for world GDP growth. This is an important reason why global managers need to understand how to decipher trade figures, as contained in the Balance of Payments. At the same time global capital flows have also exploded; these too are crucial, and also find expression in the Balance of Payments—another reason why global managers are extremely good at reading this cash-flow account.

Global companies face risk in terms of unexpected changes in foreign exchange rates. A 20 percent rise in sales abroad can be nullified by a 20 percent increase in the value of local currency, in terms of dollars, meaning that a dollar generates 20 percent less local money. Thus global managers need strong expertize in tracking forex movements, and the huge volatile forex market in general. And they face tough decisions on whether to *insure* against currency risk (through hedging, or transactions that offset possible losses), an expensive cost, or to accept the risk and manage it directly.

Global economic crises spread from one country to another through the mechanism of world trade and investment. The more closely national markets are linked, through trade and capital flows, the quicker a domestic downturn in a major country becomes global in nature. This is what happened in 2007–2009, as the crisis began in the United States, and quickly spread throughout the world.

All of this suggests that every global manager must adopt a true global perspective, tracking trade and money in all parts of the world, knowing how to read somewhat baffling tables of data that reflect such developments, while reading *between the lines* and *behind the numbers* to anticipate potential disruptions in trade, and to identify major opportunities disguised as risk.

In the previous eight chapters, our focus was primarily on economic tools. In today's world, there are major risks that are not economic in nature. Global managers must be aware of such risks. This is the subject of our next chapter—Non-economic risk.

Chapter 9

Non-economic risks

LEARNING OBJECTIVES

While the core of this book deals with economic and financial risks, and opportunities, there are many other non-economic risks that global managers must constantly monitor. After reading this chapter, readers should understand how, and why, to proactively identify, and act to mitigate the impact of non-economic risk, and to capitalize on the opportunities such risk creates. While it is not possible to exhaustively cover all types of non-economic risks that companies face, we present three of the most important risks to which managers should be increasingly sensitive, and in this manner, were sent to provide a taste of what managers' challenges are, in addressing non-economic risk. Through a series of detailed case studies, readers will be introduced to *political risks*, risks stemming from *terrorism*, and *environment-related risks*. Typically, these risks stem from outside the company. They will also learn how some companies have benefitted from the opportunities created by these risks. Examples of companies that did not properly manage such risks, and the consequences they faced, as a result, are also presented. We also briefly discuss risks that stem from sources internal to the company.

After reading this chapter, readers should be able to answer these questions:

- Besides economic risk inherent in capital markets, which is the primary thrust of our book, what other types of risks should managers track on their radar screens?
- Are there some generic tools that can be deployed to understand these risks?
- Are these risks independent of each other, or do they operate in tandem?
- What are the consequences of not managing these risks?
- Are there opportunities embedded in these risks that can be leveraged? If so, how?

Tool # 9

 Assessing and tracking non-economic risk

To ignore political risk is dangerous. To avoid it is shortsighted. To use it can be very profitable.

—Ian Bremmer[1]

INTRODUCTION

In the preceding eight chapters, we have focussed exclusively on risks and opportunities arising from economic and financial forces in global markets, and provided tools for assessing and managing those risks, and transforming them into business opportunities. But increasingly, companies additionally face challenges to their businesses, and to their business models that are inherently non-economic in nature. For example, the events of 9/11 in the United States totally transformed the businesses of airlines, as air travel collapsed overnight.

The reason non-economic risks have grown rapidly was stated succinctly by former American Secretary of State Henry Kissinger: "Economics have become global. Communications have become global. *Politics have become local.* We have expanded our knowledge ... while shrinking our perspective. This is the biggest challenge facing us."[2]

The combination of increasingly global markets—what *New York Times* columnist Thomas Friedman described as a *flat world*—and increasingly local, fragmented politics has created immense challenges for global managers. Economics is global. Politics are local. Therein lies the problem. Local politics create local risks, and indirectly, lead to terrorism, as minority groups seek independence and autonomy through force of arms and explosives. Moreover, an inherently global issue—preserving the quality of our air, water, land, and climate—flounders as countries pursue their own, narrow interests in preserving the environment. Hence, the three forms of non-economic risks addressed in this chapter all stem, we believe, in large part from the fragmented nature of local politics, which directly clashes with the complex global system of markets that has arisen. We will address such risks mainly through case studies—stories about how companies have dealt with such risks, or in some cases,

---

[1] Ian Bremmer, "How to Calculate Political Risk, Inc." http://www.inc.com/magazine/20070401/features-calculate-political-risk.html (accessed January 18, 2010).

[2] Henry Kissinger's Address, Boston University Commencement, May 23, 1999 at Boston University. http://www.bu.edu/commencement/1999/kissinger-speech.html (accessed January 26, 2010).

failed to. These three categories of risks stem from sources that are external to the business. In the concluding part of this chapter, we will also look at risk that arises from within the organization.

We first turn to the issue of political risk—how to assess it, manage it, and leverage it for business opportunities.

POLITICAL RISK[3]

There were only 62 countries in the world at the onset of World War I. A major reason was that the Great Powers—mainly Britain, along with France, Germany, Portugal, Spain, Belgium, Holland, and the United States—held colonies. At the end of World War II, there were still only 74 countries in the whole world.

But decolonization and independence movements brought a major increase. By the year 2006, there were some 192 independent countries who were members of the United Nations, and one additional *country* not belonging to the UN, the Vatican. Some 240 countries are listed by the World Bank. There are perhaps an additional 20 or 30 entities that are essentially countries, such as Chinese Hong Kong or Taiwan. Hence, the number of countries has tripled in the past 60 years. And the number is still growing.

The process of decolonization has been a source of armed conflict for decades. Many nations had to fight with force of arms to become independent. In Africa, decolonization has been especially destructive. The colonial powers have drawn almost random lines on the map, creating countries that cross common tribal, ethnic and language divisions in a random and mean-spirited fashion. The result has been rebellion, low-level warfare and economic stagnation. The massacre in Rwanda, resulting from enmity between two tribes enclosed within the same illogical *lines on the map*, is a bitter example, one of many, as is the post-election tribal violence in Kenya.

The decolonization process ended, essentially, in the 1960s, but it has become an ever-increasing source of global instability. The reason for this is clear. Once, before globalization, being a citizen of a country conferred major advantages. It gave access to finance, capital markets, trade, shipping, transport, licenses to do business, labor markets, and legal representation. But in the age of globalization, the advantages that a nation-state confers have been enormously reduced. When markets for goods, services, capital, and technology are global—world-wide in nature—one no longer needs the backbone of a nation-state. Economics, business, marketing, entrepreneurship are

---

[3] This section is based in part on R.L. Dilworth and S. Maital, *Fogs of War and Peace* (New York: Praeger Security, 2007), 33–35.

all global, as Kissinger notes. But in contrast, politics has become increasingly local. If one no longer needs the advantages of a nation-state, then loyalty and support pass to smaller and smaller units: ethnic groups, religious groups, regions, even cities. Indeed, it is no longer sensible to speak about *globally competitive countries*, but rather about *globally attractive regions and cities*—Bangalore (in the state of Karnataka), and Chennai (or Madras, in Tamil Nadu) are magnets for information technology companies, in India, but Ahmedabad (in Gujarat) is not.

There is an inherent internal contradiction between global economics and local politics. Global economics requires global politics—mechanisms to resolve disputes and organize global markets. But few such mechanisms exist. Instead, politics are now being fought at the local level. *Fragmented politics and global economics are a recipe for instability*. This is why global managers must necessarily become expert global political scientists.

There are enormous centrifugal forces at work in the world that could conceivably cause large countries to fly apart in the future. Among the candidates: Canada (split between French and English-speaking Canada), Russia (Islamic ethnic groups in Chechnya and elsewhere), and even China. While Canada held a national referendum on independence for Quebec, in other countries the process is far less peaceful and more bloody. Yugoslavia, now fragmented into several countries along ethnic and religious lines, could be replicated elsewhere in the coming decades. In the future, such conflicts, arising from local politics and global economics, will grow in intensity and in frequency. Redrawing lines on maps is rarely done without armed conflict.

Many companies have traditionally been comfortable doing business in their familiar home markets, due to perceived difficulties in dealing with different cultures, languages, legal, regulatory or tax systems, etc., in unknown markets. The anxiety stems not just from these factors, but additionally from having to deal with unpredictable events such as labor unrest or violence originating from a variety of sources; different and often unfamiliar governmental systems; and instability arising from frequent changes in governments; and many more; all of which carry significant risks, broadly classified as political risks.

DEFINITION

Political risk is the assessment of the impact that the political environment, events or decisions in a country or, indeed, a region, may have on the operation of a business, with the consequence that investors may lose their money or that the investment may not reach expectations.[4]

---

[4] Bob McDowall, "Assessing political risk—Has anything changed?" IT-Director.com, http://www.it-director.com/business/content.php?cid=6102 (accessed January 26, 2010).

Despite high political risks, many companies have succeeded in broadening their footprint, by pushing into countries other than their home countries. The ever-accelerating process of globalization energized this trend. While companies that have succeeded in moving to countries other than their home countries act as role models for other aspiring companies that seek to globalize, this still does not reduce the inherent political risks involved in doing business in countries that the company is not familiar with. Familiarity with the nature of these risks is the first step in mitigating their impact. Interestingly, it is not just moving to new countries that entail political risks. Locating new business within the home country also creates political risk. In countries such as India, with huge diversity from state to state, and region to region, there is considerable variation in the political risk profile across the country, as the recent controversy surrounding the events relating to the location of the Nano car project suggest.

Here is what can happen when a company, Tata Motors, encounters unexpected local political instability.

CASE STUDY

Tata Motors: Political Unrest Ousts Tata Nano from West Bengal[5]

 When Ratan Tata, Chairman of Tata Motors, saw millions of two-wheelers plying on the Indian roads, most bearing whole families—both parents and children, he felt a serious need to offer safer alternatives for the two-wheeler families. Thus was born the idea of producing the Tata Nano, a car that was inexpensive, safer, and an all-weather substitute for Indian families with two-wheelers. Nano, the world's cheapest car, with a price tag of about USD 2,000, was expected to expand the Indian car market by 65 percent apart from giving a boost to the Indian economy.

In May, 2006, Tata Motors announced that a new factory in Singur, West Bengal (one of India's poorest states, in the eastern part of the country) would be setup to carry out manufacturing of the Nano. No sooner was the announcement made, farmers in Singur started to oppose the acquisition of their lands by the Tatas for the car project. This soon turned into violent protests. Opposition parties in the State Assembly too disapproved

(Case Study continued)

---

[5] This case study is based on the following sources: Tata Nano, Wikipedia. http://en.wikipedia.org/wiki/Tata_Nano; *and "Talks over Tata Nano car Deadlock", BBC News, http://news.bbc.co.uk/2/hi/south_asia/7599466.stm* (accessed January 26, 2010).

(*Case Study continued*)

Tata's move. Mamata Banerjee, the leader of the opposition party Trinamool Congress, took up the cause of the farmers. Trinamool Congress insisted that Tata Motors return 400 acres of requisitioned land to the farmers. The agitation reached its peak in October, 2006, and Trinamool Congress called for a state-wide *bandh* (lock-out). The state government deployed huge police forces at the Singur site to keep the situation under control and halt protests. In December, 2006, there was large scale violence and exchange of blows between farmers and the police. Mamata Banerjee went on a two-day hunger strike in protest of the developments at Singur. Tata Motors started to express reservations about continuing the project at Singur.

Demonstrations and rallies continued through 2007, and in 2008, the High Court of Calcutta (West Bengal) approved of the acquisition of land by Tata Motors. However, the political upheavals and heavy monsoons hindered the plant construction, forcing Tata Motors to postpone the launch of the Nano to September, 2008. Agitations went unabated in 2008. On September 2, 2008, Tata Motors made a decision to stop further work at Singur. It was at this time, that Mr Narendra Modi the Chief Minister of Gujarat, a state in the western part of India that is known to be industry-friendly, is reported to have sent an SMS to Mr Ratan Tata, "Welcome to Gujarat!" Within days thereafter, the Government of Gujarat entered into a MoU (memorandum of understanding) with Tata Motors, and proposed Sanand near Ahmedabad as the new location for the Nano plant. The government of Gujarat consented to provide not only incentives that were promised by the West Bengal government, but much more. Furthermore, the land at Sanand provided for a plant with an annual capacity of 500,000 cars as opposed to 300,000 afforded by Singur. These aggressive moves by the Government of Gujarat to woo the Tata Nano project to Gujarat were essentially completed in a few weeks. The speed at which the industrially progressive government of Gujarat leveraged this opportunity is in glaring contrast to the treatment meted out to the company earlier in West Bengal.

Former MIT Sloan School of Management Dean Lester Thurow once commented that global business has changed radically. Once, he said, businesses paid taxes to governments. Today, governments pay taxes to businesses. He meant that governments aggressively wooing foreign investment and local manufacturing plants will pay very large sums to businesses to acquire their presence. For instance, Intel received a

(*Case Study continued*)

(*Case Study continued*)

> USD 600 million grant from the Government of Israel to site a fabrication plant in southern Israel in 1995. The decision was controversial, but ultimately led to Intel becoming one of Israel's leading exporters. The Government of Gujarat shows how, through alacritous statements and actions, administrations can create value for their constituents, and for the businesses they woo.

Types of political risks

There are many varieties of political risks that may impact a business. We present four of them for the purpose of illustration: change of government, violent conflicts, sanctions, and political risks to trade.[6]

- Change of government: In mature democracies, this is only to be expected each time there is a round of elections at the national or state level. From this perspective, the consequent risk is predictable, and hence can be factored into the decision-making of businesses. However, in countries that either have no democracy or very nascent democracies, changes in government can be sudden, and are often accompanied by considerable violence. In either case, change of government could result in changes in the policies, although in mature democracies, such quantum changes in policies are rare. Yet, any change in policies that have adverse impact on the business, have risk embedded in them from the perspective of businesses. The silver lining most often is that when there are changes in government, the new government is often more focussed, at least in the short term, to consolidate its political power base, and hence may not focus its immediate energies on drastic policy changes, giving adequate breathing time to business to manage any consequential risks. Another way in which business could be impacted by change in government, is through unfulfilled promises, where the government that has been swept away in the changed circumstances, might have promised certain actions that the new government might not honor. The internationally news-making Enron project in India is a case in point, where a change in the state government caused major havoc to the project, grounding it for several years. It is another matter that several years later, Enron itself was forced to wind up due to unearthing of large-scale frauds at the highest levels in the parent organization in USA.

---

[6] V. Kumar, "Political Risks in International Trade", Helium. http://www.helium.com/items/1010632-political-risks-in-international-trade, (accesed January 26, 2010).

CASE STUDY

The Enron Saga: Change in the State Government Derails Enron's Power Project in India[7]

 In 1991–1992, the Congress led government in India negotiated with Houston-based Enron Development Corporation to build a power plant in Dabhol (Dabhol Power Company), Maharashtra. The USD 2.5 billion electric power plant being built by Enron was to become the world's largest independent natural gas-fired power plant and India's largest single foreign direct investment after India embarked on its new economic reforms. The Indian economy was liberalized during the early 1990s and the country opened its economy to investments from foreign companies.

Controversy over Enron's power project had started since April, 1992. Local people were against the activities of the global energy corporation. This dragged the company into endless controversies. Many protests were being staged, environmental concerns being raised, and charges of human rights violations being filed against the company. In August 1995, the Bharatiya Janata Party (BJP)-led new government in Maharashtra scrapped the 2,015 megawatt project on the grounds of it being *anti-people*. Enron was subsequently caught up in political controversies that worried several overseas corporations who became wary of risking their funds and reputation in India's emerging markets.

Intriguingly, in January 1996, the government in Maharashtra approved the controversial power project. The chief executive officer of Enron lobbied with BJP chiefs to get their buy-in to the project. In the new round of negotiations between the government of Maharashtra and Enron, the company settled to modifying parts of the contract that were disagreeable to state officials. Enron also agreed to scale down the project cost to USD 1.8 billion. Politicians of the newly elected government faced the likelihood

(Case Study continued)

[7] This case study is based on the following sources: "Enron Power Project in India Steams Ahead, The India Budget 1996–1997. http://www.ieo.org/enron.html; "Tim McGirk. Enron's eight-year power struggle in India," *Online Asia Times.* http://www.atimes.com/reports/CA13Ai01.html; "U.S. Power Project is Derailed in India," *The New York Times.* http://www.nytimes.com/1995/08/04/business/us-power-project-is-derailed-in-india.html; "Enron India row nearing end after GE, Bechtel buy," *The Electricity Forum.* http://www.electricityforum.com/news/apr04/bechtel.html (accessed January 26, 2010).

> (*Case Study continued*)
>
> of compensating Enron by way of a stiff penalty, which could partly explain their about-turn.
>
> In May, 2001, however, Enron had to shut down the power plant because its sole customer, the Maharashtra State Electricity Board, had defaulted USD 240 million in payments. By January, 2002, the Dabhol Power Company was up for sale. Enron earned nearly two times the capital invested into the project from the sale while the Indian government had to stomach significant losses.

- Violent conflicts: These could be either external or internal in nature. External conflicts such as those between Iraq and coalition of forces led by the US, the Palestine–Israel conflict, and the flash points between India and Pakistan from time to time, are significant sources of risk that any business likely to be impacted by them, should be cognizant of. Usually they are more predictable in nature, as the build-up to such conflicts may take several months or years. Such predictability presents a time window for business to mitigate the risks it may face.

Internal conflict, which is essentially a form of civil war, such as those in Nepal, Sri Lanka, and Pakistan, could also adversely impact a business that operates in the impacted regions.

A new form of violent conflict that has reared its ugly head with increasing frequency is terrorism. We discuss this risk separately, as it needs specific attention. The reason is that while external and internal conflicts have their roots in political conflict, terrorism is beyond politics. And except for the perpetrators and mentors of the terrorist acts, terrorism is often beyond reason.

Conflicts in any form destabilize a business's supply and demand chains, and affect trade lines, impacting the ability of the business to operate smoothly, and keep up its promises to its customers. It can result in loss of human life, making it difficult to place competent people in such troubled regions. While insurance may provide financial cover for losses to a business stemming from such disruptions, it is unlikely to fully cover the loss of markets or lost credibility that a business may suffer as a result of its inability to adhere to its commitments in the wake of such conflicts. Besides, insurance covers often have several exclusion clauses, often in fine print that may result in protracted time loss in receiving compensation. Violent conflicts could adversely impact the people and property of businesses that operate in the troubled regions. It could also impact businesses that are not proximate to the troubled zones, through elaborate *teleology* (cause–effect linkages).

- Sanctions: Sanctions are actions against a country by another country, or by a group of countries acting in unison. It can result in ostracism of the affected country, wherein its normal trade links are either selectively or completely cut off. These are enacted because the affected country has not acted according to the expectation of other country/countries. The embargoes against North Korea or Iran, by the US and its allies, are examples of such sanctions. Businesses located in the affected countries can be adversely impacted, potentially being cut out of all trade links with other countries, or selectively cut off from markets or sources of raw materials. India was a victim of selective sanctions where for a few years following its second testing of nuclear weapons, all high tech purchases were denied by a consortium of countries led by USA. Impacted by this action was the prestigious Tejas LCA (Light Combat Aircraft) Project (see below), which suddenly faced the stoppage of all support in terms of know-how and components.

CASE STUDY

The Delayed LCA Project[8]

 India's ambitious Light Combat Aircraft (LCA), also named Tejas (meaning *Radiant*) project has encountered numerous delays, stretching the development efforts to over two decades. The project that commenced in 1983 under the aegis of India's Aeronautical Development Agency (ADA), has Hindustan Aeronautics Ltd (HAL) as the key contractor responsible for building the aircraft, and collaborating with several sub-contractors, and government laboratories for developing the aircraft. The then Indian government viewed the prestigious USD 21 million LCA project as a mark of the new climate of cooperation between India and the United States.

The LCA, which was to replace the Indian Air Force MiG fighter aircraft, ran into many problems very early in its development. Deficiencies in critical technology areas were detected in 1990, when the design of the aircraft was being finalized. It was decided to therefore build two technology

(*Case Study continued*)

---

[8] "US sanctions hit progress on LCA and light chopper projects," Rediff on the Net, http://www.rediff.com/news/1998/jul/13bomb.htm; "LCA Grounded Again," *India Today*, Stephen David. http://www.india-today.com/itoday/21091998/defence.html; "Hindustan (HAL), Tejas/Light Combat Aircraft (LCA) Light Multi-Role Fighter." http://www.aerospaceweb.org/aircraft/fighter/lca/ (accessed January 26, 2010).

(*Case Study continued*)

demonstrator aircrafts to resolve the design deficiencies. The first of the demonstrator aircrafts that eventually rolled out was riddled with problems in the flight control system. This proved to be the second major setback to the project.

The biggest blow to the project however came in 1998 when the Pokhran blasts (India's nuclear test) prompted the US to place sanctions, completely throwing the project out of gear. The United States put a ban on the sale of GE F404 turbofans, the all critical engine that was to be fitted into the LCA. The US also withdrew the sale of the fly-by-wire systems by Martin Meritta, a US firm. American software engineers working on the LCA project in India were retracted. Similarly, Indian software experts working at Meritta in the United States were disengaged from the project and summarily sent back home. This apart, Indian scientists and engineers carrying out testing activities of the LCA at US air bases were sent back to India. Many of them were sent back to India in *as is where is* condition, straight from their hotel rooms to the airport for their flight back to India. Many of them were put into planes in their pyjamas! Such was the haste with which the relationship between India's ADA/HAL and key technology providers in USA was terminated, exposing glaring political risks that businesses could go through, often for no fault of theirs.

With the sanctions having retarded the development of the first technology demonstrator of the LCA, India initiated development of a new jet engine domestically, a decision that resulted in additional expenses. Several delays and cost overruns were encountered which eventually led to India buying F404 engines, after America lifted the sanctions in 2001. After inordinate delays, the test flight of the first technology demonstrator was performed in January, 2001.

Since the first test flight, the LCA has undergone several phases of testing. The LCA that continues to be in the prototype phase is expected to be inducted into the Indian Air Force by around 2015.

- Political risks to trade: From time to time, primarily to enhance their political standing, or to appeal to its political constituents, a country's government can curtail import of goods and services from other countries. This could be to protect the domestic industry. It could be in response to a *sudden popular mood* against those trades. The mad cow disease, and the resulting ban on import of beef from UK, or the chicken flu, and resulting ban on poultry trade are illustrations of such responses. Additionally, vested interests in a country may persuade the government to ban imports, to protect their own markets. More recently the pronouncements of US President Barack Obama seeking to restrict outsourcing of IT services from India, have caused consternation in the Indian IT industry.

Exports could be impacted if the government of the exporting country perceives that the exports are adversely impacting the domestic prices. The ban on export of sugar from India, imposed by the Indian government in the past, from time to time, would be a case in point. A country could ban exports selectively to another country (such as India severing trade links with Pakistan during the height of hostilities with that country), if it perceives that the other country has blatantly acted against its interests. A government may also choose to nationalize industries selectively, and closely scrutinize the functioning of the industry, even imposing ban on exports or imports, in pursuance of political opportunism.

MANAGING POLITICAL RISK

Effectively managing political risks has two benefits to a business.[9] First, it helps management of the business to prepare, and anticipate possible fall-outs of political risks. From this perspective, it helps to protect investments made as well as the existing operations. It cautions about new investments being contemplated, and new operations that are planned to be rolled out. Management can proactively come up with strategies that factor the political risks into its decision-making. If the risks are perceived as being too severe, such as anticipation of severe instability in the country, the management can decide to exit the country in question, or vacate those markets. If the risks are perceived as being short-term in nature, resulting in temporary instability, suitable risk mitigation approaches can be adopted. Second, a company that is constantly scouting for new opportunities, and that is adept in monitoring political risks in its target countries or regions, can more accurately track political developments that portend boom times. It can then, with laser-sharp focus, zero in on those opportunities before its rivals, and it can aggressively take steps to capitalize on those opportunities (see Box 9.1).

---

[9] "How managing political risk improves global business performance", Pricewaterhouse Coopers. http://www.pwc.com/extweb/pwcpublications.nsf/docid/6C7FE77BCC684 D01852571620083BD9A (accessed January 26, 2010).

BOX 9.1   L.N. Mittal's Emergence as the Steel Emperor of the World

The rise of L.N. Mittal from relatively modest start to emerge as the largest player in the global steel industry is a case of leveraging political risks, and turning them into huge business opportunities. From 1989 till 2006, much of the acquisitions that Mr Mittal undertook, were of government-owned, relatively new, but sick steel plants. In countries as diverse as Trinidad and Tobago, Mexico, Canada, Kazakhstan, USA, France, Romania, Algeria, South Africa, Czech Republic, Bosnia, Macedonia, China, and many more, he demonstrated enormous entrepreneurial foresight, by converting potentially huge political risks for the respective governments, into huge opportunities for his burgeoning steel empire, in the process helping out those governments from political tight corners. He understood the political risks the governments of these countries were facing, being saddled with sick public sector steel plants. Through his growing credibility based on prior track record, he successfully convinced these governments to give him ownership of the sick companies at very attractive terms. On successful acquisition of a sick unit, he and his crack team would aggressively go about getting the house in order, and ensuring in quick time, strong financial viability of the newly acquired unit, throwing in huge cash into his growing corporate kitty. Over time, his reputation as the man with the *Midas Touch* only further enhanced his ability to continue even more aggressively, the path of inorganic growth through even more acquisitions.

Political risk has two components: shock and stability.[10] *Shock* means rapid, cataclysmic, and unanticipated political upheavals. Businesses can do precious little in terms of ability to manage the fall-out from political risk that emanates from shock. Examples could be the almost overnight disintegration of former USSR, the breaking of the Berlin Wall and resulting unification of Germany, or exposure of a major scam that brings down a civilian government, and is replaced by a military dictatorship, almost overnight. For instance, many companies that had extensive business relationships with USSR went through gut-wrenching convulsions after the disintegration of USSR.

Stability relates to the ability of the government to evolve, and implement policies in times of crisis, such as political, social, or economic crisis. For instance, the ability of India to bounce back in the aftermath of the assassination of its Prime Minister Indira Gandhi, in 1984, reflects high scores in stability.

Stability must be viewed in consonance with openness, which reflects the ease with which people, goods, services, information, and ideas flow freely in both directions both externally (with other countries), and internally (within the country). Stability in an open country has a very different connotation compared to stability

---

[10] Ian Bremmer, "How to calculate political risk", Inc. http://www.inc.com/magazine/20070401/ features-calculate-political-risk.html (accessed January 26, 2010).

in a closed country. Assessment of stability without understanding the openness of the country would thus be incomplete. The way to mitigate the risks associated with countries where long-term stability is doubtful is to evolve diversification strategies, hedging the bets, by not putting all eggs in one basket, but instead by straddling multiple countries.

Political risk is also related to the legitimacy of the government and the extent of corruption.[11] India, despite its recent phenomenon of fragile coalition politics, ranks very high on legitimacy of its government. A very elaborate election process that is conducted in a fair manner ensures that only legitimately elected Members of Parliament represent the people of their respective constituencies. At a minimum, sudden surprises with regard to changes in government are minimized when a legitimately constituted government is in place. Another major determinant of political risk is the extent of corruption. Corrupt governments are susceptible to manipulations by vested interests, and can result in greatly reduced transparency. Such governments can enact policies that result in heightened political risks to unprepared businesses.

Another significant determinant in managing political risk is the extent of bargaining power of the business, and that of the host country. The balance in the bargaining power of the business, and that of the host country will determine the effectiveness of the business in managing political risk. Factors such as uniqueness of the firm's offering, technology, size, and growth of its operations determine its bargaining power. The host country's size of market, availability of raw materials, wealth, and degree of intervention by government are some of the many factors that determine the bargaining power of the host country.

RISKS OF TERRORISM

Over the last few decades, terrorism has become much more pervasive across the world, and no person or business can assume that it would not be impacted by it. Terrorists now have the ability to strike at will, at the most unsuspecting of places, to achieve their nefarious ends. While most often, the public at large are the hapless victims of terrorist attacks, increasingly terrorists are targeting businesses as well, with the objective of spreading fear in the host country, and dissuading foreign investments into the host country. The recent attacks by highly trained and motivated Pakistani terrorists as they unleashed their dance of death in Mumbai, India on November 26, 2008, was targeted precisely to achieve the objective of derailing the economic engine

---

[11] Christina Pomoni, "Political Risks in International Trade," Helium. http://www.helium.com/items/1010632-political-risks-in-international-trade, (accessed January 26, 2010).

of India. In addition to directly targeting a business, terrorists could also throw into disarray the supply chain, as well as markets, for a business's offering, bringing the business down on its knees, as the following series of case studies demonstrate. Acts of terrorism can have significant impact on a firm's business continuity, the manner in which it conducts its business, as well as on its performance. Increasingly, companies are factoring terrorism into their strategic planning, much as they would, any other key inputs that go into crafting their strategies. We now examine three case studies of how terrorism impacts global business: 9/11, the Mumbai attacks, and IPL [India Premier League (cricket)].

CASE STUDY

Impact of the 9/11 Terrorist Attack on Businesses in America[12]

 On September 11, 2001, the worst attack of terrorism in the history of America left the country devastated. The country witnessed suicidal attacks that reduced the World Trade Centre and Pentagon to rubles. Among all other terrorist attacks in recent history, the casualties and material damages caused by the 9/11 attacks were by far the greatest. The attacks tossed up new worries, foremost among them being the fallout of the attack on America's economic outlook.

Close to 30 percent of the office space in Lower Manhattan was destroyed in that one attack, and several businesses completely wiped out. The New York City economy lost close to 200,000 jobs. The losses incurred due to destruction of physical assets were estimated at USD 14 billion, USD 1.5 billion, and USD 0.7 billion for private businesses, state and local government enterprises, and federal enterprises respectively. The cumulative loss in national income through the end of 2003 was half a trillion dollars. Insurance, airlines, tourism, other service industries and shipping were some of the sectors badly affected by the attacks. Losses to the insurance industry (including reinsurance) were estimated at between USD 30 and USD 58 billion. The short-term costs to the economy were considerable. The acceleration in defense expenditures had a bearing on the longer term growth of the economy.

(Case Study continued)

---

[12] This case study is based on: "The Economic Aftermath," *Frontline.* http://www.hinduonnet.com/fline/fl1820/18201160.htm; "Economic Costs to the United States Stemming from the 9/11 Attacks," Center for Contemporary Conflict. http://www.ccc.nps.navy.mil/si/aug02/homeland.asp (accessed January 26, 2010).

(*Case Study continued*)

The attacks also impacted the long-term potential of the global economy by raising transactions costs (higher operating costs, higher levels of inventories, higher risk premiums). According to Martin Wolf of *The Financial Times* of London, reported in the *Outlook*:

> In the second quarter of 2001, global output fell. U.S. output grew at an annualised rate of just 0.2 per cent. So did that of the eurozone. As for hapless Japan, it has slipped into its fourth recession in the past 10 years, with an annualised decline in output of 3.2 per cent. Output declined in most of emerging east Asian countries in the second quarter, the most significant exception being China. Latin America's aggregate output also shrank, led by Brazil and Argentina.

Not only was 9/11 a human tragedy but also a setback for both the US and world economies.

CASE STUDY

Unprecedented Losses to Mumbai from Terrorist Attacks[13]

 November 26, 2008 was a nightmare for India's financial capital Mumbai. More than 10 coordinated shootings and bombings ripped the southern part of the city causing much agony and destruction. The attacks, spread over four days, killed nearly 173, and wounded over 308 people. The top-end hotels Taj Mahal Palace and the Oberoi were two of the targeted sites amongst other locations. Attackers held hostages, including foreigners, for more than 60 hours in the Taj Mahal hotel. The episode that received widespread condemnation across the world left Mumbai (and India) shaken and devastated.

The estimated loss to Mumbai from the attacks was close to Rs 40 billion. In addition, there were other losses as well. Restoring the grandeur of the architectural marvel of the Taj Mahal hotel was estimated to cost over

(*Case Study continued*)

---

[13] This case study is based on: "2008 Mumbai Attacks," Wikipedia. http://en.wikipedia.org/wiki/Mumbai_attacks#Taj_Mahal_Hotel_and_Oberoi_Trident; "The Cost of Terror," *Business Today*. http://businesstoday.intoday.in/index.php?option=com_content&task=view&id=9083; "Over Rs 4,000 cr loss incurred during terror attacks," *Economic Times*. http://economictimes.indiatimes.com/articleshow/3773114.cms?in_showcase&in_showcase&in_showcase; "Carnage of November 26–29 will have moderate, shortlived impact as the country's fundamental attributes still remain." http://www.isasnus.org/articles/article-88.pdf (accessed January 26, 2010).

(*Case Study continued*)

Rs 5 billion. The travel and tourism sector took a beating, recording a 40 percent drop in arrivals. Occupancy rates of hotels in Mumbai fell by a steep 50 percent, while hotels across major cities in the country encountered a 25–30 percent drop. Other businesses that bore the brunt of the attacks included service businesses like shopping malls, multiplexes, and the television and movie industry. Footfalls took a beating in most of the malls and multi-plexes in Mumbai in the first week after the attacks affecting business of retail industry players. Losses recorded by the television and movie industry stood at Rs 100 million during the last three days of the terrorist attacks.

India, and in particular Mumbai, have weathered several terrorist attacks. However, the 26/11 attacks (November 26, 2008) were much more devastating, considering the loss of human lives, and material resources. In the short-term, the attacks had repercussions on the Indian economy, and the country would have to grapple with a higher cost of doing business for some time to come.

CASE STUDY

Conducting the Indian Premier League: How South Africa Gained due to Security Concerns in India Stemming from Terrorist Threats, and How Business took a Huge Beating[14]

In March, 2009, the second season of the India Premier League (IPL), one of the most sought after cricketing tournaments in cricket-crazy India, was decided to be held in South Africa. The multi-million dollar IPL is a Twenty20 cricket extravaganza conceived by The Board of Control for Cricket in India (BCCI). It is estimated that

(*Case Study continued*)

[14] Fakir Hassen, "IPL Huge Logistical Exercise, but will Benefit South Africa, Thaindian." www.thaindian.com/newsportal/world-news/ipl-huge-logistical-exercise-but-will-benefit-s-africa-with-image_100170874.html; Sapa, "IPL to bring economic benefits to SA, South Africa The Good News." http://www.sagoodnews.co.za/economy/ipl_to_bring_economic_benefits_to_sa_.html; Neha Pandey, "Tourism Industry worried as IPL moves out of India, IBN Live." http://ibnlive.in.com/news/tourism-industry-worried-as-ipl-moves-out-of-india/88631-3.html; "The Indian Premier League," Wikipedia wikipedia.org/wiki/India_Premier_League (accessed June 8, 2009); "IPL moves out of India," ESPN Star. http://www.espnstar.com/cricket/indian-premier-league/news/detail/item229475/IPL-moves-out-of-India/(accessed January 26, 2010).

(*Case Study continued*)

the Government of India earned close to Rs 900 million (about USD 18 million) from the inaugural tournament (also termed as the first season of IPL) played in India during April, 2008.

As the dates of the second season of IPL coincided with the 2009 Indian general elections, the Ministry of Home Affairs, Government of India, decided that it could not spare the Indian paramilitary forces to provide security to the tournament. The security threats were heightened since the tournament was scheduled in the immediate aftermath of the deadly 26/11 attacks by terrorists in Mumbai, making the conduct of the tournament extremely vulnerable to repeat terrorist attacks. The Ministry of Home Affairs maintained that the security forces would be stretched too thinly if protection was to be provided to both the elections and tournament. The BCCI too had serious concerns about the security of the overall tournament, and of the players in particular. This was further exacerbated by the Lahore terror attack on the Sri Lankan cricket team a few months before the IPL schedule.

The result of these concerns on possible terrorist attacks, resulted in the decision by the organizers to shift the venue of IPL to South Africa. This came as a boon to South Africa's economy, which had dipped to an abysmal low growth rate in the last quarter of 2008, for the first time ever in 10 years. IPL was estimated to churn close to Rs 100 billion mainly in TV rights and sponsorships. Apart from the immediate economic benefit, the games (59 matches in all) brought to the different cricketing venues in South Africa, a large number of tourists and sports fans, who poured in from across Asia. The resulting upsurge to the hotel and airline industries in South Africa was very significant. Revenues earned by individual venues on tickets, food and beverages, transport, and merchandise ran into millions of rands.

India, on the contrary, stood to lose heavily by the shift of the venue of the tournament to South Africa. BCCI lost a staggering Rs 2 billion. Having worked on the project for nine months in India, BCCI had to start again from ground zero. Organizing the logistics for the tournament in a mere 45-day timeframe across six venues was a huge challenge, and a relatively expensive affair for BCCI. Major sponsors lost out on opportunities to leverage their brands. While hotels in India were anticipating a 25 percent boost in occupancy, the tourism industry expected a 15 percent growth. The estimated loss to the hospitality and airline industry together was close to Rs 200 million. Sports goods manufacturers, merchandising companies, entertainment companies, local sponsors and other small firms together incurred lost opportunities in excess of Rs 750 million.

The reality of terrorism is that it spares no nation, and strikes at the most unexpected targets at the most unexpected moments. Increasingly, terrorists are moving from vehicle borne explosive attacks to taking people hostage. They are targeting hotels, software industry, businesses, etc., which are *soft targets*; the aim is to cripple the economy and unleash all-round fear. Businesses have no option but to be on high alert, as most top companies in India have come to realize. The security drills at top Indian IT firms, petrochemical complexes, hotels, and many more, have become very stringent, driving up the costs of doing business significantly. Companies are now beginning to have strong risk management groups focussed on addressing various non-economic risks including risk of terrorist attacks.

Terrorists typically strike when the guard is lowered. This is best illustrated in the recent Mumbai attacks. Many government agencies and even a few companies were aware that such plans were being hatched by the terrorists. Sooner or later, the guard is lowered, as it is not easy to sustain a long period of being on *high alert*. The exploding population in countries like India and pervasive indiscipline in the society at large, provide a conducive environment for terrorists to pursue their nefarious designs. The multitude of checks that companies have installed post the Mumbai attacks of November 2008, such as vehicle checks, personal frisking, and in general, very tight security drills, do not guarantee that there will be no attacks in the future. Porous international borders and neighboring countries that are not friendly, add to the threats.

From a customer–firm perspective, India is not the only option for outsourcing work to be done, be it in the services or manufacturing businesses. Foreign customer–firms have begun to hedge their bets, by insisting that service providers provide them distributed operations spread over several countries, such as India, Argentina, Eastern Europe, and many more, to mitigate any forms of risk that a country may throw up. In this scenario, it is not uncommon that the same customer–firm gets serviced from various offices. If there is a disruption of services from one of the countries, service centers located in other countries seamlessly take over. In a competitive marketplace, such proactively conceived risk mitigation processes may provide an edge over competition. It is not uncommon that large companies have multiple operating sites located in different countries. The biggest challenge in fighting terrorism is that the fight is with an enemy who cannot be seen. Eerily, fighting terrorism is akin to fighting a battle. The reality of terrorism is that a determined mind, bent on wreaking havoc, cannot be stopped. One can only deter it, or postpone it (with the terrorist waiting for the guard to be lowered).

The first step in managing the risks of terrorism is to be fully aware of the risks, followed by beefing up current intelligence and security measures.[15]

---

[15] Darragh Gray, "Is the terrorism risk level rising?" http://www.lloyds.com/News_Centre/ Features_from_Lloyds/News_and_features_2009/360/Is_the_terrorism_risk_level_rising. htm (accessed January 26, 2010).

The impact of terrorism on business can be extensive. It can alter the manner in which businesses are run. Systems such as *Just in time* inventory replenishment may have to be given up in favor of building buffer inventories. Sources of supplies may need to be changed. Choice of partners and collaborators may be more restricted. Protecting key employees will require special attention. Lot more resources may need to be spent on security regimen. All of these will doubtless increase the operating costs incurred by the firm.[16]

Tools for business continuity management rely on risk-assessment, and risk-management. Any such analysis commences from clarity on why the particular business, or any of the business's upstream (suppliers) and/or downstream (customers) entities would be of interest to terrorists. Such analysis should also assess the vulnerability of the firm's transport arrangements, communications systems, people, supplies, in-ventory, products, etc. In the era of mindless terrorism, this analysis should encompass increasingly wider circles of entities that have anything to do with the business.

Best Practice Counter Terrorism Management (BPCTM) covers a wide spectrum of a firm's operations and processes, including security. This starts with assessment of external risks and internal risks. External risks include factors such as operating in a country that is a target for the terrorists, ownership of the company and its foreign loyalties, etc. Internal factors could include disgruntled employees who could act as conduits for information to the terrorists, management style, labor relations, etc.

BPCTM is a two-stage process. First, it seeks to secure critical infrastructure through creating formidable barriers around such infrastructure, making it difficult for terrorists to access it. Second, it involves buttressing the infrastructure through systems and processes, such as tight entry protocols for personnel. Many large companies in India, such as the large IT firms, most US-based MNCs operating in India, petroleum refining units, and many more, have started moving aggressively in implementing variants of BPCTM, to mitigate the risk of terrorism.

The engineering function has a significant role in planning systems to counter terrorism. These include providing risk-assessment of the structures, as well as production and operating units, and evolving suitable risk mitigation mechanisms such as reducing reliance on just-in-time manufacturing systems, creating buffer inventories, quality checks of incoming raw materials and outgoing products for possible sabotage, creating redundant capacities at other locations, etc.

BPCTM visualizes close cross-functional working in the firm to ensure continuity of operations and services after a terrorist attack. Business continuity in the immediate aftermath of terrorist attacks, or circumvention of the effects of terrorist attacks, is done by triggering alternate production centers, suppliers, distribution channels, etc.

---

[16] Dr Mike Clark. FIEaust,CPEng, MAusIMM, "Business Continuity Management and the Terrorist Threat", Principal, M.E.T.T.S Pty. Ltd, Brisbane, metts[at]metts.com.au. M.E.T.T.S. Consulting Engineers(Infrastructure and Resource Management Engineers). http://www.metts.com.au/counter-terrorism-mngt.html (accessed January 26, 2010).

After handling the ensuing crisis, the firm needs to recover lost ground, and revert to business as usual. Once the crisis has been satisfactorily addressed, businesses typically have time to revert to business as usual. Often, during this stage, significant improvements in the organization's systems and management are implemented, based on past learning.

While there are significant additional costs for the firm in addressing the risks of terrorism, some of these costs will be offset by lower insurance premiums, as well as goodwill from clients about being assured that systems for business continuity are in place. While terrorism puts considerable costs on society in general, and on firms in particular, it also presents new opportunities for some companies[17] (see box for a case study of one such company). One thing is certain: terrorism has now become a critical issue that businesses have to deal with, in terms of how they operate, and in terms of additional costs involved in running businesses. It will continue to grow in importance in a firm's agenda. Any company that ignores the risks of terrorism does so at its own risk. A bigger debate arises on who should bear the costs for fighting terrorism: businesses, or the government?[18]

CASE STUDY

Defense, Security, Construction Sectors Make Most of the War on Terrorism—How some Companies Benefitted from the Opportunities Created by Terrorism[19]

Following the 9/11 terrorist attacks, the United States declared a new war on terrorism against Islamic militants. The US government assigned billions of dollars for states to prop up their

(Case Study continued)

---

[17] Gerry Everding, "American Businesses Play Critical and Costly role in Global War on Terrorism," December 16, 2003, News & Information—University Communications. http://news-info.wustl.edu/tips/page/normal/578.html (accessed January 26, 2010).

[18] Daniel Wagner, "The Implications of Recurring Terrorism for Business," May 2004, IRMI. http://www.irmi.com/expert/articles/2004/wagner05.aspx (accessed January 26, 2010).

[19] This case study is based on Jim Stratton, "Terrorism," Wikinvest. http://www.wikinvest.com/concept/Terrorism (accessed June 11, 2009); Jennifer Beauprez, "Defense industry perks up war on terrorism keeps Colorado contractors busy," GlobalSecurity.org. http://www.globalsecurity.org/org/news/2001/011007-attack03.htm (accessed June 11, 2009); "Private security guards play key role post 9/11." http://archives.californiaaviation.org/airport/msg36775.html (accessed June 11, 2009); "Ballooning costs and politics delay construction of 9/11 memorial," m&n. www.monstersandcritics.com/news/usa/news/article_1429983.../Ballooning_costs_and_politics_delay_construction_of_9/11_memorial (accessed June 11, 2009); "The World Trade Center—From Construction to 9/11," English Online. http://www.english-online.at/art-architecture/world-trade-center/wtc.htm (accessed June 11, 2009).

(*Case Study continued*)

security capabilities against a future assault. The US Military placed huge orders for high-tech supplies of armaments and equipment with local defense contractors who were virtually forgotten during peacetime. Thus in the wake of America's long war against terrorism, a multitude of defense contractors in Colorado (Colorado is at the heart of the US Military's satellite operations) stood ready for more business. Estimates have it that the Unites States total military spending on the war on terrorism is nearing one trillion dollars.

Local companies providing security services have also benefitted by the terrorist attacks in America. The private-security industry that defends more than 70 percent of America's most likely terrorist targets, started to bring in more professionalism and specialization into their organizations and security services. Security officers were given better training to combat attacks. The boom in private security services saw security companies deploy officers to defend many critical infrastructure establishments in the US including nuclear power plants, banks, international airports, oil refineries, dams, malls, railway lines, and other potential terrorist targets. The Stockholm International Peace Research Institute estimates the worldwide private-security sector revenues at USD 100 billion, which would continue to grow rapidly over the coming years.

Post 9/11, major construction companies were also preparing for growth as the destroyed World Trade Center, the Pentagon, and various other concrete structures in the vicinity of Ground Zero had to be reconstructed. The re-development of the World Trade Center was expected to cost more than USD 10 billion. Many architects from all over the world were invited to present blue prints for rebuilding the site. The glass towers were also to be surrounded by a memorial of September 11, the construction of which was estimated at USD 1 billion.

ENVIRONMENTAL RISKS

That human and business activities have contributed to ever accelerating degradation of the natural environment and ecosystems is now established beyond doubt.[20] The impact on a global scale of this deterioration is beginning to be felt with increasing

---

[20] Managing the Environment BMGT 4925. http://pirate.shu.edu/~bentivca/minors/Electives/Managing.htm

intensity, and this is bound to only further aggravate. Countries across the world are seeing that there is no option but to push for business sustainability. Companies that ignore this thrust will find themselves increasingly under pressure and will face intense operating risk, as the following case study on KIOCL shows, while those that pro-actively move in the direction of business sustainability will reap rich rewards in terms of better revenues, mitigate risks, and find new markets and opportunities.[21]

CASE STUDY

Kudremukh Iron Ore Company Ltd (KIOCL)—Razing Mountains and Forests for what lies Beneath[22]

 Known for its fascinating and amazing spectacle of nature, Kudremukh, in the southern state of Karnataka, is a mountain range located in the Western Ghats (mountain ranges on the western coast) in India. Dominated by enchanting deep valleys, thick evergreen forests, spectacular water falls, and breathtaking shoal grasslands, this paradise has come to be known as the *Switzerland of Karnataka*. Kudremukh is home to robust populations of tigers, elephants, king cobras, black panthers, the Great Indian Hornbill, and a variety of nocturnal Malabar Cats. The area also feeds three of the significant rivers (Tunga, Bhadra, and Netravathi), which provide drinking and irrigation water to millions of people in the southern part of India.

Massive iron ore deposits were discovered in Kudremukh as early as 1915. In 1967, the National Mineral Development Corporation (NMDC), an agency of the Central Government of India, undertook prospecting

(Case Study continued)

---

[21] "Ecosystem Change: A Source of Business Risk and Opportunity," Laden Consulting. www.landenconsulting.com/downloads/LC-CESR-brochure.pdf (accessed January 26, 2010).

[22] This case study is based on the following sources: D.V.R. Seshadri and Shobitha Hegde, 2009, *Kudremukh Iron Ore Company Limited: The Sun Sets on its Mining Operations*, Case Study, IIM Bangalore; WALHI—Indonesian Forum for Environment, 2006, *The Environmental Impacts of Freeport-Rio Tinto's Copper and Gold Mining in Papua*, a Report, May; Jagdish Krishnaswamy, Milind Bunyan, Vishal K. Mehta, Niren Jain and K. Ullas Karanth, 2006, *Impact of Iron Ore Mining on Suspended Sediment Response in a Tropical Catchment in Kudremukh, Western Ghats, India*, a Report, Forest Ecology and Management; and UNEP Islands, *Mining Impacts, Small Island Environmental Management*. http://islands.unep.ch/siemi3.htm (accessed January 26, 2010).

(*Case Study continued*)

surveys of Kudremukh. Low grade magnetite ore was detected in Aroli, Nellibeedu, and Gangrikal, which were situated on the banks of the River Bhadra. NMDC procured a mining lease for an area of 5,218 hectares from the Government of Karnataka. The 30-year lease was subsequently transferred to the Kudremukh Iron Ore Company Ltd (KIOCL), a public sector enterprise promoted by the Government of India.

By 1974, extensive mine-related infrastructure came to be established in Kudremukh. Wide roads were laid into the heart of the evergreen forests, high tension electric lines were drawn, and a new township was created to accommodate KIOCL employees, and their families. Surrounding communities however were unhappy with the developments in the virgin forest area. They viewed the imminent mining operations as an intrusion into the wilderness, and as a disruption to the ecology of the region. Local-level official agencies too disapproved of the upcoming mining activities as they believed it would displace and destroy the livelihood of local communities around the leased area. KIOCL turned a deaf ear to the initial protests raised by the district administrators and local communities. A strong lobby of interested politicians and bureaucrats nipped all such opposition raised during the early years of mining by KIOCL, thus ensuring the project implementation went forward at a brisk pace. The project got good traction because the Government of India was keen on industrial development of the country at any cost, which was the government's mantra at that time. By 1976, KIOCL grew to become Asia's largest mining and pelletizing complex.

In 1983, the Government of Karnataka declared Kudremukh as a National Park (Kudremukh National Park, KNP) under the Wildlife (Protection) Act, 1972. The primary intent of the government was to protect the rich flora and fauna of the tropical rain forests, and in particular the Lion Tailed Macaque, an endangered mammal species found in Kudremukh. KIOCL's leased mining area fell well within the precincts of the KNP.

Consequent to 15 years of operation without opposition from any quarter, KIOCL's mining operations had virtually turned a sizeable area of Kudremukh into an array of battered landscapes, had lowered the water tables, and had unleashed huge toxic wastes that contaminated the air and water ecosystems, and wreaked havoc on the natural habitat. Opencast mining activities like drilling, blasting, extraction, etc., had been causing acute air and noise pollution. The irrepressible dust during drilling and blasting posed serious health hazards to the local communities. Extensive

(*Case Study continued*)

(*Case Study continued*)

excavation, removal of top soil, discarding of tailings (which is essentially the washings from the mine area after extraction of the iron ore), and large scale felling of trees for laying slurry pipelines and creation of roads, had ruined large stretches of the land surface in the area. Silt load downstream the river Bhadra was significantly higher than the permissible limit, consequently affecting the storage of irrigation water in Bhadra Reservoir. Siltation also had considerable impact on the water quality and hydrological regime of the surrounding areas. The release of tailings into the nearby rivers was having consequential effects on the rivers and their valleys.

With a view to fostering an atmosphere of trust and goodwill among the local people, KIOCL had, over the years, initiated several community development initiatives including piped drinking water supply and health clinics to a few key towns around Kudremukh, organizing free health camps, providing funds towards improvement of select hospitals and schools, and laying of rural roads. Environment management too was high on the company's agenda. It undertook an independent afforestation program and planted close to 8 million saplings in the leased area. The Lakya Dam, two rock-filled dams, and several check bunds were constructed to store hazardous tailings, and arrest the mine wash from flowing into the river Bhadra. The mine dust was suppressed by growing a green belt along the roads, and by incessant spraying of water on mine haul roads and mine benches. Industrial effluent treatment plants, sewage treatment plants and a designated yard for disposal of municipal wastes had been established apart from ensuring the recycling of waste oils, grease, metal scrap, etc.

Despite its *green operations* and seemingly high quality environmental standards, KIOCL was ruining, to a large extent, the natural habitat of wildlife inside KNP, which was a violation of the Wildlife Protection Act. Thus in 1995, environment protection and wildlife conservation organizations mustered the courage to file a petition against the company in the Supreme Court of India. Activists also started to create awareness among the local planters and farmers about the ill-effects that the mining had been causing. They were particularly emboldened, because the 30-year lease period to the company was coming to an end, and the company was seeking an extension by a further period of 30 years. If there was a time window to bring an end to the mine's operations, these conservation organizations believed this was it. The activists along with the support of local villagers, farmers, literary and public personalities staged agitations and protests in public against

(*Case Study continued*)

(*Case Study continued*)

the mining operations. The agitations also drew the attention of the media. As an act of self defense, KIOCL presented several consultancy reports validating its green operations in the Supreme Court of India. However, the well argued case filed by the environmental organizations stood in court as the Supreme Court took the stance that mining inside a national park was antithetical to the concept of conservation. What helped the cause of the conservationists was that by this time, the environmental movement in the country picked up enough momentum, that the court constituted a *green bench* to fast track the legal hearings on environmentally sensitive cases. After elaborate deliberations, the court passed a verdict that mining by KIOCL had to be stopped by December 31, 2005, and that the company had to wind up operations within the specified date. Further to this order, the mines of Kudremukh wound down to a dead stop on December 31, 2005, essentially bringing the curtains down on the mining operations of the company.

Natural ecosystems provide visible benefits such as flora, fauna, fresh water, etc., as well as a host of not-so-visible ecosystem services such as global climate control, nutrient recycling, predictable rain patterns, and many more. World over, in the past, many of these services were taken for granted, as being available for free. With development and growth heralded by industry and business, the ability of the ecosystem services to deliver has been considerably weakened. While over 30 ecosystems have been identified, each business typically deals with a subset of them. A business depends on the proper functioning of these ecosystems to operate and be profitable. A business also impacts these ecosystem services through use of these services by its stakeholders, both internal (such as employees who run the business), and external (such as customers who use the company's products). As these ecosystem services continue to degrade, businesses face operating risks, such as higher cost of freshwater due to scarcity, unexpected storms resulting in flooding, inability to use traditional waterways for transport due to flooding, etc. Additionally there are a host of other risks that businesses have to face as a consequence, such as: regulatory pressures from governments that are becoming increasingly intolerant to environmental violations by businesses, customers walking away from environmentally insensitive companies, banks refusing to fund such companies, local organizations including NGOs filing lawsuits against such companies, etc.[23] *Going green* has thus become a business imperative.

---

[23] Corporate Ecosystem Services Review, "The Katoomba Group's Ecosystem Marketplace". http://ecosystemmarketplace.com/pages/article.tools.php?component_id=6346&component_version_id=9461&language_id=12 (accessed January 26, 2010).

While most companies address issues related to the environment through knee-jerk reactions such as controlling or preventing pollution, few have adopted a holistic issue to sustainability that is now the need of the hour. What is needed is *a vision of sustainability—a shaping logic that goes beyond today's internal, operational focus on greening to a more external, strategic focus on sustainable development.*[24] This vision is a roadmap that guides the company's environment strategies, suggesting how its products must evolve over time, and what competencies are needed to get there. Such a vision can guide a company through three stages of developing an environmental strategy: pollution prevention, product stewardship, and clean technologies.

Pollution prevention entails much more than pollution control, and originates from a belief that *Pollution prevention pays.* Pollution control involves cleaning up the waste after it is created, while pollution prevention entails minimizing and eliminating waste before it is created. Continuous improvement is an integral part of pollution prevention, much like it is in the case of Total Quality Management (TQM). A company that has incorporated pollution prevention in its strategy, and consequentially reaped rich dividends is Virchow Laboratories, a Hyderabad, India-based bulk drug manufacturer (see Box 9.2).

BOX 9.2   Virchow Laboratories Ltd

Virchow Laboratories Ltd., a flagship company of Virchow Group, is the world's largest producer of Sulfamethoxazole (SMZ), an ingredient in many life-saving drugs. With an output of 4,800 MT Sulfamethoxazole per annum, Virchow Laboratories services over 80 percent of the global Sulfamethoxazole requirement, by virtue of which it has a near-monopoly position in this drug. The company's product range includes critical high purity raw materials and intermediates such as Sodium Methoxide, Isoxamine, and N-Acetyl Sulfanilyl Chloride. Virchow boasts of being the preferred supplier to pharmaceutical giants like Glaxo Smithkline, Shionogi & Co. Ltd, Roche, Merck Generics, and Sanofi Synthelabo. Driven by the philosophy of Total Excellence since its inception in 1983, Virchow has established a state-of-the-art manufacturing facility with modern equipment that is efficient, scale-intensive, and built to serve its rapidly expanding global SMZ market. Twenty five principles of Good Manufacturing Practices (GMP) are rigorously followed in the plant. Sound environmental policies, programs, and practices have been an essential element of the company's Total Excellence philosophy. It is the first Active Pharmaceutical Ingredient (Bulk Drug) company in India to have received the ISO 14001 certification for environment management. The company believes that minimizing and eliminating waste, as well as

(*Box 9.2 continued*)

---

[24] Stuart L. Hart, "Beyond Greening: Strategies for a Sustainable World," *Harvard Business Review*, (USA, 1996).

(*Box 9.2 continued*)

recovering various by-products from unavoidable waste is a key pillar in achieving the dominant position in the world in its chosen product range. The key tenets of the company's environment management system are (source: http://www.virchows.com):

- Reduction in effluents through by-product recovery
- Reduction in emissions and particulate matter
- Ambient air monitoring
- Efficient water management for resource conservation
- Providing facilities for effluent treatment
- Documentation through Environment Procedures Manual

Product stewardship: It focuses not just on minimizing pollution during the process of manufacturing the product, but also on minimizing the negative impact of using the product during its life cycle. This requires fundamental changes in the manner in which products and processes are designed. Tools such as *Design for Environment* (*DFE*) are being increasingly used to create products that are easy to recover, reuse, and recycle.

Clean technologies: Most technologies available today are not environmentally sustainable. Environmental sustainability warrants business to invest in tomorrow's technologies that are clean and promote sustainability, and not be stuck with environmentally unsustainable technologies of the past.

There are seven concrete benefit categories from such an approach:[25]

- Meeting customer and market expectation: Customers from both business and consumer markets are increasingly seeking to buy green products from companies that have at a minimum ISO 14001 certification, that show clear commitment to continually improve on the environment front, that have clear end of life programs for their products, and that design and develop products that are energy efficient and safe to use. Products are expected to display clear environment attribute information.
- Improving market access: Due to massive increase in awareness of the public on environment related issues, governments across the world are passing new legislations and regulations that will cut off access to their markets for companies that do not comply with the new laws being passed. These laws have in-built provisions for increasingly stringent performance on the environment front for products and services. Witness the stringent norms for automobile emissions

---

[25] Lynelle Preston, "Sustainability at Hewlett-Packard: From Theory to Practice," *California Management Review*, 43, no. 3 (Spring, 2001): 26–37.

in some of the European countries (Euro-VI norms that have supplanted earlier Euro-IV and Euro-V norms). Such stringent norms make it impossible for an auto manufacturer not complying with the norms to operate in those markets.

- Increasing cost savings: Any form of waste costs money; hence environment sustainability through eliminating waste reduces costs to manufacture the product.
- Creating market opportunities: Successful companies have the uncanny ability of tracking changes in the business context, adapting to the change, and seizing the resulting opportunities. The case study of Moser Baer, a Delhi, India-based company, discussed later, that successfully changed tracks twice in response to changes in the environment, is illustrative.
- Enhancing brand image: People prefer to buy products from companies that are strong proponents of environmental responsibility. The challenge for the company is to make the relationship explicit between the company's championing the cause of environment, and its own brand image in the market place, building its brand image around environmental sustainability. The opposite is also true. As the case study ahead illustrates, Pepsi and Coke operations in India took a severe beating some years ago due to not demonstrating environmentally responsible behavior, resulting in major societal backlash that brought these companies to their knees. They had to go back to the drawing boards, and come up with environmentally sustainable approaches to their businesses. In contrast, the reputation of Philips Lighting Division (see Box 9.3) has been greatly enhanced by its launching of CFL lamps that consume a fraction of the energy needed by traditional fluorescent lamps and incandescent lamps.
- Leveraging competitive advantage: Responsible performance on the environment front is a moving target, as the bar is constantly being raised. What was acceptable and considered pioneering in terms of environmental responsibility a few years ago becomes common practice a few years hence, as competitors also implement similar processes, and as regulation tightens. To continue to be a front runner, companies have to move towards sustainability.
- Increasing shareholder value: Investors and investment firms are increasingly using performance of companies on the environment front to differentiate between firms. They are using environment drivers such as actions that a company takes on the environment front, as measures of sustainability of the business, and financially sound business strategies.

Of these seven reasons that necessitate companies to move toward environmental sustainability, the first three (meeting customer and market expectation, Improving market access, and Increasing cost savings) are minimal requirements to enable the company to remain competitive, while the last four (creating market opportunities, enhancing brand image, leveraging competitive advantage, and increasing shareholder value) truly differentiate industry leaders.

Increasingly in the future, global managers will pursue strategies that promote sustainability not just for altruistic reasons because it is right, but for profit—for survival and growth, to remain competitive, and emerge as market leaders. The case study of Suzlon is illustrative of such an approach, where the company transformed itself from a textile firm to emerge as a world leader in sustainable technologies (wind energy in this case) in a short span of a decade, and made an extremely profitable business out of it. The case studies of Moser Baer and Coca-Cola are equally instructive.

CASE STUDY

Suzlon Energy Ltd: Harnessing Wind to its Advantage[26]

 Established in 1995, Suzlon Energy Ltd is India's leading wind turbine company. Founded by Tulsi R. Tanti, Suzlon is ranked as the fifth largest manufacturer of wind turbines in the world. The company supplies over 6,000 MW of wind turbine capacity across the world, and enjoys a global market share of 10.5 percent. Headquartered in Pune, India, Suzlon has several manufacturing sites in India, mainland China, Germany, and Belgium. With annual revenues of USD 850 million, the company, maintains over 50 percent market share in India, and serves major international markets including the United States, Australia, Brazil, China, and South Korea.

A former textile manufacturer, Tulsi Tanti chanced upon an opportunity in the wind energy segment in the mid-1990s. The prospects for his textile company in Surat did not seem very bright. The business was languishing.

(Case Study continued)

---

[26] This case study is based on the following sources: 1. Suzlon Energy Ltd, iloveindia. http://www.iloveindia.com/economy-of-india/top-50-companies/suzlon.html, Suzlon Wind Energy, Wikipedia. wikipedia.org/wiki/Tulsi_Tanti (accessed June 8, 2009); Tulsi Tanti by Aryn Baker, "Heroes of the Environment." http://www.time.com/time/specials/2007/article/0,28804,1663317_1663322_1669924,00.html; "The Rise of Indian Wind Power," Spiegel Online International. http://www.spiegel.de/international/business/0,1518,559370,00.html; Robert E. Tomasson, "Harnessing Wind to generate Power for Homes." http://www.nytimes.com/1982/11/14/realestate/harnessing-wind-to-generate-power-for-homes.html (accessed January 26, 2010).

(*Case Study continued*)

Frequent power outages and escalating cost of electricity offset any profits. Frustrated with the state of electricity supply, Tanti resolved to generate his own electricity using windmills, which he believed could meet the power demands of his textile factory. He sourced two windmills from Vestas, a Danish manufacturer. Once the windmills were operational, the factory was completely off the state power grid.

Tanti had once read a report on global warming that predicted that a few of the popular tourist destinations like Maldives would be completely under water by 2050, if no efforts were made to drastically reduce the world's carbon emissions. This was an eye opener and Tanti realized "If Indians start consuming power like the Americans, the world will run out of resources. Either one has to stop India from developing, or one must find some alternate solution."[27] If wind was the solution to his textile factory, it could also be the answer to fueling the growth of other industries. This prompted Tanti to think that harnessing wind energy might just be the real business of the future, especially in a power-starved nation like India. Also, Tanti's installation of windmills for his textile factory caught the attention of several business owners, who expressed interest in adopting his solution for their plants as well. When Tanti approached his three brothers with the new business idea, they were more than convinced that it was a promising business opportunity. Tanti gradually exited the textile business, and the Tanti siblings together launched Suzlon Energy Ltd.

Today, a market leader in the renewable energy segment, Suzlon offers comprehensive end-to-end wind power generation solutions encompassing consultancy, design, manufacturing, installation, operation, and maintenance services.

With oil having political and economic problems, as well as contributing to global warming, fuels like coal causing pollution and accelerating global warming, and nuclear energy riddled with safety issues and opposition, Tulsi Tanti deemed wind energy to be the solution to the global challenge of carbon emissions and energy shortages. He has been conferred with several national and international awards for his outstanding contributions towards promoting non-conventional sources of energy. Explains Tanti: "Green business is good business and it is not just about making money. It is about being responsible. Clean and green power is the best option."

---

[27] Aryn Baker, "Tulsi Tanti," *Time*, October 17, 2007. http://www.time.com/time/specials/2007/article/0,28804,1663317_1663322_1669924,00.html (accessed March 10, 2010).

CASE STUDY

Moser Baer's Uncanny Ability to Sense Changes in Environment and Change Track: The Company's Photo-Voltaic Business to Provide Clean Energy[28]

 Founded in 1983, Moser Baer India is the world's second largest manufacturer of removable optical storage media. From being a Time Recorder unit in 1983, the company progressed into manufacturing 5.2 inch floppy disks, and then into manufacturing optical storage media, viz., Compact Discs (CDs) and DVDs. Operating in a dynamic industry such as optical storage media necessitates corporate vision, product flexibility, and resilience in strategy. Moser Baer's remarkable transition from Floppy to CD manufacturing at the right time is a case in point. Today, Moser Baer operates in diverse industries including data storage, optical media, home entertainment, consumer electronics, and more recently the solar energy sector.

The company's entry into the high-growth Photo-Voltaic (PV) business that forms the basic building block for solar energy, which is expected to become a USD 30 billion market globally by 2010, is synergistic with its existing businesses. The voluminous production of CDs and DVDs gives Moser Baer significant experience in coating thin-film silicon, a critical technology that the company's solar cells would employ. The new business would also leverage Moser Baer's core competencies in the areas of precision high technology mass manufacturing and project management. Moser Baer intends to ramp up its capacity to manufacture 600 megawatts of photo voltaic cells by 2010.

Energy is fast emerging as one of the very big challenges globally. Existing power generation approaches are riddled with the challenges of long-term growth and sustainability. Deepak Puri, the chairman and managing director, Moser Baer, explains:

(Case Study continued)

---

[28] This case study is based on the following sources: "Moser Baer Launches PV Demonstration Site In Gurgaon," *EFY Times.* http://www.efytimes.com/efytimes/fullnews.asp?edid=26521; "Moser Baer Expands into Photo-Voltaic Business," Moser Baer. http://www.moserbaerpv.in/milestone1.asp; "Will Moser Baer Become the Suzlon of Solar Energy?" Energy Alternatives India. http://www.eai.in/blog/2009/03/will-moser-baer-become-suzlon-of-solar.html; "Moser Baer: Rewriting the Future," India on Internet. http://www.indiaoninternet.com/marketing-business-news/41144-moser-baer-rewriting-future.html (accessed January 26, 2010).

(Case Study continued)

The energy scenario across the globe has become a matter of concern over the years. Heavy reliance upon the conventional fossil fuels and rising fuel prices has led to emerging energy security challenges around the World. Non-conventional energy sources like solar, wind and bio mass provide a viable, long-term, eco-friendly energy option to mankind.

With the Earth receiving many times more than the required amount of energy from the Sun, and solar energy being abundantly available for free, solar power would prove to be the most viable and environmentally sustainable alternative for power generation in the future. Moser Baer's astute ability to realize the business potential of solar energy has resulted in the company being one of the early entrants in the PV space, well-positioned to leverage the phenomenal growth of the sector, while also earning the reputation of providing clean, emission-free energy to the world.

CASE STUDY

Coca-Cola India: Embroiled in Controversies[29]

 For the most part of 2003, the world's largest soft drink company Coca-Cola had been receiving a lot of bad press in India. The Center for Science and Environment, New Delhi, confirmed, after conducting tests on the 12 soft drink brands of Coca Cola that large traces of pesticides and insecticides were present in the drinks, which exceeded the limits prescribed by the European Economic Commission. Soon to follow this allegation was a report by the Government of West Bengal, which stated that the slush and liquid effluents from Coke's bottling plants contained toxic metals and carcinogen cadmium. Similarly, the Kerala State Pollution Control Board reported pollution in the groundwater and agricultural land surrounding Coca Cola's plant in Palakkad.

The print media published several articles on the disastrous environmental impacts of the operations of Coke in multiple regions in India. Local communities in the states of Kerala, Uttar Pradesh, Rajasthan, Tamil Nadu, and Maharashtra held huge protests against Coke's bottling plants,

(Case Study continued)

---

[29] This case study is based on "Heat On Cold Drinks, Counter Currents." http://www.countercurrents.org/glo-sen190803.htm (accessed January 26, 2010).

(*Case Study continued*)

because it had depleted groundwater sources, and adversely affected the environment. Studies conducted on the samples of water effluent, and wastes (used as fertilizers by local farmers) from Coke's plants in Kerala contained excess cadmium. Villagers around the Plachimada plant in Kerala had no easy access to drinking water, and had to walk 10 kilometers, twice a day, as their wells had high levels of dissolved salts, making the water undrinkable. This forced the villagers to protest against Coca Cola, and the state government of Kerala ordered the company to cease operations at the Plachimada plant. In the state of Uttar Pradesh, villagers faced a severe scarcity of drinking water as the Coke plant had been releasing hazardous wastes, and had also been consuming groundwater in large quantities for its operations, depleting the water level.

The controversy had a negative impact on Coca Cola's financial performance in India in 2003, with the Coke brand taking a severe beating for several years thereafter.

BOX 9.3   Philips: Energy-saver Lighting Solutions[30]

Philips Lighting, one of the largest players in the global lighting market is known for its revolutionary lighting products. The company that was initially manufacturing incandescent light bulbs made a dramatic move to manufacturing energy efficient lights, capitalizing on the green trend. With a view to creating alternative lighting solutions for incandescent light bulbs, which would save energy, and reduce carbon emissions, Philips developed a range of products from energy-efficient halogen solutions to high-quality compact fluorescent energy savers (CFL) to LED-based lighting solutions. The transition from manufacturing incandescent light bulbs to energy efficient CFL lamps contributed significantly towards enhancing the Philips brand. Consumers perceived Philips to being an environmentally responsible company, and one that was focussed on enhancing the environmental performance of its products.

CFLs are four times more efficient than incandescent bulbs, last up to 10 times longer, and provide 80 percent energy savings. The company's EcoClassic range of energy-efficient

(*Box 9.3 continued*)

---

[30] This case is based on "Philips offers a choice of alternative solutions for contemporary home lighting." http://www.lighting.philips.com/gl_en/news/press/sector/2009/alternative_solutions_contemporary_home_lighting.php?main=global&parent=4390&id=gl_en_news&lang=en; "Advantages of LED Lights", http://www.lc-led.com/articles/ledlights.html (accessed January 26, 2010).

> *(Box 9.3 continued)*
>
> halogen solutions provides 50 percent energy savings. The LED lamps can operate for up to 100,000 hours continuously as against 5,000 hours of incandescent bulbs. The high operating efficiency of the LEDs result in 80 percent of electric energy getting transformed to light energy (a mere 20 percent energy is lost out as heat) which is in stark contrast to the incandescent bulbs that transform only 20 percent of electrical energy to light energy (a whopping 80 percent of the electrical energy is lost as heat).

To sum up our discussion on environmental risks: Every company should look at sustainability issues as business opportunities, and not as mere compliance to regulation, or being seen as a good Samaritan. As one observer notes: "If one is looking for a new definition of corporate social responsibility, sustainable growth is it, and it is directly related to business self-interest."[31]

BEST PRACTICES IN RISK MANAGEMENT

What constitutes best practices in comprehensive risk management, including non-economic risks? We sought a risk management process that, we believe, provides a benchmark for other global companies, and found it at Infosys. The following case study describes this process.

CASE STUDY

Risk Management at Infosys[32]

The discipline of risk management is an integral part of the business model at Infosys Technologies, India's leading IT professional services and systems integration firm. The company has made considerable progress in the field of risk management over the years. Adept at quantifying, and managing a wide range of risks from financial risks to operational risks, the company's Enterprise Risk Management (ERM) has

(Case Study continued)

---

[31] Chad Holliday, "Sustainable Growth, The DuPont Way," *Harvard Business Review* (September 2001).

[32] This case study is based on the Risk Management Report of Infosys available in the Infosys annual report (2008–09).

(*Case Study continued*)

been efficiently defending the organization against risks through tried-and-tested practices. The ERM integrates risk management practices in a broad, organization-wide approach.

The ERM practices include identification, assessment, monitoring, and mitigation of various risks to the company's business. It aims at reducing the risks that could affect the achievement of the company's business objectives in order to enhance shareholder value. With a focus on sustaining and enhancing the long-term competitive advantage of the company, the ERM is also oriented to leverage the risk-reward parity to create the greatest rewards while maintaining risks below pre-defined levels.

The range of risks

The company categorizes risks into six broad categories, within which there are different types of risks. *Strategy*: Stemming from the choices and decisions the company makes towards further improving its long-term competitive advantage and value to the stakeholders. *Industry*: Includes all those risks related to the inherent characteristics of the information technology industry including competitive structure, nature of market, and regulatory environment. *Counterparty*: Risks emanating from the company's involvement with entities for conducting business. The entities include clients, vendors, alliance partners, and their respective industries. *Resources*: Resulting risks from improper sourcing or sub-optimal exploitation of key organization resources such as talent, capital, and infrastructure. *Operations*: Inherent risks of the company's business operations including, client acquisition, service delivery to clients, business support activities, physical and information security and natural calamities. *Regulations and compliance*: Risks arising due to lack of compliance to regulations, contractual obligations, and Intellectual Property (IP) violations, leading to litigation, and loss of reputation.

The risk governance structure

The risk governance structure within the company includes the Board of Directors (comprising the executive management), Risk Management Committee (comprising four independent directors), Risk Council (comprising Chief Executive Officer, Chief Operating Officer, and Chief Financial Officer), Office of Risk Management (comprises the network of

(*Case Study continued*)

(Case Study continued)

risk managers from business units and group companies, and is led by the Chief Risk Officer), Unit Heads and the Infoscions.

The principal risk management practices

- Risk-assessment: The process involves identifying essential risks through periodic assessments, followed by prioritizing the risks, and finally chalking out necessary actions to be carried out to mitigate the risk. The procedure of identification and prioritization of risks involves conducting risk surveys across functions, and subsidiaries to get inputs on key risks, business environment scanning, and through intense discussions in the Risk Council and Risk Management Committee. Internal audit findings and risk inventory act as useful sources for risk identification.
- Risk measurement and monitoring: Dashboards created at the company track external and internal indicators pertinent to the chief risks. Trend line assessment of chief risks is done. Also, the exposure and potential impact of the risks are analyzed, mitigation plans are arrived at, and the owners for addressing these risks are determined.
- Risk reporting: A report is prepared on the chief risks thus identified. Periodic discussions are held at the Risk Council and Risk Management Committee based on the report that summarizes the trend, exposure, potential impact, and mitigation status of the risk. The company's Board of Directors too is provided regular risk updates. Entity level risks and account level risks are presented, and discussed at appropriate levels of the organization.
- Integration with strategy and business planning: The risks thus ascertained serve as important inputs during the development of the company strategy and business plan.

OTHER NON-ECONOMIC RISKS

In addition to economic risks, businesses the world over have to contend with many categories of risks that are non-economic in nature. In this chapter, we have discussed three of them in some detail, that is, political risks, risks arising from terrorism and environment risks. In each of these risks are also embedded opportunities, a few examples of which were also presented in this chapter. However, these three risks are only a few of the many non-economic risks that companies have to contend with. There are many other types of non-economic risks with which companies increasingly have to grapple. We describe some of these risks briefly in the following.

Information risk

Businesses today have to cope with very intriguing and new forms of risk. One of the big risks of companies in the technology space is information risk. Sophisticated information seekers extract vital information of companies over social settings, or through other means.

Increasingly, companies have now created the position of Chief Risk Officer, who is responsible for all forms of risk that the company faces, including risk to information security, risk to physical assets, geopolitical risks, health risks (such as pandemics like Swine Flu), and many more. The chief Risk Office takes overall responsibility of managing the company's myriad risks. This office is led by the Chief Risk Officer, who is usually an ex-serviceman (from the defense forces). Since the operation of this office requires stealth, its functioning is typically very low key from an external perspective. All risks faced by the company are increasingly being packaged into this office, so the CEO can hold one department accountable to handle all risks that the company faces. The challenge is to ensure business continuity despite the onslaught of these varied forms of risk on the business.

Newer forms of certification, specifically addressing effective risk management, such as the ISO/IEC 27001:2005 certification by ISO for Information Security Management System, adapted from British Standard (BS), have come up. This certification does not guarantee that the company is free of information risks, and hence that fraud will not happen. Such certification can at best help to win new business, and get more clients. Essentially this certification provides a third party view that all that the company is saying in terms of systems to control risks related to information are in place. This does not however guarantee that there will be no fraud stemming from misuse of information.

While it is impossible to stop frauds, companies can create check points to make a potential person who wants to indulge in fraud, to think twice. The reality is that only a miniscule fraction of employees even contemplate fraud. The overwhelming majority of employees have nothing to do with it. In such a scenario, creating awareness is the key. Companies have set up mechanisms where employees can anonymously (to safeguard their well-being) report such incidents to a central agency within the organization.

Another reality is that the frauds that are reported are a small proportion of the frauds that are actually done. Many frauds do not get reported. Companies providing services to credit card companies or banks are very vulnerable to frauds, and hence need very robust processes to prevent frauds. Many of the frauds are perpetrated over a long period of time with very small financial implications in each transaction per se. Risks in this category present themselves through one of the following three possibilities: people, processes, or technology.

People risk

While leading companies deploy reference checks of potential recruits, it is quite conceivable that while an employee may have had a clean record before joining the company, his perspectives may change after joining the company. Employees may come under ideological spell of groups with criminal intentions. Employees may get ideas of possibilities of making easy money, such as in one case, where an employee trained to prevent hacking in IT networks, used this knowledge to fraud his employer. It is thus clear that people-risk is a very big risk that companies face, and often these people are the company's own employees. The paradox for the company is how not to antagonize the bulk of well-meaning employees, and yet have processes that trap those employees who seek to indulge in fraud.

Technology risk

It includes acts such as loading information unnoticed, on a USB (pen) drive, or wiping out essential data that cripples the company, or erasing out an important presentation to a very important client, a few minutes before the presentation is set to start. Such acts continue to be perpetrated despite multiple controls that companies have put in place, such as disabling USB ports, disallowing CDs to be brought to the premise, disabling emails, preventing use of mobile phones, etc. Some companies resort to peer level controls, where peers act as conscience keepers. Companies in industries such as BPO (Business Process Outsourcing) or IT-enabled services (ITES), employ floor walkers who walk around the various locations in the company, to detect potential frauds. Sometimes, technology risks can take the form of sabotage, attempting to put the lives of key personnel in jeopardy, by indulging in sabotage of key equipment such as aircraft or cars, used for transporting top company managers.

Process risk

Most well-established companies have defined elaborate processes to ensure that each set of activities happen in a predictable manner, as envisaged. Persons wanting to indulge in frauds tend to circumvent these processes, especially if the processes are weakly defined, or if there are inadequate checks and balances. Such incidents can happen despite elaborate certifications that the company may have achieved. The huge recent fraud perpetrated by the founders of Satyam, a large Indian software company, is a case in point. At a working level, a junior employee in a call center or a BPO can memorize a password of a retail customer, and use it subsequently to indulge in fraud, although there may be well-established processes to prevent such frauds.

CONCLUSION

At the end of the day, while companies may seek to minimize non-economic risks, the truth is that such risks are real, and the consequences of such risks play out from time to time. At that stage, the ability of the company to respond rapidly, and bounce back after a setback is vital.

New types of risk constantly proliferate. Only businesses that pay highest attention to managing such risks can mitigate them. The bottom line is that each company has to come up with robust mechanisms and processes that address these, and other risks upfront, and proactively address them, rather than to be caught unawares. At the same time, companies need to build resilience—the ability to respond quickly and effectively to unanticipated risks, when they strike home. The investment company Cantor Fitzgerald offers an inspiring example. Located in the top floors of the World Trade Center, Cantor lost 658 employees who began their work day on 9/11. *That was more than 60 percent of the company's* entire *work force.* CEO Howard Lutznick kept the company intact, restored operations quickly, and while mourning, rebuilt the company and its business. He did this, in part, to enable compensation for the families of the victims. His courage provides a best-practice benchmark for global managers who encounter non-economic risks of enormous magnitude.

Chapter 10

Country "due diligence": Integrating the ten tools

LEARNING OBJECTIVES

After reading this chapter, readers should understand how to analyze the economy of a new, and perhaps unfamiliar country, or even a highly familiar one, using a systematic checklist of questions that can help analyze that country's business prospects—a process known as country *due diligence*. This checklist comprises a framework that integrates the previous nine essential tools and adds to them, non-economic factors related to culture, politics, and ethics. Readers should know why the global crisis sets the stage for major paradigm shifts in every industry, and why such shifts can create exceptionally attractive new business opportunities. Readers should know how to begin the task of exploring what these paradigm shifts imply for each industry.

Tool # **10**

 Checklist for Country "Due Diligence" Analysis

INTRODUCTION

We began our book with the pointed question of the Queen of England, Queen Elizabeth II: "Why did no-one see it [the global 2007–2009 crisis] coming?" Hopefully, in the previous nine chapters, and nine tools, we have provided readers with clear and understandable answers, along with actionable insights and tools that can lead to increased risk awareness, and the transformation of global risk into global business opportunities.

The objective of this chapter is to integrate the nine tools, in order to provide global managers with a new and powerful tool: A framework for conducting country *due diligence* (analysis of new markets), similar to how experts analyze companies that are targets for possible acquisition. A second objective is to expand on the main theme of this book, that every global risk can become a global opportunity. We will argue that the Great Depression that began in 2007–2008 will lead every industry, major and minor, to rewrite the *rules of the game*, the way in which business is conducted, and that this reshuffling of the deck can create huge opportunities for global managers, and entrepreneurs wise enough to anticipate the new paradigms and position themselves to benefit from them.

We begin with a case study of the country that has perhaps been hit hardest by the global crisis, Iceland, and two women who have turned impossibly huge risk into major business gain. After studying one of the world's smallest countries, we follow it with a case study of the world's largest nation, China, perhaps one of the major winners in the global crisis.

CASE STUDY

Iceland—From Crisis to New Business Venture

ICELAND'S CRISIS

 Arguably, Iceland has been the country hardest hit by the global crisis. This tiny nation with only 306,694 people spread over 103,000 sq km, saw its banks expand rapidly throughout Europe, attracting deposits, and paying high-interest rates (especially, to depositors in the United Kingdom) while incurring high risk in their investments. Iceland's three major banks collapsed when global capital markets declined. Compared to its size, Iceland saw a banking collapse larger than any country has ever experienced. *The Economist*[1] calls it "the biggest collapse (relative to the size of the economy) any country has ever suffered." In January, Iceland chose a woman Prime Minister to lead it out of the crisis, Johanna Sigurdardottir.

- In the wake of the collapse, the market value of stocks on Iceland's exchange fell by more than 90 percent, Iceland's currency plummeted, and a severe economic recession ensued, which led to social unrest, and the resignation of the Prime Minister.
- Many young Icelanders, who have never known unemployment, are expected to lose their jobs as businesses shut down. Corporate Iceland is technically bankrupt because of its foreign debts. It is unable to

(Case Study continued)

---

[1] "Cracks in the Crust, Iceland," *The Economist* (US), December 18, 2008. http://www.highbeam.com/doc/1G1-190341819.html (accessed January 28, 2010).

(*Case Study continued*)

    refinance loans because the new capital controls mean all credit to the country has dried up. In 2009, Iceland's GDP fell by about 10 percent.

- At one stage, Iceland's Prime Minister noted the real possibility of national bankruptcy—inability of Iceland to pay its massive debts. By mid-2008, Iceland's external debt amounted to 50 billion euros, 80 percent of which was owed by Iceland's banks, nearly six times Iceland's annual Gross Domestic Product of 8.5 billion euros.

- More than half a million depositors in Icelandic banks, living outside Iceland, (more than Iceland's entire population) found their deposits frozen as governments debated about deposit insurance liability. The government of the Isle of Man alone paid out half its reserves, or 7.5 percent of the island's GDP, in deposit insurance.

ICELAND'S OPPORTUNITY

Most global managers, after reading the above, would see the word Iceland, and react with fright, and flight. But two audacious Icelandic women, Halla Tomasdottir and Kristin Petursdottir, Chair and CEO, respectively, of Audur Capital, thought differently. Here is their story, in their own words:[2]

"We founded our company to incorporate feminine values in the world of finance. Women will represent a formidable financial force in the future. We want to unlock the potential value in women. This opportunity is too good to miss."

"We did not like the bonus culture of modern financial institutions. Regulation should come from within, from the internal ethical values of the business. We believe in market forces tempered by humanity. Women will have a big role in restoring balance to the wreckage of the financial system. Much of the credit crunch crisis came from masculine attitudes. Men were responsible because they sold things they did not understand."

Men are responsible

"Overwhelmingly, it's been men at the decision-making tables. If it had been women, the troubles would not have been as big. Token women have

(*Case Study continued*)

---

[2] BBC, Global Business, "The women who want to save banking," Interview by Peter Day, May 18, 2009 (BBC World Service, London, UK). Peter Day spearheads the BBC World Service program Global Business.

(*Case Study continued*)

no choice but to behave as the rest of the group. If you had several women in senior management, with greater diversity, the decision-making quality would have been better. Women think differently. We are not the same as men. We bring different things. They should be valued. A business that does not take advantage of women in boardrooms or key executive teams is missing an opportunity. A world with only women would be equally imbalanced. We need the balance, it brings healthier debates and decisions."

Risk aware

"It's not the role of women to clean up the mess. We are saying, it's so important to have a system where men and women work together. Women tend to bring a lot of things to the table. They are risk aware, not risk averse. Men tend to be risk takers. Women think more long term. They think about the team, not only themselves. They think more about the people. Women see other business opportunities than men do. I'm saying that women on the Board will look at more things than just financial profits. They will ask different questions, they will consider more stakeholders. It's about the wellbeing of the employees. It's not about the narrow definition of shareholder value. Women are ready to ask stupid questions. That was not allowed any more. Risk awareness means you won't take risk you don't understand. So you will ask questions. Tokenism isn't helping. One woman on a 10-person board is not helpful. As tokens, you can either belong by behaving like men, or be marginalized. Behave like men, women are told. But to be yourself? You need the support of one or two more women. *Three is a critical number*. Three women is much better."

"In Iceland, banks were taken over by people with little experience in banking. There was a great influx of people seeking higher returns, there was an orgy of extravagant lending, at home and abroad."

"It was a group of alpha males that caused this crisis. In general, most women in Iceland work outside the home, over 80 %. We have well-educated women, but on an executive or Board level, we are male-dominated. It is slowly changing, but not fast enough."

"I don't think it is right that women should clean up the mess. The men should clean up the mess after themselves. We will take part. But it's not

(*Case Study continued*)

(Case Study continued)

our job to clean up, and then they come back and start the party all over again. It has to be balanced, we have to do it with the men."

"The crisis we are going through now can be an eye-opener, men will understand we need something else. It is such a good example of when you have homogeneous decision-making, a group of only alpha males, City Bankers, men on Wall Street—business have to realize the value of diversity. I hope this crisis will make people come to their senses."

Audur capital

"What was it like to launch a new financial services company so close to disaster? We founded the company two years ago. It took time to get shareholders in. We didn't get our license until May 2008. The cracks were beginning to show. The system was about to tumble. We were risk aware. We saw the risks. *Everywhere you look, assets are being shredded. But this is a buying opportunity. We can buy at the rock-bottom prices you are seeing if you are risk-aware, and wait out the situation. We are careful when we enter into investments, at a slow pace.*"

"Our values are indeed different. Human financial services provider—we are more human, we value different things than typical financial services. For instance, we do not due typical due diligence. *We do an emotional due diligence.* You can present anything in Excel. It is down to the people, their culture, their values. What is a good investor? Just money? A good investor brings more than money. Also, emotional capital. You can squeeze the blood out of a turnip, but it is better if you can make something flourish. We use both our rational minds and our EQ, to release value from our investments. It is smarter, and more long-term. The soft side of the business is actually the hard side of the business. *We find investment opportunities based on our emotional due diligence.*"

"Our values got us through the crisis. We tripled our wealth management business during the crisis, when others were losing business. One of our values is straight talk. We told our clients things that were not spoken honestly elsewhere. We believe in being authentic. It is in our DNA. Some will love it. Others will not. We are not worried. We are the place for those who want that kind of value-driven business that will build relationships on long-term thinking."

CASE STUDY

China: Major Winner from the Global Crisis

 The world's most populous country, and (measured by PPP) second largest economy, has apparently become a major winner, perhaps *the* winner, from the global crisis. China is acting quickly to seize opportunities, according to accounts in the *New York Times* and *Washington Post*.

- China is using its vast dollar reserves to buy up contracts for energy, and other natural resources. "The sheer scope of the agreements," the Post's Ariana Eunjung Cha declares, "marks a shift in global finance, roiling energy markets and feeding worries about the future availability and prices of those commodities in other countries that compete for them, including the United States."[3]

- The New York Times' Keith Bradsher notes that China is using its nearly USD 600 billion economic stimulus package to make its companies better able to compete in markets at home and abroad, to retrain migrant workers on an immense scale, and to rapidly expand subsidies for research and development. Construction has already begun on new highways, and rail lines that are likely to permanently reduce transportation costs. The scale of this construction is enormous, covering nearly all of China. When completed, China will have a spanking new, efficient transportation system in place of its old antiquated one.[4]

- While American leaders and the Federal Reserve struggle to revive lending (see Chapter Six), Chinese banks lent more in the last three months than in the preceding 12 months. Since Chinese banks are mainly state-owned, when the state tells them to lend money, they do so, unlike banks in Europe and America.

- China is also making it easier for companies to acquire foreign firms. The commerce ministry is now leading its first mergers and

(Case Study continued)

[3] Ariana Eunjung Cha, "China uses global crisis to assert its influence", Washington Post Foreign Service, Thursday, April 23, 2009. http://www.washingtonpost.com/wpdyn/content/article/2009/04/22/AR2009042203823.html

[4] Keith Bradsher, "China's Commodity Buying Spree", *New York Times*, June 10, 2009. http://www.nytimes.com/2009/06/11/business/economy/11commodity.html

(*Case Study continued*)

acquisitions delegation of corporate executives to Europe; the executives are looking at companies in the automotive, textiles, food, energy, machinery, electronics and environmental protection sectors. For instance, a Chinese industrial machinery firm, Sichuan Tengzhong, announced on June 3, 2009 that it had acquired the Hummer brand from General Motors.

Standing out in the above details is this key fact: At a time when the global economy as a whole is contracting by 2–3 percent annually, and with foreign trade down by almost half, China's economy (which is export-driven) will grow by more than 7.5 percent in 2009, as China substitutes its domestic demand in place of foreign demand. When the dust from the global crisis settles, China's economy will be well positioned to compete in world markets.

RISK AWARENESS

A striking phrase stands out in the words of Iceland's Halla Tomasdottir and Kristin Petursdottir. It is *risk awareness*. These two words embody the main message of our book. Learned articles and books about the economics of finance analyze risk affinity or risk aversion or risk premiums. But above these important ideas rises the notion of risk *awareness*, simply being *aware* of the varieties of risks, especially *systemic risk*, and including non-economic risk, that are present at any given moment, and that are evolving from embryonic to full-blown. The key purpose of the 10 tools described in this book is to heighten risk awareness, through independent thinking, and constant visual tracking of vital economic *risk indicators* with the 10 tools.

DEFINITION

Risk Awareness

The ability to accurately and independently track and assess all varieties of risk, global and local, economic and non-economic, in an ongoing systemic fashion, and to act on that awareness, both to avoid burgeoning risk, and to seize unfolding opportunities that the risk presents.

The key to insightful risk awareness is, as has been often emphasized throughout this book, a systemic global approach to risk, which sees the *big picture* of global markets and understands how each market, each country, each industry is related to the others. If anything has been more fatal to risk management, it has been a piecemeal approach that analyzes individual risks and markets and assets without fully integrating them. Therefore, this chapter focuses on taking the individual nine tools and putting them together, into a single framework that enables analysis of individual countries, or, alternately, the entire system of global markets. We call this process *due diligence*, after the concept used to describe how experts analyze businesses prior to a possible takeover.

CHECKLIST FOR COUNTRY DUE DILIGENCE ANALYSIS

Global managers may have experienced being part of an organization that acquires another company, or is acquired by one. The investigatory process that precedes a takeover is known as due diligence. It is exhaustive, and often exhausting. In part it exists to avoid legal liability, lest the takeover fails, and leads to shareholder litigation. But mostly due diligence seeks to ensure that management knows precisely what it is acquiring, and avoid unpleasant surprises.

Country due diligence is similar. Global managers who seek to do business in new geographies should follow a similar, thorough investigatory process. What follows is a kind of template, or framework, for analyzing the risks inherent in doing business in a new and perhaps unfamiliar market. When global managers do their homework well, they will be able to spot risks in markets where others see only opportunities, and in turn find opportunities where others see only risk. China is a good example. One of the earliest American companies to invest in China was General Electric (GE) found opportunities when others saw only risk. In global investment, as with management of technology, there is a classic dilemma of *first-entrant advantage* (the advantage of being first, in a market, or in a new technology), and *second-entrant advantage* (the advantage of being second, or third, and thus learning from the mistakes of the pioneers). The resolution of this dilemma depends on solid fact-gathering, and employment of the nine tools. Integrating those tools creates the tenth:

Tool

Checklist for Country "Due Diligence" Analysis
Here are some of the key questions that managers must answer, in exploring the business opportunities in a new country:
(Tool continued)

(*Tool continued*)

Macro accounting

- How large is the country's Gross Domestic Product (GDP) and GDP per capita, measured in dollars, at prevailing exchange rates, and also using purchasing-power-parity exchange rates that reflect the real, underlying value of the currency?
- What does its *GDP cash flow* look like—the sources of GDP and its uses, the proportions of GDP bought by households, governments, businesses and foreigners?
- Is the country's GDP growing? How fast? How is the annual increase in GDP—the *growth dividend* used: for consumption, for investment, or for exports?
- Is the country present- or future-oriented as measured by how the GDP divides up between personal and government consumption, and investment and net exports?
- How large is the country's net addition to its stock of buildings, machines and equipment, and how does it pay for that investment—out of its own saving, or through borrowing the savings of foreigners?
- Overall, is the country investing abroad, or are foreigners investing in it? Where are its citizens and businesses investing abroad, how much, and in what way? Who, how much, and in what form are foreigners investing in the country? How have these patterns been changing?
- What key components of demand are driving the country's GDP growth, or slowing it?
- How fast is the country's capacity to produce goods and services (potential supply of GDP) growing, relative to demand growth? If demand is outpacing productive capacity, is there a threat of future inflation?
- How much of each additional GDP dollar is spent by households on personal consumption, and how much is saved? How have these important proportions been changing?
- How large is the budget deficit as a proportion of GDP? Are exports bigger or smaller than imports? How important is trade, and net exports expressed as a proportion of GDP?

Money, interest, and inflation

- How does the country shape its monetary policy? Who is responsible? What are its key considerations?

(*Tool continued*)

(*Tool continued*)

- How fast is the money supply growing? How is the rate at which that money changes hands (velocity) changing?
- Is the Central Bank's monetary policy currently making it easier, or harder, to borrow money? Are *real* (inflation-adjusted) interest rates rising, or falling? How is this affecting GDP? Historically, are *real* interest rates relatively high or relatively low?
- Does the Central Bank have the freedom to lower interest rates, or is it seriously limited in this by the need to maintain a fixed exchange rate relative to another currency?
- In general, what degree of political pressure and influence is exerted on the Central Bank when it sets monetary policy and interest rates? How independent is it?

Cycles and trends

- What is the current direction and magnitude of the two key macro-economic forces: prices and output? How have they been changing in recent years? How high is unemployment? How has it been changing?
- Is there inflation? How much? Is inflation driven mainly by demand-pull forces (rising spending)? Or by cost-push (rising wages, interest rates, energy prices, taxes, and cost of materials)?
- What is the current level of inflation-adjusted common stock prices? How does this compare with historical levels? Are common-stock prices justified by underlying profitability, and future earnings prospects of the country's businesses?
- Is a recovery from the global recession likely soon? Are there any signs of this recovery now? How effective is the government's fiscal and monetary stimulus plan?
- How large and how efficient are the country's capital markets—specifically its equities (common stock) market?

Dollars and deficits

- Is foreign trade important to the country's economy? Who are the country's main trading partners?

(*Tool continued*)

(Tool continued)

- Is the current account of the Balance of Payments in deficit, or in surplus? How has this deficit or surplus been changing in recent years? If in deficit—does this signal a future drop in the value of the country's currency, relative to the dollar?
- Is the country's official (legal) exchange rate bigger, or smaller, than the *underlying* (purchasing power) value of the country's currency relative to the dollar? Is there a *black market* in foreign exchange, and if so, how high are black-market rates relative to official ones?
- Are exchange rates fixed or floating? If they are floating, are they a cause of inflation? How sensitive is the country's exchange rate to speculative buying and selling? If they are fixed, is the current fixed exchange rate stable, or will there be devaluation (decline in the currency's value)?
- How are the twin deficits (budget, trade) changing, and how are these changes affecting overall disposable income?

Integrating the tools

- For this country, which variables serve as leading indicators, by signaling changes in business activity well in advance of economic downturns? What are such indicators currently signaling?
- How do long-term interest rates currently compare with short-term ones? Is the difference between short-term and long-term interest rates currently large, or small, and does this signal an impeding recession?
- Do businesses and consumers have money, or can they borrow it easily? Are they optimistic and willing, and ready to spend? What is the country's overall mood?
- Is the country truly democratic? Is it politically stable internally? Is it involved in potentially explosive disputes with neighboring countries? Is there a large, restive underclass?
- Does the country have national energy? Can individuals become wealthy through innovation and entrepreneurship? How well-educated are the people?
- Is your personal sense of the country's character and direction, based on your own observations and insights, consistent with the business profile provided by answers to the checklist questions? If intuition and analysis differ, which is right?

ACTION LEARNING

 Pick a country—any country. Conduct a *due diligence* analysis of that country, using the 10 tools and the checklist in this chapter. Be sure to analyze the data well, but also look *between the lines* and *behind the numbers*. State whether this country is a promising target for business and investment in the short run and in the long run. Why or why not?

Some suggestions for analysis: Vietnam; Australia; Kazakhstan; Ireland; Turkey; Democratic Republic of Congo; South Africa; Brazil; Guatemala; Taiwan.

For data sources, see Appendix: Helpful Resources—Where to Find the Data You Need.

BEYOND MACROECONOMICS

While the macro tools described in this book are powerful instruments for analyzing countries, there are other non-economic dimensions of a country worth examining as well. Together with macro tools, they make a powerful combination. Here is a list of just a few of them:

- Demography: How rapidly is population growing? What is the age structure of the population? What fraction of the population is under age 15? Over age 65? What fraction of the population live in cities and urban areas? Is there outmigration or inmigration? One of the major future trends in the major industrial countries is the ageing of the population. *This will have important political and business implications.* Japan, for example, has a rather old, and ageing, population. India's population is relatively young; so is Iran's.
- Health and education: What is the average life expectancy of men and women? Child mortality rates? What fraction of youths completes primary and secondary school? University? What fraction of the population is literate?
- Energy and resources: How high is energy consumption? Where are energy sources—especially, oil and coal—obtained from? Are there natural resources?
- Environment: Is the environment protected by strong policies? Is there ecological awareness?
- Political system: Is the country democratic? Is it politically stable? Are business and government allies or adversaries? Is political power concentrated or diffused?

- Society and culture: Is the country individualistic or collectivist? Egalitarian or hierarchical? Is there gender equality? Is there a strong work ethic? *Religion*: What are the major religions? Are there religious beliefs or taboos that could affect your products and marketing. *Language*: Do its people have a common language, or do they speak many dialects. *Values and attitude*: How do its citizens view foreigners? How do they feel about globalization and competing in global markets?
- Competitiveness: How does the country rank in the tables of world competitiveness? How well does the country compete in global markets? How has this ranking changed? What are the country's competitive strengths and weaknesses?
- Corruption: How honest, or dishonest, is the business system and the political system.
- Freedom: How free are the country's markets? How well can individuals and companies pursue their business interests without the constraints of excessive regulation or bureaucracy?

In many ways, the current global crisis represents a fundamental change in the way customers regard the companies from whom they buy, and for whom they work, the way governments perceive the businesses and banks they regulate, and the way businesses themselves perceive their markets, and how they function. We now proceed to discuss this key point.

GLOBAL PARADIGM SHIFT: TRANSFORMING RISK INTO OPPORTUNITY

It is not a global *recession*. It is a global paradigm shift. For political leaders, managers, investors and working people, there is a huge difference.

We believe that this key point is at present not understood. Businesses and government policy are guided on the assumption that we are experiencing a downturn, a business cycle, like many others in the past, one that perhaps is a bit more severe, and one that will pass.

This is wrong. If businesses and public policy continue to build on this wrong assumption, the global economy will remain mired in deep quicksand, and bailout, and recovery plans will fail. A paradigm shift is a massive change in the rules (mostly unwritten) under which businesses operate. We are in the midst of such a shift.

In 1962, Thomas Kuhn, philosopher and historian of science, wrote a small book titled *The Structure of Scientific Revolutions*, in which he defined and described scientific revolutions as *paradigm shifts* (a term he did not invent but described very precisely). His concept applies today with great force to global business.

DEFINITION

Global Paradigm Shift—A revolutionary change in the way managers, governments, and consumers perceive technology, products, regulation, and the unwritten *rules of the game* in the global marketplace. Paradigm shifts are characterized not in terms of changes in fundamental facts but in the way those facts are perceived and interpreted.

A business cycle is a decline in GDP, lasting about a year, accompanied by rising unemployment, followed by a recovery, led by consumer spending. The global *rules of the game* remain unchanged.

We saw such a downturn in 2001–03. Many high-tech companies saw their share prices drop by 75 percent or more. Many companies now seem to assume that the current crisis is just another chapter from the same book. Many myopic managers hope and trust that when the dust settles, it will be *business as usual*.

But this is misguided. Here is why. Entire industries are facing a collapse and radical change.

- Financial services: Investment banks have overnight become bank holding companies, subject to tougher regulations. Hedge funds are disappearing. Venture capital funds are drying up and closing. This key industry must be rebuilt under new rules, and when it is, it will look utterly different. It will be smaller and far less self-centered, returning to serving industry rather than having an industry serve it.
- Consumer electronics: AU Optronics, the world's third largest flat panel display producer, based in Taiwan, had factories that worked at 100 percent capacity in 2007. Today they are at 60 percent and the chairman of the company reports that markets are *frozen*. That 60 percent will drop to 40 percent soon, or less. The consumer electronics industry itself recently had its annual convention and trade show; industry leaders projected *flat* sales in 2009, at USD 171 billion. *They are delusional.* Sales will decline sharply. They are in denial. Many of the weaker companies will disappear, as will the companies that make the products they sell.
- Restaurants and retail: Many units are closing. Retail outlets are closing. Small businesses are failing. In past recessions, most business failures occurred during the recovery, when companies that failed to manage the downturn well found they could not compete. In this crisis, companies are going broke during it,

in part because they cannot get credit. Banks have money but do not lend it, because they need the money to shore up their depleted capital. Central Banks can push money into the system as much as they wish, but they cannot force banks to lend it. Many businesses have failed to realize that they must manage by cash flow, not profit and loss, because profitable businesses fail if they run out of cash, and cannot pay urgent debts.

Management education: Every business school teaches innovation, but few practice it. Management education will require major innovation, to adapt to the new post-crisis world, and to equip managers with new, relevant and powerful tools they will need. Managers will need newfound awareness of global finance; no longer can this be left to their Chief Financial Officer. They will need to be aware of ethical issues. They will need to understand politics and related regulatory issues, which will grow in power and intricacy. They will need to understand how global business works, how global markets are inter-related, and how to track them on an ongoing basis.

This is not a recession. It is a paradigm shift. A new world system will emerge. When? How long will it take? How much human suffering will result? For how many years?

True optimism is based on cold realism. Only if we face the facts, can we—as managers, investors, working people, heads of families—act wisely. Only if our political leaders face the facts will they act decisively and wisely. And as long as we believe we are having just a temporary recession, or even depression, this will not happen.

CASE STUDY

General Electric and the New Paradigm: "Reset"!

 Recently, General Electric's CEO Jeffrey Immelt spoke to GE's annual meeting on April 27, 2009. Most such addresses are humdrum. Immelt's was exceptional, with a strong message for innovators. Summarized in one word, Immelt called for "RESET"! The changing paradigm for GE's businesses requires the company to *reset* its entire way of doing business. Immelt's clarion call should be heeded by every single company, and every single global manager.

In Immelt's own words:

- "I believe we are going through more than a cycle. The global economy, and capitalism, will be *reset* in several important ways.

(Case Study continued)

(Case Study continued)

- The interaction between government and business will change forever. In a reset economy, the government will be a regulator; and also an industry policy champion, a financier, and a key partner.
- The financial industry will radically restructure. There will be less leverage, fewer competitors, and a fundamental re-pricing of risk. It will remain an important industry, just different.
- There are other resets as well: the diminished role of the automotive industry; a prolonged downturn in housing; a decline in the prominence of alternative investments; and the nature of executive responsibility and compensation. You get the point."

Successful companies won't just "hunker down"; they will seek out the new opportunities in a reset world.

The *reset* button initiates a restart. This is exactly what is happening in global markets. It is a source of enormous opportunities for global managers able to identify the new paradigms, and act on those insights.

Managers who read quarterly financial statements will know that each such statement is required by law to contain a *forward looking statement* that identifies in detail potential risks to the predictions the statement contains. These risk *shopping lists* are not just *pro forma*; they contain valuable insights. Here, for instance, is the forward looking statement of Microsoft. It is worth patiently reading the fine print.

CASE STUDY

Microsoft: Third Quarter 2008 Earnings Statement

 RISK ANALYSIS

Forward-looking statements

Statements in this release that are *forward-looking statements* are based on current expectations, and assumptions that are subject to risks and uncertainties. Actual results could differ materially because of factors such as:

1. challenges to Microsoft's business model;
2. intense competition in all of Microsoft's markets;

(Case Study continued)

(*Case Study continued*)

3. Microsoft's continued ability to protect its intellectual property rights;
4. claims that Microsoft has infringed the intellectual property rights of others;
5. the possibility of unauthorized disclosure of significant portions of Microsoft's source code;
6. actual or perceived security vulnerabilities in Microsoft products that could reduce revenue or lead to liability;
7. government litigation and regulation affecting how Microsoft designs and markets its products;
8. Microsoft's ability to attract and retain talented employees;
9. delays in product development and related product release schedules;
10. significant business investments that may not gain customer acceptance and produce offsetting increases in revenue;
11. unfavorable changes in general economic conditions, disruption of our partner networks or sales channels, or the availability of credit that affect the value of our investment portfolio or demand for Microsoft's products and services;
12. adverse results in legal disputes;
13. unanticipated tax liabilities;
14. quality or supply problems in Microsoft's consumer hardware or other vertically integrated hardware and software products;
15. impairment of goodwill or amortizable intangible assets causing a charge to earnings;
16. exposure to increased economic and regulatory uncertainties from operating a global business;
17. geopolitical conditions, natural disaster, cyber attack, or other catastrophic events disrupting Microsoft's business;
18. acquisitions and joint ventures that adversely affect the business;
19. improper disclosure of personal data could result in liability and harm to Microsoft's reputation; and
20. outages and disruptions of online services if Microsoft fails to maintain an adequate operations infrastructure.

Note that the number 1 risk in the list is the risk to Microsoft's business model. This recognizes that a *global paradigm shift* (for example, to open architecture operating systems, where, say, Linux could massively replace Windows) is seen by Microsoft as a major risk. Awareness of this risk is the first step toward managing it. *These risk shopping lists are of no value, unless each item in them is internalized, assessed and managed, throughout the organization, not just at the highest levels.*

An industry hard hit by the global downturn is the newspaper business. In a recession, businesses slash their advertising expenditures. In the United States, newspapers have seen advertising revenues fall by about half. Few businesses can survive for long when their revenues are cut by 50 percent. This rapid fall in revenue could have been anticipated. It should have been seen as a paradigm shift. But in general, it was not, as the following case studies indicate:

CASE STUDY

Paradigm Shift in Newspapers: *News without Paper?*

 The Rocky Mountain News is a venerable 150-year-old newspaper that went bankrupt in 2009. It could have avoided bankruptcy, in the face of a 50 percent fall in advertising revenues. One expert noted that subscribers to American newspapers fell from 60 million to 50 million in the past decade—but subscribers to Internet editions rose from about zero to 75 million! The newspaper industry faces bankruptcy—even though it has more clients, more subscribers! Why? Because like the music industry, it has failed to adapt to the changing times. It treated the Internet not as savior but as fierce foe. It failed to observe an obvious enormous paradigm shift. What a tragedy. Only a small handful of newspaper managers seem to see the light.

Here is a headline, from February 27:

Rocky Mountain News published final newspaper on Friday, Feb. 27.[5]

It could have been different. Global managers might have seen the paradigm shift in time. Here is a new and happier headline.

Rocky Mountain News doubles profits Paper boosts subscribers, slashes costs, with new format-paperless paper.

Now, how can reality be changed to make the headline true?

In the sharp downturn, which saw the US economy contract by 6.2 percent in the last quarter of 2008, advertising revenues have plummeted. Newspapers and

---

[5] http://www.cbsnews.com/stories/2009/02/27/national/main4835015.shtml, (accessed January 30, 2010).

magazines everywhere are losing fortunes, and some are closing their doors. To keep Rocky Mountain News alive, we must slash its costs by half. Indeed, many businesses now face that same huge challenge.

How in the world can that be done?

By *printing* a paperless paper. Deliver the paper every morning, at 4 a.m., to each subscriber, electronically, downloaded to an electronic book (say, Amazon's Kindle 2) provided free of charge by the newspaper, in return for a year's subscription. Every newspaper in the world that is printed on paper can instantly cut its costs in half, and save the world's forests, by becoming paperless and digital. Even when Kindle 2 is priced at USD 399, Rocky Mountain News could still make money if it gave them away in return for a multi-year subscription. A supplementary business could be selling downloaded books, music, and movies. In time this business could grow far bigger than the newspaper.

Why, then, don't papers do it?

They will. The global crisis may not always be the direct cause of paradigm shifts in industry, but it is *always* a force multiplier that accelerates the speed at which such shifts take place. The necessity to slash costs radically, as revenues dive, will force newspapers to abandon paper. And in every single industry, there will be equally radical shifts in business designs.

Not far from Colorado, in the state of Washington, one newspaper understands the paradigm shift. It is the Seattle Post-Intelligencer. Here is what the *International Herald Tribune* wrote on March 17, 2009:[6]

> SEATTLE: The Seattle Post-Intelligencer planned to produce its last printed edition Tuesday and become an Internet-only news source, Hearst Corp., said, making it by far the largest American newspaper to take that leap. But The P-I, as it is called, will resemble a local Huffington Post more than a traditional newspaper, with a news staff of about 20 people rather than the 165 it had, and a site with mostly commentary, advice and links to other news sites, along with some original reporting. Other newspapers have closed and many more are threatened. But the transition to an all-digital product for The P-I, announced Monday, will be especially closely watched in an industry that is fast losing revenue and is casting around for a new economic model.

> And the way that The P-I is changing might hint at a path for future newspaper closings. To some extent, in shifting its business model, it will enter a new realm of competition. It will compete not just with the print-and-ink Times, but also with an established local news Web site, Crosscut.com, a much smaller nonprofit organization that focuses on the Northwest. The move shows how some newspapers, in the future, may not vanish but move the battle from print to the digital arena.

---

[6] William Yardley and Richard Pérez Peña, "Seattle newspaper drops the 'paper,'" *International Herald Tribune*, Tuesday, March 17, 2009.

Had Hearst not made this decision, the survival of *The Times* was unlikely, said Jill Mackie, vice president for public affairs at *The Times*.

The P-I lost $14 million in 2008. Hearst announced in January that if it could not find a buyer, it would cease printing. Few people expected a buyer to emerge. Hearst hopes to capitalize on the healthy Web traffic The P-I already has—about 1.8 million unique visitors a month, according to Nielsen Online. It usually outranks the online readership of *The Times*, despite a smaller print circulation: 118,000 on weekdays last year, compared with 199,000 for *The Times*.

We clearly believe we are in a period of innovation and experimentation, and that's what this new SeattlePI.com represents, said Steven R. Swartz, president of Hearst's newspaper division. We think we'll learn a lot, and we think the Seattle market, being so digitally focussed, is a great place to try this.

David Brewster, the publisher of Crosscut, praised Hearst for creating new journalism, rather than completely shutting down The P-I. "There's definitely room", he said. Seattle will be quite a vital place.

The total number of readers of American newspapers has risen substantially. But its composition has shifted in the past decade, with a decline of some 10 million newspaper subscribers in recent years, and an increase of some 20 million online readers. This shift did not happen overnight. It occurred over time. It comprised a powerful signal that the nature of the newspaper business was changing. Some entrepreneurs recognized this shift. For instance, the *Huffington Post* is an online news organization launched on May 9, 2005, that today has many millions of readers. Many in the traditional paper-based newspaper business missed the trend. The results were often fatal.

ACTION LEARNING

 Readers are invited to consider:

- What is the paradigm shift for your industry? What is your evidence?
- What actions are you taking to prepare for, and implement, it? What opportunities present themselves in this paradigm shift?

CONCLUSION

In writing *Global Risk/Global Opportunity*, we pursued an agenda that we reveal only now, at the conclusion. It is this:

Like many professions, economics maintains a kind of monopoly status by surrounding its body of knowledge with complex jargon and intricate mathematics—language spoken only by the inner circle of economists. The tools of macroeconomic analysis are often presented by economists as complex and inaccessible to managers, requiring the special expertize and special knowledge of professionally trained economists for proper use.

This is untrue. The basic tools of macroeconomic analysis—those presented in this book—are exceedingly simple, direct, and uncomplicated. They can be understood by every manager and employed successfully to track risk, to assess minds, markets and money, and to identify hidden opportunities. In this book we seek to end the monopoly on macroeconomics held by macroeconomists.

We urge global managers to become expert amateur economists. We urge you, our readers, to prepare for the next global crisis—which is inevitable, because the fundamental causes of the current one have not even begun to be corrected—by building a personal set of indicators for tracking minds, markets, and money that you follow constantly and consistently.

We recommend that after the next crisis, when the Queen of England, or another public figure asks why no one saw it coming, you, our readers, will be well prepared to say: No one? *I saw it*, and prepared for it, and leveraged it for my own gain, and that of my organization, and its workers. I saw the global risks, and also saw the opportunities they embodied. And I did this by using the 10 essential tools for tracking minds, markets, and money.

APPENDIX: HELPFUL RESOURCES—WHERE TO FIND THE DATA YOU NEED

Where does one find the large amounts of up-to-date data needed to apply the economic tools for tracking global markets?

World Bank Indicators: The World Bank, located at 1818 H. Street, NW Washington DC, 20433, USA, provides CD-ROM version of its World Development Indicators database. It provides detailed annual data, starting in 1970, for some 500 different variables, and 209 countries and regions, for economic, social and demographic categories. These data usually lag a year or two (for instance, the database available in August, 1997 included date up to 1995, starting in 1970). They include the main macroeconomic indicators, including detailed GDP figures, money supply, trade and capital flows, and prices. A major advantage of World Bank data: They are measured in consistent fashion, using standard definitions, so that in general, one can compare, say, GDP per capita for different countries. The data are also available (for a price) online.

A few key countries that are not World Bank members, like Taiwan, are missing. The countries for which detailed data are provided are:

Albania, Algeria, Antigua and Barbuda, Argentina, Armenia, Australia, Austria, Azerbaijan, Bahamas, Bahrain, Bangladesh, Barbados, Belarus, Belgium, Belize, Benin, Bhutan, Bolivia, Botswana, Brazil, Bulgaria, Burkina Faso, Burundi, Cameroon, Canada, Cape Verde, Central African Republic, Chad, Chile, China, Colombia, Comoros, Congo, Costa Rica, Côte d'Ivoire, Cyprus, Czech Republic, Denmark, Djibouti, Dominica, Dominican Republic, Ecuador, Egypt, El Salvador, Equatorial Guinea, Estonia, Ethiopia, Fiji, Finland, France, Gabon, Gambia, Georgia, Germany, Ghana, Greece, Grenada, Guatemala, Guinea, Guinea-Bissau, Guyana, Haiti, Honduras, Hong Kong, Hungary, Iceland, India, Indonesia, Iran, Ireland, Israel, Italy, Jamaica, Japan, Jordan, Kazakhstan, Kenya, South Korea, Kuwait, Kyrgyz Republic, Laos, Latvia, Lesotho, Liberia, Lithuania, Luxembourg, Madagascar, Malawi, Malaysia, Maldives, Mali, Malta, Mauritania, Mauritius, Mexico, Moldova, Mongolia, Morocco, Mozambique, Myanmar, Namibia, Nepal, Netherlands, New Zealand, Nicaragua, Niger, Nigeria, Norway, Oman, Pakistan, Panama, Papua-New Guinea, Paraguay, Peru, The Philippines, Poland, Portugal, Qatar, Romania, Russia, Rwanda, Sao Tome and Principe, Saudi Arabia, Senegal, Seychelles, Sierra Leone, Singapore, Slovak Republic, Solomon Islands, Somalia, South Africa, Spain, Sri Lanka, St. Kitts and Nevis, St. Lucia, St. Vincent and the Grenadines, Sudan, Surinam, Swaziland, Sweden, Switzerland, Syria, Tajikistan, Tanzania, Thailand, Togo, Tonga, Trinidad and Tobago, Tunisia, Turkey, Turkmenistan, Uganda, Ukraine, United Arab Emirates, United Kingdom, United States, Uruguay, Vanuatu, Venezuela, Vietnam, Western Samoa, Yemen, Zaire, Zambia, Zimbabwe.

IMD World Competitiveness Yearbook: This database appears annually, and provides rankings of some 80 countries, along with underlying data for many hundreds of variables, across four competitiveness dimensions: economic performance, business efficiency, government efficiency, and infrastructure (including education, science, and technology). It is published by the Swiss business school in Lausanne.

Organisation for Economic Co-operation and Development (OECD): This organization, which arose out of America's Marshall Plan aid to Europe in 1947–1948, comprises 27 countries, that together account for over half the world's GDP. The member countries are: Australia, Belgium, Canada, Czech Republic, Denmark, Finland, France, Germany, Greece, Hungary, Iceland, Ireland, Italy, Japan, Luxembourg, Mexico, The Netherlands, New Zealand, Norway, Poland, Portugal, Spain, Sweden, Switzerland, Turkey, the United Kingdom, and the United States. A database provided as computer files exists for these countries.

The Economist: This remarkable weekly magazine, published in London, and available all over the world, offers weekly updates of key macroeconomic variables for both developed countries, and emerging markets. The variables for which data are given include: GDP (including a GDP forecast from time to time), industrial production, retail sales, unemployment rate, inflation, producer prices, wages and earnings, money supply, interest rates, stock prices, trade balance, exchange rates, and foreign exchange reserves. The developed countries listed are: Australia, Austria, Belgium, Britain, Canada, Denmark, France, Germany, Italy, Japan, The Netherlands, Spain, Sweden, Switzerland, and the United States. The emerging-market countries are: China, Hong Kong, Indonesia, Malaysia, The Philippines, Singapore, South Korea, Taiwan, Thailand, Argentina, Brazil, Chile, Columbia, Mexico, Venezuela, Greece, Israel, Portugal, South Africa, Turkey, Czech Republic, Hungary, Poland, and Russia. *The Economist* also provides country surveys, available online.

Financial Times, *Wall Street Journal*: These global publications have excellent online editions with search capabilities.

The CIA Website provides useful information on a wide range of countries: www.cia.gov

Corruption Perception: Transparency International's website provides an ongoing annual index of *corruption perception* (CPI), measuring how global managers perceive the degree of corruption in a long list of countries: www.transparency.org

Freedom: The Heritage Foundation offers an annual index of freedom, which measures the degree to which "individuals are free to work, produce, consume, and invest in any way they please, with that freedom both protected by the state and unconstrained by the state": www.heritage.org/Index[7]

Ease of Doing Business: The World Bank sponsors a website that provides detailed information on *ease of doing business*, across a long list of business activities, including: land registration, starting a business, closing a business, firing an employee and suing or litigating. See: www.doingbusiness.org.

---

[7] The Link Between Economic Opportunity & Prosperity, 2010 Index of Economic Freedom. A product of Heritage Foundation and *Wall Street Journal*. http://www.heritage.org/Index (accessed January 30, 2010).

Index

About the Authors

Shlomo Maital is a Senior Research Fellow at the S. Neaman Institute for Advanced Studies in Science and Technology, Haifa, Israel. He has over 40 years of teaching experience in various prestigious universities across the world, like, MIT, Rotterdam School of Management, EDHEC Business School, and European School of Management and Technology. He was a summer visiting professor at the MIT Sloan School of Management's M.Sc. program for 20 years and taught over a thousand R&D engineers from 40 countries.

Professor Maital was the co-founder of SABE—Society for Advancement of Behavioral Economics. He also served as Director of the National and Economic Planning Authority, Economic Ministry, Government of Israel. He has taught managers from 200 Israeli companies.

His current research focusses on how to build creativity "muscles"—carry out regular brain exercises to stimulate innovative pragmatic ideas that change the world.

Professor Maital has authored and co-authored eight books: *Executive Economics: Ten Tools for Business Decision Makers* (1994), and *Managing New Product Development and Innovation: A Microeconomic Toolbox*, co-authored with Hariolf Grupp (2001), to name a few.

D.V.R. Seshadri is an Adjunct Faculty at the Indian Institute of Management (IIM) Bangalore. His areas of interest are Business-to-business Marketing, Corporate Entrepreneurship, and Strategy. He holds a B.Tech. (Mechanical Engineering) from IIT Madras (1978); M.S. (Engineering Sciences) from University of California, San Diego; and a Fellow (Doctorate) title from IIM Ahmedabad, with specialization in Production and Quantitative Methods. He has over 15 years of industrial experience prior to joining academics since 2000.

Over the last 10 years, he had developed numerous case studies and authored a number of research papers in his areas of interest. He is also co-author of a book, *Innovation Management*, with Professor Shlomo Maital, published by Response Books (a division of SAGE Publications), India. He teaches extensively in the various programs at IIM-B in his areas of interest. He also teaches at IIM Ahmedabad in the one-year executive MBA program. He also teaches extensively in various Executive Development Programs at IIM Bangalore. He works closely with several companies, providing them training and consulting services in his areas of expertize. He is a highly rated teacher and trainer.